"North America has been one of the slowest geographies to develop coaching supervision, but the Editors and Authors of this book have done an amazing job in developing coach supervision across the Americas, north and south. The book offers a wide range of experience and practical advice to coach supervisors and supervisees that we can all benefit from."

**Professor Peter Hawkins,** *Global thought leader;*
*bestselling author on coaching, supervision and*
*systemic team coaching*

"As one of the very early voices of coaching supervision in the Americas, I am excited to see this thorough and rich exploration of the present and future of this important contribution to professional coaching. The book offers clear evidence that the once resisted idea of coaching supervision is now melting away. Across all the issues explored here, the center point of supervision shines brightly – deep and resonant presence and relationships informed by intense and ongoing curiosity."

**Samuel P Magill Sr,** *Co-director and founder, Coaching*
*Supervision Academy – North America*

"A book title that aptly reflects what the reader can expect. An exciting new text in Coaching Supervision for a growing market. The vastness of the Americas is captured by honouring the diversity of culture that deserves the wider scope given to the definition of supervision. Refreshing new authors in the field bring together sensitivity, knowledge and practical offerings in illustrating why supervision makes sense … and it doesn't end there with the promise of more to come with ideas for future research topics that are destined to expand the knowledge base promoting the case for supervision. A wonderfully crafted contribution for the expansion of supervision practice in the Americas."

**Lise Lewis,** *EMCC Past President; EMCC International*
*Special Ambassador; Founder of Bluesky International*

"In this book the editorial team have undertaken a project to explore and extend the discussion of coaching supervision in the Americas - a project that I know is close to their hearts. As a collection, it is a welcome addition to the coaching supervision literature, in particular for its diversity of voices and its intent to celebrate that diversity in the interests of developing the discipline."

**Dr Peter Jackson,** *Co-director, International Centre for*
*Coaching & Mentoring Studies, Oxford Brookes*
*Business School*

"This book opens a window into the bigger conversations in coaching supervision. It amply demonstrates the potency of this growing practice. While 'Coaching Supervision: Voices from the Americas' is rooted in a particular context, it speaks vividly to the global community of coaches, mentors and supervisors. There are new and refreshing voices in these chapters, voices that skillfully address the real-world reflections that occur every day in supervision: reflections on complexity, cultural context, collective trauma, spirituality, systemic thinking and coach education. Read this book for new insights into well-established supervision models and tools, but also for understanding how coaching supervision embraces contemporary professional and political discourses."

**Edna Murdoch,** *Director, Coaching Supervision Academy*

"This rich and panoramic view of practice, research and education by a dedicated group of coaching supervisors offers a very timely and valuable insight into the results of comprehensive work undertaken by the ACSN to bring this practice to life in the Americas. The chapters take account of the complexities of a diverse cultural milieu and will inform and inspire readers from both within our field and the wider community that supervisors wish to serve."

**Fiona Adamson,** *Co-founder of Coaching Supervision Academy; co-author of Mindfulness-Based Relational Supervision, Mutual Transformational Learning*

"In parallel to the fields and practices of coaching and coaching supervision, this book offers—with great generosity of heart and wisdom—ways forward to a better future. While coaching supervision in the Americas is in a nascent state compared to the UK and Europe, we are clearly seeing differences (and similarities) that can inform the evolution of this field where art and science combine. This collection of ideas and practices is an important contribution to the coaching supervision space."

**Kathleen Stinnett,** *MCC & certified coaching supervisor; author of The Extraordinary Coach book*

# Coaching Supervision

This edited collection brings together an impressive and international array of coaching supervisors to highlight the unique cultural and contextual aspects of coaching supervision in the Americas, exploring current theory, research, and practice.

Offering fresh insights into a growing field, Francine Campone, Joel DiGirolamo, Damian Goldvarg, and Lily Seto expertly present the nuances of coaching supervision principles and practices in the Americas. The book is organized into three parts. Part 1 introduces the range of cultures and values that inform approaches to and beliefs about coaching supervision in the Americas, such as racial justice, working with indigenous communities, and providing culturally sensitive coaching supervision. Part 2 presents adaptations of coaching supervision models and methods to align with Americas contexts, as well as uniquely introducing an original model for coaching supervision rooted in an Americas perspective. Incorporating theory with practitioner's experiences throughout, Part 3 presents chapters that offer avenues for increasing awareness and interest in coaching supervision in the Americas, including chapters on coach wellbeing and the developmental journey of the coach.

Coaching supervisors work across borders and boundaries, and this book will extend supervisors' understanding of the various contexts in which they are working. It is essential reading for coaching supervisors, educators, trainers, mentors, and coaches, and it will be of interest to practitioners and graduate students in organizational development and those who oversee internal coaching programs.

**Francine Campone Ed.D., MCC** is a coach, mentor, supervisor, and coach educator. She has published numerous studies and book chapters on coaching and coach development.

**Joel DiGirolamo** is the International Coaching Federation Vice President of Research and Data Science and has published numerous articles and book chapters in the field of coaching.

**Damian Goldvarg** is a Master Certified Coach, Certified Supervisor, and Past President of the International Coaching Federation. He has 30 years of experience working in more than 50 countries. He trains coaches, and mentors coaches and supervisors worldwide.

**Lily Seto, MA, PCC, ESIA** is a global coach, coach supervisor, and team coach. She appreciates the diversity in all that we do as coaches.

# Coaching Supervision

Voices from the Americas

**Edited by Francine Campone,
Joel DiGirolamo,
Damian Goldvarg, and
Lily Seto**

NEW YORK AND LONDON

Cover image: Getty Images

First published 2023
by Routledge
605 Third Avenue, New York, NY 10158

and by Routledge
4 Park Square, Milton Park, Abingdon, Oxon, OX14 4RN

*Routledge is an imprint of the Taylor & Francis Group, an informa business*

ISBN: 978-1-032-19375-5 (hbk)
ISBN: 978-1-032-19374-8 (pbk)
ISBN: 978-1-003-25888-9 (ebk)

DOI: 10.4324/b23130

Typeset in Bembo
by MPS Limited, Dehradun

# Contents

# Foreword

As social beings, we usually want to help others. One of the many forms this can take is coaching, whether envisioned as a professional practice or as part of other helping roles, like physician, nurse, manager, teacher, cleric, or even parent. But the mere intention of wanting to help and the act of coaching others does not mean it will be effective or useful.

Humility and intellectual integrity are key in the continuing development of a field such as coaching. As a result, although we want coaching to work, we have to admit that while there is little published data or evidence that coaching as a practice is effective, a few studies have shown positive impact on something other than client satisfaction. Although client satisfaction is important, as a sole consequence it could be the result of cognitive dissonance reduction (i.e., a justification by the client for the time or money spent). In light of other published studies of the efficacy or durability of changes as a result of psychotherapy, teaching (i.e., post-secondary education), or training, we can be humble that wanting to help and spending time and effort as well as money does not result in sustained change as much as the invested efforts would be expected.

Studies in the field of coaching have suggested that a client's openness to change may be affected by the process and mechanisms used in a coaching conversation. For example, neurological evidence shows us that using the client's larger sense of purpose or personal vision as the context for coaching conversations and initial discussion, activates parts of the brain in which a human is open to new ideas, change, and another person, such as the coach. In contrast, starting a coaching process focused on a problem or goal has a somewhat opposite effect and activates parts of the brain that suppress that openness. Of course, addressing and discussing specific "presenting problems" or specific goals may be useful in a later stage of the coaching process and relationship.

We suspect from other studies that the current psycho-physiological state of the coach will affect the emotional contagion on the state of the client. If the coach is feeling stressed or worried about something, it will arouse comparable feelings in the client even if the coach thinks they are not expressing or showing it consciously. What we have called the renewed state (i.e., activation of the Parasympathetic Nervous System) of the coach becomes vital to attentive, sensitive, and caring interactions with the client.

Coaching supervision, as a regular reflective practice with a trained professional, is essential to renewal and to the personal growth and sustainability of the coach. As demonstrated often in related fields like psychotherapy and teaching, coaches must be able to review and reflect on their recent experiences and their own current state for sustainable, positive comportment. Insights gained through such reflection effectively help the coach to more effectively support the client and the wider system within which we work.

Supervision, or the practice of the coach having their own coach or a reflection partner with whom they meet regularly, helps to provide at least three basic functions. First, it can be restorative. The conversations with the supervisor can help the coach with periodic renewal and reinforcing renewing practices. Second, such conversations can help the coach continue their lifelong learning. They can explore specific techniques to help a client with difficult situations or an unusual client mood or style. It can invoke additional training, exploration of new techniques, and practicing new questions or activities to use in coaching. This also includes coaches looking at their own blind spots and biases. Some of these may be from their family, culture, values, training, and prior socializations.

Third, coaches can bring their ethical dilemmas to supervision, thus enhancing ethical practices. It provides another expert professional's view about situations. Supervision even helps the coach navigate ethical dilemmas not encountered previously or bring unrecognized dilemmas into awareness.

Coaching and coaching supervision in various cultures are affected by the norms, values, and beliefs of those cultures. This book is the first in a series examining such practices and exploring how the cultures in which they occur may be influencing them. The chapters in this book raise and discuss many controversies and sensitive topics. The Americas, or Western Hemisphere, is a collection of many cultures, languages, economic, and political systems. Every human immigrated to these lands starting thousands of years ago. As different waves of immigrants continued and continue to arrive, it is a land of diversity of every type imaginable. While a source of innovation, such diversity is also a challenge to the weaving of a social fabric. Not all of the ideas expressed in this book can be assumed to be shared by all of the authors. But it is in the spirit of open inquiry and dialogue that these sensitive topics are discussed, noting areas of difficulty and suggesting a variety of ways forward.

This valuable compendium is provocative, insightful, and totally human! It can certainly help you as a coaching supervisor, to the coaches you help and to their clients.

Richard E. Boyatzis
July 12, 2021

# Preface

The idea for this book originated with Damian Goldvarg and Lily Seto, who created and facilitate The Americas Coaching Supervision Network (ACSN). The Americas are comprised of North, Central, and South America.

Damian and Lily invited Francine to take the role of lead editor for the book and thus, the project was born. Francine currently serves as lead for ACSN Research and has published in the coaching literature. Joel DiGirolamo was invited to join the editorial team because of his past and current research activities in the field of coaching supervision. His involvement is also relevant in light of the International Coaching Federation's (ICF) recognition of supervision as an on-going reflective practice that is consistent with the updated ICF Core Competencies and Team Coaching Competencies. The four of us have worked collectively in reviewing contributions and framing the book as a next step in ACSN's role of building the coaching supervision community in the Americas.

We reached out to the over 300 coaching supervisors from across the Americas to propose book chapters. In the interest of inclusiveness, we accepted all fully formed chapter proposals. Many of these authors are first-time authors and so, represent new voices in the literature of coaching supervision. The editors and authors of this book have come together in service to a shared vision: To present theories, models, perspectives, and experiences of coaching supervision as they have emerged in the diverse and multi-faceted contexts of our work. We also want to acknowledge the contribution of colleagues who volunteered to serve as reviewers for first draft chapters: Hermann Ditzig, Kathryn Downing, Ana Pilopas, Janet Sheppard, and Larissa Thurlow.

The growing number of participants in ACSN webinars and annual conferences has demonstrated a clear need to explore and explain how coaching supervision is unfolding in the Western Hemisphere. The ACSN is entering its sixth year; in 2020, the participant list includes over 300 members from 25 countries around the world. This network is open to supervisors, coaches, and others interested in the topic of supervision. The objectives of this community are:

- To raise awareness about coaching supervision in the Americas
- To build a community of coaching supervisors here in the Americas.

We acknowledge the key role played by ACSN in supporting this work. There is no cost to join the ACSN or to participate in the webinars and all are welcomed. Members are predominantly coaching supervisors and coaches, and there are some coaching providers as well. The primary activities of this network include:

- To deliver monthly webinars facilitated by global presenters.
- To host an annual conference. The 4th annual conference was held virtually in 2021 and brought together over 150 participants from 125 countries.
- To provide information, resources, recordings from monthly sessions on our website: https://americassupervisionnetwork.com/
- To conduct research
- To offer, on the website, a directory of fully qualified coaching supervisors along with video recordings of the monthly webinars.

For more information or to be added to the ACSN mailing list to stay up to date:

- The ACSN website: www.americassupervisionnetwork.com. Please visit and feel free to reach out to Lily and Damian.
- Lily Seto: lilyseto@telus.net
- Damian Goldvarg: damian@goldvargconsulting.com

Francine Campone
Joel DiGirolamo
Lily Seto
Dr. Damian Goldvarg

# Introduction

*Francine Campone*

The Americas cover vast territory: Geographically, politically, culturally, racially, and socioeconomically. Geographically, the territory extends roughly 8700 miles from north to south, encompassing tundras, rain forests, mountains, plains, grasslands, and dense urban areas. The languages of the Americas are as diverse as the topology, including 30 Indigenous languages still spoken in Canada, the United States (US), Central and South America. While Spanish, English, and French dominate the category of languages introduced by colonizers and subsequent waves of immigrants, large communities in the western hemisphere speak Portuguese, Arabic, Creole, Mandarin, Dutch, German, Polish, Punjab, Tagalog, Vietnamese, Korean, Italian, and dozens of others. Historically, the peoples of the Americas comprise successive waves of inhabitants, beginning with the Indigenous peoples and followed by colonists and both voluntary and involuntary generations of immigrants.

Given this diversity, how can we presume to present "Voices from the Americas?" This complex collection of landscapes, histories, and languages forms the ground and provides the context for the practice of coaching and coaching supervision in the Americas. To open the "seventh eye" systems perspective in coaching supervision, it is necessary to understand that what unites us in the Americas is our diversity. Imagine, for example, a coaching supervision group that is an embodiment of this diversity. The participants include:

- A Black coach who was born in the Jim Crow south and is active in Black Lives Matter.
- A Latina psychologist coach living and practicing in Mexico City.
- A coach whose parents survived the Holocaust and fled to New York after World War II.
- A coach who grew up in rural Kentucky with a father who worked in the coal mines.
- A coach whose grew up on a First Nations reserve after her people were removed from their traditional land.
- A coach who came from Mumbai to Boston to attend graduate school and stayed in the US.

DOI: 10.4324/b23130-1

The coaching supervisor for this group will find elements of participants' cultures, languages, history, and possibly intergenerational trauma emerging in the supervision process. The chapters in this book offer coaching supervisors insights that will increase their effectiveness in working with such a diverse group. The chapters will also help coaches working in the Americas to better appreciate the diversity of cultures in their own and neighboring countries.

The editors of this book are pleased to bring the voices of many first-time authors into the literature and conversation about coaching supervision. When we are truly committed to diversity and inclusion, we must be open to and willing to reflect on and understand the lived experience of others. While these authors write from their lived experience and that of their clients, it's important to recognize there is no one-size-fits-all answer to coaching and supervision that is truly inclusive. These chapters are intended to stimulate reflection and conversations with clients, colleagues, and ourselves.

While supervision has been a standard method of fostering professional development and quality assurance in fields, such as psychotherapy, education, and nursing, supervision in coaching is relatively recent. Publications in the field of coaching supervision have emerged from a small number of authors, predominantly in the United Kingdom and Europe. Recently, the International Coaching Federation, which is the dominant credentialing organization in the Americas, acknowledged the role of supervision in coach development and grants continuing education credits for credential renewal. The first recognized coaching supervision training program in the US began in 2013; there are now four accredited coaching supervision training programs in the US. The Americas Coaching Supervision Network began in 2017 as a community of practitioners and has grown to over 300 members. Thus, we offer this publication to enrich the literature of the coaching supervision field, extend the understanding of the supervision process, and provide useful models and data applicable to work in a heretofore underrepresented sector. This book introduces several new voices to the literature of coaching supervision, first time authors who are sharing their lived experience as well as expertise informed by their lived experience.

The book is organized in three sections: Who we are, how we work, and how we learn. One consistent theme throughout all of the chapters is diversity. Our shared humanity is manifested in myriad ways that are shaped by history, language, and culture. A second theme that we see is that words matter, as evidenced by the freight that "supervision" carries in the US and for the attention to nuance and precision of Ontologically oriented Latin America. The implication for practitioners is clear: Working effectively as coaching supervisors requires close attention to context and willingness to customize and adapt as needed.

The opening chapters present three aspects of this sprawling Americas landscape: Cultural diversity, perceptions of coaching supervision, and systems perspectives. The second section discusses key issues and offers models and techniques for working with individuals, groups, internal coaches, virtual technology, and creativity. The final section of the book explores the potential uses of coaching supervision as part of a coach's evolution from learner to professional practitioner.

The complexity of the Americas is on display in the opening section of the book. Given the cultural diversity of the 55 countries that comprise the Americas, cultural awareness, cultural sensitivity, and inclusiveness are essential. Escalante sets the stage with an overview of the cultural kaleidoscope of the Americas and those aspects that manifest in coaching and supervision processes. Honoring the diversity, Escalante offers models to help practitioners understand and frame the constellations of cultural values and perspectives that influence behaviors, meaning making, decisions, and relational dynamics. Seto, Lowish, and Prefontaine offer insights gained through work with Indigenous communities in British Columbia. The interconnected, synergistic, and dynamic worldview that is central to Indigenous culture predates by centuries the current framing of systems theory prevalent in coaching, supervision, and related literature. The chapter explores the implications for coaches to attune to and understand the diversity and nuances of Indigenous cultures as well as the impact of history and intergenerational trauma.

Diverse cultures engender diverse perceptions. Three chapters address the extent to which perceptions of and attitudes toward coaching supervision in the Americas are ambiguous. The global survey results reported by McAnally et al. show the extent of this ambiguity. In particular, the results suggest that coaches in the Americas tend to conflate coach mentoring and coaching supervision, especially as presented in coach training programs. A small percentage of respondents are currently engaged in either individual or group supervision and their perception of the benefit tend toward the pragmatic: Solving problems and expanding skills. This conflation and the need for extensive education about coaching supervision is echoed in the results of a study by Goldvarg, Seto, and Eustice. Their study resulted in five key sources of resistance among respondents and offers five strategies for addressing those issues. Lopata addresses the innovation driven, entrepreneurial spirit of the Americas with a single case that describes how a "disrupter" organization in the coaching industry came to adopt coaching supervision as a value proposition for their services. The case describes how experiencing supervision allowed the organization to identify the benefits to the coaches, the organization's clients, and the organization itself.

Like our colleagues elsewhere, coaching supervisors in the Americas offer systemic perspectives and models. The two chapters that conclude this section of the book demonstrate two very different frameworks for systems work in the Americas context. Agüero and Sturich reflect the philosophical and Ontological orientation that has gained a foothold in South America. Within this framework, the supervisor supports the supervisee to examine the "structure of living beings, functioning dynamics and ways of communicating and interacting." The authors present the underlying assumptions of an Ontological approach as well as six elements of the model. In contrast, Tennyson's pragmatic, organizational orientation leads readers through an experience of introducing a systemic developmental approach to an organization, the lessons learned and adaptations made to suit her US clientele. She pinpoints three aspects of coaching culture in the US that stimulated these adaptations and spotlights organizational values and norms that influence the adoption of coaching supervision.

The second section of the book—How We Work—offers a variety of models and methods addressing internal, group, and individual coaching supervision. These chapters focus on specific models for supervision and innovative ways of supervising. Giglio's Tri-Lens model offers a framework for coaching supervision that emphasize the restorative function of supervision, nurturing coach well-being and resilience, and supporting coaches to expand their abilities to address the personal, relational, and systemic aspects of the coach's experience. Chamow and Evans similarly offer a model for the restorative function of coaching supervision. Browning, Fitzsimmons, and Arnold start the section with a comparative study introducing coaching supervision into two different types of organizations: Corporate and government. Their observations gain an added dimension through a reflective discussion of their experiences with an experienced coaching supervisor working in the UK and Europe. Harrison and Bizouard studied the effect of supervision on coaches in North and South America. The coaches in the study share a number of characteristics, transcending location, and culture. Their chapter presents a comprehensive overview of supervision literature and identifies specific benefits as the coaches experienced them. The magic referred to in Harrison and Bizouard's title is echoed in DeLay and Giglio's model of co-presencing in a group supervision setting. Group presence is offered as an open space that allows stories and insights to unfold. The authors describe each step of the process and support the theoretical model with specific examples. Similarly, Goldvarg and Seto use a transcribed group session to illustrate how Hawkin's seven-eyed model can be operationalized as well as examples of supervision practices that align with the EMCC standards.

Goldvarg and Turner present the results of their study on the uses, benefits, and challenges of using virtual technology in supervision, while acknowledging that the global pandemic has driven an increasing number of practitioners to this modality. The authors conclude their chapter with specific recommendations that address both practical and ethical issues. One finding suggests that virtual technology may be useful in expanding creative approaches to supervision, a topic which Warman takes up in her chapter. She presents the underlying premises of creativity in coaching supervision and the outcomes of a small study.

The final section of the book addresses the development and education of coaches and the potential roles for supervision in those processes.

McLean's research articulates a developmental path for coaches and identifies the uses of coaching supervision appropriate to each developmental stage. Her research reflects the experiences of 60 coaches and compares trends across groups with different years of experience as supervisees. Wright's chapter draws on research and experience to make the case for supervision as an important element in continuing professional development. Her chapter, in particular, reinforces the case for supervision for internal coaches. Espinal and Rodriguez present the findings of a study on the effects of introducing coaching supervision into a coach training program. The authors discuss their initial hypotheses and findings and offer recommendations to coach educators on how to best incorporate supervision into their programs.

Like the continents themselves, this book covers a vast territory, exploring some new areas and adapting familiar ideas to new situations. It is our hope that readers will enjoy the journey and perhaps find new and open spaces for their own exploration.

Francine Campone, April 2021

# Section I

# Who We Are

# 1 Multi-Systemic Fields Model for Culturally Sensitive Coaching Supervision

*Ana L. Escalante*

## Introduction

As we all know, the world has been transformed in the past year not only by a pandemic that has taken more than a million lives, but also by the accelerated ecological, social, economic, political, and technological changes that it has forced into being.

Old ways of seeing and interpreting are no longer of use. Our identities are being transformed as we navigate this new world that is giving birth to a new era in human history.

North, Central, and South America are not the exception. The rise of this new era has brought forward old problems in the region: radical movements such as White supremacy and extreme communism, drug cartels, and issues of women's safety, extreme poverty, corruption, and inequality, to name a few.

In the midst of this, the region has an incredible history and beautiful cultural heritage, which I am convinced has not yet been shared with the world: family values, open heartedness, warmth, and a strong sense of spirituality, among other qualities.

As a multicultural region, the Americas reflects a kaleidoscope of cultures and values that are determined not only by each country's history, socioeconomic, and political status, but also by a myriad of subcultures that are vibrant and visible in each country. As our world embraces globalization, the rising importance of family, community, and tribal affiliations have become crucial to providing a sense of identity, security, and belonging to many individuals.

The myriad of cultures present in the Americas influence how individuals define power, personal and collective visions, and possibilities that can significantly impact the coaching supervision experience. Coaching supervisors are bound to create and hold a space where these diverse perspectives can be brought to the surface and explored in the context of coaching.

What conditions are required for the practice of coaching supervision in this changing world? What are the moral dilemmas that a coaching supervisor may encounter in our region?

The ethical conversation is an essential element in coaching supervision as

DOI: 10.4324/b23130-3

ethical predicaments and considerations are part of the day-to-day practice of coaching. Coaching supervision should provide a space where coaches can develop and even improve their ethical maturity and decision-making.

This chapter aims to provide a model for culturally sensitive coaching supervision that can serve as a framework for the analysis of value systems coaches may encounter in the Americas. The proposed model is based on five ethical approaches aimed at creating a system of analysis for ethical dilemmas in our profession.

Using survey data obtained from coaching supervisors in the Americas, I share examples of coaching supervision in the region and approaches supervisors reported using when coming close to ethical dilemmas.

At the end of the chapter, I provide some case studies that may help to exemplify this culturally sensitive coaching supervision model and some coaching supervision ethical dilemmas in the Americas.

## Culture and Values as Fields of Influences

Cultural values are a shared symbolic system of behaviors, meanings, and expressions that organize the activities of a particular society and its individuals. (Majaguabsar, 1983, p. 11). They create a symbolic order in the relationships that hold together a society or a small group, providing a sense of wholeness of life, wealth, spiritual heritage, and a common sense of purpose (UNESCO, 1980, p. 19).

As supervisors, we "are participants in the three-cornered meeting that is supervision. We bring our own culture and its assumptions with us as do the other two participants, the coach and the coachee" (Turner 2019, Atwood 2014 in Turner 2019 p. 41).

Professor Peter Hawkins advises that to fully understand the repercussions of cultural differences in supervision,

> we need to discover and acknowledge the particular norms, prejudices and assumptions that we can fall into. We cannot exclude ourselves from the field of inquiry and neither can our supervisee. This exploration includes the power dynamics between us, and between our supervisee and their coaches, both those given to us by our role and by our culture. (Turner & Palmer, 2019, p. 41)

Ryde et al. (2019) applied the intersubjective system theory (IST) to the study of coaching supervision. IST questions challenge the notion that individuals have a "separate mind," but that we exist within an intersubjective context or "field" that changes continuously as different field influences arise. The self is fluid and only exists as an organizing principle within the relationship and within the context of a community. Self, therefore, is co-created through the field of our relationships:

The meeting between the coach and the coachee and between the supervisor and supervisee are therefore co-created. What happens between us does not "belong" to either of us. It is often thought that one of the jobs of the coach or the supervisor is to try to decide if what we are experiencing or feeling "belongs" to us or to our coachee or supervisee. This idea looks different when seen intersubjectively. If we co-create our experience then it belongs to both of us and, in fact to the wider world we inhabit. (Ryde et al., 2019, p. 48–49)

The dynamic, fluid, and mostly unconscious nature of the field of culture and values of the supervision triad—supervisor, coach, and client—required the development of an explicit model that supervisors could hold for a more objective and conscious analysis of the coach's presenting situation.

## Culturally Sensitive Coaching Supervision Model

What does it mean to be vulnerable, intimate, and connected in a coaching and coaching supervision relationship? Is there a way to differentiate the ethical dilemmas that are encountered in different regions? Is there a differentiated symbolic order that holds together the relationships in the supervision triad? What is our sense of wholeness, understanding, connection, ethics, and purpose and how does this impact the supervision process?

In the following pages, I analyze four ethical frameworks for culture and value influence in the Americas that are the foundation of my proposed multi-systemic culture fields model for coaching supervision. These include:

1   The World Values Survey (WVS)
2   Individual versus collective cultural assumptions
3   Deontological versus consequentialist framework
4   The seven-eyed model of coaching supervision

## World Values Survey (WVS) in the Americas

The World Values Survey (WVS) is part of an international research program devoted to the scientific and academic study of social, political, economic, religious, and cultural values of people in the world. Researchers used WVS data to create a global map of values that classified societies and world regions.

Political scientists Ronald Inglehart and Christian Welzel (2005) analyzed WVS data and found two major dimensions of cross-cultural values variation in the world:

•   Traditional versus secular-rational values
•   Survival versus self-expression values

These values influence people's attitudes toward democracy, gender values, religion, happiness, life satisfaction, and individual agency. The value differences between societies around the world show a pronounced culture zone pattern that reflects different historical pathways of how entire groups of societies entered modernity. These pathways account for people's different senses of existential security and individual agency, which in turn account for their different emphases on secular-rational values and self-expression values (Tausch, 2015).

A two dimensional global map of values was generated for the Americas. In this, we find that Canada, most of the US, and Latin America are societies with **traditional and self-expression values** (Welzel et al., 2003). Their value system emphasizes:

- Religion, parent-child ties, deference to authority and traditional family values.
- Rejection of divorce, abortion, euthanasia, and suicide, with high levels of national pride and a nationalistic point of view.
- Prioritizing environmental protection, tolerance of foreigners, gays and lesbians and gender equality, and rising demands for participation in decision-making in economic and political life.

These results have important implications for the coaching supervision process. Values can add magnitude and strength to individual positions and perspectives in the coaching supervision process. Therefore, values should be shared with openness and treated with respect, with the aim of creating the most benefit to the client and the ethical maturity of the coach.

## Individual versus Collective Cultural Assumptions

WVS results confirmed the Americas as collectivist rather than individualistic societies. An individualistic society is rooted in the individual whose value system aims to develop the individual well-being and self-realization. A collective culture is rooted on family or community values, with people that honor their collective context and the role that they play in it (Ryde et al., 2019).

I propose that coaching supervision practices and purposes differ according to collectivist or individualistic values. In individualistic societies and cultures, the aim of coaching and coaching supervision is to help individuals better know themselves and resolve personal difficulties. By contrast, coaching supervision in a collectivist culture aims to foster the personal development of coaches in connection with systemic relationships.

Although we can observe both tendencies in the Americas, I hypothesize that the tendency in North America is toward the individualistic values that stress personal development, with the exception of Indigenous communities in North America. Latin American countries and their Indigenous communities may be more inclined to collectivist culture and values that stress personal development and identity in connection with family, friends, community, and other networks.

## Deontological versus Consequentialist Framework

Philosophically speaking, ethical predispositions and decision-making can be divided in two broad categories: formalism or deontological (Kantian) approach and consequentialism or teleological approach (Barak-Corren & Bazerman, 2017). Ethical predispositions are foundational to how people reason, shaping both moral awareness (Reynolds, 2006) and moral decision-making (Brady & Wheeler, 1996).

**The formalism framework** presumes that by acting according to a categorical imperative or in harmony with universal maxims, one necessarily acts morally. Ethical dilemmas are therefore resolved by following a list of ethical rules and principles that can assure the moral resolution of any situation. An example of this would be coaching codes of ethics.

However, there may be situations of conflicting imperatives where the formalistic approach may be insufficient. These are instances when taking action based upon a set of rules may lead to negative consequences. This complication is one that leads to the consequentialist theory.

**The consequentialism framework** focuses on the outcomes of an ethical dilemma as the main influence guiding decision-making. It holds the consequences of one's conduct as the ultimate basis for any judgment about the rightness or wrongness of a particular behavior. Thus, from a consequentialist standpoint, a morally right act (or omission from acting) is one that produces a good outcome. Rightness is based upon the maximization of well-being.

However, there remains a question of how to measure the moral consequence or outcome of an ethical decision. Is it pleasure, the absence of pain, the satisfaction of one's preferences, professional conduct, the client's interests, or a broader notion of common good?

Recently, a formal scale to measure formalism and consequentialism, the Ethical Standards of Judgment Questionnaire (ESJQ), was developed and validated for the general population by Love et al. (2020). The ESJQ is a formal instrument divided into two subscales. The formalism subscale (six items) captures the tendency of an individual to make ethical choices based on a set of rules that determine whether a decision or behavior is good or bad. The consequentialism subscale captures the tendency of an individual to make judgments and evaluate ethical choices based on outcomes, or the net utility of the choice (Love et al., 2020).

This questionnaire was used in a survey with coaching supervisors in the Americas. The outcomes are explored in the next section.

## Deontological versus Consequentialist Coaching Supervisor Study in the Americas

A survey was sent to several coaching supervisor networks in our region to explore if there was a tendency toward a formalist or consequentialist approach in the coaching supervisors. The survey was available through SurveyMonkey in English and Spanish and was open for four weeks from November 8 to December 10, 2020. The ESJQ was included in the survey as well as questions regarding ethical dilemmas and sample cases. A sample of the survey questions is attached at the end of the chapter.

An invitation to participate in the study was sent to 28 individual coaching supervisors listed on the ICF website as supervisors in the region and 11 graduate cohorts from the Goldvarg Consulting Supervision certified Spanish program and posted to the Americas Coaching Supervision Network LinkedIn site. A total of 17 coaching supervisors answered the survey. They possessed 14 years of coaching experience and 3.3 years of practice in coaching supervision, on average. Respondents reported their ICF coaching credentials as: One Associate Certified Coach, 11 Professional Certified Coaches, and five Master Certified Coaches. Further demographics of the survey respondents are presented in Table 1.1.

The results of this modest study are shown in Table 1.2, which displays the total sum of points for each subscale as well as the average responses of both scales using a 5-point Likert Scale from Strongly Agree (5) to Strongly Disagree (1).

*Table 1.1* Sample Demographics of Coaching Supervisors that Answered the Survey by Country

| Country | Nationality | Average of Years Practicing Coaching | Average of Years Practicing Coaching Supervision |
|---------|-------------|--------------------------------------|--------------------------------------------------|
| USA | 3 | 19 | 2 |
| Argentina | 4 | 11 | 4 |
| Brazil | 2 | 15 | 3 |
| Chile | 1 | 15 | 8 |
| Mexico | 5 | 14 | 3 |
| Peru | 1 | 11 | 4 |
| Venezuela | 1 | 12 | 2 |

*Table 1.2* Total Sum and Average point for Each Subscale for the 17 Supervisors that Answer the ESJQ

|  | Formalism Subscale | Consequentialism Subscale | Difference |
|--|--------------------|---------------------------|------------|
| Total Sum | 52.83 | 63.67 | 10.83 |
| Average | 3.11 | 3.75 | 0.64 |

These results aligned with several studies that show formalism and consequentialism are not the opposite ends of a continuum (Brady, 1985), but distinct and related constructs (Greene et al., 2008; Greene et al., 2001; Love et al., 2015).

The results showed that although supervisors in the Americas used both ethical approaches, there was a tendency to lean toward consequentialism or teleological predisposition, which may have shaped supervisors' reason in both moral awareness and moral decision-making. This means that when making an ethical decision, the supervisors in our region consulted applicable rules or ethical codes, but put more emphasis on decision-making that maximized well-being within a particular situation.

Independently of the ethical presuppositions of the supervisor, it is well advised that the coaching supervisor include the code of ethics as part of the general agreement for coaching supervision. This will provide a framework for the coaching supervision relationship that may guide the analysis of ethical dilemmas by the supervisor, the coach, and the client, themselves.

## The Seven-Eyed Model

Professor Peter Hawkins applied his seven-eyed model (Hawkins et al., 2020, p. 35) to study the impact of cultural factors on the coaching supervision triad as well as on the relationships between the three coaching supervision participants (the fourth element for cultural and value dynamics). As Hawkins and Turner (2020) describe:

At the heart of systemic supervision is the recognition that we cannot see any system, be it the individual client, the team and organization they are part of etc., without in some way, being part of the system we are seeing and understanding. Second, we cannot see the whole of a system we are part of, only the system as it appears in and through our perspective (p. 152).

Given that culture and value influences are mostly unconscious and not visible to the coach, it becomes necessary to make this conversation explicit and bring forward all assumptions that are shown, shared, and managed in the supervision relationship.

## Multi-Systemic Culture Fields Model for Coaching Supervision (MSCF)

Following the systemic approach, we can observe multiple layers of cultural values at play in any coaching and coaching supervision relationship and process. The dynamics of culturally sensitive coaching supervision are perceived not only through the language, meanings, and interpretation of the participants, but also through the emotional tone and physical reactions the coaching conversation may produce.

After a thorough review of the literature of culture and value influences in the coaching process, I crafted a multi-systemic fields model to help analyze the complex dynamics of the coaching supervision triad.

**Multi Systemic Fields Model
for Cultures and Values**

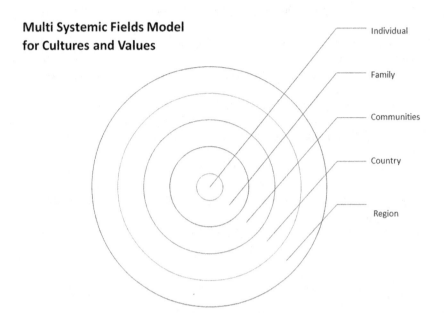

*Figure 1.1* Multi-Systemic Fields Model for Cultures and Values.

There are at least five levels of conscious and unconscious fields of cultural influences at play in the supervision triad: client–coach–supervisor. See Figure 1.1.

Each of these levels creates a cohesive conglomeration of interrelated and interdependent cultural influences on the worldview of any given individual. Many studies have found significant value differences depending on a multiplicity of factors (Tausch, 2015; Welzel et al., 2003; Palmer, 2019).

Table 1.3 further describes each of the cultural fields of influence at play in coaching supervision.

The combination of cultural and value influences creates a unique and fluid worldview. This is reflected in the perceptions, thinking, language, behaviors, actions, practices, decisions and dilemmas of the client, the coach, and the coaching supervisor; these influences are present in the supervision system at any given time.

Adapting the seven-eyed model (2020), we represent the dynamics of the MSCF model for supervision as depicted in Figure 1.2.

When analyzing the coaching supervision triad in the MSCF model, we understand multiple, complex systems are interacting together to create fields of possibilities within the coaching supervision environment. The following questions and reflections may guide us in exploring the dynamics of culture and values within a culturally sensitive supervision process:

*Table 1.3* Cultural Fields of Influence at Play in Coaching Supervision

| Culture and Values | Multi-Systemic Fields of Influences |
| --- | --- |
| Individual | Basic living conditions, health, race, identity, generation, personal history, education, income, gender preferences, social status, and existential security, languages, religious belief systems, etc. |
| Family | Family traditions, race, history, ancestors, language, health, economic status, social and existential security, values, etc. |
| Communities | The chosen communities that the individual belongs given either from the family or for the personal identities, i.e., religious, gender, hobbies, sports, etc. |
| Country | History, economic and political development, climate, government approach, leadership, traditions, legal and social norms. |
| Region/Environment | Geography, ecology, climate, history, language, eastern/western philosophical approaches. |

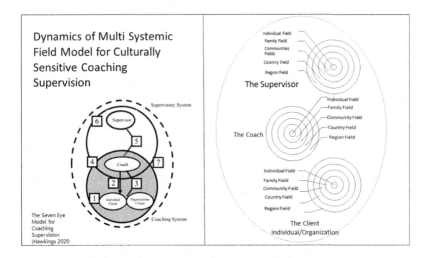

*Figure 1.2* Dynamics of Multi-Systemic Field Model for Culturally Sensitive Supervision.

1   **The individual client situation:** What cultural values influence individual behaviors, interpretations, mindset, sense of possibility, emotional expressions, purpose, and vision of future?

2   **The coach's interventions for the coachee:** What interventions are interpreted as ethical or not ethical for both parties? What does a particular word or intervention mean, given the cultural context of the participants?

3   **The coaching relationship:** What unconscious cultural influences are at play in co-creation of the relationship and in the interventions of the coach?

4   **The coach:** What conscious and unconscious cultural processes, meanings, and emotional reactions are at play in the inner world of the coach that modify the coaching process and relationship?

5   **The supervisory relationship and parallel process:** Which histories, emotional reactions, body reactions, or sensibilities are triggered that mirror the culture and values of the supervision triad?

6   **The supervisor:** What cultural conscious and unconscious processes, meanings, and emotional reactions are at play in the inner world of the coaching supervisor that modify the coaching supervision process and relationship?

7   **The wider contexts:** What cultural and values influences frame the coaching supervision and coaching conversations and processes? What does race mean to me? Do I have a particular prejudice against or predisposition for people of a particular race, gender, sexual preference, economic status, etc.?

The integration of the cultural and value fields model opens or closes possibilities in the supervision process. What are we listening for or not listening for during coaching supervision? What are we emphasizing and what are we ignoring? What unconscious cultural beliefs are brought into coaching supervision that are not challenged? What emotional reactions are expected and even expressed and what emotions are considered inappropriate in a particular culture? All these subconscious and almost invisible cultural presuppositions shape the field on which the coaching supervision conversation is occurring, shaping coaching supervision relationships and results.

For example, a coach shares a case in which the client is experiencing poor basic living conditions, high levels of corruption in her community, economic, and gender inequities. The client has just discovered that her husband has been having an affair for some time. This raises an ethical dilemma for the coach. Integrity may mean something quite different to the supervisor, coach, and client. What does this situation mean for each person? What emotional reactions are triggering? What conscious or unconscious judgments are made by each member of the triad? Is she a weak or a strong woman if she stays? And how might this change if she leaves? What consequences may appear in the multi systemic fields of the client's life and her future if she makes the decision to stay or to leave? What is expected in her family? What is expected in the family of the coach? And in the supervisor value system? Does the decision to stay or leave need to be made from a deontological or a consequentialist framework?

We all have cultural blind spots that prevent us from observing a situation as it occurs within the coaching supervision triad. Working in our personal, cultural blind spots as supervisors is necessary to create integrity, trust, strong relationships, and happy societies (Escalante, 2020). Respect for diversity and multiculturalism enables coaches and coach supervisors to form profound connections with colleagues, clients, and even with our own spiritual dimensions.

## Case Studies

Next, I present three case studies I designed with reflection questions based on the multi-systemic cultural fields model, which offer practice opportunities to consider some of the ethical dilemmas a coaching supervisor in the Americas may encounter. In the first case study, I present my own reflections using both formalist and consequentialism perspectives.

### Case Study 1

Lorena, a professional coach practicing in Mexico brought an ethical dilemma to coaching supervision that emerged in her coaching practice. Pedro was a tall, handsome 17-year-old man who convinced his parents to sponsor his coaching process to explore his career options and the type of university he would like to attend.

During the coaching process, Pedro disclosed his heavy use of marijuana. The dilemma shared by Lorena was whether she should reveal this situation to Pedro's parents, who were sponsoring the minor's coaching process.

Using the formalism versus consequentialism decision-making approach, the coaching supervisor could analyze this situation in two ways:

a  The formalist perspective: The coach consults the code of ethics and the regulating laws of the profession and acts accordingly. For instance, statement 5 of the ICF code of ethics, reads:

> Have a clear understanding with both Clients and Sponsors or interested parties about the conditions under which information will not be kept confidential (e.g., illegal activity, if required by law, pursuant to valid court order or subpoena; imminent or likely risk of danger to self or to others; etc.). Where I reasonably believe one of the above circumstances is applicable, I may need to inform appropriate authorities. (ICF, 2020)

b  The consequentialism perspective: The coach analyzes the client's privilege of confidentiality, the client's ability and resources for self-care, the multiple consequences of revealing this information to the family, the coaching relationship viability, and finds other ethical solutions such as referrals, client's self-disclosure of the problem, or client's voluntary enrollment in a rehab program.

MSCF Model Questions for Reflection:

- What confidentiality privileges should be granted to the client? To the coach? To the supervisor?
- Do the parents have the right to know about marijuana abuse by their son?
- Does the use of marijuana interfere with the coaching agreement and results? If not, does the coach need to keep addressing this issue during the coaching practice?
- Who is the authority in this case that may define the course of action? The parents? The ICF? The client? The coach? The supervisor?
- Is the use of marijuana legal in the state or country where the minor lives?
- May the supervisor take a different approach depending on the country where the coaching process is taking place?
- What prejudices, judgments, or values do the coach and supervisor hold about the use of marijuana by a minor? How does this affect the coaching process?

### Case Study 2

Johana was an experienced coach who brought to group supervision the case of Rosa, a successful Colombian 45-year-old entrepreneur. She had been coaching Rosa every other week for more than a year. Rosa had come to coaching with the purpose of balancing her personal and business life, which was quite demanding. Her business had doubled in the last year and the effort to sustain the company's growth had taken a toll on her family life and her general health. She felt irritated and tired all the time and had been gaining weight.

The coaching process had been successful in helping Rosa create balance in her life; however, Rosa reported concerns about her team being stressed out, somewhat disorganized and irritated. During the last session, Rosa requested that Johana come to her business as a human resources consultant and develop some trainings and interviews with her company's direct line of executives.

Johana brought the possibility of consulting for her client's business to coaching supervision. She already had the knowledge and skills to perform the job and knew the company through the eyes of the owner.

MSCF Model Questions for Reflection:

- Is there a conflict of interest? If so, might this conflict of interest be perceived as less relevant in Latin America than in the US or Canada?
- If Johana accepts the double role of coach and business consultant to Rosa's company, what ethical dilemmas could she encounter during the performance of her responsibilities?
- Is there a legal framework that prevents Johana from taking on both roles?

- Is there an ethical code of conduct that regulates this situation?
- How would the relationship between the supervision triad be affected if the coaching supervisor recommended against Johana taking the consulting case, even though she needs the money?
- What values, if any, are at stake in this case regarding the coach, the coaching supervisor, and the client?
- What is the role of the coaching supervisor if the supervision triad participants were from different culture, countries, or subcultures and had different approaches to this situation?

### *Case Study 3*

Sonia was the mother of two. She had been practicing coaching for more than a decade and had recently become a coaching supervisor. During her last coaching supervision session, she learned that Rocio, her new supervisee, had been coaching a client for more than six months. The client recently disclosed to Rocio their membership in a drug gang. After this disclosure, Rocio stopped feeling secure around her client and wondered what she should do. On the one hand, she felt a commitment to help the client's well-being. On the other hand, she felt vulnerable, angry with her client for the late disclosure, and unsure how to proceed. She preferred to terminate the case, however, she wanted to do it in a professional and secure way.

MSCF Model Questions for Reflection:

- What are the boundaries between the ethical confidentiality of the coach and the legal responsibilities?
- What are the legal responsibilities of the coaching supervisor?
- What are the supervisor's and coach's values, beliefs, and feelings around this case? How may these affect the coaching supervision?
- What unconscious values processes, meanings and emotional reactions are at play in the inner world of the coach that may modify the coaching process and relationship?
- What are the personal ethical responsibilities of the coach? Should the coach disclose her feelings to the client? If so, why?
- What influence do culture and cultural values play in framing coaching supervision and coaching conversations and processes?

## Conclusion

We create our social reality by distinguishing distinctions. In modern society, older polarizing paradigms classified humans as black-yellow-white; gay-straight; poor-rich; good-evil. These distinctions benefitted those who had power. From this worldview emerged a polarized, discriminatory world that produced separation, brutality, and the killing of more than 203 million people from war and oppression in the 20th century (Bassouni, 1997).

We are now entering a new era. One that emphasizes inclusion, unity, diversity, and greater respect for the different. We have invented languages that attempt to stop our blindness and create equality and the dignify, all: "LGBTTTIQ," "economically disadvantaged," "overweight," "politically correct," "race/ethnicity," "cultural heritage," "police brutality," "human rights," and many others. This is our attempt to diminish the separation between us, making us one human race. For all of us the real challenge is to embrace a bigger heart and understanding, giving birth to a new, more gentle society.

Supervision is a sacred space where this new paradigm can be held. A sacred space for healing the healers. A place of vulnerability and learning. A space where everyone is respected and honored.

We, as supervisors sustain the responsibility of embracing the challenges that our supervisees face, with open eyes, humility, and honest hearts.

Ethics is now multi-systemic and, in my view, is the context in which we are giving birth to this new field of possibilities. A space in which we can heal each other through respect, justice, and love. No one is left out.

Supervision ethics must create a relational space where coaches are welcomed and can make themselves whole again. A place where coaches are not asked to be right, but to be brave; a space where vulnerability, humility, and deep learning can occur.

Ethics for multi-cultural supervision must hold this sacred space where we can listen with gentleness and a not knowing heart to the worldview of our clients and our client's clients.

If we, as supervisors, are able to create a space where the wholeness of coaches can be embraced, we will be giving an incredible gift to the world. Coaches who are whole will, in turn, make a space for wholeness for the clients they serve.

It is time to wake up. Coaching supervisors are called now to contribute to the attempt of humanity to sing a new, old song. The song embodied by Beethoven's 9th Symphony (*Ode to Joy*) and sung by saints and sages: The song of brotherhood that urges us to honor ourselves as much as the other.

## References

Atwood, G. E., & Stolorow, R. D. (2014). *Structures of subjectivity: Explorations in psychoanalytic phenomenology* (2nd ed.). The Analytic Press.

Barak-Corren, N., & Bazerman, M. H. (2017). Is saving lives your task or God's? Religiosity, belief in God, and moral judgment. *Judgment and Decision Making, 12*(3): 280–296.

Bassouni, C. M. (1997). Searching for peace and achieving justice: The need for accountability. *Law and Contemporary Problems, 59*(4): 9–28.

Brady, F. N. (1985). A Janus-headed model of ethical theory: Looking two ways at business/society issues. *The Academy of Management Review, 10*(3): 568–576.

Brady, F. N., & Wheeler, G. E. (1996). An empirical study of ethical predispositions. *Journal of Business Ethics, 15*(9): 927–940.

Greene, J. D., Morelli, S. A., Lowenberg, K., Nystrom, L. E., & Cohen, J. D. (2008). Cognitive load selectively interferes with utilitarian moral judgment. *Cognition, 107*(3): 1144–1154.

Greene, J. D., Sommerville, R. B., Nystrom, L. E., Darley, J. M., & Cohen, J. D. (2001). An fMRI investigation of emotional engagement in moral judgment. *Science, 293*(5537): 2105–2108.

Hawkins, P., & Turner, E. (2020). *Systemic coaching.* Taylor and Francis.

Inglehart, R., & Welzel, C. (2005). *The human development sequence.* Cambridge University Press. Online publication date: September 2012.

International Coaching Federation. (2020). *ICF code of ethics.* https://coachfederation.org/ethics/code-of-ethics

Love, E., Salinas, T., & Rotman, J. (2020). The ethical standards of judgment questionnaire: Development and validation of independent measures of formalism and consequentialism. *Journal of Business Ethics, 161*: 115–132.

Love, E., Staton, M., & Rotman, J. D. (2015). Loyalty as a matter of principle: the influence of standards of judgment on customer loyalty. *Marketing Letters, 27*, 1–14.

Majaguabsar, M. (1983). Preservation and further development of cultural values. *The UNESCO Press and La Baconniere, 4*(1): 11.

Palmer, S. (2019). *The heart of coaching supervision: Working with reflection and self-care (essential coaching skills and knowledge).* Taylor and Francis.

Reynolds, S. J. (2006). Moral awareness and ethical predispositions: Investigating the role of individual differences in the recognition of moral issues. *Journal of Applied Psychology, 91*(1): 233–243.

Ryde, J., Seto, L., & Goldvarg, D. (2019). Diversity and inclusion in supervision. In E. Turner, & S. Palmer (Eds.), *The heart of coaching supervision: Working with reflection and self-care (essential coaching skills and knowledge).* Taylor and Francis.

Tausch, A. (2015, March 31). Towards new maps of global human values, based on world values survey (6) data. doi:10.2139/ssrn.2587626

Turner, E., & Palmer, S. (2019). *The heart of coaching supervision: Working with reflection and self-care (essential coaching skills and knowledge).* Taylor and Francis.

UNESCO. (1980). International thesaurus of cultural development. http://vocabularies.unesco.org/browser/en/about

Welzel, C., Inglehart, R., & Klingemann, H. D. (2003). The theory of human development: A cross-cultural analysis. *European Journal of Political Research, 42*(3), 341–379. doi:10.1111/1475-6765.00086

## Appendix 1

Ethical Standards of Judgment Questionnaire (ESJQ) by Love et al. (2020)

C1 When people disagree over ethical matters, I strive for workable compromises.

C2 When thinking of ethical problems, I try to develop practical, workable alternatives.

C3  It is of value to societies to be responsive and adapt to new conditions as the world changes.

C4  Solutions to ethical problems usually are seen as some shade of gray.

C5  When making an ethical decision, one should pay attention to others' needs, wants and desires.

C6  The purpose of the government should be to promote the best possible life for its citizens.


F1  Solutions to ethical problems are usually black and white.

F2  A person's actions should be described in terms of being right or wrong.

F3  A nation should pay the most attention to its heritage, its roots.

F4  Societies should follow stable traditions and maintain a distinctive identity.

F5  Uttering a falsehood is wrong because it wouldn't be right for anyone to lie.

F6  Unethical behavior is best described as a violation of some principle of the law.

Spanish Translation of the ESJQ sent to the American supervisors

C1  Cuando la gente no está de acuerdo sobre cuestiones éticas, me esfuerzo por lograr compromisos viables.

C2  Cuando pienso en problemas éticos, trato de desarrollar alternativas prácticas y viables.

C3  Es valioso para las sociedades responder y adaptarse a las nuevas condiciones a medida que cambia el mundo.

C4  Las soluciones a los problemas éticos suelen verse en una escala de grises

C5  Al tomar una decisión ética, se debe prestar atención a las necesidades, deseos y deseos de los demás.

C6  El propósito del gobierno debería ser promover la mejor vida posible para sus ciudadanos.


F1  Las soluciones a los problemas éticos suelen ser en blanco y negro.

F2  Las acciones de una persona deben describirse en términos de ser correctas o incorrectas.

F3  Una nación debe prestar la mayor atención a su herencia, sus raíces.

F4  Las sociedades deben seguir tradiciones estables y mantener una identidad distintiva.

F5  Decir una falsedad está mal porque no sería correcto que nadie mienta.

F6  El comportamiento poco ético se describe mejor como una violación de algún principio de la ley.

# 2 Walking With Our Indigenous Clients and Colleagues

*Lily Seto, Mary Prefontaine, and Leanne Lowish*

This chapter seeks to explore the value that coaching supervision brings to coaches working with Indigenous clients and the impact coaching supervision has on the ability of the coach to understand more deeply the client and the broader system.

## Who We Are and How This Came to Be

We are a group of coaches, who support leaders and teams in Indigenous communities and organizations. Coaching clients in these communities and organizations are mostly Indigenous people; other clients are White or people of color. These clients are, for the most part, grounded in Indigenous culture, worldviews, and traditions.

This chapter emerged from conversationswith five coaching supervisors and six coaches from Canada, the US, the UK, Australia, and New Zealand, all of whom are interested and appreciative of Indigenous worldviews.

Two of the authors of this chapter are coaching supervisors, and a third author is a coach. We share how coaching supervision has played (and continues to play) a critical role in our work with Indigenous clients. We hope this chapter generates further dialogue on the responsibility coaches and supervisors have to fully understand how dominant cultures, worldviews, biases, and coaching techniques may not serve us or the clients whose cultures and histories are different from our own.

In our part of the world, we are aware of a small number of Indigenous coaches. To our knowledge, none are coaching supervisors. We hope our shared experience spurs a call to action within the coaching industry to invite Indigenous coaches to coaching supervision training.

The author of *Sand Talk: How Indigenous Thinking Can Save the World*, Tyson Yurkaporta, wrote and built each chapter of his book around oral culture exchanges with diverse people, all of which made him uncomfortable. He called these exchanges yarns; "I yarn with those people because they extend my thinking more than those who know what I know … . Yarns are like conversations but take a traditional form that we have always used to create and transmit knowledge" (2020, p. 14).

DOI: 10.4324/b23130-4

In this chapter, we speak about coaching supervision within the specific context of our work with Indigenous cultures in BC, Canada. We seek to honor Indigenous cultural values and ways of living by sharing our experiences through a series of yarns with clients, coaches, and coaching supervisors. Most of our coaching conversations felt uncomfortable. From this discomfort, we discovered insights about ourselves, the coaching practice, and how coaching supervision was critical in the process of supporting coaches and their clients in this community.

## Our Invitation to You

We would like to extend this yarn to you, our readers, by sharing our insights and asking you to consider more deeply your own cultural biases and worldviews. We provide a few prompts for further thinking and to help you grow a deeper awareness of yourself and others.

All the coaches, clients, and supervisors we yarned with gave expressed permission to share their stories and insights. The coaches and supervisors are recognized at the end of this chapter. Client identities are confidential.

## The Context of Our Work

By some estimates, the Indigenous population in BC comprises of more than 200 First Nations[1] as well as Inuit and Métis (Muckle, 2002).

The first encounters between Europeans and Indigenous people happened in the late 1700s. These encounters brought disease to Indigenous people and increased dependence on settlers (Muckle, 2002). Colonization, which started in the late 19th century, introduced a dark period of history in BC (and Canada). Indigenous children were removed from their homes and sent to residential schools that were set up

> based on the notion that assimilation was best for First Nations people and that the best method of assimilation was to remove children from their homes and teach them the ways of Euro-Canadian society in schools where they also lived. (Muckle, 2002, p. 67)

Cases of physical, mental, and sexual abuse were documented at residential schools. The residential schools also resulted in "the loss of many traditional life ways, including languages and knowledge about healing, parenting and social relations ... leading to family breakdowns" (Muckle, 2002, p. 68).

In the early 2000s, the Canadian Government introduced a National Centre for Truth and Reconciliation to review the impact of the residential school system. Many Indigenous people considered the residential school system an attempt at genocide. This focus on reconciliation and national healing is the ground from which we introduce four key considerations for coaching and coaching supervision related to Indigenous communities.

### Intergenerational Trauma

History is an important factor to consider in the context of coaching and coaching supervision as it informs how and why some Indigenous clients live with direct or intergenerational trauma. As one Indigenous client in coach training shared:

> What really struck me as an Indigenous person was the notion that Indigenous people not only feel broken in themselves ... but the greater society has made us broken in some way. We need fixing. We need help. We need handouts. And from internal ... I am broken, I am less than, I have to work harder.

She further asserted that she needed to be seen as whole and capable of being healed and coached on her goals.

***Do you consider your own personal or intergenerational trauma and that of your clients when coaching or providing coaching supervision? Why?***

### Cultural Safety

Another insight we gained related to the importance of cultural safety. As another Indigenous client shared:

> Any time I am in a new situation, I know that I am checking the situation out at a very fundamental level within me. I am constantly scanning my situation and asking myself, am I feeling safe? Do I feel threatened? And I base my response through this lens.

In our exploration of cultural safety, we felt the following statements best describe cultural safety and how essential it is to establish in coaching:

> An environment which is spiritually, socially and emotionally safe, as well as physically safe for people; where there is no assault, challenge or denial of their identity, of who they are and what they need. It is about shared respect, shared meaning, shared knowledge, and experience, of learning together with dignity and truly listening. Unsafe cultural practice is any action that diminishes, demeans or disempowers the cultural identity and wellbeing of an individual or group. (Williams, 1998, p. 7)

According to the First Nations Health Authority (FNHA), cultural safety is "an outcome based on respectful engagement that recognizes and strives to address power imbalances inherent in the system. It results in an environment free of racism and discrimination, where people feel safe" (2021, p. 5).

An Indigenous client stated, "Cultural safety can only be defined by the person receiving the coaching."

*As a coach or coaching supervisor, do you actively reflect on cultural safety? Why? How might you think about cultural safety with more intention?*

### Relational Practice

One way cultural safety can be facilitated is through relational practice: "When an Indigenous person enters the space of another, they are warmly welcomed, respected, encouraged to feel comfortable, and empowered to express their thoughts, feelings and needs in a way that is culturally appropriate" (Speck, n.d. p. 8).

We learned that when we greet an Indigenous person and engage with them in relational practice, we need to take all the time needed to honor the relationship. Our attention as coaches must to be focused on the client's need to share how they feel and what is present for them, and accept how long this might take. This upfront relational practice must be complete before they can enter goal-setting and actioning. Sometimes the client gains insights through the relational practice and any storytelling that accompanies it.

Nuts amaht is considered a Coast Salish truth: "The Aboriginal concept of Nuts amaht refers to a worldview in which all living and nonliving things are seen as connected" (FNHA Values booklet n.d). This appears in the statement "all my relations." When a speaker makes this statement, they recognize the principles of harmony, unity and equality. As one client described:

> It's a way of saying that you recognize your place in the universe and that you recognize the place of others and of other things in the realm of the real and the living. In that it is a powerful evocation of truth.

*What does it mean to you to be in relational practice, to be holding as truth the idea of "all my relations"? What would need to change in you and your practice to fully embrace relational practice as described?*

Through our participation in yarns or exchanges, we explored and practiced cultural humility, considered

> processes of self-reflection to understand personal and systemic biases and to develop and maintain respectful processes and relationships based on mutual trust. Cultural humility involves humbly acknowledging oneself as a learner when it comes to understanding another's experience. (First Nations Health Authority, n.d. #itstartswithme p. 7)

One coach shared in supervision that it was humbling to own "not knowing" and to have the courage to ask when you do not know or understand, and offer an apology when you have said something out of ignorance.

*What does cultural humility mean to you? Can we claim to have cultural humility? Or is it witnessed only by another? How do you engage in cultural humility with yourself and others?*

## Experiencing Coaching Supervision With Respect to Indigenous Clients and Communities

As coaches and coaching supervisors, we found that what often got in the way of practicing humility (so we could work in relational practice) were our unconscious biases—views of the world that are often so subtle, we are unaware of them. The quotes that follow illustrate how easily we found ourselves influenced by our conscious and unconscious biases and assumptions and how we used coaching supervision to explore them.

*As you read these, notice what comes up for you. Do you or have you held similar views?*

The following quotes are from coaches who worked with coaching supervisors and Indigenous clients.

"To be invited to work in the Indigenous community by a fellow professional was a considerable honour for me. This sector of community was of interest and importance to me for many reasons, but primarily as a social equality imperative. As a seasoned coach, skilled in the International Coaching Federation core competencies, I felt prepared for this assignment. Basically, my initial assumption was that credentials and experience were enough, but they were not. I came to understand that the cultural and historical context is a foundational imperative when working with Indigenous clients."

"Coaching supervision was designed into the body of work. My initial assumption was that coaching supervision was 'nice to have,' but not essential. I quickly learned it was critical to navigating and observing my own self-direction within the coaching experience. The client's ability to stand in her experiences of trauma as an Indigenous woman demanded I was fully aware of trauma triggers in myself. Supervision gave me a safe place to process and clear anything that arose in me."

"The Indigenous Canada program on history and culture (offered through the University of Alberta) helped to educate me on the long history of oppression of our First Nations, which is still experienced in Canada today. The impact of colonization on legal and cultural human rights, coupled with the intergenerational trauma must be considered when coaching anyone of Indigenous heritage. The assumption I held was that I knew enough about this history when in reality, I will never know enough."

"Somewhere in session two or three I began to feel completely inadequate as a coach. I felt awkward, out of step with the client. It was the client who sliced to the truth that the questions I asked and the reflections I made did not hit the mark. At one point, the client said something to the effect, 'This is your word not mine.' The honest comebacks startled me and left me feeling unsettled, and it was through coaching supervision I uncovered my assumptions. The unconscious bias I held was that coaching language—words and phrases common to this field—would be accepted when working with any client when, in fact, it was the thing that tripped me up and disabled connecting with the client."

"As a sole proprietor of a coaching and consulting business, I held an assumption that I had to navigate client work alone. What I discovered with this experience was that having a coaching supervisor provided a safe place to speak of my fear of failure and sort new ways to work with my Indigenous client."

"The gift coaching supervision gave me was beyond consolation or sage advice—it was a broader perspective. This supervisor asked powerful questions, such as: 'What are you really here to do together?' Their powerful question reminded me that we were in a relationship, and like all relationships, it is a dance. When you are fully present, completely with the other, moving to the beat of the music, you dance well together. The minute you leave the present moment or try too hard or use a dancing technique, you lose the flow and magic of dancing. The assumption I held as the coach was that my technique and my process was the right way when in fact, I needed to let go of thinking I was the lead dancer."

"One of the best lessons came to me when an Indigenous client stated: 'I don't need you to hold space for me. I can hold my own space. I need you to stand with me and be beside me on this journey.' I had always assumed I must hold space for the client, which in retrospect is a notion of superiority and one that I need to learn to let go of."

"I was comfortable, and experienced, in working with a community of people whose worldview, history, and social norms were like my own—it was a colonized (or Western world) view. This worldview did not include the depth and breadth of oppression or trauma experienced within Indigenous communities. This new knowledge erased my assumption that I knew enough about cultural safety and trauma-informed practice to work with any client and propelled me to educate myself in new ways to better serve my clients".

"Supervision helped me to hold myself not only in the context of being the coach but in a broader relational context beyond just two people in the experience. Like in dancing, skill is not enough. You need to be fully attuned to the other and fully attuned to the space in which you are dancing. When you are aware of this, you are one with everything in and around you. We may not be 'Nuts amaht' until we enter the third space together, where we align with all that is present. Without the coaching supervision, I am not sure I would have explored fully the change required in me to be fully aligned in such a powerful manner."

As captured above, the coaches needed to see where their unexplored assumptions and unconscious biases were inhibiting them from being fully present, open, and available to what was arising in client sessions. This can be extremely uncomfortable as it involves a fundamental shift. As humans, we are hardwired to maintain homeostasis and to keep ourselves comfortable and in the familiar. This work requires letting go of all you know and stepping into the unknown. We believe it is essential to have coaching supervision support in doing this; otherwise, you will only go as far as you feel comfortable. A coaching supervisor helps you step into the abyss!

*In what ways are you as a coach and/or coaching supervisor exploring your assumptions and unconscious biases? How is what you are doing reinforcing your world views?*

## Working With Coaches With Respect to Indigenous Clients and Communities

As we became more aware of the conscious and unconscious biases we held and our limited worldview, our conversations grew uncomfortable at times. However, we learned that as coaches and coach supervisors working with Indigenous clients, we need to see uncomfortable conversations as the norm in order to foster greater self-awareness across multiple levels.

Another key lesson was the importance of being in relational practice, which we defined (for our coaching and supervision purposes) as a way of being that is steeped in cultural humility and includes the willingness to examine one's own emotional triggers particularly related to our own and others' trauma (direct and intergenerational); understanding the history of oppression of Indigenous people in Canada; and the ability and intent to stand in a value system that is cause-driven.

*As you read this, notice your thoughts, feelings, and somatic reactions. What are you sensing about this work?*

The following quotes are from coach supervisors who serve coaches with Indigenous clients.

"In many ways, some of my assumptions as a [coach] supervisor mirror many of the assumptions of the coaches. Having worked with Indigenous clients for several years, I was aware of some of my unconscious biases I tripped over as a coach. Now as a coaching supervisor, I am constantly doing work on my own trauma and the historical context of Indigenous people in Canada. I work with an Indigenous mentor on worldviews and culturally significant topics that help inform my practice. I am not sure how one can be an effective coach or supervisor in this space (or any other culturally diverse space) unless we are consistently exploring more deeply our own identity, biases, and trauma. These are key to building psychological safety and trust to do the important work that emerges. It truly is a dance of the unknown. I am also aware that while there are now a growing number of Indigenous coaches, there are currently no Indigenous [coach] supervisors in Canada that we are aware of."

"At any given time, we need to dance the dance that the supervisee brings into a session, which means that as a [coach] supervisor, I need to hold the bigger system in mind and be able to inquire about salient points related to the concepts of 'all my relations' and Nuts amaht."

"In some cases, the coaches I have supervised initially expressed concern about whether they have what it takes to coach in this space, as they see their Indigenous clients possessing deep spirituality and connection with all things around them. There is some awe about this. As I see it, the coaches and clients may come from different worlds, but their hearts are joined."

"The beauty of coaching is that it is a shared journey of learning, as is supervision. Both the coach and the coach supervisor work with relational and somatic ways of knowing, ways also deeply [em]bedded into Indigenous peoples' way of life. We both bring a deep appreciation of the ancient practices that play a part in their ceremonies and rituals, their dance, music and art, which are unique to each community we work within and each client we work with."

"Coaching in such communities is psychologically and spiritually demanding and as such, asks that in [coaching] supervision, it is our responsibility to ensure that the coach attends to their self-care. I believe that without attending to one's soul's journey, a coach or [coach] supervisor will miss a foundational element of their practice. Our souls need space to emerge, to reveal our frail humanity, to accept all of who we are, and to develop self-compassion. A compassionate coach is then free to work with what is emerging, free from fear of having to fix problems, and free to engage in the messiness of their work and their life with love. [Coaching] supervision that attends to the soul is a spiritual practice."

"Another theme that emerges in coaching supervision is the notion of setting goals and taking actions. In an Indigenous context, I am often reminded that a common worldview is considering the impact of actions to future generations. In some cultures, it is called Seven Generations thinking, and it is about how we are being good ancestors. One coaching client spoke in supervision about their experience as 'It's you and me in the coaching and supervision conversation, and I don't need to know about the ancestral context of my Indigenous clients to work in this space.' What he is not realizing is that ancestral learnings and elders and knowledge keepers are part of the development process. An elder is a person who has accumulated a great deal of wisdom and knowledge throughout his or her lifetime, especially in the tradition and customs of the group. They strive to show by example—by living their lives according to deeply ingrained principles, values, and teachings. In Indigenous culture, elders are the essential link to the past and to the future. Elders provide continuity and complete the 'circle of life' so that individuals, family and extended family, and community view them-selves, and subsequently behave, as a confident and complete whole. Not all older or elderly people are considered elders."

"Given the difficulties stemming from colonialism (intergenerational trauma, poverty, a legacy of challenges in society), it may be easy to step into the role of rescuer, either as a coach or even coach supervisor. Ensuring that everyone in the system is still held in unconditional positive regard (i.e., capable, resourceful, adult) is an element to be mindful of. Both the coach and coach supervisor must be aware of trauma and use trauma-informed methodologies when appropriate. Additionally, as professionals we need to be prepared to refer the client to other support systems such as therapists or the elders and traditional healers within the client's own community. It is also the shared responsibility of the coach and coach supervisor to consciously commit to questioning where power, rank, and privilege may be impacting relationships and the work."

As we explored where power, rank, and privilege surfaced in the work, we were reminded of the work of Paulo Freire:

> No pedagogy which is truly liberating can remain distant from the oppressed by treating them as unfortunates and by presenting for their emulation models from among the oppressors. The oppressed must be their own example in the struggle for their redemption. (1970, p. 54)

As coaches and coaching supervisors, we believe to work effectively with relational practice, cultural humility, and cultural safety, and maintain a deep connection to everything ("all my relations"), it is essential to identify a coaching supervisor who has experience working with diverse cultures (and if possible, Indigenous worldviews). As one coach shared:

> There's a sense in this work that you are working in unknown territory, and you have no clue that you are in the unknown territory because oftentimes we are working from our unconscious biases. So, it's critical to have a reflection partner to ensure that we are self-adjusting our worldview.

We all have our own identities, coaching models, and maps that guide us during a coaching or coaching supervision session. One challenge in relying upon identities, models, and maps is that sometimes we hold them as the truth rather than a guide to take us forward. And sometimes we believe our map is the right map and renders us all-knowing. Based on the experiences described in this chapter, we're invited to hold lightly our identities, models, and maps and call on something deeper, less directive. We prepare ourselves by arriving without attachment to our identity, model, map, or worldview and instead, trust and rely upon our own deep connection to everything, our "all my relations."

## Finding Our Way Forward

As we reflected on our journey, the following concepts, insights, and ideas emerged. Consider how these might support you in relational practice with your clients. We invite you to take these into supervision to further explore!

### Knowing Spiritual Attunement

There is a deep reverence for "the Creator" within Indigenous culture and oneness—that everything is connected, including all beings, all of nature and all that is both visible and invisible. By some definitions, attunement is a vibrational connection to the divine. We invite clients to find their own rhythm and place within this worldview that fully respects their inner wisdom and ways of knowing.

### Willingness to Explore Our Unconscious Biases

Being aware, owning our unconscious biases, and exploring how they feed into our worldview as coaches and coaching supervisors is paramount. As one coaching supervisor shared:

> As coaches and coaching supervisors, we have an opportunity to pause and have the conversations that are uncomfortable; to step into an opportunity to address systemic racism. Supervision is a safe place to talk about racism and to unpack our unconscious bias.

We believe in "calling people in" to have the conversation and do the work rather than calling people out, which has the potential to trigger shame and judgment on both sides. "Calling in involves conversation, compassion and context. It does not mean a person should ignore harm, slight, or damage ..." (Ross, 2020).

### Being Trauma Informed

Equally important is being aware that trauma exists in everyone, is always present, and often is not visible. Being trauma informed is knowing and exploring your own trauma and recognizing the signs of trauma in others.

In exercising a "trauma-informed approach" (TIP), we maintain awareness that someone (a coach, client, or coach supervisor) may have experienced trauma (directly or indirectly) and that certain behaviors may have developed to cope with the trauma. This understanding can shift how we support clients on their journey and make it easier to build trusting relationships and foster confidence.

### Working With Parallel Processes

Parallel processes are dynamics that happen in a session between the coach supervisor and the coach mirror or parallel what is unfolding for the client or within the system (Searles, 1955;in Sumerel, 1994). Tuning into parallel processes can enable us to sense what is happening in the larger emotional field. This information is accessed through our bodies and feelings (somatic listening) and can help us better support the client and coach within the wider system.

### Sense-making and Listening Somatically

There is a different type of observing, perceiving, listening, and sense-making which enables us to access different kinds of wisdom:

> To sense-make our way into understanding the world differently, so it might be possible to behave differently, is to go into the difficult task of

non-prose, non-explicit exploration and the body, memory, and mind re-find their reflections in the surrounding world. (Bateson, 2020, p. 1)

### Lean Into Not Knowing

As we walk beside our Indigenous clients, we need to be open and vulnerable in a whole new way. It takes courage and deep respect for ourselves and others to continuously embrace and be open on our journey together. Being fully vulnerable is to admit to not knowing and allowing yourself to stand on the precipice of the unknown, open to learning the way forward. This can be uncomfortable and the pull to being the expert—knowing, solving, fixing, saving, rescuing—can be strong, especially when we allow our hearts to open. What we may also experience in opening to our vulnerability is shame. Acknowledging shame and being open to its presence requires deep courage and compassion. Brene Brown asserts that "shame resilience is about moving from shame to empathy—the real antidote to shame" (2018, p. 136). Whatever emerges, we need to be ready to dance with the client in this space.

## Conclusion

It is a moral imperative that coaches work with a coaching supervisor when serving clients from Indigenous communities. Our experiences demonstrate that working with a coaching supervisor can expand a coach's capacity to be with not knowing in a way that allows relational practice to develop. In turn, this can create sufficient cultural safety to engage in the important work that's needed. As one coach supervisor described: "You have to have the capacity to dance in the unknown as a coach supervisor, and as a coach, because it's always emerging and changing."

We encourage those who serve Indigenous clients to find and work with a coaching supervisor or an Indigenous mentor to strengthen their practice and grow greater awareness of their biases and worldviews.

We also invite our colleagues and leaders in the coaching profession to take an active role in including and supporting the development of more Indigenous coaches and coaching supervisors within the profession.

Finally, as a closing question: How does the coaching and coach supervision community accelerate the training and inclusion of more diverse coaches and coach supervisors into this space? There is an ethical and moral imperative to do so. This is a question to be answered in our future work together as a community of coaches and coaching supervisors.

**The authors acknowledge with gratitude the contributions the coaching supervisors and coaches who were interviewed.**

## Note

1 First Nations is a term used to identify Indigenous Canadian Peoples who are neither Inuit or Métis.

## References

Bateson, N. (2020). The squishy mud of warm data—Where senses find senses. *Medium*. Retrieved June 18, 2021, from https://norabateson.medium.com/the-squishy-mud-of-warm-data-where-senses-find-senses-6888da67b941

Brown, B. (2018). *Dare to lead*. Random House.

First Nations Health Authority. (2021). *Cultural Safety and Humility*. https://www.fnha.ca/wellness/wellness-and-the-first-nations-health-authority/cultural-safety-and-humility

First Nations Health Authority. (n.d.). *Values and how we live them*. Booklet published by First Nations Health Authority.

First Nations Health Authority. (n.d.). #itstartswithme: Creating a climate for change. https://www.fnha.ca/Documents/FNHA-Creating-a-Climate-For-Change-Cultural-Humility-Resource-Booklet.pdf

Freire, P. (1970). *Pedagogy of the oppressed*. Herder and Herder.

Muckle, R. J. (2002). *The first nations of British Columbia*. UBC Press.

Ross, L. J. (2020, November 19). What if instead of calling people out, we called them in? *New York Times*. https://www.nytimes.com/2020/11/19/style/loretta-ross-smith-college-cancel-culture.html

Speck, W. (n.d.). *Indigenous cultural competency—A conceptual framework for building a culturally safe organization*. Aboriginal Organization Development MCFD.

Sumerel, M. (1994). *Parallel process in supervision*. (EDOCG9415). ERIC. https://www.counseling.org/resources/library/ERIC%20Digests/94-15.pdf

Williams, R. (1998). *Cultural safety—What does it mean for our work practice?* Northern Territory University. https://www.utas.edu.au/__data/assets/pdf_file/0010/246943/RevisedCulturalSafetyPaper-pha.pdf

Yurkaporta, T. (2020). *Sand talk—How indigenous thinking can save the world*. Harper Collins.

# 3 Coaching Supervision: A Study of Perceptions and Practices in the Americas

*Kimcee McAnally, Lilian Abrams,*
*Mary Jo Asmus, and Terry H. Hildebrandt*

Relatively little research has examined the adoption, benefits, and practice of coaching supervision[1] in the Americas. Prior research has focused primarily on the United Kingdom (UK) and Europe, where over the past 40 years, supervision has grown to become an expected and often required best practice for coaches (Hawkins & Turner, 2017; Turner & Hawkins, 2016). Despite the large number of coaches in the Americas, very little is known about the practice of coaching supervision in the Americas, since previous studies had few participants from this region (Hawkins & Turner, 2017; Turner & Hawkins, 2016).

To address this gap, our research team embarked on an analysis of this emerging best practice and conducted this study in 2018–2019. Our team consisted of four trained and experienced executive coaches, applied researchers, and coach supervisors, who worked actively as coaches, supervisors, and had obtained routine coach supervision, themselves. Additionally, our team coaches were among the first coaching supervisors trained in the Americas. As such, we believe that proper coaching supervision assists coaches to improve themselves and their coaching practices, for their own betterment and that of their clients.

We used the largest dataset on coaching supervision available to analyze and describe the responses of almost 500 coaches from the Americas. This exclusive focus on coaching supervision data provided a new and unique contribution to the literature, highlighting key characteristics of this practice as it begins to grow in the region. Our study also provides a useful baseline for future research investigating the growth of coaching supervision in the Americas over time.

## Research Questions

For this study, we analyzed survey data to answer the question: "How is coaching supervision currently being utilized in the US and the Americas?" In investigating the coaching supervision experience, we collected data to address the following, additional questions:

DOI: 10.4324/b23130-5

- How do coaches in the Americas find a coaching supervisor?
- What are the benefits of supervision?
- What do coaches experience under individual and group supervision?
- How frequently are individual and group coaching supervision sessions attended?
- What challenges and topics do coaches bring to individual and group supervision sessions?
- What do coaches expect to pay for individual and group supervision?

Collectively, these questions represent how executive coaches in the Americas find, experience, and expect to compensate their coach supervisors.

Given the wider usage and understanding of coaching supervision in the UK and Europe, our research utilized the European Mentoring and Coaching Council's (now EMCC Global's) 2018 definition of coaching supervision (EMCC, 2020). EMCC Global is a world leader in accrediting coaching supervision training programs as well as credentialing individual coaching supervisors.

> Supervision is the interaction that occurs when a mentor or coach brings their coaching or mentoring work experiences to a supervisor in order to be supported and to engage in reflective dialogue and collaborative learning for the development and benefit of the mentor or coach, their clients and their organisations. (EMCC, 2020, para 3)

EMCC Global's definition has been widely adopted, adapted, or has contributed to the coaching supervision definitions of such professional associations as the International Coaching Federation (ICF), the Association for Coaching (AC), the Association for Professional Executive Coaching and Supervision (APECS), among others.

## Methods

Data were collected using an online survey link that was distributed as widely as possible to coach and coach supervision networks, worldwide. We aimed to obtain responses from as many coaches as possible, regardless of whether or not they had already received supervision. Survey data were gathered between March and July, 2018. A total of 1,280 coaches participated, of which 497 coaches reported living in the Americas. Other respondents reported living in the UK, Europe, Asia, and elsewhere. More detail about the survey methodology and results, along with the survey questionnaire can be obtained in the referenced literature (McAnally et al., 2020b).

The survey questionnaire had 27 questions that covered supervision experiences, perceptions, and demographics. Demographic characteristics of both coaches and their coaching supervisors are detailed below.

| AMERICAS (497) | |
|---|---|
| **North America (476)** | **South America /Caribbean (21)** |
| Canada (44) | Argentina (3) |
| Mexico (5) | Brazil (13) |
| United States (427) | Columbia (1) |
| | Curacao (1) |
| | Paraguay (1) |
| | Peru (1) |
| | Uruguay (1) |

*Figure 3.1* Geographic Locations of Respondents.

## Results

### Our Sample

The majority of the 497 respondents were from the US (427) and Canada (44). As seen in Figure 3.1, there was limited study participation by coaches from Spanish- or Portuguese-speaking countries. It is unclear if the lower participation rate was due to fewer coaches in these countries, less utilization of coaching supervisors, a language barrier as the survey was only available in English, or other reasons.

In addition to country, we indexed the proportion of coaches who reported working either internally or externally to their client organization(s). Respondents could check more than one category in response to this question. Results indicated that most respondents served as external coaches (438) at least some of the time. Others reported serving as internal coaches (47), coach supervisors (48), or clinicians (39). See Figure 3.2, below.

Since coaching supervision is not yet widespread in the Americas, we were interested in the number of years respondents received supervision. Not surprisingly, most respondents (86%) reported having been supervised for less than five years. See Figure 3.3. Respondents indicated that their supervision was not always continuous; in other words, some indicated that they received supervision on an intermittent basis. Respondents who received less than a year of supervision often noted that this took place during their initial training as a coach, rather than as part of an ongoing professional development program.

### Where Do Coaches Find a Supervisor?

Respondents were asked how they initially found their supervisor(s). See Figure 3.4.

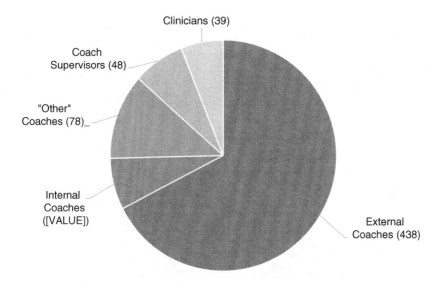

*Figure 3.2* Type of Coach.

Note: Participants could select more than one option.

As some respondents had more than one supervisor, they were able to enter multiple responses. Consequently, the total number of responses exceeded the sample size. Most respondents indicated their supervisor was someone they already knew from a coach training program or another source. We determined this by analyzing respondents that selected "Other" for this question; in fact, these participants often indicated that the coaching supervision took place as part of a training program, rather than as part of continuing professional development.

Based on these results, we believe it is possible that respondents defined coaching supervision differently from our definition. Many of our respondents may have confused it with ICF mentor coaching received during their initial coach training program. This possible difference and confusion in definitions was not anticipated by the authors and is an area requiring further investigation and research.

Secondary approaches respondents used to find a coaching supervisor included having known them from a professional organization or from personal referrals. It is interesting to note that prior personal exposure to a coaching supervisor was the most utilized method. Many coaching supervisors in the Americas promote their supervision services through presentations and networking events to coaches. Yet, these events were among the least frequently mentioned methods for identifying coaching supervisors. However, as these networking and presentation activities have been inaugurated relatively recently in the Americas, future research will reveal if it proves more effective over time.

| Years in Supervision | Number of Responses (295 coaches) | Percent to Total | Year Groupings |
|---|---|---|---|
| < 1 | 78 | 26% | |
| 1 | 65 | 22% | |
| 2 | 57 | 19% | 5 years or less = 253 coaches (86%) |
| 3 | 23 | 8% | |
| 4 | 15 | 5% | |
| 5 | 17 | 6% | |
| 6 | 6 | 2% | |
| 7 | 3 | 1% | |
| 8 | 3 | 1% | 6 -10 years =24 coaches (8%) |
| 9 | 4 | 1% | |
| 10 | 8 | 3% | |
| 11 | 1 | <1% | |
| 12 | 2 | 1% | 11 -15 years = 8 coaches (3%) |
| 15 | 4 | 1% | |
| 17 | 1 | <1% | |
| 18 | 4 | 1% | 16 years or longer = 9 coaches (3%) |
| 20 | 2 | 1% | |
| 25 | 3 | 1% | |

Figure 3.3 Years in Supervision.

### Benefits of Supervision

Respondents were asked to describe the benefits of coaching supervision and were offered a checklist of possible responses. The results are reported in Figure 3.5. As might be expected, "working through a client challenge" was the most popular choice. Interestingly, "developing my coaching skills" was an almost equally popular second choice, and also the primary focus of ICF's mentor coaching program. The consideration of client cases may initiate self-reflection during supervision. Additionally, supervision can lead a coach to develop new skills during or after the self-reflective discussion. These skills and insights expand the coach's self-awareness and under-standing of their role in the coaching process and can strengthen their ability to effectively work with clients. This phenomenon corresponds to the formative aspect of Proctor's (1987) three-part description (formative, normative, and restorative) of the functions of coaching supervision.

Next, we explore individual coaching supervision in the Americas, elaborating on the coach experience, supervision frequency, topics discussed, and fees.

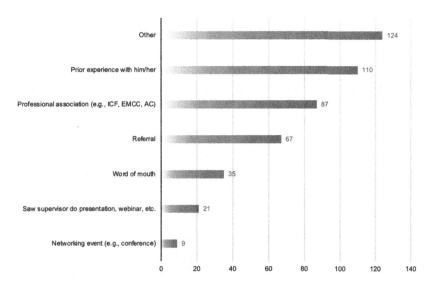

*Figure 3.4* How Coaches Found Coaching Supervisor(s).

Note: Participants could select more than one option; Most of the "Other" responses indicated that the coaching supervision took place as part of a training program.

## Individual Coaching Supervision

Coaching supervision typically takes place in either an individual or group format. Supervision that takes place individually, meaning solely between a coach and their coaching supervisor, provides that coach with more time, focus, and ability to reflect solely on themselves and their practice from different perspectives. The focus of each meeting depends solely upon that coach and their practice, as opposed to sharing their supervision time and focus with other coaches (McAnally et al., 2020a). As compared to group coaching supervision, this method was the most frequently cited by respondents. Almost twice as many coaches worked individually with a coaching supervisor than used group supervision in our sample.

## Experience of Individual Coaching Supervision

Respondents were asked if they had worked with an individual coach supervisor, either currently or in the past. Of the 484 coaches who responded, only 20% reported "currently working individually with a coach supervisor." This left 80% (391) who reported that they "currently do not work individually with a coach supervisor." Interestingly, almost two-thirds (63%) reported "working with an individual supervisor in the past," even if only in the context of a training or certification program (37%) (not depicted in Figure 3.6). Only 17% reported that they had "never worked with an individual coach supervisor."

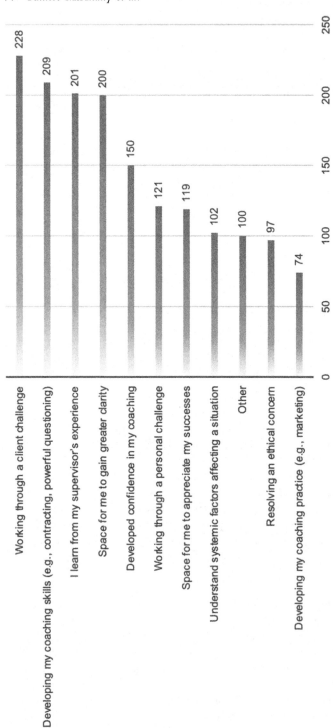

*Figure 3.5* How Coaches Benefitted from Supervision.

Note: Participants could select more than one option;

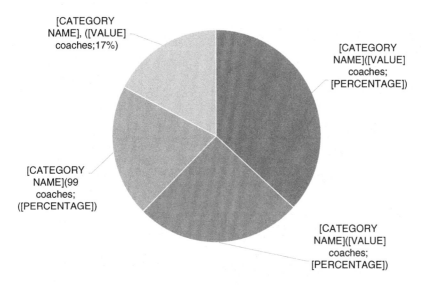

*Figure 3.6* Experience With an Individual Supervisor.

We believe the write-in comments may partially reflect the ICF mentor coaching they received in their coach training programs, rather than true coaching supervision as defined by EMCC Global. Based on these findings, it's clear that coaching supervision is still in a growth stage in the Americas, especially as compared to the UK and Europe where it is more established (McAnally et al., 2020b).

### Frequency of Individual Coaching Supervision

The goal of coaching supervision is to provide coaches with a safe, supportive space to reflect, consider, celebrate, and ultimately improve upon themselves and their coaching practice. Ideally, coaches use this time and relationship to explore, learn, grow, and develop as coaches, including recognizing their skills and achievements. The coach and their coaching supervisor need meetings at regular intervals in order to build the depth of trust necessary to foster meaningful results for the coach.

For this reason, respondents were asked about the frequency of their individual coaching supervision meetings. The most common meeting frequency was "once a month" (42%). Roughly half as many (19%) reported receiving supervision as needed. This response was followed, respectively, by "every two weeks" (13%), and "other" (12%). Some 8% reported receiving supervision "every two months" or quarterly (4%). It appears that our respondents most often found monthly sessions of individual supervision best met their needs (Figure 3.7).

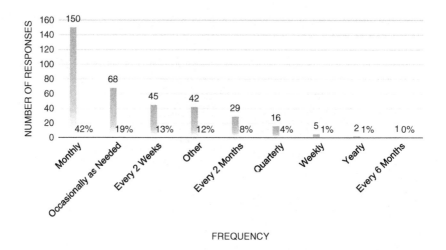

Figure 3.7 Frequency of Individual Coaching Supervision Sessions.

### Individual Supervision Session Topics

Respondents were asked about the types of challenges or situations they brought to their individual coaching supervision sessions. Because multiple discussion topics were possible, respondents could choose more than one response. The most frequent response was "client-related issues, challenges, and situations" (271). Often, beginning the supervision session by discussing a specific client situation can lead a coach to reflect on various aspects of their "being" as a coach. It was not surprising that the second most common response was "issues, challenges, and/or situations that related to me personally as a coach" (169). Similar, but somewhat less frequent supervision topics were "questions about my own skills and competencies as a coach" (133) and "emotional reactions I have had in or about my coaching work" (124), as well as "developing my practice" (123), "habitual patterns I wanted to change in my coaching style" (121). Fewer respondents reported discussing personal well-being, ethical issues, or the value of coaching during these sessions. Discussing client situations and challenges can be a starting point for addressing other topics of importance to coaches during their individual supervision sessions (Figure 3.8).

### Individual Supervision Fees

Given that coaching supervision is a newer practice in the Americas, we were curious about the amount that coaches might consider an appropriate hourly fee for this service. According to respondents, although the range was wide, the average fee for individual supervision within the Americas region was USD 201 (Figure 3.9).

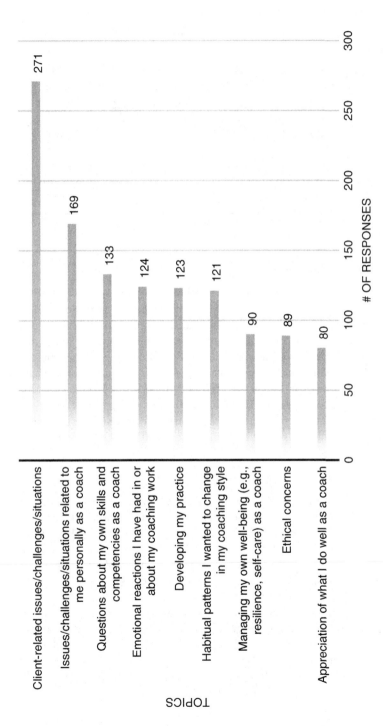

*Figure 3.8* Challenges Brought to Individual Supervision Sessions.

| | Average Fee | Range | Median | Mode | Number of Responses |
|---|---|---|---|---|---|
| TOTAL AMERICAS | $201 | $0-$625 | $200 | $150 | 251 |
| US | $204 | $0-$625 | $150 | $150 | 207 |
| Canada | $173 | $0-$400 | $181 | $250 | 28 |
| Mexico | $250 | $200-$300 | n/a | n/a | 2 |
| LATAM | $214 | $100-$350 | $200 | $ | 14 |

*Figure 3.9* Individual Supervision Fees.

### Group Coaching Supervision

Group supervision is common for psychotherapists, counselors, and other professionals. For coaches, however, group coaching supervision is less common than individual supervision (Pinder, 2011). Group supervision can take a variety of forms, but generally it features one coach supervisor working with multiple coaches simultaneously. The processes used by the supervisor during the session may vary depending on the preferences of the group or the supervisor. Typically, two or three coaches receive focus during a single group supervision session. Coaches engaged in this format thus have the opportunity to observe and learn from each other as well as receive focus during the supervision conversation (Pinder, 2011).

### Experience of Group Coaching Supervision

Respondents were asked if they were working or had worked with a group coach supervisor. Almost half of the respondents (46%) indicated they had not worked with a group coaching supervisor. About a third (34%) of the respondents reported they had experienced group supervision within the context of a training or certification program. The smallest segment of coaches reported that they either "currently worked with a group coach supervisor" (11%) or had in the past (9%).

As noted above, we believe these results may reflect some confusion by respondents. As few training programs in the Americas offer true supervision, (as defined by EMCC Global) we wonder if many of the respondents who reported working with a group coach supervisor actually experienced other types of development in a group format, such as ICF mentor coaching, or targeted case analysis, or other practices (Figure 3.10).

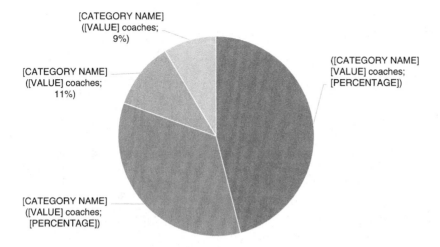

*Figure 3.10* Experience with Group Coaching Supervision.

### Frequency of Group Coaching Supervision Sessions

As coaching supervision is meant to provide ongoing learning, growth, and development for coaches, this requires ongoing and regular meetings between coaches and their group coach supervisor. When queried about the frequency of their group coaching supervision, most respondents reported meeting monthly (37%), "occasionally as needed" (14%), "every two weeks" (12%), or "quarterly" (8%). Remaining respondents reported meeting on an alternate schedule ("other"), "weekly" (3%), "every two months" (5%), or far less frequently.

Coaches and coaching supervisors, whether group or individual, negotiate the frequency of supervision they prefer. As with individual supervision, a coach's caseload may influence the frequency of their supervision sessions (Figure 3.11).

### Group Supervision Session Topics

Trained coaching supervisors know that one way to stimulate reflection is to ask coaches to consider possible discussion topics in advance, be they related to a particular client case study or to some other personal coaching-related challenge. This is one way individual and group coaching supervisors can help coaches identify and work through thoughts, emotions, and other experiences that occur during their coaching work.

In our research study, respondents were asked what challenges or situations they brought to their group coaching supervision sessions. Respondents could choose more than one response. Like coaches who

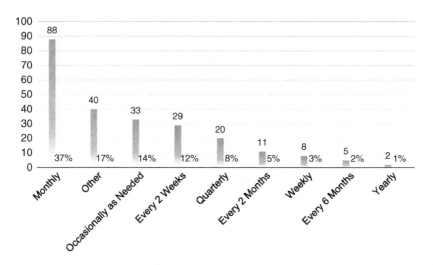

*Figure 3.11* Frequency of Group Coaching Supervision.

received individual supervision, respondents of group coaching supervision indicated "client related issues/ challenges/situations" (166) were the most commonly shared topic. This was followed by "issues/challenges/situations related to me personally as a coach" (106), "questions about my own skills and competencies as a coach" (95), and "habitual patterns I wanted to change in my coaching style" (71). Fewer respondents reported discussing practice development, processing emotional reactions, well-being, or ethical concerns, among other topics (Figure 3.12).

### Group Supervision Fees

Respondents were asked what would be the most appropriate fee for an hour of group coaching supervision. While the range was wide, the median fee within the Americas was USD 100 (Figure 3.13).

## Discussion

Coaching supervision is still new to the Americas, and much research remains to be conducted to better understand its characteristics. Among many possibilities, two issues stand out: The conflation of coaching supervision, as defined by EMCC Global, with ICF mentor coaching or other coaching developmental practices and research to help the coaching community better understand how coaching supervision continues to emerge in the Americas.

The growth of coaching supervision in the Americas is taking place in a region where ICF is the predominant professional association for coaches. For accreditation by the ICF, coach training providers are required to

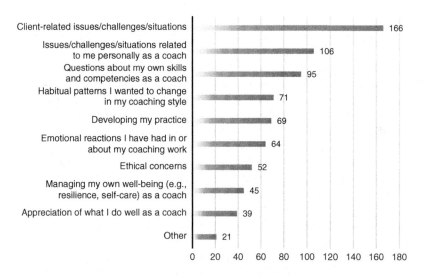

*Figure 3.12* Group Supervision Topics.

|  | Average Fee | Range | Median | Mode | Number of Responses |
|---|---|---|---|---|---|
| TOTAL AMERICAS | $145 | $0 -$750 | $100 | $100 | 142 |
| US | $144 | $0-$500 | $100 | $100 | 114 |
| Canada | $116 | $25-$200 | $100 | $100 | 15 |
| Mexico | $150 | $100-$200 | n/a | n/a | 2 |
| LATAM | $186 | $50-$750 | $100 | $100 | 11 |

*Figure 3.13* Group Supervision Fees.

ensure their trainees receive 10 hours of ICF mentor coaching, which are narrowly focused on aspects of the ICF coaching competencies. There are no required ICF mentor coach trainings; rather, mentor coaches are only required to possess an ICF credential at the same accreditation level for which the applicant is applying. Although there are mentor coaching competencies, there is no required mentor coach training or certification. This means that in the Americas, the only individual attention paid to a particular coach's practice typically occurs early in their career, pre-credential, and often by a mentor coach with a competency-specific focus.

In contrast, coaches who maintain regular coaching supervision may only use up to a limited number of their coaching supervision hours to renew their ICF credential. For the ICF in the Americas, then, receiving coaching supervision serves as only one, non-required possible option by which a coach can earn their continuing coach education (CCE) credits, since ICF does not require ongoing coaching supervision for either a coach's initial credential or that credential's renewal. Working with an ICF mentor coach may be considered only an "initial event," designed to help a new coach master the ICF core competencies for coaching, and/or to fulfill a requirement to obtain an ICF credential. Coaching supervision, on the other hand, is a long-term commitment by a coach to their own self-development, over the lifespan of their coaching career. ICF expectations differ significantly from leading UK and European coach professional associations (e.g., EMCC, APECS, Association for Coaching), which require coaches receive regular, ongoing supervision from trained coaching supervisors, for initial accreditation and renewal.

After analyzing data for this study and reflecting on our experience as coaching supervisors, we noticed initial confusion about the practice of coaching supervision, relative to ICF mentor coaching. Given the ICF's predominance in the Americas, respondents who reported receiving coaching supervision may have conflated this form of supervision with ICF mentor coaching. That said, our respondents may also have been employing a broader definition of "coaching skills" than reflected in ICF mentor coaching, which typically focuses on the ICF coaching competencies and their application to the structure and content of coach conversations with their clients.

In retrospect, it is not surprising that there was confusion around who might be called a coaching supervisor. Some respondents reported working with a coaching supervisor as part of their coach training program, or as part of their work improving on ICF competencies. Very few coach training programs in the Americas employ trained coaching supervisors and supervision practices. We have heard anecdotally that some ICF mentor coaches call themselves coach supervisors, despite a lack of training or informed coaching supervision practice. We are likewise aware that in practice, ICF mentor coaches may at times stray into processes and topics typically employed in coaching supervision. Clear boundaries and better understanding of the differences between mentor coaching and coaching supervision and their requirements would be useful for all members of the coaching profession in the Americas. Given the growing awareness of proper coaching supervision, future research could help clarify the distinctions between mentor coaching and coaching supervision in the Americas. For example, one research question could explore what types of activities or exercises the coaching supervisor and coach engage in during supervision sessions. Another question could identify terminology used by coach trainers when mentor coaching or providing feedback to coaches on their coaching skills as related to ICF core competencies.

Another point to highlight from our study results is that coaches who work with a coaching supervisor appreciate exploring many different areas of their practice, including ethical conduct. Coach learning typically extends beyond any immediate client situations that are initially discussed and are applied to other present and future client situations via the coach's increased personal insights and appreciation for themselves and their practice. As in the UK and Europe, we suggest that coaches in the Americas should obtain regular coaching supervision from a properly trained and certified coaching supervisor. Further this best practice should be required for all those seeking a coaching credential or renewal, over the lifespan of their coaching practice.

Given the usefulness of supervision, it is notable that many respondents had yet to work with a coaching supervisor. Various reasons were given for this, including 29% of respondents who reported "I belong to peer networks where I can get support when I need it." Some 14% indicated "it is not required by the organization I work with" and 14% of respondents chose "I do my own reflective practice." Smaller proportions of respondents reported: "I do not feel I need it" (11%) and that "it is not required by the professional association (e.g., ICF, EMCC, AC) to which I belong" (11%).; 9% who indicated: "I am not familiar with supervision." Another 8% reported: "I discuss issues with my coach" as a reason. Smaller proportions cited the perceived expense of coaching supervision or challenges identifying an appropriate coaching supervisor. It is notable that these coaches feel their needs are met by other methods, they do not know what supervision is or feel they need it, and/or their client organization(s) or professional associations have not required it.

Trained coaching supervisors employ a range of tools and methods that other practices and practitioners do not replicate and according to our data, result in broader learning than other methods. As coaching supervisors, we personally have witnessed the growth and benefit our coaches have gained from coaching supervision. Likewise, we have seen those who observe or experience coaching supervision in action are more likely to understand and adopt it. When there is broader knowledge and understanding of the benefits of coaching supervision or certifying associations and entities adopt this best practice, we expect it will become the norm for coaches in the Americas, as it has in the UK and Europe.

There is work to be done to assist Americas coaches to take advantage of coaching supervision as well as to differentiate this practice from other learning methods. Additional research is needed to assist the elevation of coaching supervision to place among various continuous professional development methods for coaches. For example, identifying the specific benefits gained from coaching supervision and how it differs from ICF mentor coaching would help clarify use of the practice. Other important research questions could examine the practices that ensure coaches feel safe during supervision; advance understanding of how cultural contexts affect supervision practice in the Americas and detail the ways in which supervision affects coaching practice, among others.

While clear and appropriate boundaries and points of differentiation need to be maintained, what might we learn from the supervision practices performed for clinical practitioners, such as clinical psychologists, LCSWs, and other psychotherapists? Ongoing supervision for clinicians has long been recognized as valuable and necessary. How might coaching supervisors learn more that is useful from our clinical colleagues about their use and practice of supervision? Further investigation and collaboration in that direction would prove fruitful for coaching supervision.

Finally, as in the early days of coaching, there are no widely known expectations or requirements for anyone to call themselves a coaching supervisor in the Americas, at present. In the Americas, what standards and requirements would be beneficial to be considered a properly trained, credentialed, effective coaching supervisor? How much coaching experience should be required? What training content should be required, specifically, for coaching supervision? What elements, models, processes, practices, or behaviors should a coach master and demonstrate before they begin supervising other coaches? In what ways might the knowledge base for effective coaching supervision be made conceptually and practically clear and separate from the ICF's mentor coaching? Research that addresses these questions and others will greatly assist in advancing the practice and effectiveness of coaching supervision in the Americas.

## Conclusion

Since this research study is an early examination of the state of coaching supervision in the Americas, the low adoption rates indicated by the coaches in this sample were not surprising. We look forward to future surveys that examine similar topics and note any changes. While areas of confusion currently exist about the definition and practice of coaching supervision in the Americas, there are many areas of opportunity for further research to help the practice grow and ultimately strengthen the coaching profession in the Americas.

## Note

1 "Coaching supervision" is synonymous with what elsewhere is called "coach supervision." The choice at times to use "coaching supervision" herein is to emphasize our reference to the coach's whole being, as well as the coaching practice for which they are receiving supervision, rather than simply referring to their coaching work alone.

Those interested in similar data drawn from a global sample of respondents and our findings can access these at www.coachingsupervisionresearch.com.

# References

European Mentoring and Coaching Council. (2020). *Supervision*. https://www.emccglobal.org/quality/supervision/

Hawkins, P., & Turner, E. (2017). The rise of coaching supervision 2006–2014. *Coaching: An International Journal of Theory, Research and Practice*, *10*(2), 1–13. doi:10.1080/17521882.2016.1266002

McAnally, K., Abrams, L., Asmus, M. J., & Hildebrandt, T. H. (2020a). Coaching supervision. In T. H. Hildebrandt, F. Campone, K. Norwood, & E. J. Ostrowski (Eds.), *Innovations in leadership coaching: Research and practice* (pp. 395–417). Fielding University Press.

McAnally, K., Abrams, L., Asmus, M. J., & Hildebrandt, T. H. (2020b). *Global coaching supervision: A study of the perceptions and practices around the world*. https://coachingsupervisionresearch.org/wp-content/uploads/2020/02/Global_Coaching_Supervision_Report_FINAL.pdf

Pinder, K. (2011). Group supervision. In T. Bachkirova, P. Jackson, & D. Clutterbuck (Eds.), *Coaching and mentoring supervision: Theory and practice* (pp. 196–204). McGraw Hill.

Proctor, B. (1987). Supervision: A co-operative exercise in accountability. In M. Marken & M. Paynes (Eds.), *Enabling and ensuring: Supervision in practice* (pp. 21–23). National Youth Bureau and the Council for Education and Training in Youth and Community Work.

Turner, E., & Hawkins, P. (2016). Coming of age: The development of coaching supervision 2006-2014. *Coaching at Work*, *11*(2): 32–36.

# 4 Resistance to Coaching Supervision in the Americas

*Lily Seto, Damian Goldvarg, and Sarah Eustice*

Coaching supervision is a growing discipline, globally, and is relatively new to the Americas—North, Central, and South America. As leaders in the supervision community, we have observed resistance to coaching supervision as a persistent theme of discussions in the Americas. In community and network gatherings, this resistance showed up in conversations about growing the awareness around coaching supervision. This sparked our interest in investigating the underlying sources and reasons for this resistance and the strategies that coaching supervisors implement to overcome them. In this chapter we share the findings of a survey conducted in 2019.

## Research on Supervision

To better understand this resistance and learn more about what supervisors in this part of the world might do differently to engage coaches, we conducted a qualitative study to investigate this phenomenon. The original research was presented at the International Conference on Coaching Supervision at Oxford Brookes University (Seto & Goldvarg, 2019a), and the Americas Coaching Supervision Network Conference in 2019 (Seto & Goldvarg, 2019b). Updates to our research were presented at EMCC Global's annual supervision conference in 2020 (Seto & Goldvarg, 2020).

### Definitions

#### Supervision

According to EMCC (n.d.), coaching supervision is a reflective practice where a coach brings their work and client cases into a space to reflect on. The purpose of this reflective practice is to develop as a coach in service of the clients, their organizations, and the larger system. ICF (n.d.) says, "Supervision is a collaborative learning practice to continually build the capacity of the coach through reflective dialogue for the benefit of both coaches and clients." Further, in the updated ICF core competency framework, under the new competency *Embodies a coaching mindset*, there is a

DOI: 10.4324/b23130-6

standard that focuses on "the importance of developing an ongoing reflective practice to enhance one's coaching" (ICF, 2019).

*Resistance*

We define resistance as behaviors, attitudes, and comments that reject or minimize coaching supervision as a valuable practice for the development of the coaches. Feedback was received during the aforementioned conference presentations about looking into other words such as reluctance or hesitancy, which may better reflect the sentiments from coaches who do not embrace this reflective practice.

## Methodology

The purpose of this research study was to investigate resistance among coaches, what was behind the resistance, and strategies to mitigate the resistance. We distributed a survey to the Americas Coaching Supervision Network (ACSN) member list. At the time of the survey dissemination, the network included 150 members mainly from the Americas. The survey consisted of three open-ended questions:

What kinds of resistance have you encountered when seeking supervisees?

What strategies have you applied when facing resistance to enrolling in coaching supervision?

What are some strategies that can be employed to increase the acceptance of coaching supervision in the Americas?

## Sample

In total, 58 coaching supervisors provided responses (~39% response rate). Forty-three respondents (81%) were from the Americas. This included 20 from the US, 10 from Canada, and 13 from Central and South America. The remaining 15 were from Europe and Asia. There was a range of experience among the coaching supervisors, from less than a year to nearly 20 years of coaching supervision.

## Analysis

Data were collated and imported into qualitative data analysis software. The first level of analysis was an open coding, line-by-line analysis, yielding 37 codes. A balance emerged in the top 10 most frequently identified codes between strategies [S] and areas of resistance [R] for coaching supervision.

They are presented in the order of significance discovered during the qualitative analysis:

- Educating or explaining supervision, what it is and is not [S]
- Lack of awareness and understanding [R]
- Discussing, sharing benefits of supervision [S]
- Experiencing it to understand it [S]
- Cost [R]
- Professional organizations(s) lack of support, promotion, or requirement [R]
- Research and outcomes (more needed) [R]
- Active promotion by coaching supervision practitioners [S]
- Growth and development (resulting from supervision) [S]
- Fear of being vulnerable [R]

The second level of analysis was thematic coding: A process of arranging codes into related categories based on their conceptual similarities. This stage of analysis involved a two-step process. First, three authors individually reviewed the 37 codes and generated a list of themes. Then, the authors came together to review the themes and came to a consensus on a final list of themes.

## Results

The final categorization consisted of six themes: Three related to resistance (awareness and understanding, expenditures, and vulnerability) and three themes around strategies for countering that resistance (educating and explaining, exposure to and experiencing, promotion and professional support). The themes are further described below. Excerpts from these data accompany each theme to convey the views of respondents in their own words.

## Resistance Themes

### Awareness and Understanding

The main resistance to coaching supervision among respondents was linked to a lack of awareness and understanding about what it is, the use of the word *supervision*, and where it is situated in the professional development of coaches. Respondents encountered confusion in distinguishing the role of a supervisor from that of a coach, mentor coach, therapist, or peer source of support. This is not a new finding. In fact, in a study conducted by McAnally et al. (2020), the majority of respondents indicated that they belonged to peer groups where they could get adequate coaching supervision.

Coaching supervision has often been conflated, specifically in the Americas, with organizational supervision. It has generally been seen as connoting power or control over someone when in fact, coaching supervision is the co-creation of a reflective space between the coach (i.e., supervisee) and coaching supervisor (Hawkins & Schwenk, 2006).

*Excerpt:* "Supervision is not well established or recognized in North America."

*Excerpt:* "A visceral reaction to the word supervision as meaning manager or boss."

A lack of understanding and awareness of what coaching supervision is, or the benefits it can provide, may manifest in different ways. One way it presented itself was through a coach exhibiting a sense of mastery and ultimately, thinking supervision was unnecessary.

*Excerpt:* "I'm an MCC. I don't need it."

*Excerpt:* "I already had coaching mentoring. Why have supervision?"

### Expenditures

Although the term seems self-explanatory, expenditures emerged as the second leading area of resistance to coaching supervision. Expenditures refer to the cost, time commitment, and effort required of a coach to engage in coaching supervision. In instances in which the coach did not yet fully understand the benefits of supervision, cost compounded their resistance to engaging in it.

*Excerpt:* "As they [coaches] mainly earn a living through billable hours, they need to see the value of giving up client time for supervision."

*Excerpt:* "Coaches do not want to pay for what they do not need; [it is] not valued."

### Vulnerability

Being open and transparent about one's coaching practice can be uncomfortable, bringing on a sense of feeling exposed. This can especially be true if there are unknowns about the supervision process and the space in which a coach is asked to be vulnerable. For some, the concept of coaching supervision may bring with it a fear of judgment or shame. One respondent noted that coaches might feel like the supervisor would "see what they are doing wrong." Yet, supervision is meant to be a reflective practice where the coaching supervisor helps to create and maintain a container of safety, rather than a place of judgment.

*Excerpt:*    "Not fully embracing development or openness to change [that often results from being in a supervisee role]."
*Excerpt:*    "Fear of being evaluated or assessed by the supervisor."
*Excerpt:*    "Careful strategies that build on the tenets of a safe container [in] a one-on-one or small group setting."

## Strategy Themes

### Educating and Explaining

Not surprisingly, respondents often provided strategies to mitigate the different types of resistance they identified. While lack of understanding or awareness were the most common sources of resistance respondents cited to enrolling in coaching supervision, many respondents recommended providing education and explanation as a strategy to counter that resistance. Some respondents acknowledged that the term "supervision" was inherently problematic and recommended changing it. However, no concrete suggestion of replacement terms accompanied this recommendation. This is an example of how education about supervision can help advance the discipline.

*Excerpt:*    "I think the word supervision is the first barrier."
*Excerpt:*    "Maybe finding a different word other than supervision. Unlikely, but since it's so early [and supervision is a relatively young discipline], why not?"

There are several ways the field could expand understanding and awareness of coaching supervision and its benefits. A coaching supervisor might have a conversation with a potential supervisee to explore their personal beliefs or assumptions about supervision. Another approach might be to provide them with actual materials such as a link to an explanatory article, an educational video, or the website of a professional organization that offers training in coaching supervision.

*Excerpt:*    "Provide more information and distinctions between coaching, mentoring, and supervision."
*Excerpt:*    "[I'm] currently working with a local colleague, running webinars to educate the market."

Another highly recommended strategy was for coaching practitioners who had engaged in supervision to educate others by having conversations and leading discussions about it. They could share stories and examples from their own experiences as a supervisee to help coaches realize the value of coaching supervision.

*Excerpt:*   "Thought leaders in the fields of coaching and supervision should continue to talk about its benefits."

*Excerpt:*   "There is a very present disconnect here that can lead to defensiveness and [cause the coach to] shut down. It's made it hard to get coaches on board. Once they see the value, they get it, but they don't come in initially understanding the purpose and process."

### Exposure and Experience

Closely related to the strategy of expanding education and awareness was the recommendation by respondents that coaches have the opportunity to experience coaching supervision as a supervisee. This strategy was recommended to help coaches better understand it. The pro bono sampling of a supervision session has often been offered by coaching supervisors as a way to actively promote the reflective practice and its benefits.

*Excerpt:*   "We need to invite more people to try it at least once. For free."

*Excerpt:*   "Offer to engage with them in one-on-one for one session so they can experience what it might be like."

Coaching supervision can take place in a group or individual setting. However, some supervisors recommended a group supervision setting as an introduction that allowed coaches to participate by observation if they were not quite ready to actively participate as the supervisee.

*Excerpt:*   "I always offer an experience sample [like offering an initial group session for free] so that people can feel what it gives them and so far they have signed up."

*Excerpt:*   "Demonstrate as much as we can so people can get a live sense of it.

Different approaches are worth doing to show the variety so coaches see a possible way they could be supervised."

### Promotion and Professional Support

Two methods of promotion emerged from these respondent data. The first method involved coaching practitioners and professional organizations acting in an ambassador-type role for the profession where they educate and advocate for supervision. The second method involved industry marketing.

We've identified and briefly discussed how coaching supervisors actively promote the discipline by offering a supervision experience or educational materials. Respondents also recommended that professional coaching organizations promote the importance of supervision by making sure it was incorporated into regular activities, such as annual conferences, chapter meetings, monthly newsletters, and webinars, to name a few. This intentional and consistent promotion would allow for increased visibility and exposure to coaching supervision.

*Excerpt:*    "Getting the word out there by various means – through the local chapters, social media, [and] articles that illustrate the value."

*Excerpt:*    "Thought leaders in the fields of coaching and supervision should continue to talk about its benefits."

Some respondents noted that coaching supervision might not be considered important from a marketing perspective and thought that should change. This lack of marketing presence around the value of supervision was seen as problematic for both professional development and for large organizations that have coaches with corporate clients. Supervision was seen as a way to not only support their coaches, but also their clients: A way to reflect on those relationships through a systemic view.

*Excerpt:*    "Could be more marketing ... more social media presence ... publish in US based magazines and professional bodies, newsletters, blogs, etc."

*Excerpt:*    "The advantages of a step back to overview what is going well in coaching and mostly what are the blind spots that are in the way (the coach's way, the client's way and his employee's way)."

The concept of making supervision mandatory for coaches also surfaced in these data, but with mixed views. There were respondents who believed supervision should be mandatory for the sake of the profession, as it would contribute to the overall professionalization of coaching. Others supported introducing coaches to supervision, but ultimately allow them to choose whether to continue. Respondents from both views proposed to incorporate supervision as part of coach training programs, as was often done with coach mentoring.

*Excerpt:*    "Offer a module on coach training courses to describe and demonstrate to coaches during their preparation for the field."

*Excerpt:*    "I also believe coaching supervision is a choice. It's very helpful, and yet I don't believe it should be mandatory."

Supervision was not only considered a reflective practice by respondents, but a continuum of reflection. Coaching supervision was described as an invitation for coaches to grow and develop their own reflective practice.

*Excerpt:*    "Reflection on experience is the most powerful way to learn at an advanced level."

*Excerpt:*    "There is somewhere to reflect on their [coach's] practice in such a powerful way."

## Discussion

Although coaching supervision is a widely accepted ethical practice in the Americas, the word "supervision" tends to carry with it an organizational hierarchical connotation. Hawkins (2018) made the point that coaches in the US mostly come from the corporate world where the word supervision carries a connotation of this hierarchy. Whereas in Great Britain and other parts of the world, many coaches come from the helping professions (e.g., counseling, psychology, social work, etc.) where supervision is an accepted and encouraged practice. Indeed, in some professions, supervision is mandatory. It is also worthy to note that EMCC Global, the Association for Coaching (AC), and other coaching associations require supervision as part of ongoing professional development (EMCC, n.d.; AC, n.d.). According to our study findings, some strategies to mitigate this connotation and resistance, such as promotion and opportunities to participate in live demonstrations, have already begun to emerge throughout the coaching profession, specifically in the area of coaching supervision.

In 2016, Seto led a team that delivered coaching, mentor coaching, and coaching supervision demonstrations to over 45 ICF chapters and events around the world. Goldvarg has also facilitated numerous demonstrations around the world. Now, the discipline is seeing more coaching supervisors facilitating coaching supervision demonstrations and offering webinars across the Americas in English, Spanish, and French languages. These efforts have created a noticeable shift in the acceptance of coaching supervision in the region. Coaching supervisors are noticing that more coaches are reaching out to discuss or engage in coaching supervision. Additionally, the ACSN membership increased by 30% to almost 300 members in 2020. For coaches to experience the value that coaching supervision adds to the coaching profession, we extend an invitation to coaching supervisors in the Americas to continue to offer presentations and demonstrations in their various networks and local ICF chapters.

The practice of coaching supervision has been growing for more than 15 years in Europe. Whereas, in the Americas, it is a recent practice that started to develop after the first formal training facilitated by the Coaching Supervision Academy in 2013. In 2021, we are aware of four coaching supervision programs that are accredited through EMCC Global and operate in the Americas. As more coaching supervisors are trained and offer their services in the Americas, and as more coaches and companies learn about the value and importance of coaching supervision, the practice will grow rapidly.

Nevertheless, coaching supervisors may still encounter resistance from coaches who have misguided assumptions about supervision or associate it with management and quality control rather than as a reflection process for professional growth and self-development.

## Conclusion

This chapter presents some of our key findings surrounding resistance to supervision in the Americas. These include a lack of awareness and understanding of its benefits and reservations about the time, energy, and costs required for coaching supervision, and challenges surrounding vulnerability. Across varying levels of experience, coaching supervisors shared what they encountered in and around their supervision engagements. Strategies offered to overcome resistance were drawn from their lived experience, what they have employed or where they see opportunity for change, including: Educating and explaining what supervision is and is not, exposing coaches to the experience of coaching supervision as a supervisee, and increasing promotion and professional support for the practice. Whether it is a coaching supervisor who is inspired to offer a supervision experience pro bono, or a coach who may be curious to learn more about the benefits of supervision, we present this qualitative study to the larger coaching community to help inform, empower, and encourage others to actively engage, promote, and further study of this reflective practice.

## References

Association for Coaching. (n.d.). *Accreditation at a glance.* https://www.associationforcoaching. com/page/AccreditationataGlance

European Mentoring Coaching Council. (n.d.). *Supervision.* https://www.emccglobal. org/quality/supervision/

Hawkins, P. (2018, September 25). *The why, what and how of coaching supervision* [Webinar]. Americas Supervision Network. https://americassupervisionnetwork.com/

Hawkins, P. & Schwenk, G. (2006). Coaching supervision [Event Report]. The CIPD Coaching Conference, Chartered Institute of Personnel and Development. https:// researchportal.coachfederation.org/Document/Pdf/abstract_2716

International Coaching Federation. (n.d.). *Coaching supervision.* https://coachfederation. org/coaching-supervision

International Coaching Federation. (2019). *Updated ICF core competencies.* https:// coachfederation.org/core-competencies

McAnally, K., Abrams, L., Asmus, M. J., & Hildebrandt, T. H. (2020). *Global coaching supervision: A study of the perceptions and practices around the world.* https:// coachingsupervisionresearch.org/wp-content/uploads/2020/02/Global_Coaching_ Supervision_Report_FINAL.pdf

Seto, L., & Goldvarg, D. (2019a, May 11). *Resistance to supervision in the Americas.* [Conference presentation]. 8th International Conference on Coaching Supervision 2019, Oxford Brookes University, Oxford, England. https://www.associationofcoachingsupervisors.com/ community/events/95/8th-international-conference-on-coaching-supervision-2019-0mjlq

Seto, L., & Goldvarg, D. (2019b, December 16). *Resistance to supervision in the Americas.* [Conference presentation]. Americas Coaching Supervision Network 2019, Virtual. https://www.youtube.com/watch?v=VAJHWR6jw_M&ab_channel=DamianGoldvarg

Seto, L., & Goldvarg, D. (2020, June 1). *Resistance to supervision in the Americas*. [Conference presentation]. 26th Annual EMCC Global Mentoring, Coaching and Supervision Conference, Virtual. https://virtual2020.emccconference.org/speakers/damian-goldvarg-lily-seto/

## Author Bios

**Sarah Eustice** is a communicator, researcher, and evaluator with over 15 years of experience in the fields of public health, education, and professional coaching. She has worked in an array of settings, including academic, government, and nonprofit institutions. Sarah currently serves as the Assistant Director of Academic Research at the International Coaching Federation.

**Damian Goldvarg** has 30 years of experience in executive assessment and coaching, leadership development, talent management, facilitation, strategic planning, and team-building services. Originally from Argentina, he has extensive experience working with people from different cultures and social backgrounds. He has worked with individuals and organizations in over sixty countries, including the Americas, Europe, Africa, and Asia, offering services in English, Spanish, and Portuguese.

Damian is a master certified coach and received his Ph.D. in Organizational Psychology from Alliant University in California. He is also a professional certified speaker (CSP) and an accredited coach supervisor (ESIA) and facilitates certifications on professional coaching, mentor coaching, and coaching supervision. He was the 2013–2014 International Coaching Federation Global President and received the 2018 ICF Circle of Distinction Award for his contribution to professional coaching worldwide and the 2019 Supervision Award from the European Coaching and Mentoring Council.

**Lily Seto** is a global leadership coach and coaching supervisor with many years of experience. She holds a Masters in leadership and training and holds memberships and credentials with the International Coaching Federation (ICF–PCC) as well as with the European Mentoring and Coaching Council (EMCC), Supervision ESIA, and senior individual coaching and team coaching. Lily has been facilitating both internal and external supervision groups since 2013. She is also the co-lead for the Americas Coaching Supervision Network, which has over 300 members from 25 countries.

# 5 The Business Case for Coaching Supervision: An American Tech-Enabled Coaching Platform's Drive for Quality

*James A. Lopata*

## Introduction

AceUp is a technology-based executive coaching business based in Boston that partners with a network of over 300 coaches and leverages online technologies to deploy coaching more broadly throughout organizations, at scale, measurably and affordably.

Our company is one of several—including Pluma, Torch, CoachHub, and BetterUp—that have launched innovations for the coaching industry through the use of technology in the past decade. Most of these are based in the US. They've distinguished themselves from older coaching companies such as Coach Source, The Center for Creative Leadership, and Korn Ferry, by emphasizing technological innovations that bring greater transparency, access, and ubiquity to the coaching market—sometimes referred to as the democratization of coaching.

We conducted confidential, competitive research in 2020 and validated our platform through hundreds of conversations with coaches and coaching supervisors who worked on it. Our platform is the first and only platform of its kind to require that participating coaches receive coaching supervision. We also engage coaching supervision as a key element of the company's core value proposition. AceUp provides coaching supervision to both benefit coaches and to ensure system-wide consistency and quality in coaching for its organizational clients.

Since AceUp currently hires coaching supervisors trained by Damian Goldvarg Associates, which is affiliated with the European Mentoring and Coaching Council (EMCC), all coaching supervisors follow EMCC's coaching supervision competencies and guidance. Although the International Coaching Federation (ICF) is the predominate professional coaching association in the US, it does not offer the same level of professional codes and competencies as EMCC. Consequently, AceUp defines coaching supervision using EMCC's definition:

> Supervision is the interaction that occurs when a mentor or coach brings their coaching or mentoring work experiences to a supervisor in

DOI: 10.4324/b23130-7

order to be supported and to engage in reflective dialogue and collaborative learning for the development and benefit of the mentor or coach, their clients, and their organizations (2021).

This chapter offers a case study of what happens when a coaching platform provides complimentary coaching supervision and makes it an obligatory activity of all participating coaches and central to the company's core value proposition to clients.

The following chapter was written using documentation from internal surveys conducted by AceUp as well as observations and conversations with key stakeholders who are involved in designing, implementing, participating in, and evaluating coaching supervision with AceUp. These stakeholders include coaches, coaching supervisors, coaching supervision clients, employees, and corporate client stakeholders such as Learning and Development (L&D) Directors and Chief Human Resource Officers (CHROs). By sharing our subjective data, I hope to advance the conversation concerning coaching supervision and show how our company is rolling out innovative coaching supervision practices in larger organizational settings.

Bachkirova et al. (2020) cited six groups with stakes in coaching supervision: 1) the coach, 2) the client receiving coaching, 3) the organization providing coaching, 4) the organization sponsoring the coaching, 5) the coaching profession, and 6) the wider system. This chapter primarily explores considerations of the organization providing coaching with some secondary focus on the organizations sponsoring coaching, and coaches. I employ the following structure for the case study described below:

1   What led AceUp to use coaching supervision as a key defining characteristic of its value proposition?
2   What key elements have contributed to the successful implementation of coaching supervision for the company and its clients and coaches?
3   Based on AceUp's lessons learned, what considerations are key to the future of coaching supervision both in the company and the coaching industry?

Since AceUp experiments frequently and iterates quickly, I briefly describe how the company's focus evolved from a focus on individual coaching supervision to ultimately, group coaching supervision for coaches on a single company engagement.

AceUp launched in 2015 out of the Harvard i-lab incubator as an online marketplace connecting coaches to clients. In 2017, the company pivoted to exclusively offer business-to-business engagements in which large-scale executive coaching programs were made available to serve hundreds of employees, affordably.

To address corporate needs, AceUp leveraged a highly select pool of high-end coaches. Relying on its connections to Harvard University and the Institute of Coaching, it attracted premier coaches with long histories of coaching success, who commanded high compensation, and mostly eschewed working in imposed coaching formats.

AceUp used four key criteria to evaluate and curate coaches:

1    Well-recognized coaching credentials such as Associate Certified Coach (ACC), Professional Certified Coach (PCC), or Master Coach Certification (MCC) from the ICF.
2    Five or more years of executive coaching experience.
3    Five or more years of corporate executive experience.
4    Demonstrated coaching success via validated client testimonials.

AceUp further curated its coach network by watching for top coaches who yielded a high satisfaction rate from clients. We measured satisfaction using a scale of one to five and looked for coaches who achieved the highest rating (very satisfied) among 90% or more of their past clients. These coaches also demonstrated a client engagement rate of 90% or more, as measured by the percent of clients showing up for at least one coaching session per month on an annualized basis. These top coaches tended to balk at imposed coaching methodologies. They had their own methodologies and approaches they had acquired over time and worked. As one coach put it: "Look, I get results. I'm working for you because you don't impose structures on my coaching" (AceUp, 2020).

One corporate client validated our approach. The client had tried a few different coaching companies in parallel before transferring all of its coaching business to AceUp. "We went to these other firms for coaching," the client said, "and we got a method. We came to AceUp for coaching and we got results."

Unfortunately, it was challenging to say that the coaches simply "got results." Corporate decision makers often felt more comfortable knowing a consistent methodology was being employed by coaches.

To address this, AceUp determined three key criteria that corporate buyers of coaching sought in the coaching they purchased.

### Quality Coaching

Demonstrating quality had been pretty standard in the coaching industry. In surveys conducted by AceUp, we found after six months of coaching, 98% of clients said they "feel more confident in their ability to succeed in their role" as a result of their coaching (based on a 5-point Likert scale).

### Consistency of Coaching Experience

Most coaching firms promised consistency through the use of standardized coaching methods. Since AceUp's coaches focused on results more than methods, it was a challenge to demonstrate consistency.

## Low Maintenance Administration and Management of Coaching Programs

Managers in HR and learning and development had their hands full. Many were frustrated managing multiple coaches who were personally chosen by executives; it demanded too much oversight and customization. Particularly, when issues arose, they did not want to be handholding. They wanted coaching that would not tax their limited internal resources.

These comments were heard repeatedly from L&D directors, CHROs, and other HR leaders that many AceUp staff encountered. As an L&D head of a global, 50-year-old, 15,000- employee technology company described: "The days of me coordinating multiple, customized solopreneur executive coaches for C-Suite are over. My staff can't handle that anymore." An HR director for a global pharmaceutical company said: "My coaching solutions need to be off-the-shelf, ready-to-go, with no ongoing maintenance by me and my team. I'm exaggerating a bit, but our executive leadership expects coaching to be a smooth process with no hiccups anymore."

How could a coaching platform guarantee low maintenance and high quality without standardized methods? After a few inquiries from coaches about complicated coaching situations (described in the next section), which were resolved through the intervention of a certified coaching supervisor, AceUp's leadership decided to introduce a more intentional coaching supervision protocol within the company.

## Individual Coaching Supervision

The first complex coaching situation arose when an AceUp coach discovered that the two employees she was coaching had a direct reporting relationship at the company. Furthermore, the two clients were talking about each other in their coaching sessions. The coach did not know if they were aware she was coaching both of them and did not want to break confidentiality by sharing this. But she worried about what it might mean if they found out. The coaching supervisor helped her navigate and resolve the situation by creating a climate of trust in which she was able to reveal the coaching relationships to the clients.

In another instance, a coach approached the CEO of AceUp with concerns related to an AceUp client. The coach was not comfortable breaking the client's confidentiality to share specific details, so the CEO referred the coach to a coaching supervisor. Reflection in supervision revealed that coaching was not the optimal intervention for the client at that time. As a result, the coaching supervisor helped the coach navigate a respectful withdrawal from the engagement.

A third case concerned a breach of confidentiality. An HR director alleged that a coach had shared privileged information about one client's intention to leave the company with another client. The coach denied this, but there was no way for the coach to defend himself since he was bound by the ethics of confidentiality. Yet, the clients, the coach, the HR director, and AceUp all had stakes in the matter.

A coaching supervisor was brought in to process the case with the coach. This enabled the coach to have a voice and place to process his truth and accept that the client's perceptions were beyond his control. Upon further processing, the coach declared to all parties that as a PCC-certified coach with the ICF, he took ICF's coach competencies and ethics guidelines seriously and firmly believed he had never violated them. AceUp stood behind the coach and has continued to deploy him on other assignments. AceUp was also able to let the client's perception stand even as the coach was removed from the assignment at the client's request.

This case demonstrates an instance in which there was no clear-cut, easy solution or strategy for preventing a future recurrence (such as creating better legal contracts or written policies). Only the intervention of a trained coaching supervisor allowed for a workable win–win–win outcome.

In all of these cases, a coaching supervisor assisted in resolving the issues expeditiously. Based on these initial results, stakeholders at AceUp became convinced of coaching supervision's benefits to its clients, its coaches, and to the company.

The company decided to formalize coaching supervision. To do this effectively in a large-scale manner, the company's leadership team decided to roll out formal group coaching supervision.

## Group Coaching Supervision

Just as many of AceUp's experienced coaches balked at imposed coaching methodologies, some of them also resisted the idea of being supervised. An example of a common objection came from one coach, who said: "This supervision thing feels like an additional unnecessary burden that simply complicates coaching."

However, some coaches had experienced coaching supervision and welcomed the idea.

We decided to experiment with regular, 90-minute "drop-in" coaching supervision sessions for coaches interested in exploring their practice in a voluntary, safe, confidential, group setting. We dropped "supervision" from the title and called the group sessions, "The Green Room." This was a metaphor taken from the entertainment industry, whereby an offstage room is provided to foster relaxation and open discussion among performers when not on stage.

The Green Room was structured as formal coaching supervision and used the following format: First, a gathering exercise such as a short meditation began the session. Then the team engagement rules were co-created, such as agreeing to safety and confidentiality (it was made explicit that, with the exception of major themes or legally required reporting, nothing discussed in the coaching supervision session would be shared back to AceUp or anyone else). The coaches shared round robin a summary of prospective cases to explore and the group chose which case to explore first. At this stage, the case or cases were explored. When discussion of cases concluded, individual takeaways were shared by each coach about what they learned to apply to their own coaching. Finally, the coaching supervision session was evaluated by coaches who shared impressions and thoughts for improvement.

This format was derived and adapted from group coaching supervision sessions deployed in the coaching supervisor's training program. It also follows Brigid Proctor's participative typology for group supervision, which is described as "supervision *with* the group" (Proctor's emphasis), whereby the supervisor "is responsible for supervising and managing [the] group" (Proctor, 2008, page 32).

One of the most significant questions that came up early with coaches concerned confidentiality. Specifically, how can coaches talk about clients in a group setting while maintaining confidentiality? All coaching supervisors hired by AceUp were trained to meet EMCC competencies. To address this concern, coach supervisors and coaches were asked to agree to the Association for Coaching (AC) and EMCC Global Code of Ethics, which states: "Members will share with clients that they are receiving supervision and identify that the client may well be referred to in this context anonymously. The client should be reassured that the supervision relationship is itself a confidential relationship" (2021).

The Green Room format proved popular and durable. Each session attracted an average of three to six coaches the first few months it was offered. This allowed time for strong contracting at the beginning and meaningful exploration of two or three cases during the session, with engagement from all coaches. When sessions began attracting 10 or more coaches, the balance between scalability and significant learning diminished rapidly.

To address this challenge, the company upgraded the group coaching supervision program in 2019 to require that coaches sign-up for groups in advance and limit session attendance to no more than six coaches at any given time.

AceUp also began experimenting with group coaching supervision specific to a cohort of coaches all working with clients at a single company. This model will be discussed in more detail, below.

Many of the themes that emerged from the Green Room group coaching supervision sessions concerned sharing ideas and best practices for dealing with specific coaching situations. Following EMCC's three functional categories for coaching supervision—developmental, resourcing, and qualitative—I describe some of the issues that surfaced, below.

1   **Developmental.** Many coaches, particularly less experienced coaches, were eager to hear how others worked through difficult situations, such as when a client gets in a rut and just seems to want to talk. These

developmental discussions not only provided applied learning opportunities for individual coaches, they also resulted in the organic creation of a common coaching framework and set of best practices or AceUp approach to coaching. There is no need for the company to impose a coaching methodology. The coaches are co-creating an AceUp coaching framework, themselves. As one coach wrote: "[Coaching supervision] creates connection and an important dialogue around the challenges, successes, and opportunity for growth as individual coaches and a more aligned collective consciousness of understanding."

2  **Resourcing.** Many coaches brought concerns about how to balance the business of coaching, (e.g., wanting to please the company to acquire more clients) with the need to coach without an agenda. As one coach noted: "I tend to treat my AceUp clients differently than my private clients. Sometimes I feel extra pressure to coach well with an AceUp client, which can make me choke and not do my best work."

3  **Qualitative.** Conflict of interest issues continued to emerge in group coaching supervision. As a result, we recommend a fourth category be added to EMCC's three functional categories: The Systemic Function. This category provides important emphasis on the larger system, which can take time to emerge in discussion. Related questions that arose included how to best handle different understandings of the contract by various stakeholders, and how many larger systemic issues or themes must a coach know in order to effectively coach a client.

What transpired in group coaching supervision sessions was initially treated as confidential and nothing was shared with the company. Eventually, short reports were filled out and submitted to AceUp. These reports were designed to capture the common themes and issues that surfaced in coaching supervision so future improvements could be guided by qualitative evidence.

One of the key benefits of group coaching supervision was that coaches were able to share and identify with what other coaches were going through. This reassured many coaches that they were not alone in their anxieties. While it is difficult to measure the precise impact of this on the coaches and the wider system, coaches revealed that such sharing allowed them to relax and worry less about their own anxieties and focus more on client needs. This was reflected in the words of one coach who appreciated coaching supervision for the "normalization of challenges I thought 'only I have'."

### Group Coaching Supervision for Coaches on a Single Company Engagement

At the same time the coaching supervision Green Room was launched, another group coaching supervision experiment commenced with several coaches who were collectively coaching at a single company. The approach and format of these sessions was inspired by a chapter from Michel Moral's

(2011) *A French Model of Supervision*. In particular, Moral points to parallel processes that can manifest among coaches in coaching supervision that often reflect what is happening in a coached organization. "Coaching an organization means managing different interventions, at different places, at the same time, through different people in more than one language," writes Moral. "Hence it follows that the coaches have to create a mirror image of the client organization." (p. 69).

An early group coaching supervision session involving several AceUp coaches who were coaching employees at a single organization demonstrated this phenomenon of parallel processes. The session included two coaches who were separately coaching a boss and a direct report. In the middle of the session, the boss's coach turned to the direct report's coach and stated: "Well, your client is doing (such and such behavior) and you should tell your client that they really need to be doing (such and such) things differently."

Coaching supervision revealed that a parallel process was playing out. In their language and responses to one another—one coach telling the other what to do—the coaches reflected a relationship dynamic similar to that shared by the boss and the direct report. In pointing out the parallel, coaching supervision allowed for a deeper exploration of the organizational dynamics and helped the coaches bring greater awareness to later coaching sessions with their clients. While maintaining client confidentiality, the coaches' newfound awareness elevated the level of coaching inquiry to a systemic level. One coach reported asking their client in the next session: "What might your boss say if they heard the conversation we are having in this session?" The subsequent response by the client created an "aha moment" that accelerated the coaching process. What better way to explore systemic issues than in a group coaching supervision session where the organizational parallel processes are allowed to emerge and be analyzed by professional coaches?

These organization-specific coaching supervision sessions have proven powerful for coaches. One exemplary quote from AceUp's, 2020 coach survey, read: "[Regarding coaching supervision] with coaches that have clients at the same organization as mine, the real value has been in hearing the common/different threads our clients are dealing with and collaborating with other coaches." Another surveyed coach called it "symbiosis."

As demands on coaches increased, regular participation in group coaching supervision became a challenge. This led AceUp to conduct a cost-benefit analysis of coaching supervision to determine how much time and resources were needed by the company and its coaches to invest in this beneficial activity, and still deliver a high quality client experience.

## Coaching Supervision Business Modeling

AceUp coaches are required to receive coaching supervision at least once a year and this is provided by AceUp at no cost to coaches. Companies that purchased coaching from AceUp did not see coaching supervision as a separate line item in billing. Rather, coaching supervision is considered part of the critical support structure at AceUp and covered within the corporate expense structure. Consequently, AceUp needed to justify the expenditure of resources on this activity internally and determine the highest return on investment (ROI) for coaching supervision. Or, put another way, AceUp needed to determine the least amount of coaching supervision required to create the greatest value. Key questions included: How many times per year should coaches get coaching supervision? How much time would be required per session? How many coaches per session would be optimal? How often should coaches be required to present a case? What thresholds of engagement are required of coaches to harvest benefits for clients, specifically on coaching engagements with multiple coaches?

The company used EMCC guidelines to establish a baseline. EMCC guidelines recommended coaches participate in at least one hour of coaching supervision for every 35 hours of coaching or at a minimum, participate once per quarter.

In 2019, AceUp introduced coaching supervision requirements that called on coaches to receive coaching supervision once per year. Coaches with five or more clients were required to present a case at least once a year. Coaches with fewer clients could also present cases as long as coaches on multiple engagements had satisfied their requirements, first. Sessions were 90 minutes long and included up to six coaches. Sessions were offered as many times as needed to ensure all coaches could attend up to four times per year.

Anecdotal feedback received by the company included comments that requiring coaching supervision once a year seemed more like a marketing gimmick than something meaningful. Fortunately, coaching supervision proved popular: Close to 60% of engaged coaches attended at least two coaching supervision sessions in the last two quarters of 2019.

In mid-2020, a new coaching supervision framework was rolled out. Coaches were asked and encouraged to sign up for 90-minute group coaching supervision sessions at least once per quarter. Coaches could attend open Green Room or company-specific sessions. And each engaged coach, regardless of number of clients, was asked to present at least one case per year.

By the end of 2020, 100% of engaged AceUp coaches had attended supervision at least once that year and 76% had attended on a quarterly basis; 85% of coaches had presented cases at least once in 2020.

At the same time, AceUp added a fourth criterion for vetting coaches: the ability to collaborate with other coaches. Part of the vetting process began to include a modified group coaching supervision session whereby coaches were evaluated based on how they worked in a collaborative coaching environment.

Consequently, coaches who were attracted to a collaborative atmosphere showed up more often in applications. The quality of the coaching pool at AceUp increased.

In fact, coaches began to cite coaching supervision as a benefit of joining the company. These coaches did not see coaching supervision as a burden; they saw it as a benefit. As one coach noted in the 2020 end-of-year survey, in offering coaching supervision, AceUp "stands out from other vendors who do not offer this" (AceUp, 2021).

## Benefits of Coaching Supervision

Coaching supervision has been clearly demonstrated to benefit at least three key stakeholders: coaches, the client organization, and the company.

First, coaches benefit as they do from all forms of supervision. Namely, they receive the opportunity to work through complicated client interactions in a safe space, to learn new ways to improve their practice, and to refresh themselves as coaches. In 2020, AceUp's annual coach survey revealed 87% of coaches surveyed were satisfied with coaching supervision (the highest rating), 13% were neither satisfied nor dissatisfied. None of the surveyed coaches reported being dissatisfied with coaching supervision.

Second, the benefits to client organizations continue to prove valuable. Group coaching supervision for coaches serving a single company involves organically co-creating a coherent approach to coaching. Group coaching supervision allows themes to emerge that can be related back to the organization's primary decision makers concerning the engagement. This effectively creates an internal coaching department for the coached organization. The coaches understand the organization intimately. At the same time, it affords the client organization all the benefits of professional external coaches who are focused on coaching and not burdened by the organization's internal agendas. This allows for best-matched coaching practices specifically fit for the coached organization. In this way, the organization itself becomes coached.

Currently, AceUp is experimenting with expanding the coaching supervisor role to also serve as a kind of "theme catcher." While maintaining client confidentiality, coaches have an ability to reflect back to the coached organization through a coaching supervisor: "Here's what we are hearing about some significant themes from your organization." Furthermore, powerful coaching questions can be asked of the organization's key stakeholders through a coaching supervisor.

For example, one organization had leadership that wanted employees to focus on developing a "growth mindset." Yet, a survey of clients at this organization ranked "growth mindset" as 13th of 16 priority areas to work on. From coaching supervision, coaches unearthed deeper themes that included identifying a "culture of nice" at the organization and a climate that impeded productivity as staff felt unsafe (psychologically) and unable to communicate freely. Other surveys and discovery activities had not revealed these conditions. When shared with the client organization's executive team, they decided to model the growth mindset they expected of their employees. They investigated the coaches' reflections with employees and found them to be true. Leadership embraced these insights and shifted the organization in response.

Third, AceUp continues to realize benefits from coaching supervision as the company has grown. We've found that allowing coaches to mix and match in various coaching supervision group sessions has created a unique culture whereby more coaches get to know each other in different times and spaces. This has fostered a trusting environment at AceUp that has grown and a new "AceUp way" of coaching has developed. Whether this type of curated community approach can be sustained as the company grows has yet to be determined.

## Conclusion: Considerations for the Future

Many questions and opportunities for innovation remain. Here are a few:

1   How is coaching supervision scaled for consistency and quality? As AceUp grows, more coaching supervisors will be brought on. Currently, AceUp relies on three coaching supervisors. Consistency and quality concerns are handled through monthly, one-hour sessions that loosely follow group coaching supervision formats. These sessions involve exploring coaching supervision cases as well as ad hoc discussions of questions that emerge from working in a startup environment.
2   What outcomes can be expected of coaching supervision and how can these be best articulated to all stakeholders? How can the value of coaching supervision be better conveyed to coaches, organizations, clients, and others who may question it?
3   What actual value can be abstracted from coaching supervision and passed on to stakeholders, while maintaining confidentiality? As noted earlier, AceUp is experimenting with a model of coach supervisor as "theme catcher." What other methods are available to directly connect coaching supervision to client development without losing the safety and confidentiality so crucial to outstanding coaching supervision?
4   How can coaching supervision further interact with other engagement activities, such as survey data collection from clients and coaches, business update calls with organizational decision makers and other activities? How can coaching supervision best be integrated into the overall coaching engagement?
5   How can we better measure the impact of coaching supervision on the client? Further, AceUp is exploring how to better connect coaching supervision to the value proposition provided to client organizations. Bachkirova et al. (2020) captures some of the most important questions in this area when it comes to group coaching supervision:

[P]ractice seems to have followed some principles from theory outside of coaching supervision which may not have been explicitly operationalized or fully articulated in the translation to the coaching supervision domain. It would seem that the concept of collective intelligence may provide useful insights into group work. Systems theories are also articulated at a very coarse level in application to coaching supervision (Lawrence, 2019) and a more extensive translation to the domain would be warranted. Also implicit in this development would be more explicit and extensive incorporation of complexity theories (p.13).

6  Finally, what makes for the most effective coaching supervision? A necessary corollary to this question is: How to optimize the quality and frequency of producing effective outcomes? As Tkach and DiGirolamo (2019) note: "Some forms of supervision may be more helpful than others." In particular, they cite a study that demonstrated "group supervision may be more beneficial than one-on-one … and more frequent and longer sessions (but not 'very long') may be more advantageous than shorter, less frequent sessions (Wilkins & Antonopoulou, 2018)" (Tkach & DiGirolamo, 2019, page 4).

In addition to determining the most effective modalities for coaching supervision, is also necessary to consider the cost-benefit analysis that produces a maximum return on investment. While longer sessions may be more fruitful, some thought must be given to the cost-benefit tradeoff of frequent and long coaching supervision sessions versus coach time spent in the field.

AceUp believes that coaching supervision will continue to be a core element of its value proposition. We continue to work with clients and other stakeholders to leverage the extraordinary potential that coaching supervision offers to clients, organizations, coaches, and the entire system touched by the coaching industry. Perhaps the greatest area of growth is harnessing group coaching supervision to help explore systemic coaching, particularly by seeing, identifying, and exploring parallel processes. With professional coaches taking on parallel roles in a safe, confidential group space, a kind of off-site lab is created. This reflective environment allows for deeper insights and more powerful paths to emerge for all stakeholders, particularly the client organization. I believe this may be the most promising area for development and remain excited to innovate and see how others innovate coaching supervision for the benefit of all.

James Lopata is a consultant for AceUp as Vice President of Coaching Supervision and has played a leading role in helping the company build out its coaching supervision framework.

## References

AceUp. (2020, May 21). *AceUp coach advisory council* [Meeting notes].
AceUp. (2021, January 14). *AceUp year end report on coaching supervision*. AceUp.

Bachkirova, T., Jackson, P., Hennig, C., & Moral, M. (2020). Supervision in coaching: Systematic literature review. *International Coaching Psychology Review*, *15*(2): 31–53.

EMCC Global. (2021). *Quality standards*. https://www.emccglobal.org/quality/supervision.

Lawrence, P. (2019). What happens in group supervision? Exploring current practice in Australia. *International Journal of Evidence Based Coaching & Mentoring*, *17*(2): 138–157.

Moral, M. (2011). A French model of supervision: Supervising a 'several to several' coaching journey. In T. Bachkirova, P. Jackson, & D. Clutterbuck (Eds.), *Coaching & mentoring supervision: Theory and practice* (1st ed., pp. 67–77). Open University Press.

Proctor, B. (2008). *Group supervision: A guide to creative practice* (2nd ed.). SAGE.

Tkach, J. T., & DiGirolamo, J. (2019, February). *ICF supervision literature review: 2018*. https://coachfederation.org/app/uploads/2019/03/SupervisionLitReview2018_MAR15-1.pdf

Wilkins, D., & Antonopoulou, V. (2018). What does supervision help with? A survey of 315 social workers in the UK. *Practice*, *31*(1): 1–20.

# 6 Ontological and Systemic Coherence Model in Coaching Supervision

*Alicia Agüero and Angelica (Tani) Sturich*

## Introduction

Supervision, currently in full development, is gaining legitimacy and expanding considerably throughout Latin America, thanks to the emergence of training programs and related literature. In this regard, Peter Hawkins stated that: "[In 2006] I co-directed the first field research into the development of Supervision. The encouraging results of this study, which were updated in 2015 and 2017, showed that the activity had grown significantly, both in the UK and in other places in Europe, southern Africa and Asia, Australasia, although to a lesser extent, in North America. In South America the development of Supervision was also slow, largely due to the lack of good quality literature and training programs ..." (Goldvarg, 2017, p. 15).

In our coach training school in Argentina (A&T Organizational Coaching), supervision has been a common but informal practice since 2000. It has gained considerable importance and presence since we were trained as supervisors in 2016. As such, we offer supervision to coaches from Argentina as well as to participants of our training program, who bring to their sessions issues related to ethics, contracting or other cases that affect their professional performance. At the beginning, we had no specific model. Then, we applied strategies based on a series of models and eventually, a few years ago, we started using the ontological and systemic coherence model.

To understand the model described in this chapter, it is important to show foundations, principles, schools of thought, and theoretical developments of the Ontological approach, what it is based on, the areas it covers and its effectiveness.

The Ontology of Language and Ontological Coaching were developed mainly in the Americas and Spain. They are based on modern philosophy, human and natural sciences (particularly biology), and various fields of culture.

Currently this model adds to the contributions already made by the Ontology of Language. It is the first coaching supervision model with an Ontological and systemic basis, which proposes a specific and particular way of supervising while articulating the contributions made by the Ontology of Language.

DOI: 10.4324/b23130-8

In this chapter, we invite the reader to discover a model that is relevant because it comes from a field—mainly philosophical and biological—that is different from those of the supervision models that are common in our field.

## Theoretical Foundations of the Ontology of Language

The Ontology of Language is the discipline that studies the human being as a linguistic being. It undertakes the great challenge of rethinking what it means to be human and coming up with a new approach to the human phenomenon. It provides an interpretation of what being human means, of the dimensions that we all share, and those that constitute our particular way of being. In recognizing the central role played by language in the creation of our lives, our identities and the worlds in which we live, the Ontology of Language introduces a powerful interpretation of the human being and phenomena related to social coexistence.

The foundations of this conception arise mainly from the contributions of philosophers such as Nietzsche, Wittgenstein, and Heidegger, among others and from representatives of the field of biological sciences, such as Humberto Maturana and Francisco Varela.

It is worth noting that there have been different interpretations of what it means to be human, depending on the moment in history. Ontology traces back to ancient Greece. Approximately 25 centuries ago, Heraclitus, a voice from the Greek world, would claim that the foundation of everything we see, of all experiences, is not in being; he would claim that "becoming" is the main characteristic of existence and that everything is undergoing a transformation process, being is just a brief moment in it.

In the 20th century, important developments in biology, philosophy, anthropology, sociology, and even quantum physics took place, which provided rigorous academic foundations for the development of the Ontology of Language.

Coaching is referred to as Ontological when it arises from interpreting a person's way of being, performing new actions, and leaving behind old ways of being as a result of an Ontological intervention. The Argentine Association of Professional Ontological Coaching (AACOP) defines the discipline as "a profession committed to the expansion of personal, organizational and social potential, based on ontological learning within a constructivist framework and a systemic perspective" (AACOP, 2017, p. 28).

Humberto Maturana's research on the nature of perception provides the biological foundation. Fundamental concepts in Maturana's work, such as the observer, language and emotion, cognition, the act of distinguishing and consensual domains, provide the Ontological proposal with new perspectives on the structure of living beings, their functioning dynamics, and the way people communicate and interact (Maturana & Varela, 1994).

The notion of observer constitutes a key aspect of Maturana's theory. He points out that given our biology, the way we perceive the information in the world around us (what others say, whatever happens, experiences, etc.) is always imbued with our interpretations of how we see life. What we observe in a given situation largely depends on the type of observer we are (Maturana & Varela, 1984).

Not only do human beings perceive the world through their senses, but they also perceive it from their distinctions. When we distinguish, we separate something from a background to observe it. Language then enables us to distinguish characteristics of the world and develop shared understandings, which are essential in constructive human relationships.

The interpretation that "language describes reality" has been challenged based on the so-called linguistic turn, which enables us to maintain that language generates reality. In other words, not only does language have a descriptive role, but it also constitutes and actually *generates* reality (Echeverria, 1997).

Different branches of philosophy have contributed to this new understanding of language. In different parts of the American continent, the "continental philosophy" and "analytical philosophy" developed proposals that converged in the Ontology of Language.

Following Echeverría (2006), the 20th century was marked by two great philosophical trends: Analytical philosophy and continental philosophy. Both were great movements that witnessed main advances, from a philosophical point of view.

Analytical philosophy evolved mainly in the Anglo-Saxon world (Great Britain, the US, Germany, and Austria) and developed a special interest in the issues of language and the way we think. For example, this philosophy maintains that language is understood as generative of identities, relationships, commitments, possibilities, different futures, and different worlds. Leading exponents of analytical philosophy included Bertrand Russell (1872–1970), G.E. Moore (1873–1958), Ludwig Wittgenstein (1889–1951), and J.L. Austin (1911–1960).

Continental philosophy developed more strongly in continental Europe. Starting from the philosophical reflection on human existence and associated problems, it has several main pioneers, such as Feuerbach (1804–1872), Nietzsche (1844–1900), Martin Buber (1878–1965), and Heidegger (1889–1976).

Within the Ontology of language, some of the most relevant authors are the following: Baruch Spinoza (1632–1677), who proposed that instead of exaggerating the role of reason, it is necessary to understand the importance of emotions; Friedrich Nietzsche (1844–1900) who, among many reflections, invites us to see that to rethink the human phenomenon, it is important to affirm change, transformation, and becoming; Martin Heidegger (1889–1976) stated that language is the home where a human being dwells; and Martin Buber (1878- 1965), who wrote that as human beings we constitute ourselves and become human beings from our dialogues and conversations with others, ourselves, and the mystery of life. David Hume

(1711–1776) contributed to the field saying that experience is the key to knowledge and Ludwig Wittgenstein (1889–1951) expressed that all language is a way of life, therefore language and life cannot be separated. Closer in time, J. L. Austen (1911– 960) shared the reflection that language generates realities, transforms worlds, and allows human beings to transform themselves. Lastly, John Searle (1932–) established the speech acts, or the ways in which human beings interact with themselves and with others.

Influenced by the work of authors mentioned above, Fernando Flores, and later Rafael Echeverría, elaborated concepts on the Ontology of Language.

Fernando Flores appears as the key reference in the development of the Ontology of Language. He established the first Ontological conversational proposal in the world, and generated a paradigm change in the way of communicating and in social relations. His work is mostly focused on the organizational context (Flores, 1989, 1994, 1998, 2017).

Echeverria (1997) deepened the development of the Ontology of Language by contributing postulates, principles, models, and distinctions that have established a rigorous philosophical framework as well as a guide for Ontological observation and intervention. He is the author of other theoretical models and contributions, such as the understanding of a learning model that includes the human being and the system in which it interacts, and the development of conversational skills.

## Ontological Assumptions of the Supervision Model

The Ontological assumptions of the supervision model that are taken into consideration are the following:

1   The human being and the system are being and maintain coherence.

This implies that we are not immutable in our living, but we constitute ourselves moment after moment and impact the system where we belong.

By system, we understand a dynamic network of relationships in interdependent interaction with other relationships. The expression *being* was coined by Heidegger. As regards the person, Heidegger conducted considerable research into the field of being (Heidegger, 1991). He used the word "Dasein" to refer to "being-in-the-world" and to the particular way of being that human beings and systems are, as particular types of observers.

2   The human being is linguistic, interpretive, social, and learner.

The characteristics of a person listed in this premise requires some clarification. The person is **created in language**. Thus, language takes precedence over reason. The latter is a particular language game and to understand it, it is necessary to understand the character of the language.

Language has an active and generative capacity: It makes things happen, besides enabling us to talk about them. Language creates realities and generates being. It allows us to shape our identity and the world we live in.

Likewise, the human being is an interpretive being that does not have biological mechanisms that allow him to have perceptions corresponding to how things really are. Interpretation is vital to human existence and it is from our interpretations that we see the world.

Human beings are **social** beings. **We live in coexistence with others.** We constitute ourselves as individuals from the system of relationships that we maintain with others. Communities with different languages constitute different people. We are the result of an already constituted language within which we grow.

We are ultimately **learning** beings. Learning is fundamentally experiential and social, and transforms the identity of the human being. Being is a transient moment of becoming. Being and soul are not immutable. The main emphasis is on transformation and change, since the way of being is not determined. In turn, it enables endless inventions from action. Our actions enable us to transform ourselves into different beings.

The creation of learning relationships such as supervision, makes transformation possible within those relationships and in systems of which they are a part. We have the chance to communicate through language, we live in social environments and interpret and learn from each experience.

3    The human being presents three basic observation domains: Language, body, and emotion. They are irreducible and maintain Ontological coherence.

Human existence recognizes three primary domains: language, body, and emotion, which provide a better understanding of the person. The world we observe is different according to our language, body or physical behavior, and emotionality. Below, we further define these concepts.

### *Language*

The way we are in conversations and the distinctions we have define how we see a given situation. Our use of language creates our reality, and changes in it can generate a more effective one.

### *Body*

Gestures, voice, postures, and movements evidence themselves in different body dispositions. To consider the body in learning implies increasing our chances of becoming a more powerful observer and achieving more effective changes.

### Emotion

We are always in some emotional state that "colours" the way we see the world. Observing our own emotionality and that of others makes it possible for us to self-regulate and generate new ones.

Changes in one domain (language, body, or emotion) produces changes in the others, which leads to the adoption of a new coherence in the person. If these changes are not short-lived, they produce transformations that allow a different being to emerge.

4   We apply the Principles of the Ontology of Language in the supervision model presented below. The first and second principles of the Ontology of Language refer to the Observer, while the third one refers to the System.

First principle: *"We do not know how things are. We only know how we observe them or how we interpret them. We live in interpretive worlds"* (Echeverría, 1997, p. 151).

Second principle: *"Not only do we act according to how we are, (and we do), but we also are according to how we act. Action generates being. We become according to what we do"* (Echeverría, 2010, p. 209).

Third principle: *"The action of every entity results from its own structure and that of the system where the entity operates. This defines its scope of possible actions. Within that scope, however, it is usually possible to introduce transformations in both structures. These actions, in turn, allow for other actions that were not possible before"* (Echeverría, 2010, p. 201).

The four assumptions explained above are the context for the development of the Ontological and systemic coherence model in coaching supervision that we introduce later in this chapter. The reader will be able to appreciate its application in each of the areas we propose.

## Ontological and Systemic Coherence Model in Coaching Supervision

The participants in the supervision session are supervisor and supervisee: Two fellow coaches who meet to reflect on a topic or a case raised by the supervisee, who will express what they want to work on. From that point on, any reflections, questions, comments, or other points will include supervisor and supervisee as well as client and their system(s).

The order of these areas is only for the purpose of their presentation in this chapter. In practice, during the supervision session, they are taken into consideration and adapted without a prior order, according to the concerns or needs expressed by the supervisee. All the questions refer to any of them, delivered in an order appropriate to the specific supervision session.

This model has been tried and tested for five years with participants of the coach training program and with coaches in individual and group

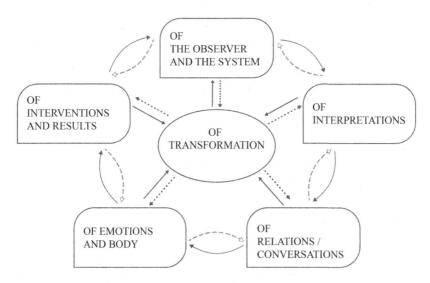

*Figure 6.1* Ontological and Systemic Model of Coaching Supervision.

sessions, and proves to be inclusive, integrative, and applicable to all the situations or issues (ethics, contract, responsibility, interpretations, etc.) we have had the honor to supervise (see Figure 6.1).

## Model Areas

The model consists of six areas presented individually, below. These sections describe each area and what each comprises, and include general and specific possible questions for the supervisor to ask the supervisee.

## Area of Observer and System

In supervision, reflecting about the kind of coach or supervisor we are being with each client enables us to understand more deeply how we are observing; what kind of observers we are being, our distinctions and the size of world we perceive to coach or supervise the way we do.

Reflection is enriched by taking a closer look at the systems in which coach, client, and supervisor intervene and the effect they have on each one.

The notion of observer relies on the systemic approach, just like the systemic approach accounts for a way of observing. Coherence of both system and observer is shown in such a way that one notion is supported by the other. The observer can be seen as the result of a systemic view of the individual and the system offers a particular way of looking at reality and of a particular type of observer.

In supervision, it is important to know that when looking at a system, supervisor, supervisee, and client will observe different systems. We further define these terms, below.

Observer: The distinction refers to the fact that every human being observes things from their own perceptions, emotions, and expectations, which defines the type of observer we are. The way we see things is only the way we see things, not the way they actually are.

System: This distinction aims at a way of observing or interpreting that focuses on finding relationships between different elements and giving them a particular meaning. For instance, community where we belong, family into which we were born, and others. The systems where we participate affect the type of observer we are, our actions, and results.

## Possible Questions in this Area

- What limitations of the system, supervisor, supervisee, or client is it necessary to express and recognize?
- What system, supervisor, supervisee, or client connections need to be made?
- What mental maps of the supervisor, supervisee, or client need to be clarified?
- What is the purpose of this supervision? How does it connect with other aspects of life?
- What new ways of thinking as a coach connect me with a systemic perspective?
- How are we observing what we observe?
- What can you do with your client that is effective given their way of being?
- What can we bring to the session for the benefit of the client?
- What would you need to complete and let go of?
- What is your gut feeling telling you?
- What is your challenge?

## Area of Interpretations

The process of interpreting or making assessments generally follows these steps: We pick out what demands our attention and we consider important; we quickly, and often times automatically, make sense of what we choose; we draw conclusions or interpret what happened according to the way we see the world; we take actions based on the conclusions we have drawn. In this regard, Argyris (1991) develops the concept of the ladder of inferences and defines it as a mental path of increasing abstraction that leads to erroneous beliefs.

The world of possible interpretations is as diverse as the individuals in it, each person has their own and particular interpretations and these impact at least three aspects:

- **In language**, through opinions, which can be automatic.

Many times this is done unconsciously, for example by saying: I don't like this; if I do this it is not correct; this is not appropriate for me. However when we interpret, there is a commitment to act in a certain particular way. This interpretation has a direct impact on how and what one is willing to do.

- **In listening,** because what we perceive colors our interpretations.

This process happens so fast that it can lead to wrong conclusions if we fail to check our interpretations.

- **In the emotional world,** interpretations about any situation often determine actions. They trigger emotions and these are related to predispositions to do or not to do.

Learning to explore interpretations in the supervision session is key to transformational learning, as it is possible for supervisees to generate and choose other interpretations leading to greater capacity for action.

One of the simplest and most effective interventions to accompany the supervisee's reflection is to invite the supervisee to tell the difference between facts and interpretations. This makes it possible to recognize what is immutable. For example: There are 100 people in a room (fact). What can be changed? The interpretation: 100 people may be a lot for some, or only a few for others.

By asking questions related to this area in supervision, it is possible to find out what members of the system, the supervisee or the client, think. Some examples could include: "Being incompetent or making mistakes is not right," or "it is important to always know the correct answer," or "we must not waste time and quickly understand what we are asked," "asking for help is frowned upon," "it is necessary to control the situation," or "uncertainty is bad," and so on.

This domain shows a summary of the beliefs, values, and expectations resulting from the interpretive worlds of all the parties involved in supervision.

## Possible Questions in this Area

- What interpretations need to be discussed or examined?
- What interpretations are either limiting or enriching the session?
- What barriers or obstacles are we going through in the session?
- What do your interpretations about other people say about you? (Remember that when we point out what we observe about others, we are actually speaking more about ourselves than about them).

- If you opened a door that allowed you to go through your assumptions, what would you see, or where would it lead you?
- How can we bring the perspectives of stakeholders (customer or system) to the session?
- What were you thinking when the client spoke so fast or slow or at a speed different from yours?

## Area of Relationships and Conversations

In this area, relations are explored: Client with stakeholders and the organization; coach and client; supervisor and supervisee.

The type of relationship we have with a person depends on the quality of our conversations. This is how conversations become the gateway to improving relationships. We can change our relationships by changing our conversations (Agüero & Sturich, 2001).

Conversations and relationships open the door to generating new realities and creating what does not yet exist. Conversing is a relational dance. It is moving around with others while creating a rhythm and a constant association.

Supervision is a phenomenon that can only occur in the relationship between supervisee and supervisor. It occurs in their connection as they listen to each other, in the shared reflection, in the relationship they both build by generating a conversation that includes dignity and autonomy. In such a relationship, it is possible for both to share experiences, expectations, beliefs, assumptions, arguments, and emotions as well as what happens to them in the "here and now" in a vulnerable way in order to better serve the supervisee, their client, and system.

This area also includes contracts, either formal or informal, as expressions of the relationship created and maintained between the different actors. We clarify our association through contracts, as the "framework" of a safe and free relationship.

Contracting is key to ethical considerations between the parties involved. By way of example, we establish agreement on how the balance between support and challenge will be reached, how feedback will be given, and other elements. The contract can also detail logistics or practical aspects in the relationship, limits and confidentiality, work alliance, learning styles, mutual responsibilities, ethical issues, and any other element that contributes to building a mutually satisfactory relationship.

In the context of supervision, various contracts are addressed: Between supervisor and supervisee, between coach and client, and even with stakeholders.

Moreover, it is important for supervisors to recognize their vulnerability. The supervisor is committed not only to listening to what the supervisee wants to achieve, which at times can be painful, curious, or creative, but also to showing their own vulnerability and being able to share what they feel and what happens to them in the here and now.

In supervision the conversations that generate possibilities for supervisees are those of abundance, power, and love; they are also inclusive, creative, helpful, and generous conversations.

## Possible Questions in this Area

- What would the client want the supervisor and supervisee to discuss?
- What relationships need to be examined, including that of supervisor and supervisee?
- What "voices" need to be heard?
- What would be possible if we looked at our relationship (supervisor–supervisee) differently?
- How would you describe the relationship you have with the client?
- How would you describe our relationship (supervisor–supervisee)?
- What is happening between us (supervisor–supervisee) here and now that you can relate to what is happening to you with your client?
- Regarding the contract, what do I need to know about you? What do you need to know about me? What balance do you need between support and challenge in our supervision? What do you understand by confidentiality? What else should I ask you to ensure a safe and peer-to-peer relationship?
- If you were dancing with your client, what would the dance be like? Who would propose new steps and who would follow?
- What does your client value about what you do and what do they need you to develop?
- Is the personal aspect interfering with the professional one? In that case what can we do?

## Area of Emotions and Body

We might say that **emotions and moods** are predispositions to carry out certain actions or to behave in one way or another. They define spaces for possible action for those who experience them and also for those relating to them (Echeverria, 1996).

Emotion is triggered by the interpretation of an event and this leads to a certain predisposition for action. By way of example, we can think of joy when we are promoted and surprise when we hear unexpected news.

Moods show the continuity of certain emotions as they are an expression of the fundamental predispositions and orientations in life. For example, optimism, resentment, serenity, and acceptance either open or close possibilities for us by defining what actions and ways of acting in the world are possible or impossible. They have a direct influence on performance and on the undertaking of actions. They are contagious and can be designed.

Cultural and historical narratives have power over the emotionality of human beings. If we think of the "gender narrative" or the "diversity narrative" or the "inclusion narrative," all of them have informed human beings about what emotions they can or cannot feel and express.

Even without knowing the various historical-cultural narratives, they nevertheless determine the emotions that we are allowed to feel and express. We grow up learning that some emotions are not legitimate and even fear we will be unable to manage them.

A key aspect of a supervisor is to expand the range of emotions that can be felt and expressed appropriately in different contexts. The supervisor must develop a greater sensitivity to their own personal moods and those of others, and identify whether it is the best mood for the session or design one that enables them to collaborate in an effective way. It is important for the supervisor to learn how to manage and show vulnerability, which is regarded as being able to express emotions authentically.

Human beings use the **body** to express themselves, and they perceive external sensations through it. The body makes it possible to perform certain movements that will surely show the emotions that are being felt.

We can observe that in certain body spaces there is no possibility of certain interpretations or emotions. In a body with a depressed posture, e.g., there is no room for joy or optimism. So, the way we stand up and walk, our gestures, and movements reveal our way of being in the world and how we "are being."

Certain bodily dispositions connect us with conversations and emotions that enable us to perform some actions and not others. Each disposition shows different structures (eyes, breathing, muscle tone, dynamics, sounds, etc.), and have certain emotional states.

Emotions occur in the body specifically in the brain limbic system, which generates bodily action. Emotions are explained in language, hence the coherence generated by the domains of observation. Movement that allows us to act, create, and relate appears through emotions.

In supervision, it is important to intervene in the body, which is the observable domain: Proposing changes in breathing, posture, and focus to name just a few. These influence the other observation domains presented in this chapter (emotion and language), while reflecting on emotions and moods. Facilitating emotional observation by relating it to the possibilities of action makes it possible to broaden expectations and results.

This area allows us to connect with the coach and generate an intimate space where two fellow coaches reflect together.

## Possible Questions in this Area

- What emotion is expressed in the session?
- What emotion do I feel as a supervisor?
- What emotions do I recognize? Which ones do I allow myself to express as a supervisor?

- What happens in my body or in the supervisee's? Do I let myself express it?
- What do I feel, or what does my body feel that I can share here and now at the service of the client, the system, or the supervisee?
- When you said that word I felt something very chaotic or important or uncertain in me. How does that sound?
- I am feeling confused/angry/sad/etc. How does this relate to whatever is happening to you or your client or the system?
- I feel tension in my shoulders/arms/legs. Does this make any sense to you?
- What fears/angers/sadness/confusions/are we not facing?

## Area of Interventions and Results

This area refers to exploring the interventions made and the results achieved not only in the supervision session, but also in the session that took place between coach and client, as narrated by the coach to the supervisor.

Supervisor and supervisee reflect on what worked and what did not work in the session, what might be done differently, and assess potential advantages and disadvantages.

As regards interventions, it is interesting to explore the most common ones and those that the coach or supervisor have decided not to carry out and why. Reflection generates new ideas that can be applied in the next session with the client to create new realities and possibilities by observing the interventions and results and sharing experiences to find different ways to act or achieve different results.

Exploration in this area can lead to discovering similarities between what is happening in the supervision session and in the coaching sessions. These can include tendencies to use the same dynamics or modalities or examples in both cases. For example, coaches might seek to quickly find new actions in supervision and lead the client to that same terrain in the coaching session. The supervisor's ability to become aware of this modality and articulate what is being observed, provides valuable information for the coach's reflection. In addition, it enables them to compare the results obtained in these circumstances against new ones.

The possibilities of intervention are endless. In addition to questions oriented to "what" or "who," there is the use of metaphors, analogies, images, colors, drawings, photos, and other tools that the supervisor can contribute to the session. The timeliness and relevance of the intervention is a learning opportunity in the supervision session and for subsequent sessions between coach and client.

Results are also a matter for reflection in this area, specifically those developed in the Area of Transformation. Working between peers, sharing and reflecting together, supervisor and supervisee share interpretations, emotions, and challenges that lead to completely new results.

## Possible Questions in this Area

- What do new results in the improvement of connections (between you and the client, the system or me) bring you?
- What actions do you think need to be taken?
- What are the changes that you need to generate and how will you do that?
- What strengths and areas in development do I observe in my interventions with the client?
- What are the observable results referring to stakeholders (supervisee, client, system)?
- What would we allow ourselves to think of and reflect on if we were not attached to the results?
- How do you want to explore that concern?
- If your client were in the session now, what do you think they would like us to talk about?
- What would "effective results" mean to you (supervisee), your client or other stakeholders?

## Area of Transformation

This is the area in which all the above areas converge. Transformational learning aims to modify the particular way of being of those who intervene. It is the area where the different learnings converge so that coaches can expand their resources and professional possibilities, while impacting and transforming the systems where they operate. The supervisees who become aware of their lack of self-confidence and of the possibility of showing themselves as they are, produce an impact on themselves, on their clients and on the systems in which they participate when coaching clients from a newly acquired state of confidence.

We think of transformation as a result of Ontological Learning, considering the levels of learning proposed by Argyris (1991): One-way and two-way learning. These are later called first-order learning and second-order learning in models developed by action design and Echeverría (1997).

In this regard, Echeverría proposes in his model that we evaluate each of the results we obtain from our actions, to see whether they are the ones we want to achieve or not. Echeverría (2010) notes, upon assessing the results and not achieving the expected ones:

- If actions are changed and more effective results are achieved, first-order learning occurs.
- Exploring and changing the observer makes it possible to reach second-order learning.
- When new behaviors are achieved in the way of being and the observer's nucleus has been changed, there is transformational learning.

Each of the levels impacts on the system.

Otto Scharmer introduced his readers to the theory and practice of the U process. He refers to the process of "letting go and receiving" for transformation to take place. This process requires courage to let go of values, expectations, beliefs, and theories that have been at the heart of our lives. Also courage to accept the consequences of new ways of making sense of events. The resulting creation of meaning has consequences in our relationships (Scharmer, 1997).

The connotation here is important because it is not only the supervisee, the client or the system that decides to cling to all the above or to transcend and embrace new ways of making sense. It is also the supervisor.

To facilitate this experience it may be valuable to ask oneself: What do I want to keep? In this way, what emerges is what is important for the individual or the system.

The scope of transformation resulting from the work carried out during supervision makes it possible for stakeholders to observe differently with new perspectives, perceptions, and meaning.

Supervisors are expected to work on continuous learning and seek their own transformation showing coherence in their own being, to have impact on the supervisee, the client or the system.

As the model shows, we believe that transformational learning can occur in supervision from reflection in any of the areas, since all the areas converge in the area of transformation. We believe the deepest learning occurs here.

## Possible Questions in this Area

- From what you observe in your being a coach, what would you like to keep?
- From what has been reflected in this supervision, what aspects do you recognize you have learned as a coach?
- What are the strengths you have identified as a coach?
- What new ways of making sense of experiences have you found?
- What new connections or ways of thinking systemically flow from the supervision relationship?
- What new challenges do we face in our practice today?
- How do we make our work as supervisors reach high quality standards?
- How do you suggest we can celebrate our learning?

## Case Study

A coach brings the following case to supervision: His client is the director of operations in a multinational company that has been through a cultural change process, from process-centered to client-centered.

The coach holds regular sessions with the supervisor regarding this client. His interventions include training and coaching sessions for area members as well as for the director, who after several months decides that he will not continue with the sessions and that only some of the area members will.

The coaching process takes one year. Two months before the end of the term, the director is dismissed and a new director takes over without knowledge of the cultural change or the characteristics of the work done.

The presentation of this case summarizes situations brought to sessions by the supervisee and the results that were produced in the organization. These results arise from progress reports the coach presented quarterly in the organization, during the year covered by the process. To facilitate the understanding of the application of the model in this case study, they are presented separated by scope.

In the supervision sessions, the coach brought different **situations to work on,** which are presented below with reference to the model elements.

In the area of observer and system of our intervention, one of the issues was that the director who worked with the coach and was unable to form a team that would foster cultural change. This was due to resistance among the company's employees. Another issue related to the area of relationships and conversations that we worked on was the definition of the most suitable profiles for each new role. Moreover, there were no clear agreements regarding key leadership roles, which relates to the area of interventions and results in our work. At the beginning, we observed the area of emotions and body, which were resignation, uncertainty, and distrust; however, after the director was changed, the emotions were surprise, confusion, and doubt about the future. The company's initial road map had deadlines that had not been met for different motives and in our work, this was the area of interpretations. In addition, there was concern in the team because they had yet to meet the new director and did not know how to agree on the continuity of the contract. This relates to the area of emotions and body.

The **results observed** in the supervision sessions according to the model areas are indicated below.

Regarding the Area of Observer and System: There was evidence that the process of cultural change (to define a client-centered culture) is understood by the different observers. What could be observed was the adaptation of the system to the new leadership styles that developed, and the definition of roles for each employee who joined the new area.

Regarding the Area of Interpretations: The interpretive framework was consistent with the client-centered culture. In addition, this framework gave rise to the development of tools to define the new leadership styles required (eight were defined), as well as ways of assessing and indicators for each style.

Regarding the Area of Relationships and Conversations: The area meetings included an agenda prioritizing the user's point of view and their opinions regarding the service they receive. Verification of the service quality reported by the user was carried out through the implementation of tools. It must be noted that before the change of director, a meeting was held to deliver the report that included areas of learning, development, and future opportunities.

Regarding the Area of Emotions and Body: The necessary moods, ambition, acceptance of uncertainty, and other emotions were addressed and managed regularly for the proposed change, as well as the design of the body dispositions of trust, autonomy, and decision.

Area of Interventions and Results: The interventions and results achieved (based on the vision) were verified periodically.

Regarding the Area of Transformation: The members of the area evidenced new connections related to the client center. The early stages of a cultural change integration in the system was reported.

## Conclusion

We regard supervision as both an art and a discipline. As an art, it allows endless interventions of different degrees of creativity. As a discipline, it has its own strategies. It provides opportunities for transformation in all participants, both directly in the supervision session and indirectly as clients or systems. It can bring about a change in mindset or behavior rather than just transferring ideas or knowledge. Reflection is the main learning tool. It helps participants make new connections and think systemically.

In the presentation that we made of this model at the 3rd Supervision Congress (May 2020) we stated before concluding that:

> *The journey that we started at the beginning in the coaching practice invites us to a new journey every time, in this case, to the journey of supervision that we share with you today. Because the journey became the dream of creating an inclusive and peaceful world. And today more than ever, a world where action and coordination of actions are essential. This supervision journey that we discover is a one towards creating value for ourselves and for others, where who we are and what others are, take place in conversations that we must work on ... A journey in which coherence of who we are and who we want to be, as observers and as systems, is a permanent job and leads us to transformation. In short, a journey, where everything leads us to the same destination: Love.*

The model presented in this chapter is applied in the supervision session and the learnings are later applied in the coaching practice. We have verified that its use leads to the generation of a safe space, which presents an adequate balance between challenge and support and aims at achieving the purpose of supervision: Transformational learning.

We invite all coaches to actively participate in supervision. It is a journey where coherence of who we are and who we intend to be, both as observers and systems, is never-ending work and will definitely lead us to transformation.

# References

AACOP. (2017). *Significación del coaching Ontológico, Constructivista y Sistémico.* Leven Anclas.

Argyris, C. (1991). *Teaching smart people how to learn.* Harvard Business Review.

Agüero, A., & Sturich, A. (2001). *Diseñando conversaciones.* Editorial Consultora.

Aguero, A., & Sturich, A. (2007). *Formación en coaching ontológico: Coach personal – Coach organizacional – Fundamentos, reflexiones y propuesta.* Editorial Consultora.

Echeverria, R. (1997). *Ontología del lenguaje.* Dolmen.

Echeverria, R. (2006). *Actos de lenguaje – Volumen I – La escucha.* JC Saez Editor.

Echeverria, R. (2007). *Por la senda del pensar ontológico.* Ediciones Granica S.A.

Echeverria, R. (1996). *El observador y su mundo.* JC Saez Editor.

Flores, F. (2000). *Abrir nuevos mundos.* Santillana.

Flores, F. (1994). *Creando organizaciones para el futuro.* Dolmen.

Flores, F. (1989). *Inventando la empresa del siglo XXI.* Dolmen.

Goldvarg, D. (2017). *Supervisión de coaching.* Ediciones Gránica S.A.

Heidegger, M. (1991). *El ser y el tiempo.* Fondo de Cultura Económica Argentina.

Maturana, H., & Varela, F. (1994). *El arbol del conocimient.* (10th ed.) Lumen Universitaria.

Maturana, H. (1997). *Emociones y lenguaje en educación y política.* Dolmen.

Maturana, H. (1991). *El sentido de lo humano.* Dolmen.

Scharmer, O. (1997). *La teoría U.* Editorial Eleftheria.

Searle, J. (1986). *Actos de habla.* Ediciones Cátedra.

Solomon, R., & Flores, F. (2001). *Building trust.* Oxford University Press.

Stuart, C. (1938). *The tyranny of words.* Harcourt Brace.

# 7 Applying a Systemic Developmental Approach to Coaching Supervision: Experiences from the USA

*Sarah Tennyson*

## Introduction

Coaching supervision is a growing practice in the Americas (Hawkins & Turner, 2017), yet there are few data or research studies about supervision in an American context. In the Americas, the supply side of coaching supervision appears to be growing—as demonstrated by the number of coach supervisor training programs, conference sessions, communities of practice and now this book, the first of its kind focused on the American context. On the demand side, there appears to be a range of needs that can be met—at least, in part—by coaching supervision or adaptations of coaching supervision approaches.

In this chapter, I draw on my experience from my coaching supervision and leadership development practice in the US to suggest that systemic, developmental approaches from coaching supervision can be usefully adapted to support the development and resourcing of coaches and leaders in organizations and help them respond to the complex challenges they face.

Survey data indicate that coaching supervision is less prevalent in the Americas than in other countries (Hawkins & Turner, 2017; McAnally et al., 2019) and indeed most of the coaches whom I have supervised in the US are new to coaching supervision. They come with experiences from mentor-coaching or co-coaching and may be confused or put-off by the terminology of supervision (Bachkirova et al., 2011; Wright et al., 2020).

In my US practice, group supervision seems to be an attractive starting point for coaches and organizations engaging with coaching supervision for the first time. From there, they may decide to engage in individual or peer supervision, often in addition to continuing with group supervision. For example, in 2017 the Association for Talent Development (ATD) New York Chapter offered peer group supervision facilitated by a qualified supervisor, free of charge, to its members. This initiative attracted sufficient participants to establish three groups, initially comprised of many highly experienced and qualified coaches, most of whom had not experienced coaching supervision before.

The systemic developmental approach holds the primary purpose of coaching supervision as helping coaches see more than they can currently

DOI: 10.4324/b23130-9

see. It is based on the premise that "coaches can only bring to supervision that which is currently in their awareness and emphasizes the importance of helping coaches notice what they cannot currently see in themselves, their clients, their client organizations and each of the respective systems of which they form part" (Wright et al., 2019, p. 109). This approach draws on adult development theory (Kegan, 1994), systems theories applied to coaching (Lawrence, 2019b; O'Connor, 2020; Cavanagh, 2012), and Isaacs' conceptualization of dialogue (1999).

A systemic developmental approach to coaching supervision is particularly relevant to coaches and leaders today, supporting them as they adapt to meet the challenges of our complex, interconnected, and changing world (Wright et al., 2019). A complex, uncertain world presents us with situations for which our existing knowledge and skills are inadequate. Kegan and Lahey (2009) describe this as being "in over our heads" where a person's complexity of mind does not match the level of complexity they face in the world. This was felt acutely by many in 2020 as they strived to make difficult decisions and communicate effectively in the face of the unprecedented combination of challenges found in the US context[1]. Developing greater mental complexity cannot be learned or taught through training, but rather emerges from cycles of experience and reflection.

Using the cycle of developmental supervision (described in detail in Wright et al., 2019), a supervision session starts with an *issue* brought by a supervisee, following which the *issue* and *focus areas* are explored through *dialogue*. In one-to-one supervision, this *dialogue* occurs between the supervisor and supervisee whereas in group coaching supervision all supervisees are invited to participate. During the *dialogue,* the supervisor helps the supervisee examine the *issue* from multiple perspectives and facilitates subject-object shifts in the supervisee's perception and understanding of the material they are exploring. Through this *dialogue*, the supervisee may start to gain new awareness, insight, or see things they had not previously seen. The *dialogue* is an emergent—rather than a linear—process, requiring the supervisor be mindful and aware of their own self as the instrument of coaching supervision, and to balance developmental challenge with appropriate support.

However, it became apparent to me through practice that to engage in the *dialogue*, the supervisee(s) and supervisor must first have a shared understanding of coaching supervision and, over time, expand the breadth of perspectives they bring to each issue that is discussed in a coaching supervision session. In the US context, with so many coaches being new to coaching supervision, I found that I needed to adapt the approach in a number of ways: provide education about what coaching supervision is and the different formats available for supervision; establish the containing space in which supervision sessions can be held; design a scaffold for teaching how to be a supervisee and how to contribute effectively as peer-supervisors in a group setting; and adapt the rationale for engaging in coaching supervision to different motivations of different supervisees.

This chapter starts with a brief overview of coaching supervision in the US context and a summary of a systemic developmental approach to supervision. Next, two different applications of this approach will be described using examples from my supervision practice in the US. The first section shows how I adapted the approach to a coaching supervision group for coaches and the second shows how my colleagues and I adapted the approach for leaders in corporate organizations. Throughout the chapter, I make suggestions for future research to support coaching supervision practice. Finally, this chapter concludes with a summary for practitioners.

## Application to Coaches

In this section, I describe some ways in which I adapted the systemic developmental approach to coaching supervision to group coaching supervision. I give examples from a group that met monthly for 90-minute sessions via video conference.

### *Education about Coaching Supervision*

During the contracting phase, I provided a document summarizing my perspective on what coaching supervision is and the systemic developmental approach. Prior to the first session, I invited supervisees to complete a short self-reflection on areas of strength and what they find most challenging about their coaching practice. From this I could see themes that applied across the whole group and was able to make reference to these as patterns that emerged across multiple cases.

At the first session, I facilitated a discussion based on their reading of the summary documents to create a shared understanding of supervision within this group. Across multiple groups I have found this to be vital in the US context where 1) supervision is not yet widely practiced and the terminology can cause confusion; 2) not all coach training programs have the same theoretical underpinnings in psychology that are found in coaching supervision; and 3) specialized coaching practices exist in organizations such as sales, change, or team coaches. These coaching specialties may not have an historical or a theoretical link to the counseling and therapeutic practices that have informed coaching supervision. Nonetheless, my experience with these coaching specialties suggests that these coaches and their practices can also benefit from engaging with supervision. This offers an opportunity for coaching supervision practitioners to adapt and respond to the needs of the US market.

### *Establishing the Containing Space for Supervision Sessions*

Initially, I focused on establishing the process and the container in a similar way to the supervision practices described by Lawrence (2019a). In practice, this meant setting up a structure, process, and contracting for how the group would engage. The aim was to form and maintain a containing space in each session in which the supervisees learn how to bring forward an issue and the peer supervisors (facilitated by the qualified supervisor leading the group) learn to help them determine focus areas and engage in a dialogue that leads to greater awareness and insight. As both a leader and participant, I've observed this process unfold similarly across supervision groups in the US, Australia (where the groups studied by Lawrence were located), and internationally.

### Scaffolding Learning about being a Supervisee and a Peer-Supervisor with a Systemic Lens

Over two 90-minute sessions, we used the same process with three different group members' *issues* and I judged that the container was well formed enough to introduce the seven- eyed model (Hawkins & Schwenk, 2011) to help them take additional perspectives on each case and scaffold systems thinking (Wright et al., 2019). After a short overview of the model, I suggested that each group member take and apply one of the seven eyes to pay attention to in the next case. In subsequent sessions, we rotated the seven eyes allocating a different mode to each person for each case. This is an adaptation of the method suggested by Lucas (2020) and my experience in the US accords with her suggestion to allow sufficient time to work slowly with groups who are unfamiliar with the model, building their understanding before applying it to a case. Coaches from countries where coaching supervision is more commonplace (e.g., UK) are more likely to already be familiar and have experience applying the model and holding multiple lenses in mind as the case is presented.

During the first few sessions it was noticeable that the supervisees presenting an *issue* were looking to the group for "best practice" and to learn from other coaches' experience. Putting it in the language of the seven-eyed model (Hawkins & Schwenk, 2011), both the presenter and the group were in mode 2 (the coach's interventions) seeking to find practical actions for the coach to take. Questions about the case itself were mostly coming from mode 1 (the client and their context) as the coaching supervisors in the group sought to understand the client and their situation in detail. As we worked together, it was noticeable that the group expanded their perspective on the *issues* and *focus areas* brought by the supervisees, the questions that were asked by the group, and the content of the *dialogue*. For example, I noticed the group increasing self-awareness and reflexivity by identifying how the *issue* was impinging on the supervisee's identity as a coach ("I'm here to help; why don't you want my help; see how I'm helping you"). The group also engaged in discussion about ways to enhance their reflective practice outside of the supervision group, e.g., with reflective writing (Lucas & Champion, 2020). The group became more attuned to the parallel processes between the coaching engagement and what was happening in the coaching supervision session, for example the tangled dialogue that ensued among members of the group mirroring the confusion of the coach when they talked about their client. The coaches started to incorporate a greater number of psychological theories into their conceptualization of their coaching engagements. For example, one group applied goal theories to a case in which the coach felt their client was not making much progress. The dialogue included recognition of the influence of wider systemic factors, such as the impact of the way internal coaches were evaluated and measured for performance on how they practice as a coach. Finally, the group became more skilled at identifying ethical dilemmas whereas previously they had not been seen. For example, a coach in possession of confidential information was able to see that it put them between the client and the manager or sponsor. Similarly, the head of an internal coaching practice saw how role and boundary conflicts emerged when they served as the coaching supervisor to their own team.

### *Adapting to Different Motivations for Engaging with Supervision*

As the practice of coaching supervision in the US continues to grow (Hawkins & Turner, 2017), it is interesting to consider what motivation and rationale for coaching supervision may be most effective in the US context. In my experience providing supervision in the US, I've noted four reasons for wanting to engage in supervision. First, there were coaches (internal or external) curious to experience supervision as part of Continuing Professional Development (CPD). Second, there were coaches (internal or external) who sought out coaching supervision in order to meet the accreditation requirements of a professional coaching body (e.g., AC, EMCC). Third, those who led internal coaching practices and wanted to be "world-class" saw coaching supervision as playing a role on their continuous quest for improvement and learning. Fourth, coaching supervision was attractive to support managers and other professionals such as HR, who provided coaching (formally or informally) within the organization.

Professional coaching bodies appear to play a role in influencing individual coaches to engage in supervision. My experience with coaching supervision groups in the US mirrored my experience with international groups of coaches from the UK and Europe, namely that participants were partly motivated to participate to fulfill the requirements for accreditation or to maintain their status with a professional coaching body. This is more likely to be seen outside of the US in places where the dominant professional coaching body mandates supervision. That said, while the extrinsic motivator of fulfilling such requirements may initially trigger engagement, consistent with the research, I have found that once coaches experienced supervision they valued it (Hodge, 2016) and chose to attend for more intrinsic reasons such as commitment to their ongoing personal and professional development or their desire to develop greater self-awareness, capacity, and capability as a coach. (Grant, 2012; Hawkins & Turner, 2017; Wright et al., 2020).

My experience with organizations in the US that have invested in supervision for their internal coaches suggests that quality assurance and the desire to enhance professionalism were influential factors. This is similar to other countries such as Australia, where clients who purchased coaching viewed the primary purpose of supervision as quality control (Lawrence & Whyte, 2014), and the UK case study of supervision at Deloitte (Champion, 2011), which reported that coaching supervision was introduced as a way to build the credibility and expertise of the internal coaches and to enhance their quality, competence, and professionalism.

Making a business case for investment in supervision can be challenging given the lack of evidence of the impact or efficacy of coaching supervision (Bachkirova et al., 2011). Much like the challenges of trying to establish a return on investment for coaching, isolating coaching supervision as a variable for study is extremely difficult (Lawrence, 2019a; Bachkirova et al., 2011). An important question for organizations is: how does coaching supervision fit or compliment the organization's coaching philosophy and corporate values? For example, my early conversations with the decision-maker in one organization found traction when we connected coaching supervision to their desire to build a best-in-class internal coaching practice and their wider corporate values of pioneering innovation and early-adoption of new practices in their industry.

### Perception of the Value of Supervision

A recent study (Wright et al., 2020) used the systemic developmental approach to supervision with mostly North American coaches and found seven key themes and insights regarding the supervision experience. These included: The coaches valued talking through their coaching issues and being listened to; they reported that coaching supervision had a positive impact on the coach, client, and client organization; they gained new insights and learnings (research, frameworks, resources, tools, and techniques); coaches found new, bigger systemic perspectives emerged from supervision; coaching supervision increased self-awareness, understanding of themselves as coaches and the relationship dynamic, which helped them to reframe their perspective on challenges and issues; coaching supervision deepened their understanding of their inner self and experience, which built their confidence as a coach; and coaches were motivated and inspired to learn and grow and engage further in professional development.

Personal communications from members of my US practice accords with these themes. Additionally, anecdotal feedback from internal coaches indicated that their engagement with supervision enhanced both the effectiveness of their coaching as well as the perception of the coaching practice with senior executives. Many found the effectiveness of their coaching practice was enhanced following supervision as they were better able to see instances when their internal coaching methodology worked well and when it did not. With greater awareness, they could continuously refine their methodology, and develop and expand their personal and professional coaching self.

### Suggestions for Further Research

Further research is needed to investigate the decision-making process surrounding coaching supervision and influential factors driving these decisions by individual coaches and organizations within the US. Questions to answer, include: To what extent are these decisions expressions of US culture? To what extent might the purpose, process, value, and benefits of coaching supervision differ among individual coaches and organizations across global cultures and contexts? How might perceptions of coaching supervision change with experience among individual coaches and within organizations? Future exploration could expand upon this to investigate how coaching supervision emerges from and nurtures an organization's learning culture (Hawkins & McMahon, 2020).

Concluding this section about my experience of applying the systemic developmental approach with coaches, I have found that the greatest adaptation needs to be made in the contracting phase, education about supervision, supporting supervisees in learning how to be a supervisee or peer-supervisor, and in connecting with the motivation and rationale for engaging in supervision that makes sense in the US coaching context.

In the next section, I describe the experience my colleagues and I had applying and adapting the systemic developmental approach to supervision to work with leaders in organizations in the US.

## Application to Leaders

In this section, I first provide a brief overview of the theoretical rationale for applying approaches from coaching supervision to developmental work with leaders. Then, I describe how we applied the cycle of developmental supervision and revised it through three adaptations. The first adaptation involved changes to the language and terminology of supervision. The second involved revising our approach to the culture of US corporate organizations. In the last adaptation, we created a tool to scaffold systemic perspectives in leaders as they engaged in the dialogue.

### Rationale for Applying Approaches from Coaching Supervision

The dramatic, globally interconnected events of 2020 tested leaders, coaches, and practitioners of every helping profession to their limits. As one coaching leader put it to me at the end of the year with an ironic smile: "I cannot believe the challenges I brought to our coaching sessions a year ago. I thought those were the biggest problems I had. Turns out they were simple."

Coaching supervision is, itself, an adaptation of a practice that originated in counseling and psychotherapy (Gray & Jackson, 2011). It is no surprise, therefore, that coach supervisors have started thinking about how coaching supervision can be applied usefully to others. Patterson (2019) argued that supervision is an intervention that has a powerful application to leaders and people practitioners in roles other than that of a coach, and that its relevance now is greater than ever before. In a follow-up action-research study, Patterson et al. (2020) conceptualized and investigated a distinct practice of one-to-one "executive reflection," based on theories from leadership, executive coaching, and coaching supervision that: "provides a creative and reflective space and generative oasis for Leaders to gain deeper insights and awareness ('helicopter-vision') that includes themselves, their work, their relationships and with their wider environment at work" (p. 8).

With leaders, our aim was to adapt the systemic developmental approach to coaching supervision and foster dialogue among peers that generated new insight and thinking to create new pathways forward on the leaders' *issues*. Simultaneously, by participating in the sessions, leaders developed a strong peer support network and grew their capability as leader-coaches. Although we did not use the terminology of executive reflection, our practice aligned closely with the aims and process described by Patterson et al. (2020).

Our experience adapting this supervision approach was similar in some ways to the experiences I described in the previous section. We provided education to leaders around the purpose, process, and possible outcomes of engaging in these sessions. There was a need to help leaders learn how to bring issues forward and how to enhance their contributions so that the sessions had greater value than simply sending a small group of experienced, smart executives out for lunch and inviting them to talk about their challenges. Keeping this comparison in mind brought to life the importance of having a qualified supervisor facilitate the sessions and supports the view that coaching supervisors need knowledge and skills over and above those of a coach (Bachkirova et al., 2011).

We used the cycle of developmental supervision to guide the process, with leaders bringing an *issue*, deciding on *focus areas* for exploration and engaging in co-created *dialogue* with the coaching supervisor and the group.

### Adapting Language and Terminology

The terminology of "executive reflection" may be more appealing to US organizations than the language of "supervision," which has a specific meaning in organizations implying oversight and control. "Executive reflection" follows intuitively from concepts that are already familiar and well-established in the marketplace such as executive coaching, executive leadership programs, executive MBA, etc.

The three functions of coaching supervision are most often labelled qualitative, developmental, and resourcing (Hawkins & Smith, 2006) or formative, normative, and restorative (Inskipp & Proctor, 1993). However, we found that we needed language that resonated better with leaders inside organizations, such as Lawrence and Moore's (2019) three functions of evaluation, support, and reflective practice/development. The evaluation function serves to identify blind spots in the leader's practice, to identify and address skills gaps, and ethical issues. The support functions help refuel leaders in what can be emotionally draining work and help them to process their feelings. The function of reflective practice is purely developmental and facilitates both personal and professional growth.

### Adapting to the Culture of US Corporate Organizations

The strongest resistance in the organizations where we have applied this approach appeared to be related to the fit between the approach and the organization's culture. Concerns about "fluffiness," pace, and a perception that these sessions might be quasi-psychotherapy rose quickly to the forefront of discussions with clients. We faced a paradox introducing this practice into a corporate organizational culture where fast action, few words, and reducing interventions to their "essence" dominated. Yet, what leaders needed was a "thinking environment" (Kline, 2015). A thinking environment provides time and space to take new perspectives, become mindful, gain clarity, generate new ideas, and examine underlying assumptions and beliefs that may be getting in the way of business decision-making. In one example, after a series of group sessions where leaders had applied this approach to their own *issues*, a participant reported that at first they "hated it." But after a few sessions they could see how the dialogue was changing as a result of actively, consciously looking at the *issue* from multiple perspectives and considering the relationships between various parts of the system. At the end of the program, this participant reported that he would be taking the tool back to his team and using it with them.

## Creating a Tool to Scaffold Systemic Perspectives

Inspired by the way we had used the seven-eyed model in other supervision settings, we created a tool for leaders to take different lenses on each case (Figure 7.1). This is similar in concept to other methodologies that help make things that are subject become object. In this context, we were interested in supporting the development of systemic competence (O'Connor, 2020) and thus adopted lenses that reflected different parts of the system.

Feedback from groups with whom we have used this approach indicated that using lenses in the *dialogue* enabled exploration of diverse perspectives on the leaders' strategic and tactical challenges, and the relationships between different aspects of a situation. This, in turn, created the possibility of new pathways forward on the *issue*.

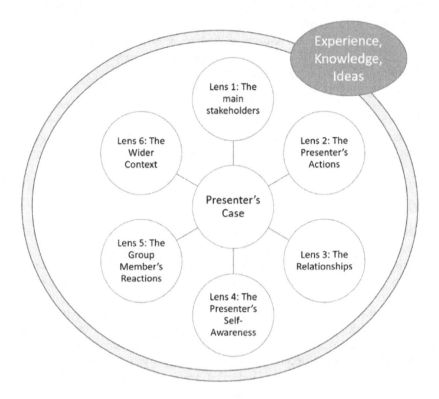

*Figure 7.1* Six Lenses for Reflection and Dialogue on Leaders' Issues.

Note: *Six Lenses for Reflection and Dialogue on Leaders' Issues. Copyright 2018 by Angela Wright and Sarah Tennyson. CEC Global LLC. Reprinted with permission.*

A more robust study could validate this feedback and help make more generalizable theories and frameworks that could be applied broadly in the US context. In the longer term, we would like to study the impact of this approach on the vertical development, perspective-taking capacity, and systemic thinking capabilities of the leaders who participate. A study based on the coaching ripple effect (O'Connor & Cavanagh, 2013) could also help us understand whether this intervention has an impact beyond the individual leaders who participate.

This adapted approach invites questions about the extent to which it is appropriately classified as coaching supervision, as defined in the coaching literature, or whether it could be conceptualized as a distinct intervention. Given the recency of coaching supervision as a field of study and practice, it is exciting to explore different ways in which the practice of supervision is emerging.

In conclusion, we observed that revising the language used to describe this type of developmental intervention and in engaging with clients to address a corporate culture that demands fast action were important adaptations. Specifically, we adapted our approach by creating the six lenses tool and found that, consistent with research from coaching supervision, leaders valued this approach and wanted more of it once they tried it.

We observed the supervisor's understanding of a leader's context, capacity, and capability was far more important than their coaching or facilitation skills in ensuring the sessions served all three functions of supervision.

The groups we ran involved multiple sessions over a period of three months or longer. Only with a regular cadence and a commitment to the ongoing developmental process can the sessions effectively serve all three functions of supervision. We believe it is important for the groups to run for multiple sessions over a period of time to engage with the developmental aspect of the systemic developmental approach to supervision. Without this, the developmental aspect of the approach could fall short and result in sessions that facilitated problem-solving, rather than the leaders' ability to think systemically, to "see more."

## Conclusion

A substantial body of literature highlights the increasing complexity of the world in which leaders and coaches operate, the requirement to make decisions faster with either an overwhelming amount of data or little data, and a high degree of uncertainty. Leaders—and by extension coaches—are under pressure to operate with fewer resources and deliver ever-higher standards, to stay ahead of the competition, and to withstand whatever demands are made with personal resilience and grace. Hand-in-hand with these observations is the question of how to support coaches and leaders to effectively function—even better, to thrive—in such a world. The role of coaching supervision in responding to this need will continue to evolve as it is applied and studied in different organizational cultures and countries with diverse coaches and leaders.

A number of authors have made the case for systemic thinking and the application of systems theories to coaching as a necessary step in developing the practice to better support today's leaders. Our experience applying the systemic developmental approach to supervision appears to offer a pragmatic intervention that aids the development of systemic competence and enhances systemic thinking (O'Connor, 2020). This is relevant where there is an explicit goal of developing systemic thought, such that leaders and coaches can evolve new ways of seeing, sense-making, acting, and engaging to achieve their challenges or goals.

Additionally, there is a notable rise in developmental coaching, which has similar goals of developing greater systemic thinking and competence in leaders. Developmental coaching is underpinned by adult development theories, supporting leaders' mental complexity, perspective-taking capacity, and understanding of self. By extension, some authors have argued that coaching supervision must necessarily take a systemic perspective (e.g., Bachkirova et al., 2011) and that the supervisor must attend to their own reflexivity and the match between their own current level of adult development, the level of their supervisees, and the complexity of the supervisee's world.

In this chapter, I have drawn on experience from my supervision and leadership development practice in the US to illustrate how systemic, developmental approaches from coaching supervision can be usefully adapted to support the development and resourcing of coaches and leaders in organizations and help them to keep fit-for-purpose.

Until coaching supervision becomes more widely understood and an accepted part of practice in the US, prospective supervisees will likely need help identifying and articulating their supervision needs. I have found this to be the case with individual coaches and with organizational decision-makers. Lawrence and Moore (2019) provide a useful framework for this, suggesting that a supervisee first figure out whether they are seeking supervision to support the development of their competence, capability, or perspective and then consider what they want the supervisor to provide: Evaluation, support, or reflective practice. Providing prospective supervisees with opportunities to experience supervision is important in helping them become more aware and better articulate their own preferences and needs for development and support.

## Note

1 An illustrative but not exhaustive list includes the COVID-19 pandemic, widespread reactions to racial injustice, a divisive political climate, disruption to schooling and care services, job insecurity, the devastation of entire sectors of the economy, and record-breaking climatic events.

## References

Bachkirova, T., Jackson, P., & Clutterbuck, D. (Eds). (2011). *Coaching and mentoring supervision: Theory and practice*. Open University Press.

Cavanagh, M. (2012). The coaching engagement in the 21st Century: New paradigms for complex times. In S. David, D. Clutterbuck & D. Megginson (Eds.), *Beyond goals: Effective strategies for coaching and mentoring*. Gower Publishing.

Champion, C.K. (2011). Beyond quality assurance: the Deloitte internal coaching supervision story. In T. Bachkirova, P. Jackson, & D. Clutterbuck (Eds.), *Coaching & mentoring supervision: Theory and practice* (pp. 281–289). Open University Press.

Grant, A. M. (2012). Australian coaches' views on coaching supervision: A study with implications for Australian coach education, training and practice. *International Journal of Evidence Based Coaching and Mentoring, 10*: 17–33.

Gray, D., & Jackson, P. (2011). Coaching supervision in the historical context of psychotherapeutic and counselling models: a meta-model. In T. Bachkirova., P. Jackson., & D. Clutterbuck (Eds.), *Coaching and mentoring supervision: Theory and practice* (pp. 15–27). Open University Press.

Hawkins, P., & McMahon, A. (2020). *Supervision in the helping professions* (5th ed.). Open University Press.

Hawkins, P., & Schwenk, G. (2011). The seven-eyed model of coaching supervision. In T. Bachkirova, P. Jackson, & D. Clutterbuck (Eds.), *Coaching & mentoring supervision: Theory and practice* (pp. 28–40). Open University Press.

Hawkins, P., & Smith, N. (2006). *Coaching, mentoring and organizational consultation.* Oxford University Press.

Hawkins, P., & Turner, E. (2017). The rise of coaching supervision 2006–2014. *Coaching An International Journal of Theory Research and Practice, 10*(2): 1–13.

Hodge, A. (2016). The value of coaching supervision as a development process: Contribution to continued professional and personal wellbeing for executive coaches. *International Journal of Evidence Based Coaching and Mentoring, 14*(2): 87–106.

Inskipp, F., & Proctor, B. (1993). *The art, craft and tasks of counselling supervision. Part 1: Making the most of supervision.* Cascade.

Isaacs, W. (1999). *Dialogue and the art of thinking together: A pioneering approach to communicating in business and in life.* Doubleday.

Kegan, R. (1994). *In over our heads: The mental demands of modern life.* Harvard University Press.

Kegan, R., & Lahey, L. (2009). *Immunity to change.* Harvard Business School Publishing Corporation.

Kline, N. (2015). *Time to think: Listening to ignite the human mind.* Cassell.

Lawrence, P. (2019a). What happens in group supervision? Exploring current practice in Australia. *International Journal of Evidence Based Coaching and Mentoring, 17*(2): 138–157. 10.24384/v0d6-2380

Lawrence, P. (2019b). What is systemic coaching? *Philosophy of Coaching: An International Journal, 4*(2): 35–52. 10.22316/poc/04.2.03

Lawrence, P., & Moore, A. (2019). *Coaching in three dimensions: Meeting the challenges of a complex world.* Routledge.

Lawrence, P., & Whyte, A. (2014). What is coaching supervision and is it important? *Coaching: An International Journal of Theory, Research and Practice, 7*(1): 39–55. 10.1 080/17521882.2013.878370

Lucas, M. (2020). Working with the seven-eyed model. In M. Lucas (Ed.), *101 coaching supervision techniques, approaches, enquiries and experiments* (pp. 292–294). Routledge.

Lucas, M., & Champion, C. (2020). Reflective writing. In M. Lucas (Ed.), *101 coaching supervision techniques, approaches, enquiries and experiments* (pp. 76–79). Routledge.

McAnally, K., Abrams, L., Asmus, M. J., & Hildebrand, T. (2019, April 25). *Coaching supervision: Global perceptions and practices.* EMCC Conference, Dublin, Ireland.

O'Connor, S. (2020). Systemically integrated approaches to coaching: An introduction. *Philosophy of Coaching: An International Journal, 5*(2): 40–62. 10.22316/poc/05.2.04

O'Connor, S., & Cavanagh, M. (2013). The coaching ripple effect: The effects of developmental coaching on wellbeing across organisational networks. *Psychology of Well-being, 3*(2). 10.1186/2211-1522-3-2.

Patterson, E. (2019). Supervision's oasis for leaders and people practitioners. In J. Birch, & P. Welch (Eds.), *Coaching supervision: Advancing practice, changing landscapes* (pp. 176–187). Routledge.

Patterson, E., Arnold, J., & Hodge, A. (2020). *Report from an action research inquiry to explore the relevance and value of 1:1 executive reflection to leaders in a global, virtual and diverse world.* Coach 4 Executives, Alison Hodge and Centre for Reflection and Creativity Ltd.

Wright, A., McLean Walsh, M., & Tennyson, S. (2019). Systemic coaching supervision: Responding to the complex challenges of our time. *Philosophy of Coaching: An International Journal*, 4(12): 107–122. 10.22316/poc/04.1.08

Wright, A., van Vliet, K., & Tennyson, S. (2020, February 15). *Experiencing coaching supervision: A study in understandings of supervision, value & benefits* [Conference presentation]. University of Sydney Evidence Based Coaching Psychology Conference, Sydney, Australia.

# Section II

# How We Work

# 8 Supervision in Globally Challenging Times: Supporting Coach Well-Being by Reflecting Through Three Lenses

*Ken Giglio*

## Introduction

The current tumultuous and changing global environment has impacted us all in different ways. In the US, in particular, we have been affected by the devastating impacts of the pandemic as well as racial injustice and its re-verberating effects in our society, from ongoing protests to deepening political and racial divisions. The murder of George Floyd on May 25, 2020 was a tragic, life-ending moment for one Black man who had survived the COVID-19 virus and a harsh reckoning for our society in the US. The entire global community is watching the US and experiencing to varying degrees their own cultural introspection when it comes to race relations. Racial inequity has produced significant trauma for the Black community and a compassionate response for all of us who want to see a just world. The uncertainty and turmoil brought about by the COVID-19 pandemic has caused a spike in anxiety and depression among US adults; rates among adults grew 20% higher than pre-pandemic levels (Statista, 2020). The assault of COVID-19 around the globe has also shed a harsh light on US racial inequity as Black populations suffered disproportionately and have had a higher mortality rate than White populations due to the systemic challenges of higher levels of poverty (Kim & Bostwick, 2020).

Coaches in this environment are dealing with clients who are leading teams through the complexity of the pandemic and its ripple effects. The organizations in which coaches work, particularly in the US, are also grappling with racial injustice in the workplace, leading to an increased focus on diversity, equity, and inclusion. Past traumas are being reignited by current events, such as the Black coach who lived through apartheid and now experiences bouts of fear from seemingly nowhere (Van der Kolk, 2015). Or the leader who left the violence in their South American country many years ago and now recoils physically when seeing the Capital riot, because the trauma is still present in her body (Walker, 2013). Another example is one of my supervisees, who feels helpless and emotionally drained in parallel with her exhausted client, who is an executive and

DOI: 10.4324/b23130-11

young mother struggling with a big job and young children all quarantining in a small apartment.

As coaches and coach supervisors, how do we steady and center ourselves within this external storm happening in our world and on our doorstep in the US? How do we remain well and resilient for ourselves and for our clients in the work we are called to do? In this chapter, we explore how well-being is fostered through mindful reflection in coaching supervision as a support for coaches in our challenging global landscape. Today, being emotionally settled, aware, and agile has become particularly important for coaches and supervisors as they engage with stressed and overwhelmed clients and client systems (David, 2016). To illustrate the supervision strategies that can be implemented to address these issues, I present The Tri-Lens Coaching Supervision Model, a specific model for coaching supervision that facilitates the well-being of coaches. The Tri-Lens is built on Buddhist principles and psychology and supported by the latest research and thinking in neuroscience and social psychology.

Coach well-being is one of the three functions of supervision, which are described as qualitative, developmental, and resourcing by Hawkins and Shohet (2007). Well-being is aligned with the resourcing function and supports coaches in acknowledging and understanding the emotional impact of their client work. This supervision function is also identified as restorative (Proctor, 2008), and nuturative (Cochrane & Newton, 2018). I discuss the ways in which the Tri-Lens leverages mindful reflection, with particular attention to how the resourcing function instills emotional well-being in coaches and fosters experiential learning (Kolb, 1984).

Hawkins and Shohet (2007, pp. 12, 25–26) identified "sustaining one's own resilience" or well-being as a key capacity of reflective practice for helping professionals including coaches, and suggest practitioners map their own resourcing system. The authors talked about external resources, like supportive people and things that enable learning and creativity to flourish, and they touched on the criticality of an internal emotional monitoring system for increasing awareness and resilience (Hawkins & Shohet, 2007). In this chapter, I build and expand on the resourcing function of supervision and how the well-being of coaches depends on their internal resourcing. From this inner source of awareness and presence, as framed through the Tri-Lens, I explore the well-being of coaches as it is connected to being "fit for purpose and practice" (Brockbank, 2008).

As coaches look inside themselves for the resources that will foster well-being in the midst of shifting and often difficult client circumstances, here are some key reflection questions:

- *What destabilizes us emotionally in our work with clients and how can we use the reflective practice of coaching supervision to recenter and ground?*
- *How do we, as coaching supervisors and coaches, allow our inner resources to come through and be in best service of our clients and client organizations?*

- *How can coaches access their inherent well-being and natural resilience and add practical ways to be a "well" coach for their clients as they face these challenging times?*

## Well-Being & Ill-Being

There has been extensive research in the field of well-being, and a growing field of inquiry into resilience factors that support human beings to live individually and collectively in good mental, physical, and social health (Liu et al., 2020). Well-being is more inclusive, broader in scope, and more culturally centered, as opposed to "wellness," which often refers to programs offered to employees. Researchers have studied and documented what brings about stress and burnout among psychology professionals for decades (McCormack et al., 2018) and research on physician burnout has continued to be of keen interest under the COVID-19 pandemic (Flynn, 2020). Since the beginning of the pandemic, many researchers have launched studies to examine the relationship between the virus and the mental health of various populations (Newey, 2021). However, there is a dearth of research focused on coach and coach supervisor well-being in the current environment and in general, around the resourcing function of supervision and its effectiveness in supporting coaches and coaching supervisors (Amour, 2020).

In an effort to elevate resourcing, the "neglected third leg of supervision," as Peter Hawkins calls it, I present the Tri-Lens Coaching Supervision Model as a mindful, reflective path to well-being through examination of self, other, and system (Palmer & Turner, 2018). Resourcing is a foundational function as it enables and facilitates the two other functions—development (harvesting learning from reflective practice) and qualitative (increasing the quality of the coaching work) (Hawkins & Shohet, 2007).

Among the many ways to define well-being, studies coalesce around self-perceived health, longevity, healthy behaviors, mental health, physical illness, social connectedness, productivity, and factors in the physical and social environment (Hicks et al., 2013). Ongoing research in the connected fields of well-being and resilience links these elements to potential genetic factors integrated with environmental aspects of our development (Stacey et al., 2020). Chief among these well-being influencers is our family along with socioeconomic status, community culture, and workplace environment (Centers for Disease Control and Prevention, 2018).

What happens when a coach shows up with unhealthy stress that has been absorbed from their clients and client organizations? How will a coach develop awareness of how they are experiencing fear and anxiety about the client, organization, or their coaching in general? Stress can become chronic, resulting in burnout that makes it difficult to return to a state of well-being (Flynn, 2020). The signature signs of burnout are emotional exhaustion, depersonalization or cynicism, and reduced personal accomplishment (Maslach et al., 2001). Coaches can find themselves on the road to burnout, and the resourcing function of coaching supervision serves as a shelter in the emotional storms that sometime emerge from client work. Studies show that the work of well-being in coaching supervision results in a coach's return to engagement. This is the opposite of burnout and characterized by vigor, dedication, and absorption (Schaufeli et al, 2002). These engaged behaviors are signs that a coach is working from Source.

The stress responses of the "Four Fs"—fight, flight, freeze, fawn—have been well studied and understood (Walker, 2013; Tovote et al., 2015). Fawning is not as well studied and means excessive pleasing to stay in another's good favor. It is often witnessed in, and is a byproduct of, co-dependent, abusive relationships (Walker, 2013). The stress that produces one of the Four Fs is usually caused by an external event (trauma can be reignited by memory), while the response (chiefly fear or anxiety) is the internalized, conditioned complex of thinking and emotion that has physically changed the brain over time (American Psychological Association, 2020; Feldman Barrett, 2020; Jasanoff, 2018). The Four Fs framework is a good starting place for coaching supervisor and supervisee to explore any emotional disruption stemming from the coach's work. This can include reflective practice that touches on the coach's reactions and triggers to stressors in their coaching environment. All is in play and numerous factors related to well-being and ill-being are considered, such as a self-narrative of "not good enough" (Cochrane & Newton, 2018). For the coaching supervisor, a compassionate, measured approach is best as a full picture of the trauma and associated shame the coach has lived through cannot be known (Holloway, 2016; Smith, 2019). Frequently, coaches may be unaware of their own reactivity.

## Mindful Reflection & Well-Being

Building a coach's capacity for well-being as they encounter constantly shifting and sometimes unsettling client situations is the work of reflective practice within the resourcing function of supervision (Hawkins et al., 2019). One such reflective approach is that of mindfulness, which can be defined as paying attention in a particular way: On purpose, in the present moment, and nonjudgmentally (Kabat-Zinn, 1994). I be using the terms mindfulness and mindful reflection in a broad sense, which includes embodiment; it also includes, but is not exclusive to, meditation.

Mindfulness is most firmly rooted in Buddhist psychology (Welwood, 2002; Goldstein, 2016). Therapeutic and counseling disciplines have adopted mindfulness techniques in work with clients, and the tradition of mindful coaching and presence-based coaching is firmly rooted in the coaching field (Hayes & Smith, 2005; Senge et al., 2004; Silsbee, 2008). Evidence of the effectiveness of mindful reflection for facilitating well-being at the emotional and social levels has been increasing within the fields of neuroscience and social and evolutionary psychology (Feldman Barrett, 2020; Wright, 2018.)

Mindful reflection is a practice and resource coaching supervisors can use to increase awareness, deepen insight, and build resilience and well-being within coaches during challenging times. Below are mindful reflective practices adapted from and built on the three principles of Buddhist psychology—*impermanence* (nothing lasts; everything changes); *unsatisfactoriness or suffering* (being unsatisfied, as in not realizing our desires or being unable to avoid what repulses us); and *non-self* (there is no permanent identity or central self) (Goldstein, 2016). These principles provide the constructs and experiential platform for enabling mindful reflective practice within coaching supervision. Working from a shared understanding and awareness that constant change, uncontrollable challenges, and self-centeredness impact virtually all client work, enables coaches to gain perspective, lessen stress, and build capacity for well-being.

The Tri-Lens is an adaptable framework for integrating mindful reflective practice based on the three principles that can be brought into supervision dialogue. The Tri-Lens supports increased clarity and objectivity by allowing for a truer seeing of our ourselves, our clients, and our clients' systems.

### Everything Changes and is Always Changing

The impermanence of our experiences becomes evident upon stepping back to observe and reflect on how what is happening now lasts only in a present that cannot be crystallized or contained—it's all process and flow. Without reflection, insight, and acceptance that everything is constantly shifting and changing, we are at the mercy of our urgent tendency to seek certainty, closure, and permanence (Kruglanski & Webster, 1996). The consequences for practitioners caught in this loop of temporary but false psychological safety is resistance to deeper, more transformative change, and the seeking of certainty to allay fear and anxiety (Schaefer, 2018).

Nothing is static in the natural world and this is reflected in human interactions. Each season has its qualities, and every day has its wonders of growth and fullness or decline and death (Prentice, 2020). Our underlying need for certainty and control in our coaching work is amplified when external circumstances are volatile and uncertain. Our well-being suffers when we hold on too tightly to anyone or anything with the expectation that it will last. It is during these times when we most need an ongoing acknowledgment and acceptance of the truth that everything changes.

### Present Experience is Where All the Action Is

Robin Shohet, co-creator of the seven-eyed supervision model, sees coaching supervision as a time for reflection on what happens when a coach is not present with their client (Shohet & Shohet, 2020). We all mind travel, wandering away to a should-have past or need-to future as our client sits unwittingly in front of us, unaware of the drama playing out in our heads. The coach might be asking their past self: "Did I ask the best question and provide enough direct feedback?" And the future self is chattering: "I need to get this leader to understand their peer is really an ally." Core work in supervision is paying attention to what triggers coaches to "go away in my mind," as one supervisee put it. Present experience, moment-to-moment in our sessions with clients is the point at which discovery and insight can occur. When we mind travel to the past or future, we experience emotions that exhaust us—anxiety, fear, doubt, shame—all adding to ill-being and disallowing our essential coach, our best resourced self, to shine through with our clients (Goleman, 2013; Goldstein, 2016; Shohet & Shohet, 2020).

Working with supervisees to support them emotionally means at times guiding them through mindfulness practices that settle their emotions. Conscious breathing from our core, roughly two inches below our belly button, or belly-breathing, is one way of centering ourselves during emotional storms. Silence and stillness are other approaches that allow a sense of settling and grounding so that the coach and coaching supervisor can clear their minds and fully see what's going on with the client work.

### How We Relate to Events is More Important than the Events Themselves

How we think about and feel in response to what is happening in our environment can be managed with increased awareness. A healthy, internal locus of control is a state of centeredness and agency (Rotter, 1966). It is the pivot point between being well and unwell. The vicissitudes of life confront us every day; life by its nature brings ups and downs, happiness, and suffering. This state of being unsatisfied with what's happening in our world easily finds its way into coaching and supervision conversations when the systems around us create stress. When we become aware of our emotional and reactive patterns to the ever shifting and challenging environments around us, we increase our internal resources and capacity for inner calm and centeredness.

The current COVID-19 crisis has generated more individual and collective fear around the world in a single year than we've possibly encountered in a generation. Our capacity for well-being in this environment rests on our interpretations or the stories we create about challenging events as well as our emotional responses to them, all of which are key aspects of our conditioned minds (Goldstein, 2016; Bridges, 2004). According to research by the neuroscientist Feldman Barrett (2017), to work with and master our emotions we need to increase our emotional literacy by identifying our emotional experiences at the granular level. This "granularity" training matches mindfulness practice as it requires we notice and sense what is occurring in our mind and body as it is happening (Feldman Barrett, 2017, 2020).

### Selflessness is Noticing the I, Me, Mine Way We Live and How We Suffer for It (Goldstein, 2016)

In my career as an executive coach and coaching supervisor, I often hold a space for leaders and coaches who are struggling and emotionally unsteady in their work. What I hear are versions of the personalization—I, me, mine—of their professional experiences, with examples like: "I am my own worst enemy," "if I could only stop getting in my own way," "they are making it hard on me," "it's mine to lose," and "my ego is getting in the way."

At the center of this expressed ill-being is our sense of self. Self is a construction of who we are at any given time and place in our lives. Self—our understanding of ourselves, our world and all those in it—is given to us by our parents, communities, and schools during our formative years as children. In this pre-reflective state, script or self-stories take root and become our identities (Welwood, 2002). These identities are constructed by our earliest selves and are what social psychologists refer to as multiple selves (Ellemers et al., 2002). These selves are perpetuated, adapted, and reconstructed as we go through life with stories of self, and they give us the illusion of solidity and control within ourselves and our world (Henriques, 2014).

Understanding non-self or selflessness is challenging at the conceptual level; however, there is ample evidence from neuroscience, and agreement among evolutionary and social psychologists that "the conscious self is not some all-powerful executive authority" (Feldman Barrett, 2017; Wright, 2018, p.77). Our conscious experience and sense of self is constructed in real time within our social and systemic contexts to support our survival and yet, it also gets in the way of connecting us with ourselves and others, causing emotional disruption (Edelglass, 2009; Feldman Barrett, 2017). The work of coaching supervision can build on this scientific understanding of non-self and when coupled with the concept of impermanence, can help coaches gain insight into their emotional well-being. For example, the coach who states, "I am my own worst enemy," can be gently challenged in reflective dialogue to investigate who this enemy is and if he or she exists other than as constantly changing feelings.

Blending scientific perspectives of mindfulness with the principles of Buddhist psychology creates a new framework for mindful reflection within coaching supervision that instills a state of awareness and presence within the practitioner, with others, and with the systems in which clients and coaches work: The Tri-Lens Coaching Supervision Model.

## The Tri-Lens Coaching Supervision Model

Models and frameworks for supervision are helpful for communicating ideas and theories. They describe concepts and can simplify complex topics (Proctor, 2008). They also provide guideposts for thinking about the

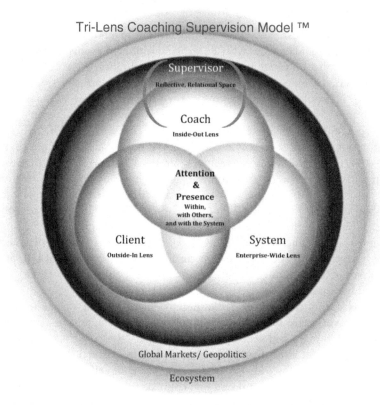

Tri-Lens Coaching Supervision Model ™

*Figure 8.1* Tri-Lens Coaching Supervision Model.

content of supervision work within particular contexts and chart a process toward developmental goals.

The Tri-Lens (see Figures 8.1 & 8.2) started out as a mindful reflection model. I built the framework from the inside out; it evolved organically from the intersection of my mindfulness practice of 25 years and my coaching and coaching supervision work. I had been striving to maintain attention and presence in my work from the start, growing my awareness of myself as a coach, awareness of my clients, and my clients' organizations as systems.

As a supervisor, I wanted a framework that was simple and straightforward, easy to understand, and practical to use for reflective practice. It needed to easily translate to supervisees as they engaged in collaborative inquiry about their client work. The model needed flexibility, rigor, and the breadth and depth to hold theoretical, psychological, and scientific underpinnings. In these globally challenging times, I also wanted a framework that helped me gain perspectives about the constantly shifting and volatile systems that could potentially impact my coaching and supervision work.

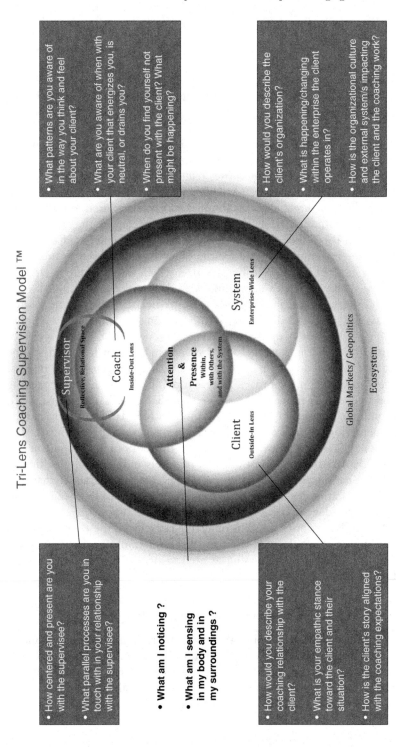

*Figure 8.2* Tri-Lens Coaching Supervision Model.

As we review the Tri-Lens, it is good to keep in mind that all models have their limitations. "All models are wrong, but some are useful" (Box & Draper, 1987, p. 424). Resonance and usefulness are more important than any model being right. The Tri-Lens meets these criteria. I've leveraged the Tri-Lens in my practice as have supervisor colleagues in their practices. I have also given presentations on coaching supervision using the Tri-Lens before major global coaching and coaching supervision accrediting bodies, in North American and around the world.

Viewing how we experience our coaching work through three frames is familiar, intuitive, and part of many organizational change and development models: individual, team, enterprise; self, client, and system; leading self, leading others, leading culture (Asumeng, 2015 & Hamilton, 2012). These mental models of threes allow us to quickly orient our attention, thinking, and actions without undue complexity. The center of the Tri-Lens is grounded in the principles of Buddhist psychology highlighted earlier. It provides the integration needed for the supervisor and coach to mindfully reflect together in a space of calm presence, which allows a fuller picture to be revealed around what's happening with the coaching work.

The Tri-Lens integrates and builds on pioneering supervision models such as the seven-eyed model of supervision by Hawkins & Shohet (2007) and Proctor's supervision alliance model (2008). The work of Schon (1984) in *The Reflective Practitioner* has also informed its development as reflection on action and reflection in action is central and integral to the Tri-Lens. This approach fosters mindful reflection on a coaching session and in real time during the session. Scharmer's theory u (2007), adds another theoretical brick to the model's foundation in how it supports centering in not knowing, with an open mind, open heart, and open will. This not knowing occurs at the bottom of the u, an in-between space of letting go of our past mindsets and ways of operating to allow an opening for a letting come of the emergent future (Scharmer, 2007). In addition, working with the Tri-Lens in coaching supervision cultivates the development of a coach's internal supervisor (Casement, 2002). This is the inner mindful reflective capacity of the coach when in session with a client. It plays the role of internal monitor supporting our real-time learning and increasing awareness of our emotional steadiness and focus during sessions.

### Center—The Viewfinder of Attention & Presence

The Tri-Lens center is the pivotal starting and returning point for mindful reflection during coaching supervision. It is the grounded, still point for the mind and body of the supervisor and the coach to settle into with calm so that information or data from the three lenses—self, other, and system—can be processed and integrated in the supervision dialogue. From this center, the qualities of intentional attention and embodied presence are fostered through the Tri-Lens' mindful reflection questions: *"What am I noticing? What am I sensing in my body and my surroundings?"* These core questions facilitate a continuous flow of information about the coaching work being examined in the relational space between the coaching supervisor and coach. The Tri-Lens center viewfinder is a mindful reflector not bounded by time. The supervisor and coach work within the present moment of the supervision session, and grow the coach's capacity to reflect retrospectively "on action" and sense the emergent future through not knowing (Schon, 1984; Scharmer, 2007).

The viewfinder center is not self and can be associated with the idea of selflessness or non-self (Goldstein, 2016; Welwood, 2002), as discussed above. This ability to detach temporarily from personalizing experiences allows us to access our deeper intuition and see a truer, more objective view of our coaching. In this space of presence and not knowing, a clearer view of the stories entering the supervision conversation can emerge. The Tri-Lens center broadens and deepens the field of awareness and allows the coach and coaching supervisor to access and resource their principles and presence for well-being. This well-being is then extended to the coach while working with their clients and adds value and impact to the organization (Diochon & Louis, 2019).

## Attention and Presence Within—Self as Coach; Self as Supervisor

The self as coach lens is the view into our relationship with ourselves, whether we're the coach or the coaching supervisor. Peering into our inner landscape with a reflective partner helps us deepen our emotional awareness, sparks insight into our coaching work, and fosters well-being. The self lens is support by and aligned with emotional mastery and emotional intelligence research (Mayer et al., 2003; Feldman Barrett, 2017).

During the mindful reflection of a coaching supervision session, the thoughts and feelings of the coach are observed for clues into what is happening within the coach that may be impacting the coaching work. These self-as-coach experiences are processed in real-time with nonjudgment to better understand underlying patterns that either support or block the coach from resourcing themselves when they are with their clients.

Questions for coach reflection: *How can I take an honest look at myself? What do I notice in my thinking patterns? Is my mindset more fixed or oriented toward curiosity and growth? What do I sense in my body as I talk about my coaching client and situation? What destabilizes me emotionally in my coaching work?*

Questions for the supervisor: *How centered and present am I with the supervisee? What parallel processes am I in touch with in my relationship with the supervisee?*

## Attention and Presence with the Client

The client lens is a look at the quality and integrity of our relationships with others, primarily with the coach in the supervisory relationship. Our well-being is intrinsically connected to the health of our relationships. We feel well and grounded when we are socially and relationally aware and deeply connected with others. The client lens builds on research in the fields of relational and social intelligence (Goleman, 2007).

When looking through the client lens in supervision, a myriad of complex factors surrounding the coach's relationship with their clients can come into clearer view. Mindful reflection creates the space for deeper inquiry into the relational aspects of the coaching work as it presents itself in supervision. Questions posed in supervision can bring to light where the coach may be getting struck in their coaching conversations and allows for exploration of the why behind these limitations and strategies for making meaningful shifts.

Questions for coach reflection: *How would I describe my coaching relationship with the client? How am I attuning to the needs of my client by listening deeply and empathizing with them? How is the client's story aligned with coaching expectations? What assumptions do I have about my client? What do I notice about the client that causes me to become emotionally disrupted?*

## Attention and Presence with the System

The systems lens provides a vantage point for looking at the cultures and systems in which we work. The health and well-being of organizations and systems are constantly shifting and are interconnected with the well-being of the coach and their clients. Our capacity to be systemically intelligent allows us to see the full constellation of people interacting within and around an organization's culture and system. The systems lens is supported by research on systems intelligence (Törmänen et al., 2016) and gives the coaching supervisor and coach the widest-angle view of what is happening within the coach's work. The coach and coaching supervisor can unwrap layers of the organization's culture to better understand how the system is impacting the coaching client's view of themselves and their work. The wider systems impacting the coaching client's organization, especially during globally challenging times, can also be viewed through this lens to raise awareness and gain perspective on overt and subtle influences present in the coaching work.

Questions for coach reflection: *How would I describe the client's organization? What is happening or changing within the enterprise the client operates in? What are the cultural factors present in the broader organization that impact the client? What is happening in the business environment that might impact the client and my coaching?*

## My Case

I had been coaching for roughly eight years when I was fortunate enough to find myself sitting across from a senior vice-president (SVP) of a top, global bank. It was the summer of 2008 and the global financial markets were at the edge of collapsing. It was my first meeting with this corporate client and I was nervous because of all that was happening in the world. I also needed the work as it had been a difficult year for me, financially. The conversation was going well when I suddenly felt thirsty and my throat tightened. I was also short of breath.

I felt frozen in place, overwhelmed by my constricting throat, and now racing heart. My face felt hot. Fortunately, the SVP continued talking, telling his story and unaware anything was amiss as I suffered in silence. In that moment of intense physical reactivity, my mind told me to ask to be excused to get a glass of water or go to the bathroom. Anything to get out of that office! I went from fright mode to flight mode in seconds. In retrospect, I was having a panic attack. Fortunately, I had some ability to center myself in that storm of cortisol and adrenaline release. I was able to tolerate the physical onslaught of hormones and anxiety in my body to keep the conversation going. I was good enough to get the assignment.

Had a supervisor been working with me at that point, we might have used the Tri-Lens to retrace and process what happened during the coaching session. My supervisor would start by peering with me through the viewfinder of the model: The central point from which to notice and sense my present state—my thoughts, feelings, and sensations. Through our reflective dialogue, my supervisor and I might replay the scenario of the fight-or-flight response that I had experienced and examine what destabilized me, emotionally. In retrospect, I was conscious of my feeling of nervousness even before I entered the room. While I anticipated being nervous during that interview, this was the tip of the iceberg and relates to a pattern of constructed emotions that date back to my childhood. This emotional package contains versions and variations of fear and anxiety.

My current mindful awareness can now sense and notice to a higher degree the spectrum of my fear, from terror to tentativeness and my anxiety, from bodily dislocation to mild agitation. This capacity was hard earned over many years of noticing and sensing in mindful reflection. An embedded script is present in me. This false identity was given to me before I could reflect on my own and understand the fiction of my not being good enough. My bodily tensions reside in my jaw; I grind my teeth. I also still experience anxiety in my throat and chest. My tendency to overthink and allow a voice of judgment to hold sway over my mind can leave me feeling anxious and emotionally exhausted. In these instances, when my mindfulness is shaky, l am not a well coach.

Back in my imagined session with my supervisor, she is guiding me in a brief mindfulness practice of three full-body breaths, which helps clear the emotional residue fogging up my viewfinder. The fog is self-judgment and shame for being so anxious and afraid. We now shift our attention to the *client lens*, as the *self* fades into the background with the *system*. What is revealed as we zoom in on the client and our coaching relationship is that I have transferred my fears onto the SVP title before even meeting the leader. My emotions are settled as I see through my self-story of a scary executive, when in fact this leader is reasonable, gracious, and open to partnering.

As we shift to the *systems lens*, after some moments of silence and centering my attention and presence, I share with the coaching supervisor that the hiring firm warned me the situation with global financial markets might force cancellation of the coaching engagement. Adding to the systems in play, when I spoke with the HR partner, they indicated the SVP "may not make it." When I inquired what that meant for coaching and expected outcomes, the HR partner commented: "We'll see what happens if he can make some changes." I feel a mix of doubt and excitement as I share this with my supervisor. I feel I can help and the executive is ready to engage in the coaching, and yet, as my supervisor astutely points out, the conditions for success are barely present. I'm also made aware of my rescuer-self showing up. This is a conditioned way of thinking and acting that makes me feel valued. We talk about how my limited self-appreciation and positive self-regard could hook me in a no-win situation.

We take another look through the viewfinder at *self as coach* and I'm feeling more emotionally settled and supported. The insights into my conditioned thinking that surfaced in our reflective dialogue have given me a confident way forward. In part, this was made possible by better understanding my reactive thinking and associated anxiety as we looked through the *client* and *systems lenses*. My supervisor checks with me about the severity of my anxiety and I assure her I have the therapy I need outside of supervision to process my past trauma. We end on a note of appreciation and humor, as I note: "I got the job, what's the worst that can happen now?"

## Future Implications

There is a need for more research in the coaching supervision community. Fortunately, leaders within the Global Supervision Network and the America's Coaching Supervision Network have taken interest in addressing supervision research questions. More specifically, I recommend a research focus into the why, what, and how the resourcing function of supervision adds value for the coach, supervisor, client, and client organization. I believe all the functions of coaching supervision need study to fully understand and measure their benefits and value proposition. This is a research challenge I have committed to and look forward to supervisor colleagues joining me on this journey of inquiry.

# Conclusion

History is a retrospective interpretation of events by people who lived through them. The ways in which we relate to world-changing events impacts our ability as coaching professionals to be present and emotionally sound when working with our clients. Well-being, as the foundational function of coaching supervision, supports coaches in centering and grounding themselves as they absorb all that their clients and client organizations are going through when in crisis mode.

A coach's capacity to work and draw from their internal resources rather than effort can be facilitated in supervision by leveraging the Tri-Lens. The Tri-Lens framework allows for the supervisor and coach to look together through a viewfinder of attention and presence and three lenses—self as coach, client, and system. Shifting their view between lenses, they become curious about what destabilizes or grounds the coach emotionally. Coaches come to supervision, especially in challenging times, for a variety of reasons. A chief reason is to ensure they are showing up as the best version of themselves for their clients and client organizations. By and large, coaches are purpose-driven and client-centric and they desire to be "fit for purpose." Therefore, the question we need to be consistently asking ourselves as coaches and coaching supervisors is not "who do I want to be when I grow up?" It is: "who will I be when I wake up?"

# References

American Psychological Association. (2020, September 21). *What's the difference between stress and anxiety?* http://www.apa.org/topics/stress/anxiety-difference

Armour, M. R. (2020). Supervision's 'Three Amigos': Exploring the evolving functions of supervision and its application in the field of coaching. *Philosophy of Coaching: An International Journal, 3*(1): 23–37. 10.22316/poc/03.1.03

Asumeng, M. A. (2015). Organization development models: A critical review and implications for creating learning organizations. *European Centre for Research Training and Development UK, 2*(3): 29–43.

Bartlett, L., et al. (2019). A systematic review and meta-analysis of workplace mindfulness training randomized controlled trials. *Journal of Occupational Health Psychology, 24*(1): 108–126. https://doi.apa.org/doiLanding?doi=10.1037%2Focp0000146

Box, G. E. P., & Draper, N. R. (1987). *Empirical model-building and response surfaces (Wiley Series in probability and statistics).* (1st ed.). Wiley.

Brockbank, A. (2008). Is the coaching fit for purpose? A typology of coaching and learning approaches. *Coaching: An International Journal of Theory. Research and Practice, 1*(2): 132–144. https://www.annualreviews.org/doi/10.1146/annurev.psych.53.100901.135228

Casement, P. J. (2002). *Learning from our mistakes: Beyond dogma in psychoanalysis and psychotherapy.* Guilford Press.

Bridges, W. (2004). *Transitions – Making sense of life's changes.* (2nd ed.). Da Capo Lifelong Books.

Centers for Disease Control and Prevention. (2018, October 31). *Well-being concepts.* https://www.cdc.gov/hrqol/wellbeing.htm#four

Cochrane, H., & Newton, T. (2018). *Supervision and coaching: Growth and learning in professional practice*. Routledge.

David, S. (2016). *Emotional agility: Get unstuck, embrace change, and thrive in work and life*. Penguin Publishing Group.

Edelglass, W. (2009). Engaged Buddhism: Thich Nhat Hanh's interbeing. In W. Edelglass, & J. Garfield (Eds.), *Buddhist Philosophy: Essential Readings* (pp. 419–427). Oxford University Press.

Diochon, P., & Louis, D. (2019). *Complex situations in coaching: A critical case-cased approach*. Routledge.

Ellemers, N., Spears, R. & Doosje, B. (2002). Self and social identity. *Annual review of Psychology, 53*: 161–186. 10.1146/annurev.psych.53.100901.135228

Evans, R. (1990). William James, "the principles of psychology," and experimental psychology. *The American Journal of Psychology, 103*(4): 433–447. https://www.jstor.org/stable/1423317?origin=crossref&seq=1

Feldman Barrett, L. (2017). *How emotions are made: The secret life of the brain*. Mariner Books.

Feldman Barrett, L. (2020). *Seven and a half lessons about the brain*. Houghton Mifflin Harcourt.

Flynn, J. M. (2020). Mistakes made and lessons learned: A mid-career pediatric orthopaedic surgeon's journey to sustain energy and avoid burnout. *Journal of Pediatric Orthopaedics, 40*(6): 16–21.

Goldstein, J. (2016). *Mindfulness: A practical guide to awakening*. Sounds True.

Goleman, D. (2007). *Social intelligence: The new science of human relationships*. Bantam.

Goleman, D. (2013). *Focus: The hidden driver of excellence*. Harper.

Hamilton, M. (2012). *Leadership to the power of 8: Leading self, others, organization, system and supra-system*. Wirtschaftspsychologie.

Hawkins, P., & Shohet, R. (2007). *Supervision in the helping professions*. (3rd ed.). Open University Press.

Hawkins, P., & Smith, N. (2007). *Coaching, mentoring and organizational consultancy: supervision and development*. Open University Press.

Hawkins, P., Turner, E., & Passmore, J. (2019). *The manifesto for supervision*. Henley Business School and Association for Coaching.

Henriques, G. (2014). One self or many selves? *Psychology Today*. https://www.psychologytoday.com/us/blog/theory-knowledge/201404/one-self-or-many-selves

Hayes, S.C., & Smith, S. (2005). *Get out of your mind and into your life: The new acceptance & commitment therapy*. New Harbinger Publications.

Hicks, B., et al. (2013). Impact of coaching on employee well-being, engagement and job satisfaction. *Institute for Employment Studies*. https://www.employmentstudies.co.uk/system/files/resources/files/hrp8.pdf

Holloway, K. (2016). Exploring shame within the supervisory relationship. *Sophia*, St. Catherine University. https://sophia.stkate.edu/msw_papers/597

Jasanoff, A. (2018). *The biological mind: How brain, body, and environment collaborate to make us who we are*. Basic Books.

Kabat-Zinn, J. (1994). *Wherever you go, there you are: Mindfulness meditation in everyday life*. (1st ed.). Hyperion.

Kim S. J., and Bostwick W. (2020). *Social vulnerability and racial inequality in COVID-19 deaths in Chicago*. Health Ed & Behavior, 47(4): 509–513. 10.1177/1090198120929677

Kolb, D. A. (1984). *Experiential learning: experience as the source of learning and development*. *Englewood Cliffs*. Prentice-Hall.

Kruglanski, A. W. & Webster, D. M. (1996). Motivated closing of the mind: "Seizing" and "freezing". *Psychological Review, 103*(2): 263–283. 10.1037/0033295X.103.2.263

Liu, J. J. W., Ein, N., Gervasio, J., Battaion, M., Reed, M., & Vickers, K. (2020). Comprehensive meta-analysis of resilience interventions. *Clinical Psychology Review, 82*. 10.1016/j.cpr.2020.101919

Maslach, C., Schaufeli, W. B., & Leiter, M.P. (2001). Job burnout. *Annual Review of Psychology, 52*(1): 397–422. https://www.annualreviews.org/doi/abs/10.1146/annurev.psych.52.1.397

Mayer, J. D., Salovey, P., Caruso, D. R., & Sitarenios, G. (2003). Measuring emotional intelligence with the MSCEIT V2.0. *Emotion, 3*(1): 97–105. 10.1037/1528-3542.3.1.97

McCormack, H. M., MacIntyre, T. E., O'Shea, D., Herring, M. P., & Campbell, M. J. (2018). The prevalence and cause(s) of burnout among applied psychologists: A systematic review. *Frontiers in Psychology, 9*: 1897. 10.3389/fpsyg.2018.01897

Neff, K. (2011). Self-compassion, self-esteem, and well-being. *Social and Personality Compass, 5*(1): 1–12. https://self-compassion.org/wp-content/uploads/2015/12/SC.SE_.Well-being.pdf

Neff, K. (2015). *Self-compassion: The proven power of being kind to yourself.* William Morrow Paperbacks.

Newey, S. (2021). Covid-19 has amplified 'parallel pandemic' of poor mental health across Europe, WHO warns. *The Telegraph.* https://www.telegraph.co.uk/global-health/climate-and-people/covid-19-has-amplified-parallel-pandemic-poor-mental-health/

Palmer, S., & Turner, E. (2018). *The heart of coaching supervision: Working with reflection and self-care (essential coaching skills and knowledge).* Routledge.

Palmer, W. (2008). *The intuitive body: Discovering the wisdom of conscious embodiment and aikido.* (3rd ed.). Blue Snake Books.

Prentice, K. (2020). *Nature's way: Designing the life you want through the lens of nature and the five seasons.* Karen Fletcher.

Proctor, B. (2008). *Group supervision: A guide to creative practice.* (2nd ed.). SAGE Publications Ltd.

Rotter, J. B. (1966). Generalized expectancies for internal versus external control of reinforcement. *Psychological Monographs: General and Applied, 80*(1), 1–28. 10.1037/h0092976

Scharmer, O. (2007). *Theory U: Leading from the future as it emerges.* The Society for Organizational Learning.

Schaufeli, W. B., Salanova, M., Gonzalez-Roma, V., & Bakker, A. B. (2002). The measurement of engagement and burnout: A two sample confirmation factor analytic approach. *Journal of Happiness Studies, 3*: 71–92. https://www.wilmarschaufeli.nl/publications/Schaufeli/178.pdf

Schaefer, M. (2018). *The certainty of uncertainty: The way of inescapable doubt and its virtue.* Wipf and Stock.

Senge, P., Scharmer, C., Jaworski, J., & Flowers, B. (2004). *Presence: Human purpose and the field of the future.* Society for Organizational Learning.

Schon, D. A. (1984). *The reflective practitioner: How professionals think in action* (1st ed.). Basic Books.

Shohet, J. & Shohet, R. (2020). *In love with supervision: Creating transformative conversations.* PCCS Books.

Shohet, R. (2018). *In love with supervision: Creating transformative conversations.* Routledge.

Silsbee, D. (2008). *Presence-based coaching: Cultivating self-generative leaders through mind, body, and heat.* (1st ed.). Jossey-Bass.

Smith, J. (2019). *Coaching and Trauma.* (1st ed.). McGraw-Hill.

Statista (2020). *Pandemic Causes Spike in Anxiety & Depression.* https://www.msn.com/en-us/health/medical/pandemic-causes-spike-in-anxiety-andampdepression/ar-BB14V2Ki

Stacey, G., Cook, A., Aubeeluck, A. et al. (2020). The implementation of resilience based clinical supervision to support transition to practice in newly qualified healthcare professionals. *Nurse Education Today, 94.* 10.1016/j.nedt.2020.104564

Strozzi-Heckler, R. (2014). *The art of somatic coaching: Embodying skillful action, wisdom and compassion.* North Atlantic Books.

Törmänen, J., Hämäläinen, R. P., & Saarinen, E. (2016). Systems intelligence inventory. *The Learning Organization, 23*(4): 218–231. 10.1108/TLO-01-2016-0006

Tovote, P., Fadok, J. P., & Lüthi, A. (2015). Neuronal circuits for fear and anxiety. *Nature reviews. Neuroscience, 16*(6): 317–331. 10.1038/nrn3945

Van der Kolk, B. (2015). *The body keeps the score: Brain, mind, and body in the healing of trauma.* Penguin Books.

Walker, P. (2013). *Complex PTSD: From surviving to thriving: A guide and map for recovering from childhood trauma.* (1st ed.). CreateSpace Independent Publishing Platform.

Welwood, J. (2002). *Toward a psychology of awakening: Buddhism, psychotherapy, and the path of personal and spiritual transformation.* Shambhala.

Wright, R. (2018). *Why Buddhism is true: The science and philosophy of meditation and enlightenment.* Simon & Schuster.

# 9 Resourcing, Restoring, and Responding Through Coaching Supervision: *A Practice of Noticing, Embodying, and Cultivating Resilience*

*Sarah Evans and Alexis Chamow*

## The Backdrop

This chapter is being composed as our world is experiencing unprecedented, complex, and disorienting change and adversity. The current moment finds us amid a global pandemic; humanitarian and systemic reckonings; environmental risk and disruption; and uncertain economics that leave many questioning much about the future and their place within it. It is amid this increasingly volatile, uncertain, complex, ambiguous, and disruptive environment that coaches and their clients are working.

While the specific challenges of the moment will be addressed, there will always be forces that impact us in ways requiring more resources to navigate. Though the elements will change, we believe there is a perpetual need for coaches to cultivate resilience and have a reliably resourced version of the self to use as instrument (Bachkirova, 2016; McLean, 2012, 2019) for the circumstances faced now and those yet to come. If coaches can master themselves, they can be masterful in holding presence and space for others in full partnership as the International Coaching Federation's (ICF) competencies invite.

## Considering Resilience

We are experienced coaches and coach supervisors with a particular interest in resilience. We believe that the practice of coaching supervision and holding space for reflection, meaning making, and learning are vital for coaches to develop their capacity for service. To be effective, coaches must attend to personal and professional presence and prioritize wellness and sustainability in the demanding and more dynamic, nuanced, and systemic work in which they are engaged.

The coaching supervision relationship is a rich ecosystem where resilience can be sown, nurtured, and cultivated. To support full and responsive engagement in this immersive environment, we introduce a model of relational spaces to cultivate resilience resourcing: Facilitating the restorative

DOI: 10.4324/b23130-12

aspect of coaching supervision for the coach, and by extension, their clients. Our hope is that this resilience resourcing will accelerate the generation of support to coaches and their clients as they—we—navigate and thrive in this globally challenging environment.

In this chapter, we seek to expand the restorative function of coaching supervision, to make resilience actionable, and to support building capacity and sustainability in our work. We begin by looking at the parallels with nature and the importance of reflection in the calm. We then turn to the restorative function and resilience, including core components and capacities. We end by offering our model of relational spaces to cultivate resilience resourcing and share two case studies as illustration.

## Navigating the Storms

A couple of months into the spread of COVID-19, the notion proliferated—in the news, business circles, and social media—that "we were in this together." That whoever and wherever we were, we were all inevitably going to be impacted in some way or another. Damian Barr, columnist and author, took the notion in a more nuanced direction. He tweeted on April 21, 2020: "We are not all in the same boat. We are all in the same storm. Some are on super-yachts. Some have just the one oar" (Barr, 2020). This led an anonymous author, cited by Barr, to pen a poem that included these lines:

> *We are in the same storm, but not in the same boat …*
> *It is very important to see beyond what is seen at first glance.*
> *Not just looking, more than looking, seeing.*
> —Anonymous

This moment in history in North America, where we live and practice, finds us amid one storm after another. In our coaching supervision practices, we are witnessing coaches and their clients grappling with and being impacted by implications of COVID-19; the future of the workplace; diversity, equity, inclusion, belonging, and justice; and wellness and well-being.

The devastating pandemic exposed long-term health disparities and vicious racism. Barr's tweet came a month before the murder of George Floyd, a Black man, by a White Minneapolis police officer that sparked months of protests, inquests, and calls of "Black Lives Matter" to address systemic racism and intergenerational trauma. In May 2021, the remains of 215 Indigenous children were discovered buried on the grounds of the former Kamloops Indian Residential School in British Columbia, Canada. This heartbreaking discovery was a reminder that what some consider the past, remains in the present for those who have experienced institutionalized trauma and that there is much truth and reconciliation to confront.

In January 2021, the US Centers for Disease Control and Prevention reported a mental health crisis that will have lasting effects. The report pointed to several stressors that were creating an unprecedented storm: the ongoing COVID-19 pandemic, concerns about racial injustice, climate change, and the state of the economy. Canada's Centre for Addiction and Mental Health painted a similar picture and also reported an opioid crisis. Both Centers indicated that drug overdoses were at the highest levels in recorded history. There were significant barriers to accessing mental health supports and the need was overwhelming current systems.

The current natural and human-made environments are marked by significant and consistent disruptions. There can be great virtue there including immediate and compelling attentiveness to data we might otherwise ignore, large-scale reevaluations, and punctuated equilibrium that gives way to new, more equitable and just norms. But there is an intensity and high alert quality to these disruptions that, for many, makes a thoughtful pause challenging yet essential.

The word "storm" comes from the Proto-Germanic *sturmaz,* meaning noise, tumult (Online Etymology Dictionary, n.d.). As coaching supervisors, our aim is to acknowledge the space of storm—whatever that means for whomever is sitting before us. At our best, we provide a moment of peaceful presence in the midst of the noise and tumult. Much like the eye of a hurricane, this supervision center we establish is a place of calm. Because everything reels around it without actually converging on it, the eye of the storm is meant to be a place of refuge and preparation.

The eye of the storm sees a coaching supervision parallel in the seven-eyed model developed in 1985 by Peter Hawkins and Robin Shohet (Hawkins & Shohet, 2012). This framework for coaching supervision speaks to the author of the poem's point about not just *looking,* but actually *seeing.* We have this eye (or eyes) that when fully utilized, become tools for thoughtful examination, consideration, and preparation. Within that calm center, coaches can achieve a sense of ease within the challenge that allows them to flourish when they return to the more insecure or unstable portions of our world.

## Reflection in the Calm

We seek to create this ease by working with reflection. The Oxford English Learner's Dictionary (n.d.) identifies reflection as originating from the Latin root *reflectere*—a verb meaning "bent back." It refers to a literal bending back of light, when an image can be seen in a reflector that is still and calm; and a metaphorical bending back of time taken to consider a particular moment. In this still, calm, and reflective space, we can engage coaches in a deliberate inquiry into their practice for them to gain a deeper understanding and appreciation of self, others, and the systems in which they work, and to support them in being fit for purpose. Harvey (2015) notes,

"Being reflective on practice is the most empowering resource available for our professional development because the answers arrive inside-out as gifts of consciousness and give us the power of choice" (p. 3).

A warped reflector is like an unnatural funhouse mirror, twisting and turning what we are able to see in a way that creates confusion rather than clarity. By themselves, coaches may or may not reflect in a useful way. In coaching supervision, we aim for a view that is unobstructed. To be clear, this does not necessitate a supervision space absent of challenge; rather, it aspires to be a safe space where challenge may arrive and be met with courage, vulnerability, and heightened understanding. Sometimes the stillest water reflects back the most surprising image. Reflection evokes awareness, and awareness can activate self-regulation (Hullinger et al., 2019), which elevates capacity facing out as well as in.

In Nancy Kline's *More Time to Think* (2014), she identifies 10 components of a thinking environment. "Ease" is one component she identifies as "offering freedom from internal rush or urgency" (p. 35). As Hookham (2016) indicates, Kline teaches:

> Ease is an inside thing. You slow down. You still your internal day. You focus. You notice that you exist and that you are in this very moment and in this very room and with this very person. You 'see' them. You let yourself let them be … (p. 19)

Internal ease allows coaches to think about the emergencies outside. It is in this space of reflection where we can support coaches as they pause from serving others to reflect on their practice, rebalance, and resource themselves. Synergistically, there is ripe potential for coaching supervisors to rebalance and resource, as well.

## The Restorative Function—Resourcing, Restoring, and Responding

We acknowledge the value of the normative and formative functions of coaching supervision and are focused on expanding an understanding of the third function: Restorative (Bachkirova et al., 2011). It is in the restorative function that personal and emotional support for the coach is offered as they engage and interact with clients and the systems in which the client works to support restoring health, strength, well-being, and the human spirit. Hawkins and Smith (2013) speak of this function as a way of responding to how those "engaged in the intensity of work with clients are necessarily allowing themselves to be affected by the emotions of their clients" (p. 173). To practice sustainably, it is important to "become aware of the way this has affected them and to deal with any reactions" (p. 173).

The coaching supervision space and its conversations can support coaches to be fit for purpose as they interact with clients and client systems affected by stress, challenge, and uncertainty. Additionally, there is growing recognition in the wellness industry that well trained and resourced coaches can be a viable solution to increasing access to mental health care. The application of coaching can provide "targeted support to clients and recommend strategies for gaining mental resilience in the face of adverse events ..." (Altman, 2021).

A coaching supervisor's support can help coaches to normalize or put into context their experiences; to view other perspectives; to see what they haven't seen or to expand perspective; to explore and respond to emotions and reactions, as well as doubts or questions about self and approaches taken; to be "clean" in their work; and to compassionately attend to their personal well-being.

This restorative function supports increasing capacity for a coach to work from a core source, sustaining self and practice as well as increasing resourcefulness and resilience both in mindsets and behaviors. We agree with Hawkins (2019) that this restorative function is "both at the heart of supervision and the core spiritual practice that underpins other important elements of supervision practice" (p. 62).

## Restorative and Resilience

*Like tiny seeds with potent power to push through tough ground and become mighty trees, we hold innate reserves of unimaginable strength. We are resilient.*
—Catherine DeVrye

The literature related to resilience is vast, spans multiple disciplines, and offers a multitude of definitions (e.g., Bhamra et al., 2011; Earvolino-Ramirez, 2007; Fletcher & Sarkar, 2013; Masten & Reed, 2005). Definitions found in the literature have focused on two key elements: 1) Experiencing significant stress, strain or adversity, and 2) recovering. For example, resilience researcher Christopher Layne (as cited in Stix, 2011) stated: "It basically means that you spring back to functioning in a short period, like a steel beam, which bends under stress and returns afterward to where it started" (p. 30). Bridges (1995) offered a similar definition, "the ability to bend and not break" (p. 57). Yet, our human biology is more complex than an analogy from metallurgy, and human agency also contributes to this complexity.

For our purposes, the definitions we find more in alignment with a human-focused dynamic are those from natural systems that emphasize continuity, adaptation, and development. For example, Walker et al. (2006) defined resilience as, "The capacity of a system to experience shocks while retaining essentially the same function, structure, feedbacks, and therefore identity" (p. 2). Or, as van der Vegt et al. (2015) indicated, resilience can be framed as "the ability of systems to absorb and recover from shocks while transforming their structures and means for functioning in the face of long-term stresses, change and uncertainty" (p. 972). Rather than a return to where we started, resilience in a human-focused context sees us through and helps us evolve.

All definitions began with an experience of significant stress, strain, or adversity. In our exploration of definitions relative to natural systems, we noted more absorbing, adapting, and continuing than springing back to what was. One doesn't experience stress, strain, or adversity and remain as they were. They are in some way altered by the experience. Resilience is the foundation of the bridge that moves one from an intensely challenging experience through discovery and whatever shift follows. And in the best case, this move empowers one with increased capabilities and capacity (Lawton Smith, 2017) to see, hear, feel, adjust, and thrive.

More broadly, these definitions supported extending the two key elements (experiencing significant stress, strain, or adversity; and, recovering) by shining a light on what we believe are three additional core components of resilience, once the sources or causes of the stress, strain, and adversity are identified and assessed:

1   *Adapting* to the adversity
2   *Learning and growing* from the setbacks
3   *Resourcing* for future challenges

In part, these components are enacted by reflecting deeply and acknowledging, two actions that are present in a psychologically safe, fluid, and reflective supervision space. They are also enacted as part of the restorative function. An impactful session serves as both a container for and a pathway to resilience. If there is a priority on achieving such a mutually beneficial landscape, we must look to larger contexts to know where this specific priority lives, and how to manifest it as part of a larger and more systemic whole.

## Resilience Resourcing: A Model for Restoring and Thriving

At the center of a supervision conversation lies the supervision space, itself. The container we create to hold this space has layers and depth. The case or theme brought to the conversation draws our focus and is the place we begin, sitting atop a bedrock of calm at the center. Yet, the case or theme brought to the space does not exist in a vacuum. It is occurring in an interrelated system. The work exists in the context of the other realms around it. The conversation is a microcosm of the coach's practice, which exists in a specific coaching environment, which exists within many larger environments.

Having looked at the importance of reflection in the calm and the value of focusing on the restorative function of supervision, we now introduce resilience resourcing: A model of relational spaces that (when explored in

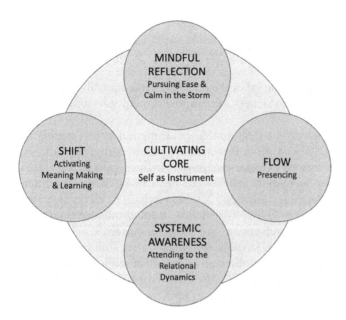

*Figure 9.1* Relational Spaces to Cultivate Resilience Resourcing.

supervision) can cultivate resilience. By activating this model (Figure 9.1), there exists potential to explore, deepen, and expand the core components and capacities of resilience as a means of *adapting* to current challenges, *learning and growing*, and continuously *resourcing* for future challenges. Coaches can strengthen their capability and capacity, and in turn, are equipped to support those they serve to do the same.

The model prioritizes a sense of readiness in the supervision space to engage, evaluate, emerge, and evolve. The following relational spaces and accompanying suggestions for action are intended to offer specific opportunities to achieve a more "ready" way of being and doing that builds rapport with our coaches and, by extension, their clients. It is in this ready, open, safe, and exploratory space that there can be a synergistic sense of resilience. This is not meant to be a prescriptive set of steps, but rather a dynamic interplay of intention and attention.

### Cultivating Core—Self as Instrument

As coaches, we know who we are is how we coach. By extension, as coach supervisors, we know who we are is how we supervise. The most important resource we need to access to engage most effectively in this work is our own fully present self.

We can show up at our most authentic and available if we make a practice of engaging in a personal assessment of our core source: Our thoughts, feelings, beliefs, intuitions, values, perspectives; our unique nature, our being, and our personal strength, literally and figuratively. "Your inner state is the foundation for resilience: the capacity for creativity, resourcefulness and skilled action, no matter what's going on around you" (Silsbee, 2018, p. 155). How are we at our core? We grow in our capacity to re-source self when we engage in the practice of intentionally cultivating our core and developing awareness and purpose around who and how we want to be.

Thinking of ourselves as energy systems and physical bodies aiming to strengthen our core, the work is meant to support a strong, yet flexible, connecting central link to enhance our power, balance, and stability. It is our core that keeps us upright and poised, helps us be at our best, and supports adapting, learning, growing, and resourcing. A weak, tight, or imbalanced core can not only lead to depletion, fatigue, and less endurance, it can also undermine our movement. We must ask ourselves, at base, who we are being, how are we presencing, and what we are doing.

Dr. Richard Schwartz (2020) observed eight C's of self leadership in his work *Internal Family Systems Therapy*. We have adapted seven of these as core energy sources per our examination of resilience capacity. As with any capacity, it begins with awareness and intentionality. To this resilience work, we also begin, as Schwartz does, with compassion.

### Courage

Courage is defined as the "mental or moral strength to venture, persevere, and withstand danger, fear, or difficulty" (Merriam Webster Online Dictionary, n.d.). Courage requires an inner strength, a whole heart, a commitment, a valor to encounter the unknown, the uncertain, and the frightening, including one's own fears and insecurities. Coaches can embody and multiply courage when they are legitimately at peace with not knowing, trusting the process and flow, going where a session takes them. They can practice courage by coming together, prepared to be fully present with a coaching mindset, through listening deeply and giving voice to whatever is emerging. *Courage requires trust, a willingness to be vulnerable and a sense that whatever it is we are heading into must be undertaken in service to a greater outcome.*

### Creativity

Elaine Patterson notes, "Creativity is an energy and a life force that defines us. Creativity is inherently who we are" (2019, p. 24). To create is to bring into existence, to make new or imagine, to design, to bring about by action. A new idea, insight, perspective, way of thinking, doing, working, or relating are all acts of creativity as are new products, art, and artistic forms. Creativity encourages positive emotions that can unlock our inner resources for navigating stress and uncertainty (Conner et al., 2018). Creativity also enhances our ability to connect abstract ideas and concepts, and come up with novel solutions. We have colleagues who have developed beautifully creative tools (e.g., Lucas, 2020; Patterson, 2019) to hold, explore, and play in the supervision space. When coach and coaching supervisor agree to engage in a creative process, the capacity to restore, re-source, and cultivate resilience can increase exponentially and in phenomenally unanticipated ways. *Under duress, it can be difficult to receive creative inspiration; but it can also be exactly where we need to go for release or to access our next steps.*

### Connection

We are hardwired for connection. We are social beings and relationships are key to human flourishing. Our interconnectedness means that changes in ourselves and in the small worlds we inhabit can have ripple effects in the larger world. As we hold and explore connection with self, others, and the world around us, we are able to shift our focus from an individual perspective to relationships, interrelationships, and patterns: To take a more systemic view. Two core competencies of coaching supervision and coaching are to actively listen and to inquire to evoke awareness. Leaning intentionally into these as discreet and actionable skills can expand our ability to connect. *When we see ourselves as part of an interconnected system, with an inter-woven consciousness, we begin to frame on a broader scale, seeing ourselves as a significant and impactful part of a whole.*

### Calm

When the external storms toss us, we can look internally to find or generate calm—our personal eye in the storm. We can literally still our system physiologically. In stillness, our senses come alive and our intuition can be laid bare. We can strengthen our capacity to tune into what is happening in the moment, to focus attention and to ground ourselves. "Without calmness, the mirror of mindfulness will have an agitated and choppy surface and will not be able to reflect things with any accuracy" (Kabat-Zinn, 2005, p. 68). *It is in the quiet, still moments when we can focus on our breath and our internal landscape that we are able to best identify what is truly impacting us, where we are truly feeling challenged, what we might most authentically need in order to meet the moment.*

### Curiosity

We are all born with an innate sense of curiosity that is stimulated as we experience wonder and as we explore, discover, and learn. As we marvel, wonder, and hold awe we can be uplifted. Curiosity is correlated with creativity and helps us adapt to uncertain conditions and external pressures. It has also been linked to greater tolerance, noncritical attitudes, unconventional thinking, and the initiation of humor and playfulness (Kashdan et al., 2013). To begin a coaching supervision session by literally asking where the curiosity lies and then going "5 whys" deep, we can get to the heart of a matter through the simple action of focusing on what draws us into a particular topic and considering how it might be explored. *When our curiosity is triggered, we are more able to view challenges as possibilities. We think more deeply and feel with more light and we are stimulated in a playful or inquisitive way to show up differently and come up with more creative solutions.*

*Clarity*

Thich Nhat Hanh (2007) and Kerry Lee MacLean (2009) have both written delightful stories teaching children (applicable to adults, too) the "Mind in a Jar" mindfulness activity to soothe and quiet the mind. Children learn that when they are experiencing high levels of emotion, by shaking up a jar of colorful glitter in water they can experience, observe, and honor all their swirling emotions and thoughts instead of just being caught up in them. As they observe the glitter slowly settle through the water, their emotions and thoughts begin to settle as well. Try it! By being calm, clear, and transparent, it becomes easier to understand, see, and to hear. We see the world through how we feel. We see things as we are. The act of attuning with a clear focus literally creates physiological changes in our system and we are better able to ground ourselves in the midst of the storms. *Seeing with clear eyes or perhaps even polished lenses creates greater clarity, which amounts to greater grounding, which leads to greater capacity to act in choice.*

*Confidence*

When external storms shake us, we can be steadied by our confidence: A belief and trust in ourselves and our wisdom. How do we value ourselves? Where do we focus? How do we stand literally and metaphorically? Confidence is a capacity that can be developed. Try something hard on purpose. Give yourself a clear space to stretch into. The simple act of the reach creates a greater sense of purpose and a greater intentionality that shows up as "confidence." Build failure into the process, so when it happens it's more "ah, there you are!" rather than "what's wrong with me that I missed that …" With confidence, we embody an openness and a growth mindset. We trust in our abilities and at the same time challenge ourselves to grow them. We can hold a conviction that we can meet life's challenges with a willingness to act. We know that we can adapt and handle the emotional outcome of any challenge. Comfort with ourselves will often precede confidence and a coach can pick up on both. *With a foundational belief in ourselves, we can be both humble before others and assertive with what we* are clear about. *Perhaps most importantly, we know when to stand in which (humility or assertion) and our sense of our own value, regardless of circumstances, is constant.*

As we comprehensively consider the restorative function of supervision, it becomes clear that it is also a *re-sourcing* function. To cultivate and offer restoration, we must be mindful of core, self as instrument, and where our original sourcing begins in the first place.

### Mindful Reflection—Pursuing Ease & Calm

The chapter section *Reflection in the Calm* offers a perspective on why we view reflection, ease, and calm as essential. We liken the coaching supervision space to a riparian area that occurs in nature: Lands along watercourses and water bodies where dry meets wet. Both are observable and another ecosystem is created.

> They are distinctly different from surrounding lands because of unique soil and vegetation characteristics that are strongly influenced by the presence of water ... all riparian areas possess some similar ecological characteristics such as energy flow, nutrient cycling, water cycling, hydrologic function, and plant and animal population. These functions give riparian areas unique values relative to the surrounding landscape. (USDA Natural Resources Conservation Service, 1996)

For coaching supervision to achieve something akin to this unique space, this co-created ecosystem, a recommendation is to return to, and begin with, breath. This can include *box breath* or inhaling for four counts, holding for four counts, releasing for four counts, holding at empty for four counts and repeating; *circle breath* or breathing in through the nose, out through the mouth on even counts; or *motorboat breathing*, a rapid inhale followed by rapid exhale through the lips assertive enough to encourage vibration of the lips as air passes. Reflection and cultivation of the unique ecosystem is most accessible to us when we are on breath.

### Flow-Presencing

As we practice full involvement in the moment, we can access the experience of flow (Csikszentmihalyi, 1990). This means tapping into an energetic exchange that moves us forward with an overall absence of resistance. A coach is "able to sharpen all their senses in order to tune into the energy vibrations of the client" (Hullinger & DiGirolamo, 2020, p. 15). As we find rhythm within, we are also iterating on co-creation with others in the coaching supervision space. Being in flow allows us to advance as in a raft going down a river—with ease, momentum, clarity of direction, and purpose. In this state, there is a loss of self-consciousness and one's sense of time evaporates. Being deeply involved in some activity that has us feeling passionate creates in us a sense of ultimate presence. When in a state of flow, our brain decreases activation of the amygdala (the fight, flight, freeze response), reducing anxiety, and encouraging greater focus.

In the coaching supervision space, this flow inducing activity is *listening* and *inquiry*. Showing up fully and completely with our whole selves for the others with whom we are sharing the space. How we listen determines what we see and how we inquire. From Otto Scharmer's (2008) four levels of listening, we are particularly interested here in the third (empathetic) and fourth (generative) levels and engaging in inquiry to evoke awareness, insight, and wise action, especially into the generative level. These levels of listening are defined below:

> *Empathetic* (a connection to people and relationships) - a move from the objective world to a deeper listening to the story of a living and evolving self. This requires an open mind and an open heart to feel what another might be feeling or seeing. An open heart gives us the empathic capacity to directly connect with another person.

> *Generative* (a connection to something larger than self) - listening from the soul and to the emerging field of future possibility. This level of listening requires us to access our open mind, heart, and open our will to act or our capacity to connect to the highest future possibility that can emerge.

### Systemic Awareness—Attending to the Relational Dynamics

As we hold and explore connection with self, others, and the world around us, we are able to shift our focus to take a more systemic view. In this, we notice the patterns and relationships within the flow, to see both the dance and the dancers. When we take the time to understand what systems are in play and how they *inter*play, we are able to focus our inquiry in the moment, and hold space for moments of discovery to emerge.

Utilizing the seventh eye in Hawkins' seven-eyed model is one way to focus attention on environmental and systemic factors. In addition, there are a myriad of frameworks attending to "circles" of communication, of influence, of function. Activating these resources can query, reveal, or confirm a sense of the role a particular system plays in the broader supervision conversation.

### Shift—Activating Meaning Making & Learning

Human beings are active construers of meaning. We are hard-wired to ask questions, seek answers, and find pleasure in making connections and making meaning. As we reflect on and make meaning of our experiences, we know we must also apply intentionality to the process. Functioning from a growth mindset, we deliberately enter a thoughtful supervision space with a willingness to be altered and transformed. We activate, embody, recognize, and integrate data that's been dropped into the space. We alter once we discover how we're moved by it. Speaking about takeaways and commitments as we leave a coaching supervision session, we codify for ourselves what we have explored, what we have gained, and how we may hold ourselves accountable for allowing it to impact us out of the session and into our future.

### Sarah's Case

I had a profound experience working with a supervisee who was an experienced coach of healthcare leaders. In the time of the COVID-19 pandemic, our conversations often focused on the unimaginable stressors present in the healthcare system and the sense of overwhelm, exhaustion, and uncertainty felt by those he coached. He spoke of his own feelings of depletion and questioned whether anything he offered as a coach mattered. He had doubts about himself, his approach, and whether coaching could make a difference at all. There was much swirling. My heart went out to him as his heart went out to those in the communities he served. I could feel the heaviness he carried. In one particular conversation, after we had begun by calmly breathing and centering (*pursuing ease and calm*), we reflected together (*presencing*) about how the wider system in crisis was being reflected in his practice and in himself (*attending to the relational dynamics*). He suddenly stopped and quietly said: "I have no more words." Previously, we had explored creative expression as a means of accessing other dimensions of understanding self and of meaning (*cultivating core and activating meaning making*). As he sat with no words, he drew a picture. He was quiet and contemplative for a long time and then shared: "There are three words ... flourish, grow, joy" (*presencing*). I would never have guessed those words given the tiny dark smudge he had drawn in the centre of the page. When I inquired, he reflected on what that meant for him (*activating meaning making & learning*). What I noticed in myself was a resonance for how he spoke of joy (*presencing*). This was not a word or experience I would have associated with him prior to this conversation. Part of the title of C.S. Lewis's autobiography rang clearly in my mind , *Surprised by Joy*. A beloved Canadian author, Louise Penny, used this same line in her Gamache novels. As I shared my musings of how Gamache interacts within his systems and how I was experiencing his "inner Gamache," my supervisee became emotional as we touched something deeply meaningful for him (*activating meaning making and learning, self as instrument*). We were both *surprised by joy*. That moment reverberated for both of us and rippled into and beyond our practices in surprising ways. He used the word "wellspring" as a descriptor for his capacity to embody and actively "flourish, grow, joy" in the most challenging of circumstances. He also spoke to how he has channeled his "inner

Gamache" within the healthcare system in which he works and how the leaders he coaches are doing the same. I, too, have been able to access an expanded core source energy which has provided me a greater clarity and capacity to adapt and respond.

### Alexis' Case

In this still virtual world, I begin with sitting at the edge of my seat, feet planted loosely on the ground, wrists on things, palms up. I inhale through the nose, exhale through the mouth (circle breath.) I ask myself a few questions: "How are you? What are you looking forward to? How will you be of service today ...?" I think for a moment about something resourceful that brings me whatever I need, be it energy, calm, or focus. I sign on to my meeting with Lisa. An educator, entrepreneur, program facilitator and executive coach, she and I worked together first as coach-client, then as supervisor-coach. One supervision session I recall as particularly impactful and resonant for both of us in the context of resilience resourcing.

About six months into the pandemic lockdown in the United States, we had a quiet and thoughtful engagement about a client of Lisa's who was working on a "blue sky" topic. In session, Lisa said she often felt out of her element when clients brought topics related to "things like figuring out life's purpose." I had a hunch and asked her permission to propose a question. She blessed it. "Is there a parallel process," I asked, "in your clients struggling to figure out their life's purpose and you doing the same? Because I think I might be doing the same ..." It was very, very quiet as we both considered. We dug down into what Lisa was going through in her life and practice (major transition) and what we were both going through as coaches in the midst of the pandemic, and questioning what really mattered right alongside our clients. We moved on to explore who Lisa was being in those coaching sessions and why this topic seemed particularly challenging. We explored different facets of her coaching and her presence that, in follow up, allowed her to bring more spaciousness to the sessions with her clients. I realized my own breath had been held with the same question, but it wasn't until we co-created the space that I could see it. We breathed together, held lots of silences, and even laughed! She came to realize it wasn't her job to have the answer to these deep questions being posed as much as it was her job to hold a safe space for the client's exploration of the question—much in the same way we were approaching the coaching supervision session. A takeaway she recalled months later was the idea of creating a "padded room in which clients could bounce around and explore," which happened to be exactly what we had created and modeled for her. Being excused from needing to have the answer meant she could also excuse others in the same situation.

We both left that session having experienced safety and challenge. We realized the partnership of safety and challenge served as the baseline for the coaching container. Lisa shared with me that exploring that space of brainstorming and creativity had enabled her to take coaching sessions to a more meaningful and impactful level. I, too, felt that session illuminated what becomes possible when we catch the wave together. We both had the opportunity to bounce around in the reflective space we co-created, and we both left feeling more resourced and resilient because of it.

## Conclusion

Given the context of today's world and the uncertainties of tomorrow, we believe there is a pressing need for coaches to prioritize sustainable wellness to be able to work effectively. This chapter provides an approach to cultivating a calm space from within, which coaches can nurture to develop greater resilience and capacity for service. In the exploration of cultivating core as a source energy, we also promote seven energy sources as part of a resilience capacity. This underscores our perspective on resilience resourcing to facilitate the restorative aspect of supervision: To support restoring health, strength, well-being, and the human spirit. As noted, our model of relational spaces prioritizes a sense of readiness to engage, evaluate, emerge, and evolve.

## References

Altman, M. (2021). *Coaches could help solve the mental health crisis: A call to broaden the mental health standard of care*. Medium. https://elemental.medium.com/coaches-could-help-solve-the-mental-health-crisis-de5ebee8a231

Bachkirova, T. (2016). The self of the coach: Conceptualization, issues, and opportunities for practitioner development. *Consulting Psychology Journal: Practice and Research, 68*(2): 143–156.

Bachkirova, T., Jackson, P., & Clutterbuck, D. (2011). *Coaching and mentoring supervision: Theory and practice*. Open University Press.

Barr, D. [@Damian-Barr]. (2020). *We are not all in the same boat. We are all in the same storm. Some are on super-yachts. Some have just one oar*. Twitter. https://twitter.com/damian_barr/status/1318802918603182082?lang=en

Bhamra, R., Dani, S., & Burnard, K. (2011). Resilience: The concept, a literature review and future directions. *International Journal of Production Research, 49*(18): 5375–5393. doi:10.1080/00207543.2011.563826

Bridges, W. (1995). *Jobshift: How to prosper in a workplace without jobs*. Addison-Wesley.

Conner, T. S., DeYoung, C. G., & Silvia, P. J. (2018). Everyday creative activity as a path to flourishing. *The Journal of Positive Psychology, 13*(2): 181–189. DOI: 10.1080/17439760.2016.1257049

Csikszentmihalyi, M. (1990). *Flow: The psychology of optimal experience*. Harper Perennial.

DeVrye, C. (2018). *Gift of nature: Inspiring hope and resilience*. Rockpool Publishing.

Earvolino-Ramirez, M. (2007). Resilience: A concept analysis. *Nursing Forum, 42*(2): 73–82.

Fletcher, D., & Sarkar, M. (2013). Psychological resilience: A review and critique of definitions, concepts, and theory. *European Psychologist, 18*(1): 12–23.

Harvey, J. B. (2015). Coaching for essence: Potential & vulnerability drive professional mastery. *Choice, 13*(2): 3–5.

Hawkins, P. (2019). Resourcing: The neglected third leg of supervision. In E. Turner, & S. Palmer (Eds.), *The heart of coaching supervision: Working with reflection and self-care.* (pp 61–82). Routledge.

Hawkins, P., & Shohet, R. (2012). *Supervision in the helping professions.* (4th ed.). Open University Press.

Hawkins, P., & Smith, N. (2013). *Coaching, mentoring and organizational consultancy: Supervision and development.* (2nd ed.). Open University Press.

Hookham, M. (2016). The thinking environment – An ideal model for homeopathic consultations. *The Australian Journal of Homeopathic Medicine, 28*(1): 18–22.

Hullinger, A M., & DiGirolamo, J. A. (2020). A professional development study: The lifelong journeys of coaches. *International Coaching Psychology Review, 12*(1): 8 19.

Hullinger, A.M., DiGirolamo, J.A., & Tkach, J.T. (2019). Reflective practice for coaches and clients: An integrated model for learning. *Philosophy of Coaching: An International Journal, 4*(2): 5–34.

Kabat-Zinn, J. (2005). *Wherever you go, there you are: Mindfulness meditation in everyday life.* (10th ed.). Hachette Books.

Kashdan, T. B., Sherman, R. A., Yarbro, J., & Funder, D. C. (2013). How are curious people viewed and how do they behave in social situations? From the perspectives of self, friends, parents, and unacquainted observers. *Journal of Personality, 81*(2), 142–154.

Kline, N. (2014). *Time to think: Listening to ignite the human mind.* (reprint edition). Cassell Illustrated.

Lawton Smith, C. (2017). Coaching for leadership resilience: An integrated approach. *International Coaching Psychology Review, 12*(1): 6–23.

Lucas, M. (2020). *101 Coaching supervision techniques: Approaches, enquiries and experiments.* Routledge.

MacLean, K. L. (2009). *Moody cow meditates.* Wisdom Publications.

Masten, A. S., & Reed, M. G. J. (2005). Resilience in development. In C. R. Synder & S. J. Lopez (Eds.), *Handbook of positive psychology* (pp. 74–88). Oxford University Press.

McLean, P. (2019). *Self as coach, self as leader: Developing the best in you to develop the best in others.* Wiley.

McLean, P. (2012). *The completely revised handbook of coaching: A developmental approach.* Jossey-Bass.

Merriam Webster Online Dictionary. (n.d.). Retrieved July 6, 2021, from https://www.merriam-webster.com/dictionary/courage

Online Etymology Dictionary. (n.d.). Retrieved July 6, 2021, from https://www.etymonline.com/word/storm

Online Oxford Learner's Dictionary. (n.d.). Retrieved July 6, 2021, from https://www.oxfordlearnersdictionaries.com/us/definition/english/reflection

Patterson, E. (2019). *Reflect to create! The dance of reflection for creative leadership, professional practice and supervision.* Ingram Spark.

Scharmer, C. O. (2008). Uncovering the blindspot of leadership. *Leader to Leader, 47*(Winter): 52–59.

Schwartz, R. C., & Sweezy, M. (2020). *Internal family systems therapy.* (2nd ed.). The Guilford Press.

Silsbee, D. (2018). *Presence-based leadership: Complexity practices for clarity, resilience, and results that matter.* Yes! Global Inc.

Stix, G. (2011). The neuroscience of true grit. *Scientific American, 304*(3): 28–33.

Thich Nhat Hanh. (2007). *Planting seeds: Practicing mindfulness with children.* Parallax Press.

USDA Natural Resources Conservation Service (1996). *Riparian areas environmental uniqueness, functions, and values.* Retrieved July 6, 2021 from https://www.nrcs.usda.gov/wps/portal/nrcs/detail/national/technical/?cid=nrcs143_014199

van der Vegt, G. S., Essens, P., Wahlstrom, M., & George, G. (2015). Managing risk and resilience. *Academy of Management Journal, 58* (4), 971–980. 10.5465/amj.2015.4004

Walker, B., Gunderson, L., Kinzig, A., Folke, C., Carpenter, S., & Schultz, L. (2006). A handful of heuristics and some propositions for understanding resilience in social-ecological systems. *Ecology and Society 11*(1): 13.

## Author Bios

**Alexis Chamow**, PCC, MFA is the founder and president of A of All Arts, Inc. Alexis facilitates live and virtual leadership and communication programs for executives, artists, entrepreneurs, and teams in transition. A of All Arts, Inc. engages individuals and groups in a range of coaching opportunities, and hosts customized workshops across industries within organizations like NBC-Universal (media-entertainment), Cal State University Northridge (education), Ogilvy & Mather (PR), Genentech (bio-tech), Microsoft (tech), and Geffen Playhouse (performing arts) among many others. She is also a Senior Director with Stand & Deliver, an international consultancy based in the Bay area that focuses on high performance communication for teams. Alexis holds an MFA in theatre from University of Texas, Austin, a coaching credential from the Center for Non-Profit Management in Los Angeles, and has completed Goldvarg Consulting's Supervision Training Program. She is an accredited PCC through the International Coaching Federation. With a background in Performance, Education, and Group Facilitation, she has crafted a unique methodology for building authenticity and connection in some of the most seemingly inauthentic circumstances. Alexis supports clients as they tap into their full communication and leadership potential, and is a staunch advocate of curiosity, discovery, and joy.

**Sarah Evans**, Ph.D. (cand), MCC, Dipl. Coaching Supervision is an executive leadership and team coach, facilitator, OD consultant, coaching supervisor, and mentor coach at Evans Leadership Group. Sarah is passionate about working with visionary decision-makers and influencers inspired by the transformative potential of coaching. She is dedicated to supporting individuals, teams, and organizations lead and thrive in complexity. Her goal is to maximize human capacity, organizational capabilities, and contributions to societal well-being. Her key working themes are relationships, resilience, results. Sarah is a Ph.D. Candidate in Human and Organizational Systems where her research focused on meaning making and leadership resilience during organizational change. She holds Master's degrees in Human and Organizational Systems; Leadership; and Counselling, as well as multiple certifications. Sarah is a coach educator at Royal Roads University's graduate certificate program in executive coaching. She is a member of the International Coach Federation, where she holds a Master Certified Coach (MCC) credential.

# 10 Internal Coaching Supervision: Insights into Two US Based Cases and Perspectives

*Jerry L. Browning, Theodora Fitzsimmons, and Jackie Arnold*

## Introduction

In this chapter, we explore how two organizations in the United States (US), one private and one public, came to introduce coaching supervision into their internal coaching programs. Jerry Browning and Theodora Fitzsimmons provide our accounts of how the need for supervision was identified, promoted, and developed in each of the organizations and the challenges that we addressed along the way. Author and Coaching Supervisor Jackie Arnold of the United Kingdom (UK), provides feedback and insights relative to the journey of bringing coaching supervision into organizations.

The cases discussed here are neither intended to be representative of private or public organizations in general, nor a comparison between public and private organizations. Rather, the two internal coaching initiatives are compared to see how coaching supervision was brought into organizations. Considering how each organization developed internal coaching initiatives was important as it informed how and where the eventual coaching supervision would be needed and introduced. What were the challenges, experiences, and conclusions?

It is our hope that our reflections and perspectives will provide important information for practitioners, while benefiting individual coaches, anyone involved in internal coaching, organizational stakeholders, and professional coaching associations considering internal coaching supervision.

## Coaching Supervision Journeys

### US Case 1: A Private Sector Organization (Jerry Browning)

Case 1 is about a private sector, Fortune 100 company in which executives who had been exposed to professional coaching wanted to build an internal coaching program to create a coaching culture in the organization that would foster leader development and performance. The approach was to embed closely knit coaching relationships within work groups. The internal

DOI: 10.4324/b23130-13

coaching program was governed by the Coaching Strategy Team (CST) who were experienced, credentialed coaches, and part of a leader development group. In 2010, I (Jerry Browning) joined the CST. As a CST member, I served as a full time coaching faculty member and was responsible for creating and delivering accredited coach training and ongoing internal coaching activities of the program.

Thirty high-level business executives comprised the inaugural cadre and they championed the internal coaching program and encouraged all managers in their business lines to participate and become leader coaches. Coaching cascaded throughout the organization with trained leader coaches conducting monthly individual coaching sessions with each of their direct reports in meetings separate from regular work meetings. Coaching became an additional performance expectation for the leader coaches, who had other full-time responsibilities. See Figure 10.1.

The internally created coach training program received accreditation by a professional coaching association, which also provided a path for the leader coaches to attain individual coaching certification credentials. Within seven years, over 300 leaders completed the robust training and coaching practice hour requirements and attained coach certifications.

In addition to coach training, the CST developed four areas of ongoing support for trained leader coaches that focused on continued professional development and education for certifications:

1   Ongoing, monthly individual coaching with a CST member.
2   Leader coaches shared coaching best practices in monthly groups facilitated by CST members.
3   CST members travelled to work settings and provided in-person oversight in tripartite settings. They observed the leader coach coaching their direct report and provided feedback in a private debrief meeting afterward.

CASE 1
Private Organization
Coaching Structure

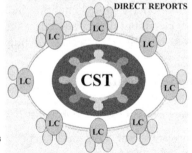

CST - Coaching Strategy Team
LC – Leader Coaches
•   **CST** members coach **LC**
•   **LC** coach **Direct Reports**
Cascading through organization

*Figure 10.1* Case 1 Private Organization Coaching Structure.

CASE 1 Private Organization Coaching Support System

*Figure 10.2* Case 1 Private Organization Coaching Structure.

4 Advanced development events were held with outside speakers to reinforce learning, foster the internal coaching community, and provide continuing education.

See Figure 10.2.

## Precursors to Coaching Supervision

In the individual coaching and oversight debrief meetings, leader coaches had private discussions with CST members to learn when and how to use specific coaching skills with direct reports. Among leader coaches who had been coaching for years, these meetings shifted away from a focus on coaching skills to challenges of coaching long term and other issues. Comments included:

> *After coaching one of my direct reports, I feel exhausted. I've thought about the differences in our DISC profiles making it difficult for me to coach them, but it seems there is something else going on.*

> *I was drawn into negative thinking when I began work with one of my high-producing teams. I went along with it at the beginning to build rapport, but now I am really uncomfortable, feeling stressed and don't know what to do.*

Like other CST members, my role was to support the leader coaches, but I started to find that the coaching skills in my toolbox were not enough. In fact, I recognized my own compassion fatigue (Mathiew, 2007) as I heard these comments. I asked other CST members if they were struggling with anything similar, and some of them reported being stressed by knowing too much about the organizational workings such as upcoming staff reductions and knowing who would lose their job. Others described getting caught in the emotions of the leaders they coached. And while the CST met regularly for our own continued professional development and to work on aligning coaching to business strategy, these dilemmas were not being brought into the discussions—neither about the leader coaches, nor about ourselves as CST members.

Having worked as a consultant with other maturing internal coaching programs, I had never seen such dilemmas before, possibly because I was never in a place where this amount of coaching was happening. "However, in an organization where internal coaching has been established for a while, internal coaches themselves look for supervision even without knowing what it is exactly that they are looking for" (Moral et al., 2017). While I did not know exactly what was needed, I wanted to learn what others were doing to support maturing internal coaching initiatives.

I transitioned out of the Case 1 company in 2017. No longer an employee, I was retained as an external consultant to continue to help the internal coaching initiative. Through my involvement in different professional coaching associations, I discovered the prevalence of coaching supervision in the UK and Europe. I remembered how supportive professional supervision was when I was a psychotherapist and a consultant in a Gestalt-based firm. After finding the US-based Oxford Brookes University Coaching Supervision program, I eagerly enrolled in the second cohort and learned new ways to help myself and other coaches. I also realized that as coaches, we assume our clients are whole and resourceful (Whitworth et al., 2007). Yet most coaches do not know how to keep themselves whole and resourceful, and that is what coaching supervision provides. Given the unique challenges facing internal coaches around confidentiality, boundaries, conflicts of interest, and dual relationships (Turner, 2018), I felt strongly that coaching supervision was needed to support internal coaches in the Case 1 organization.

## Introducing Coaching Supervision

As I began discussing coaching supervision with the CST, I found that only a fourth of the members had heard of coaching supervision. They all questioned, if they had been doing well without it for years, why would it be needed now? The word "supervision" did not fit the organizational vernacular, so I immediately decided not to use it. Instead, I introduced the CST to coaching supervision as a refining type of advanced coach development that included reflection with a trained partner to explore important professional functions. I discussed how the normative, formative, and restorative functions of supervision help build capacity in individual coaches to better handle challenges of coaching for themselves, those they coach, and the organization (Proctor, 1986).

I informed the CST that part of coaching supervision was seeing themselves as the instrument of coaching and as such, the care of that instrument was essential (Bachkirova, 2016). Experienced coaches were stunned. They had never viewed their coaching work as a practice that included themselves. In a survey I gave to the CST members, they quickly identified why they needed coaching supervision: "As internal coaches, we are insulated. Biases are part of the culture. We are too close, which makes coping with emotions difficult." At this point, I felt like I was finally making some headway in introducing supervision.

## Integrating Coaching Supervision

Training the CST in coaching supervision was important since they would become the hub for it with respect to spreading it to the leader coaches. Since funding was not available for full coaching supervision training, I explored peer coaching supervision as an alternative for the training (Turner et al., 2018). I created an introductory peer coaching supervision training program that was granted continuing education credit for coaching core competencies by the International Coaching Federation (ICF), but nothing specific to coaching supervision was recognized.

The training program presented the foundations of coaching supervision, explored how it differs from coaching and mentoring, introduced models of coaching supervision, and taught participants how to recognize self as instrument (Bachkirova et al., 2011). It promoted shifting mindsets from coach to coaching supervisor (Lucas, 2017). Reflection models (Hay, 2007) were introduced, which was particularly useful for CST members who acknowledged that their fast-paced professional setting did not readily allow time for reflection about their coaching work.

Experiential learning was fostered through fishbowl demonstrations that used real situations to illustrate coaching supervision. Each CST member engaged in supervision with an external supervisor and practiced being both a coaching supervisor and a supervisee (Turner et al., 2018) with one another. A chain format was used for the peer supervision practice so that different pairs of CST members met for each encounter, preventing reciprocal exchanges, and keeping the supervisory engagement fresh each time. Forms were created to guide each CST member in reflection (Homer, 2017) and to write about their experiences.

Posttraining surveys provided an opportunity for CST members to share positive and negative reactions. For the question, "what held me back from coaching supervision," respondents answered: "Time – another thing to do;" "scary to be vulnerable;" and "safety of relational boundaries." For the question, "what drew me to supervision," comments included: "Curiosity," "safe space to clear," and "say to reflect more deeply on my coaching sessions." After the training was complete, the CST found a monthly cadence of peer supervision to be best for members.

Finally, I wanted to help incorporate coaching supervision methods that would ensure confidentiality and psychological safety. By using metaphors (Rooney, 1992) or the "Magic Box" (Seto & Geither, 2018), participants could discuss client situations without divulging any details. Looking back, we (the CST) may not have known how to talk about our coaching challenges in a way that protected the anonymity of those involved. This may be the reason these conversations were not brought into our regular CST meetings. With some coaching supervision experience, skills, and methods of maintaining confidentiality, I hoped the CST would grow through these experiences to eventually offer this kind of support to leader coaches.

## Sustaining Coaching Supervision

Continued exploration of available options was necessary to integrate coaching supervisory experiences throughout the internal coaching community of this organization. See Figure 10.3.

While the CST continued to use peer coaching supervision to support one another, I recommended the group obtain funding for external supervisors and full coaching supervision training. The CST could use action learning (Marquardt et al., 2009) in the existing group coaching meetings to expand the knowledge of leader coaches while conducting group coaching supervisory experiences referred to as "advanced development" to further expand capabilities. Combining the existing oversight debriefs with individual coaching would be a perfect fit for leader coaches needing private coaching supervision. This would provide leader coaches the support needed to learn and develop methods for sustaining themselves as whole and resourceful coaches helping many in the organization.

### US Case 2: A Public Sector Organization (Theodora Fitzsimmons)

In Case 2, I (Theodora Fitzsimmons) established an internal coaching program in 2016 to develop leaders and build their skills for service in a

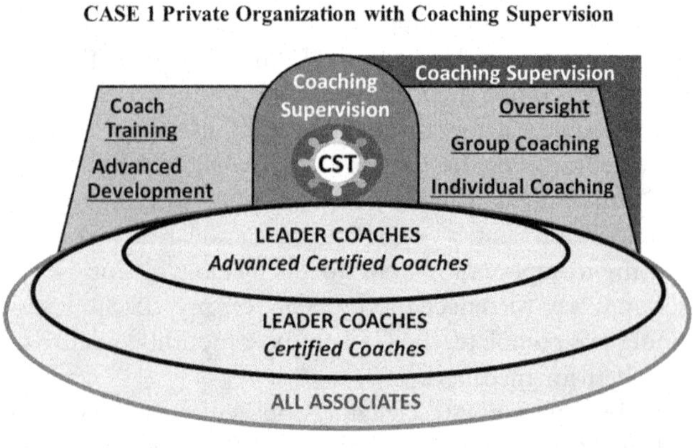

*Figure 10.3* Case 1 Private Organization Coaching Support System.

CASE 2
Public Organization
Coaching Structure

INTERNAL COACHES
*  **Formally** coach outside
   chain of command, across
   organization
*  **Informally** coach inside
   chain of command

*Figure 10.4* Case 2 Public Organization Coaching Ecosystem.

public organization. I had previously managed the external coaching contracts for those in the organization's leadership. Partnering with a senior champion in the organization, I created the path for internal coaching, marshalling resources, and garnering interest in the program throughout the organization.

I aimed to architect as much safety as possible in the internal coaching program, so the coaching could occur with a high level of confidentiality. Any employee could have formal coaching with an internal coach outside their immediate organization. I also intended to grow the program so that internal coaches would informally coach inside chains of command, bringing a coaching style of work into their activities. See Figure 10.4.

This organization historically utilized external coaches to support the learning and development of senior leaders participating in leadership training. An opportunity to test an internal coaching approach occurred in 2014 when a grant was awarded to train 22 volunteer senior executives to become Certified Professional Coaches (CPCs). The volunteers became the first internal coaches of the organization and external coaches were no longer used. In addition to full-time work responsibilities, the CPCs provided coaching to other leaders who participated in the leadership programs. In 2016, this successful first cohort led to formal investment in a multi-year contract to train up to 500 internal coaches. Again, these potential coaches would apply for training from every part of the organization and provide coaching as their time permitted. They were not required to become ICF accredited, but they were required to perform no less than 24 hours of coaching per year and to attend three Community of Practice (CoP) learning events. Subsequently, coaching had become a universal benefit for all employees in the 17,000-person organization. Additionally, the program was recognized and received the ICF Prism Award (2019) and the Association for Talent Development's Excellence in Practice Award (2018).

I established a tiered approach to provide ongoing support to coaches by delivering training in coaching topics through CoP bimonthly events. The

**CASE 2.**
**Public Organization**

**Coaching**
**Ecosystem**

*Figure 10.5* Case 2 Public Organization with Coaching Supervision

topics included ethics in coaching, advanced core competencies, and special topics. Industry experts were utilized as budget permitted to offer new concepts and perspectives. I maintained ICF Continuing Coach Education (CCE) Certification for the internal programs to enable coach trainees to receive CCE units for the internal programs they attended. An ecosystem organically emerged generating opportunity for continued growth and learning for the coaches and was further strengthened by the introduction of mentor coaches. Figure 10.5 shows the supportive ecosystem of the coaching program.

## Precursors to Coaching Supervision

From the beginning, I set myself and my comanager as points of contact for any ethical dilemmas the coaches encountered. Occasionally, coaches reached out to us to ask for guidance on how to best handle specific situations.

**Example 1:** "My coaching client is a terrible boss. I know that coaching is supposed to be confidential, but I feel a responsibility to the employees who suffer at the hand of this supervisor. What should I do?"

**Example 2:** "I had my first case of a potential suicide. I remember you taught us that we should seek help. Fortunately, there was someone in the Employee Assistance Program that day and I was able to escort the person to the psychologist."

**Example 3:** "I wonder how to handle someone who seems to need therapy? I think I can help her even though I am not a therapist. How do I know what to do?"

Scenarios like these helped me recognize that the coaches faced dilemmas with confidentiality, boundaries, and ethical issues that were unique to internal coaches. I wondered what was happening in cases in which they were not reaching out (Clutterbuck et al., 2016). Early on, I engaged resources within the organization to acquaint internal coaches with other services available to employees, such as psychologists, equal employment opportunity specialists, Human Resources professionals, legal professionals, and others. As each of these representatives presented to the coaches about their roles in the organization, they also spoke to the question: "What happens when it is not coaching, but it is 'x'?" These representatives became resources for the coaches who gained more insight on coaching boundaries. Yet, I was not sure if the coaches were utilizing these resources.

My passion for quality coaching impelled me to keep seeking resources. I researched what regulating bodies defined as important for sustaining an internal coaching program. It was then that I discovered coaching supervision. I garnered funding for training by talking about how integrating coaching supervision would help ensure safety for all concerned: The client, the coach, and the organization (see examples below). Safety in this context is related to the normative function of supervision (Hawkins & Smith, 2013) where there needs to be a focus on ethical behavior and boundaries inside an organization. When an internal coach has a dual role (see Example 2 above), there is an increased possibility of unethical behavior, stemming from bias and collusion. Examples of safety-related concerns within an internal coaching program are described below.

Safety for the Client: An internal coach who coaches 1–3 clients at a time is not going to evolve in their expertise as quickly as a coach who is dedicated full time to coaching. The client may be subject to poor coaching.

Safety for the Coach: For the same reasons as stated, the coach may be in danger of collusion or bias. They could also make an error and fall easily into mentoring or giving advice. If the coach is violating an ethical boundary, the coach could get into trouble.

Safety for the Organization: As coaches get into trouble, the organization can also be held liable.

Safety for the Profession Itself: If there are increasing ethical violations and lawsuits against coaches, it could damage the reputation of coaches in general.

I and my comanager completed training at the Coaching Supervision Academy in the US in 2019. The completion of this program opened my eyes about the need for coaching supervision in the organization. The content of this program was extremely relevant to coaching and changed my coaching practice forever. All the theories learned in supervision were directly applicable to coaching relationships, as well. Upon completing the training, I was even more committed to bringing coaching supervision into the lives and practices of the coaching cadre of the organization.

## Introducing Coaching Supervision

Socializing coaching supervision in the organization was difficult because in the organization the word "supervision" only denoted a "boss." I found there was an unnecessary resistance to the practice because of the word alone. However, I persevered and formed coaching supervision groups and did supervision one-on-one with those who were interested. While there was initial awkwardness and uncertainty among coaches about what to expect, supervision participants reported they gained value from these experiences.

I continued to promote the need for coaching supervision through webinars in which I provided demonstrations of supervision and had coaches share their experiences. Just as the internal coaching had grown organically, I wanted to provide experiential learning to make the need for supervision real for the internal coaches. I provided interviews with coaching supervision experts Peter Hawkins and Sam Magill that were shared and followed by discussions. I also conducted 90-minute CoP events where I introduced coaching supervision and demonstrated it to the participants one-on-one and through fishbowl demonstrations. Over time, I expanded the ecosystem of support for coaches with the inclusion of supervision. See Figure 10.6.

## Integrating Coaching Supervision

I held more groups as the demand increased. Small supervision groups were limited to three participants plus the coach supervisor. In the earliest sessions, participants seemed uncertain about supervision and what it entailed. They often mentioned that they had expected more coach mentoring and skill building. In a parallel phenomenon (Cochrane & Newton, 2018), I was less confident about the supervision in these early group sessions. As the supervisors became more experienced, the participants seemed to trust

*Figure 10.6* Case 2 Public Organization Coaching Ecosystem with Supervision.

supervision and anticipated the insights they would be gaining. Not surprisingly, a third round of coach groups came to supervision with a better understanding of what the experience would provide them and their evolution as coaches.

I utilized methods to help maintain confidentiality that included drawing and image cards. Additionally, under group supervision usually only one case is discussed at a time. This structure enabled other supervisees (those not sharing a case) to gain important insights without divulging information about a case they may be thinking about, as well.

## Sustaining Coaching Supervision

The work has just begun. For this organization to benefit from coaching supervision, there needs to be more of it available. I and my colleague cannot offer coaching supervision to 500 coaches. Before creating a supervision training opportunity, the organization will need to update their organizational policies to require supervision for internal coaches. Ensuring coaches follow the policy will be challenging since the requirement will be new and they have been coaching without it for quite a while.

Going forward, we face several challenges in sustaining coaching supervision. Not having an executive level champion advocating supervision (as I had had for coaching), makes it difficult to convince coaches and stakeholders of the value. In addition, there is nothing presented in the US-based coach training program about coaching supervision, and the Professional Certified Coach instructors were not, themselves, recipients of coaching supervision. Further, ICF does not emphasize coaching supervision as a *necessity* for coaches. Such conditions weaken the case for establishing coaching supervision in organizations.

At present, I'm challenged with identifying the best course of action for promoting coaching supervision. I have been encouraging more advanced coaches to consider becoming coaching supervisors on their own. I have plans to provide training in peer supervision (Turner et al., 2018), reflective practice (Reynolds, 2020; Patterson, 2019), and action learning (Marquardt et al., 2009). I have begun to lay the foundation and grow support for integrating coaching supervision as a policy requirement for coaches' continued development. As such, it will also be introduced in the initial coach training program.

## Comparing the US Cases

Although we (Jerry and Theodora) had never met or heard of one another's cases until writing this chapter, we found many parallels in our journeys. In Case 1, the internal coaching model was to train leaders to coach their direct reports. In Case 2, individual employees became certified coaches available to coach anyone in the organization. A by-product we observed in both cases was how coaches changed as leaders. Beyond these fundamental differences, we identified many similarities, which led to the eventual introduction of coaching supervision in our organizations.

We both found that adhering to coaching industry standards was important for quality. We ensured that the coach training programs were accredited by a professional coaching organization through which coach trainees could also attain individual professional coaching certification credentials. While care was taken to meet core competencies and ethics set out by professional coaching associations, we knew nothing about coaching supervision at the start. Neither of us had experienced coaching supervision during coach training in the US. We established our respective programs with a focus on quality, but with no knowledge about how coaching supervision would support quality. Each internal program was considered successful by many standards. The Case 1 organization was meeting the needs of the business and building a strong coaching culture. The Case 2 organization was internationally recognized for its success. Yet, amidst this success, we both recognized that the coaches faced dilemmas with confidentiality, boundaries, and ethical issues. We did not know quite what to do about it, until we figured out on our own that coaching supervision was needed.

We both went through the process of becoming coaching supervisors and encountered similar challenges in introducing coaching supervision into our organizations. The term "supervision" was regarded negatively, and coaching supervision was largely unknown. This reminded us of earlier periods when coaching was unknown: We needed to explain what it was, why it was beneficial, and hold onto the value we knew it had amidst resistance. Discovering ways to educate our internal coaches about coaching supervision while providing direct experiences, gradually increased interest. Over time, we also witnessed coaching supervision having an impact as coaches gained more insight about themselves and their coaching work.

From our respective organizations, amidst a lack of awareness about the practice of coaching supervision, we were challenged to convince our organizations that funding needed to be applied to the training of more coaching supervisors. It was hard to garner alliances when even coach training programs failed to promote or require coaching supervision. As a result, both coaches and their organizations were unaware of its value. As part of that system, we were also unaware until we took the personal initiative to learn more about it. As we pondered this US phenomenon, we wondered about the early days of coaching supervision in the UK and Europe, and looked to our expert co-author for insights.

## An Experienced European Perspective (Jackie Arnold)

As I (Jackie Arnold) read these US cases, I was reminded of my own journey into coaching supervision in the UK. In 2002, my global coaching business was expanding, and the needs of my clients were becoming ever more challenging. I was looking for support for the new challenges I faced and I decided to research coaching supervision. There was little to draw on as what I found was mostly clinical supervision and I felt I needed a different kind of support. I wanted to explore my coaching approach and learn what patterns I was repeating and if I was working ethically.

I had joined a large European private company as an executive coach and was feeling under-resourced by the diverse challenges being raised in the internal leadership program and the one-to-one coaching sessions. This company was facing great competition. The deadlines and resulting stress were having a considerable impact on my coaching clients, many who had to relocate from Spain, Germany, and the UK to France. This naturally brought further challenges. I eventually found and hired an experienced coach and coaching supervisor.

During this time, I had also met Edna Murdoch and Miriam Orriss through the Coaching Supervision Academy (CSA) where I enrolled in their first cohort for the CSA Diploma in Coaching Supervision in 2007. Just as it was for Jerry and Theodora, the coaching supervision training was life changing for me as a coach. It enhanced my coaching behaviors, added to, and expanded my knowledge, and provided the space for deep insights and reflection. I am delighted to see coaching supervision expanding to the US and to learn of the cases brought by Jerry and Theodora.

I noticed in both US cases, a natural inclination to set the coaches up for success emerged and led to some creative and logical internal coach support systems. When introducing coaching supervision, it had been important to consider budgets, time constraints, and the agility of the system. It was vitally important to listen to the needs of the organization to adapt while also challenge thinking where appropriate. Both cases explored what specific outcomes were required, the selection process for training, and how robust the program needed to be to ensure success.

There has also been a strong need for coaching supervision in organizations where I have worked or consulted. Internal coaches were experiencing ethical dilemmas and coming up against emotional and psychological issues they were not able to handle. Just as in the cases discussed here, I encountered coaches with dual roles that brought up conflicts of interest, split loyalty, ethical issues, problem solving, and confidentiality. I also remembered that introducing coaching supervision was difficult because some organization members had the perception of supervision as being an "over the shoulder" process and had negative experiences of supervision in the workplace. I began calling it continuous professional development and super-vision to distinguish it from clinical supervision. Also, the hyphenation helped illustrate the multiple perspectives coaches and their supervisors practice in reviewing coaching situations.

I found it important to build nonjudgmental, reflective relationships between both coaching supervisors and internal coaches in supervision. These relationships supported coaches in thinking about themselves as part of the client-coach system and the ways in which they were meeting the needs of their staff, their teams, and their impact on the organization. The coaches in regular supervision, therefore, ensured that ethical standards and quality were maintained throughout the process. The resulting supervision sessions provided deeper insights for coaches that, in turn fostered greater leadership competence, emotional intelligence, and self-awareness among coach clients in the organization.

Just as in Jerry's and Theodora's cases, I also found the need to integrate supervision in nontraditional ways. Depending on budget and coach experience, I have used peer supervision circles and triads for performance coaches. For full time internal coaches, I found the small groups format, led by a qualified external supervisor, to be the most effective.

However, I caution that an internal coaching supervisor, regardless of the experience level and where they may be, will always be part of the same system. Thus, there will be the danger of unconscious bias, collusion, and parallel process. In my view, there is a benefit to providing coaching supervision using external coaching supervisors.

In my experience it is the primary purpose of coaching supervision in any organization to rise above the system and ensure that the emotional, psychological, physical, and business needs of the coach or leader are met in the most professional, safe, and appropriate manner.

## Reflections, Key Findings, and Recommendations

### Reflections

As we reflected together and discussed our individual experiences, we realized that early on we each were unconsciously incompetent (Broadwell, 1969) with respect to coaching supervision. Particularly in the Americas, the only intentional space for a coach to engage with someone for support has been with a mentor coach who focuses on coaching competency skills. We believe many coaches are just like we were: Continuing to carry burdens from coaching, possibly without realizing it, and having no idea where to go for other support.

However, by exploring support for coaches in our professional coaching organizations, we found that many experienced coaches were providing mentoring for other coaches that was well beyond the focus of coaching skills and blurs significantly into a type of coaching supervision. While these efforts support coaches in organizations by exploring how their work impacts them coach as an individual, this level of "mentoring" is often done without coaching supervision training and no proper framework or clear approaches for conducting that kind of support. Just as professional coaching requires specific training, so does coaching supervision.

In discussions with other members of coaching supervision organizations, we found that some trained coaching supervisors in the US are blending coaching supervisory experiences into mentoring work with coaches to provide support that is needed, but still largely unknown. However, while we are all on a continuum of coaching supervision awareness and integration, it is essential to help coaches differentiate between coach mentoring and coaching supervision so that coaches can understand their needs and find the right support.

We feel both excitement as coaching supervision is becoming more available and frustration because it is not yet well known. We're again reminded of a time when coaching was unknown and how our perseverance was important to helping others. Today, perseverance is needed for coaching supervision to become understood and experienced.

### Key Findings

In bringing coaching supervision to internal coaches, we found the following:

- Engaging in training of various lengths to learn about coaching supervision helped internal coaches have a wider and deeper perspective for how and when to utilize it.
- The value of coaching supervision was better understood when it was experienced.
- For internal coaching programs already up and running, it was helpful to piggyback on existing internal coach support initiatives in the organization to introduce coaching supervision.
- Group coaching supervision that included clear contracting and the use of simple abstract practices such as the use of metaphors, art, small objects, and card activities provided the psychological safe space to process without breaking confidentiality.
- While supervision from a fully trained coaching supervision is highly recommended, organizations with limited fundin used peer coaching, group supervision with action learning, and live demonstrations to integrate the needed support through existing resources.

### Recommendations

The comparisons and insights that came from discussions between the three authors gave us inspiration and new ideas to apply going forward in our own work. We make the following recommendations for others considering coaching supervision for internal coaches. These include:

- Build coaching supervision into internal coaching programs right from the beginning.
- Inform constituents of the necessity of providing coach support through coaching supervision; this benefits culture, associates, and the business.

• Share with leaders how coaching supervisory experiences can broaden their perspectives to better identify individual and organizational needs and impacts.

Awareness of coaching supervision is increasing, but it remains more unknown in the US. According to the Global Coaching Supervision Report of 2020, 57% of coaches in Europe and Africa use coaching supervision while only 20% in the Americas do (McAnally et al., 2020). While we understand that awareness of coaching supervision is still growing in the US, as stewards of coaching, we believe that bringing coaching supervision into US organizations is paramount. More than other coaching settings, it is vital for internal coaches to have ongoing support in dealing with boundaries, confidentiality, and safety. Coaching supervision provides that insight and support.

Coaching supervision also has the power to reveal blind spots, unknown biases, gaps in knowledge, and new ways of being as a coach. It boosts confidence, resilience, and the skills to coach up and across departments. Coaching supervision also encourages greater relational behaviors in leaders such as empathy and compassion that are vital today (Arnold and Patterson, 2021). With the challenges that internal coaches experience and the need to embrace diversity at work, we agree that it is imperative every internal coach receives regular coaching supervision to sustain their capability and capacity.

The professional coaching associations in the Americas are guideposts to more than core competencies, ethics, and accreditation; they help shape the coaching profession. Our hope is that they will require equal emphasis on coaching supervision. Full coaching supervision training is now more available in North America and the US, making it more feasible to attain. More case studies, articles, research, and books on coaching supervision are needed from the Americas. While we are grateful to colleagues in Europe and the UK paving the way for coaching supervision. For too long we have relied on evidence from other parts of the world to influence our evolving coaching standards. We must also provide our own experience in the Americas so that all involved in internal coaching will grasp the value of coaching supervision to strengthen internal coaches, expand coaching cultures, and help sustain the organizations they support.

## References

Arnold, J., & Patterson, E. (2020). *Tomorrow's global leaders today: Executive reflection: working wisely in turbulent times.* Ingram Spark.

Bachkirova, T., Jackson, P., & Clutterback, D. (2011). *Coaching and mentoring supervision: Theory and practice.* Open University Press.

Bachkirova, T. (2016). The self of the coach: Conceptualization, issues, and opportunities for practitioner development. *Consulting Psychology Journal: Practice and Research, 68*(2): 143–156.

Broadwell, Martin M. (1969). Teaching for learning (XVI). *The Gospel Guardian*, *20*(41). Retrieved January 1, 2022. https://www.wordsfitlyspoken.org/gospel_guardian/v20/v20n41p1-3a.html

Clutterbuck, D., Whitaker, C., & Lucas, M. (2016). *Coaching supervision: A practical guide for supervisees.* Routledge.

Cochrane, H., & Newton, T. (2018). *Supervision and coaching: Growth and learning in professional practice.* Routledge.

Excellence in Practice Award—Association for Talent Development (May 20, 2019). Retrieved January 1, 2022. https://www.td.org/press-release/atd-recognizes-excellence-in-talent-development

Hawkins, P., & Smith, N. (2013). *Coaching, mentoring and organizational consultancy: Supervision, skills & development.* Open University Press, McGraw-Hill.

Hawkins, P., & Sohet, R. (2007). *Supervision in the helping professions.* McGraw-Hill.

Hay, J. (2007). *Reflective practice and supervision for coaches.* Open University Press, McGraw-Hill.

Homer, A. (2017). How executive coaches see value arising from peer group supervision. *International Journal of Evidence Based Coaching andMentoring*, *S11*: 101–110. https://radar.brookes.ac.uk/radar/items/9196d96e-efce-4f42-9c73-2fe56de57387/1/

Lucas, M. (2017). From coach to coach supervisor – A shift in mind-set. *International Journal of Evidence Based Coaching and Mentoring*, *15*(1), 11–23. https://radar.brookes.ac.uk/radar/items/545bafc8-58cb-4604-83a0-a70d13296373/1/

Marquardt, M., Skipton, L., Freedman, A., & Hill, C. (2009). *Action leaning for developing leaders and organizations.* American Psychological Association.

Mathiew, F. (2007). Running on empty: Compassion fatigue in health professionals. *Rehab & Community Care Medicine*, Spring, 2. https://compassionfatigue.org/pages/RunningOnEmpty.pdf

McAnnally, K., Abrams, L., Asmus, J., & Hildebradt, T. (2020b). *Global coaching supervision: A study of perceptions and practices around the world.* https://coachingsupervisionresearch.org/wp-content/uploads/2020/02/Global_Coaching_Supervision_Report_FINAL.pdf

Moral, M., Guerand, A., Desroches, J., Reveneau, C., Levey, M., Raynal Benoit, O., & Muh, E. (2017). *How to best organise supervision in a "strong coaching culture" environment?* [Conference session]. 23rd International Mentoring and Coaching Conference. Edinburg, Scotland. https://www.undici.fr/wp-content/uploads/2017/04/Edimbourg_2017__How_to_best_organise_supervision_in_a_strong_coaching_culture.pdf

Patterson, E. (2019). *Reflect to create! The dance of reflection for creative leadership, professional practice and supervision.* Ingram Spark.

Prism Award—International Coaching Federation. (October 25, 2019). Retrieved January 1, 2022. https://coachingfederation.org/app/uploads/2020/04/PrismCaseStudy_DIA.pdf

Proctor, B. (1986). Supervision: A co-operative exercise in accountability. In A. Marken, & M. Payne (Eds.), *Enabling and ensuring: Supervision in practice.* Leicester National Youth Bureau and Council for Education and Training in Youth and Community Work.

Reynolds, M. (2020). *Coach the person, not the problem: A guide to using reflective inquiry.* Berrett-Koehler Inc.

Rooney, E. (1992). *Metaphors for metamorphosis.* L.E.A.D. Consultants, Inc.

Seto, L., & Geither, T. (2018). Reflections from the field: Metaphor magic in coaching and coaching supervision. *International Journal of Evidence Based Coaching and Mentoring*, *16*(2): 99–111. 10.24384/000562

Turner, T., Lucas, M., & Whitaker, C. (2018). *Peer supervision in coaching and mentoring: A versatile guide for reflective practice.* Routledge.

Whitworth, L., Kimsey-House, K., Kimsey-House, H., & Sandahl, P. (2007). *Co-Active coaching: New skills for coaching people toward success in work and life.* (2nd ed.) Davies Black.

## Author Bios

**Jerry Lee Browning**, MS, CBC, trained in coaching supervision at Oxford Brookes University US 2nd cohort in 2018. Prior to establishing Chiron Company for organizational and individual development in 2003, Jerry managed development initiatives around the globe for L.E.A.D. Consultants, Inc., was senior consultant at Business of People, and had worked in finance, healthcare, and manufacturing. She helped build internal coaching in four organizations and provides consultancy on internal coaching from creation to sustainability. She is active in the Americas Coaching Supervision Network, Association for Coaching, Association of Coaching Supervisors, and other professional associations. Her MS in Community Counseling is from the University of Dayton, her BSC in Organizational Communication is from Ohio University. Jerry trained in psychotherapy, NLP, Constellations, MBSR, team & systemic Coaching, and other approaches. Her newest program, *Refine Peer Coaching Supervision,* is approved by ICF for CCEs. Jerry resides in Columbus, Ohio. Email: jbrowning@chironcompany.net www.chironcompany.net

**Theodora Fitzsimmons**, Ph.D., PCC, trained in coaching supervision in the 4th cohort of the Coach Supervision Academy US in 2018. Her original training in coaching was with iPEC in 2012, with additional training and certifications from Success Unlimited Network, ACT Leadership's Leadership and Performance Coach Certification Program, and Brain-Based Coaching with the Neuroleadership Institute. She serves on the Governance Board of the Federal Internal Coach Training Program and is faculty and lead trainer to the coach mentors. She manages an award-winning internal coaching program at a Department of Defense Agency in Washington, D.C. where she also maintains a CCE program for the continuing education of coaches and serves as coach mentor and coaching supervisor to these coaches. She earned her Ph.D. from Capella University in Training and Performance Improvement in 2007. In her private business, Coach Evolving, LLC she offers coaching, mentor coaching, coaching supervision, and coach training. Theodora resides in Rockville, MD. Phone: (301)602-5769. Email: theofitz@coachevolving.com

**Jackie Arnold** is an accredited ICF Executive Coach (2001) and Dip CSA Coach Supervisor (2007). She holds an RSA Dip Ed from Guildhall University and is a lecturer and an Associate for Advance HE. She runs her own coaching and supervision company "Coach4Executives" introducing 1-2-1 and group coaching and supervision programs into universities and several private companies across Europe. She holds group supervision in banking, IT, media, retail, and NHS for full-time international coaches sharing of best practice and CPD. Jackie is cofounder of The Association of Coaching Supervisors (www.associationofcoachingsupervisors.com). She contributed to *The full spectrum supervision*, co-edited with Edna Murdoch. She is the author of *Coaching skills for leaders in the workplace* (2015) and *Coaching supervision at its BEST* (2016). In 2020, she co-authored *Tomorrow's global leaders today: Working wisely in turbulent times*, based on the Executive Reflection Action Research Project with Elaine Patterson, CSA Faculty. Jackie resides in Dorset, UK. Email: jackie@coach4executives.com www.coach4executives.com

# 11 The Magic of Group Supervision

*Lynn Harrison and Martine Bizouard*

## Introduction

Given the plethora of workshops, certification programs, webinars, videos, books, blog writings, and journal articles about coaching, why would an experienced coach in the Americas want to invest in supervision? This question was fundamental to the exploratory study we conducted with coaches located in North and South America. Using a phenomenological method of inquiry, our research team conducted in-depth interviews with seasoned practitioners who had participated in supervision a minimum of six months. We wanted to understand how they perceived their learning experience, including the kind of shifts that occurred and the impact on their client work.

Supervision, from the broadest perspective, can be described as a reflective practice aimed at helping practitioners improve their work with clients and client organizations. It can take various forms, including self-reflection, meeting one-on-one with a supervisor, or participating in a group. In this study, we focused on the experience of learning in supervision groups. Coaching can be a rather solitary profession where most of the day is spent with clients and client systems, allowing little opportunity for consultation with colleagues. In group supervision, practitioners bring cases to experienced colleagues, who also bring their own coaching issues and dilemmas. With the guidance of a qualified supervisor, the group takes a structured approach, looking at situations from all different angles. This kind of collaborative, formalized learning process can be a bit daunting, as sharing becomes a more public activity; however, it also offers the potential of tapping into a larger pool of reactions, knowledge, interpretation, and experience.

The coaches in our study were from a variety of backgrounds. The common factors were that they were all certified external coaches with established practices. Although coaching supervision as a form of continuous professional development has been shown to be beneficial to coaches at all levels (Cochrane & Newton, 2018; Lawrence & Whyte, 2014; Tkach & DiGirolamo, 2017), we were particularly interested in the

DOI: 10.4324/b23130-14

perceptions of practitioners who have been coaching for several years. As Cavanagh et al. (2016) noted, supervisees have different needs at different stages of practice development. We wanted to explore the learning experience in group supervision for coaches who were no longer novices.

To ground our study in the existing literature, we drew on three main areas of research: (a) coaching supervision studies; (b) adult learning theory; and (c) group dynamics literature. Interestingly, there has not been much research regarding coaching supervision and even less that is specific to group supervision (Bachkirova et al., 2020; Tkach & DiGirolamo, 2017). Supervision in the coaching field only came to the fore in the early 2000s, when the first book on the subject was published and the first training for coaching supervisors was offered (Hawkins & Smith, 2006). Research to date has primarily been quantitative, with limited insight into the lived experience of participants. For this reason, we chose a phenomenological design, a methodology that uses in–depth interviews and observation to first probe into the thoughts, emotions, and perceptions of the individuals involved and then illuminate the common elements of the experience.

## Study Background

Although supervision has been widely used by the coaching profession in Europe and other parts of the world, it has not had the same history in the Americas (Grant, 2012; McAnally et al., 2020; Hawkins & Turner, 2017). Part of the problem, it has been argued, is that the term "supervision" does not have a positive meaning, particularly in North America. Coaches tend to associate it with oversight or critical assessment by a superior, not an opportunity for transformative growth and revitalization (McLean, 2019). Another factor may be that the hourly rate for supervision in the Americas is substantially higher than in other places (McAnally et al., 2020). In addition, it appears that many of the coaches who have had supervision tend to see it as part of certification training, and something no longer necessary after graduation from the program (McAnally et al., 2020). Similarly, depending on what they experienced in coach training, some practitioners may conflate supervision and mentoring.

Another reason given for the lack of widespread participation in coaching supervision in the Americas is that it is generally not required by employers or the governing bodies of coaching in that part of the world. Although there are differences of opinion about the value of mandating supervision (Bachkirova et al., 2011; Hodge, 2016; Salter, 2008), it is worth noting that the European Mentoring and Coaching Council (EMCC) and Association for Coaching (AC) require that coaches engage in some form of supervision for accreditation. Meanwhile, the International Coaching Federation (ICF), the governing body to which the majority of coaches in the Americas belong, recognizes coaching supervision as "an important element of a coach's professional development" (ICF, 2020), but has not made it a requirement, as it has with mentor coaching.

It has been suggested that coaching supervision has more appeal for coaches with counseling psychology backgrounds, and in recent years, an increasing number of therapists have trained to become coaches (Bluckert, 2005; Moyes, 2009). Indeed, like coaching, supervision can trace its roots back to the fields of psychotherapy and social work, where it has long been a requirement (Carroll, 2007). Butwell (2006) has argued, however, that coaching is very different from psychotherapy and so the standards of therapeutic supervision should not be "blithely transposed" to the coaching field (p. 49). De Haan (2011), on the other hand, has pointed out that issues like transference and countertransference, common topics in counseling supervision, can similarly show up in coaching. Along these same lines, Jackson and Bachkirova (2019) asserted that because of the complexity and "personal connection at the heart of coaching" (p. 21), coaches need to engage in the formalized reflexivity that supervision offers. In their view, it is essential that practitioners understand themselves, clarify their values, and develop their principles to build a practice congruent with who they are.

Over the decades, numerous models of supervision have been presented. Early informal frameworks, rooted in psychodynamics, were followed in the 1950s by more didactic models focused on skill development. In the 1970s, developmental approaches emerged with greater attention to social roles. One of the best known is the Hawkins and Shohet (1989) model, which evolved into the "seven-eyed model" (Hawkins & Schwenk, 2011). Since then, this and other conceptualizations have been adapted to reflect the concerns of the coaching field, including a focus on the systems surrounding the coach, client, organization, and supervisory relationship. The full spectrum model (2013), for example, proposes a multidisciplinary framework that, in addition to systemic thinking, draws on adult learning theory, the art of reflection, mindfulness, relational psychology, neuroscience, and other disciplines (Lewis, 2013).

Over time, various labels for the primary uses of supervision have been put forth by researchers. One of the most popular frameworks is that of Hawkins and Smith (2006), which identified three main functions of coaching supervision: (a) qualitative (providing quality control in working ethically with people); (b) developmental (building skills, understanding, and capabilities); and (c) resourcing (giving emotional support). Moral and Angel (2019) have proposed that the developmental function be further divided into *resolution*, (analysis and problem solving), and *elevation*, (self-reflection and the discussion of meaning, values, and vision). Armstrong and Geddes (2009) have questioned the validity of the qualitative area in an industry where supervisors have no formal responsibility for the ability of the supervisees. More recently, Hawkins et al. (2019) have pointed to overlaps between the functions. As an example of this, participants in Lawrence's (2019) study of group supervision reported improvements in the quality of their coaching that in turn, enhanced their feelings of confidence, which could be viewed as a form of resourcing.

In addition to models distilling the functions of coaching supervision, several definitions have been developed. As Hawkins et al. (2019) commented in their supervision manifesto, one of the challenges of studying this topic is that there is no universally accepted definition. Common to most descriptions is that it is a confidential, reflective, and collaborative process. The EMCC (2018), one of the few organizations to identify supervision competencies, put forward this definition:

> Supervision is the interaction that occurs when a mentor or coach brings their coaching or mentoring work experiences to a supervisor in order to be supported and to engage in reflective dialogue and collaborative learning for the development and benefit of the mentor or coach, their clients, and their organizations.

As this suggests, coaching supervision aims not only to support the professional growth and well-being of the coach, but to help practitioners better serve their clients and client organizations. In its definition of supervision, AC (2019) emphasized that it is not a policing role, but rather a trusting, collegial relationship in which the practice, process, tasks, and challenges of coaching can be explored. Although supervision involves reflecting on past events, Hawkins and Turner (2017) have emphasized that supervision should be forward-focused, building the coach's capacity for the future.

Several researchers have highlighted the need for coaching practitioners to develop higher-level thinking and self-awareness to meet the challenges of today's increasingly complex world (Burke, 2020; Norwood, 2020). To operate at the level of their clients, who face uncertainty and unprecedented change, coaches need to develop ethical maturity, which includes not just logic and reason, but awareness of their own motivations and emotions (Campone, 2020; Carroll & Shaw, 2013). This calls for a different kind of professional development, one that is integrative (Potter, 2020) and vertical (Kegan, 1982), challenging existing beliefs, inviting nonlinear thinking, and examining the dynamic tension between the head and the heart. As Campone (2020) asserted, "The ability to skillfully engage with a client intersubjectively, to explore somatically, to coach from one's own 'way of being' cannot be cultivated solely through a structured, didactic form of learning" (p. 428).

Coaching supervision, with its experiential focus and emphasis on self-reflection, provides a process for this deeper, transformational learning. De Haan and Regouin (1991) observed, "Supervision is mainly about you as a professional, you as a person doing the things you do professionally" (p. 20). Indeed, it can initially be difficult for coaches to see a practical experience as a personal one as well, and to recognize the connections between themselves and what occurred in the coaching. And yet, if the self is a main instrument in this work, as Bachkirova (2016) has asserted, gaining such insight is a critical part of practitioner development.

Consistent with transformative learning theory, the supervision process begins with a coach describing what Mezirow (2000) called "a disorienting dilemma" (p. 22), a situation where the practitioner is thrown off or is questioning something in their practice. The coach senses that the coaching did not have the kind of effect hoped for but cannot quite understand what has happened, or their own part in things.

The coach's description of a dilemma is then followed by critical reflection on narratives relating to the experience. Taken-for-granted frames of reference are explored through constructive discourse and, potentially, revised. When a holistic approach is taken, participants draw on not just their thoughts, but on their feelings, intuition, somatic responses, and other ways of knowing (Taylor, 2008). This subjective experience helps to build practitioners' metacognitive abilities, their awareness of what is occurring in them and around them, critical to skillful coaching with clients (Potter, 2020).

Thus, the focus is not on "how to do something," but rather on the "why" of the behavior. The coach has an opportunity to step back and see patterns that may be interfering with effectiveness. New insights lead to new actions, and even a new way of being, what Argyris and Schon (1974) referred to as triple loop learning. This experience can be emotionally intense, as learners become aware that their underlying assumptions, beliefs, and habitual practices need to change.

In group coaching supervision, where there are typically four to six practitioners meeting simultaneously with a supervisor, the coach has exposure to a greater number of perspectives on the dilemma than in individual supervision. As Proctor (2008) stated, "Groups offer both wider choice and the richness of the group unconscious" (p. 18). Different people will attribute different meanings to experiences, even if they attended the same event. In addition, the variety of participants means that it is less likely for the supervisor or any one supervisee to have common blind spots. Indeed, group supervision can address the problem of "discounting," where people tend to minimize or ignore some aspects of themselves, others, or a situation (Mellor & Schiff, p. 301). As Hay (2007) has noted, "We can spot it happening in others, but we need others to help us identify our own" (p. 34).

Group supervision also offers an opportunity to be supervised at a lower financial cost, as the fees are shared with other practitioners. Perhaps more important, however, is that it provides a way to interact with people who share a common professional background and have faced similar challenges. Passmore and McGoldrick (2009) described the sense of community experienced in supervision. Moreover, as trained coaches, group members are skilled in listening, asking questions, challenging assumptions, and helping people get into action, which supports learning. At the same time, for the group to have positive impact, there must be a trusting relationship among the members, much like the relational turn that occurs in coaching when intimacy and confidentiality are present (De Haan & Sills, 2010). Indeed, studies have shown that some coaches may be reluctant to self-disclose in supervision for fear of feeling shame (Butwell, 2006; Cohen, 2015). As De Haan (2017) pointed out, it takes courage to be willing to talk about situations that have gone awry. Corey and Corey (2006) noted that trust involves a sense of safety, but it does not necessarily entail ease. As they put it, participants "are not apt to feel comfortable if they are talking about matters of significance" (p. 139).

Supervision in a group, therefore, brings both risks and rewards. Although coaches gain insights from multiple practitioners, not just one supervisor, their challenges are reviewed in a more public light. In addition, groups can struggle with dysfunctional dynamics. Groups typically go through phases of development and, in the early stages, there can be disharmony and an over-reliance on the supervisor to manage both tasks and emotions (Tuckman, 1965). Recurring issues like inclusion, dominance, competition, and pairing with other members can also emerge (Bion, 1961; Proctor, 2008; Schultz, 1958). On a positive note, participating in a supervision group also offers coaches a here-and-now experience of group life and systems dynamics, something that can potentially be transferred to their work with clients (Lawrence, 2019).

As might be surmised, group supervision can take various forms. Similar to Berne's (1961) notion of supervising *in* a group, *with* a group, and *by* a group, Proctor (2008) identified four different types: (a) authoritative, where the supervisor supervises one group member at a time, while the others mainly observe; (b) participative, where the supervisor is responsible for supervising and managing the group, but inducts supervisees as supervisors; (c) cooperative, where the supervisor is the group facilitator and supervision monitor, but the supervisees contract to actively co-supervise and develop as a supervisory system; and (d) peer group supervision, where members take shared responsibility for supervising and being supervised. Regardless of the format chosen, the supervision must meet both the developmental needs of individuals and of the group. Collective energy is released when supervisees see their group as a mutual learning entity and self-regulating system.

## Research Question and Design

Although supervision and group supervision appear to offer valuable opportunities for coach development, empirical research measuring the actual impact of this learning on the coach's practice, clients, and client organizations is lacking at this point (Bachkirova et al., 2020). Also largely missing in the literature is the rich texture of qualitative studies, investigating the actual experience of supervision from the participants' perspectives.

Addressing this last point, we asked the following: "What is the lived learning experience of seasoned coaches in the Americas who have participated in group coaching supervision?"

To explore this question, we conducted in-depth interviews with 10 practitioners from Canada, the US, Argentina, Brazil, and Uruguay. Participants had a minimum of five years of coaching experience and had attended at least six coaching supervision sessions with a qualified supervisor. Coaches were certified in a broad range of coaching specializations including ontological coaching, co-active coaching, and executive coaching. All were external practitioners who met with the same supervisor over time in groups that were, to use Proctor's (2008) categories, participative or cooperative in format. Coaching supervision sessions were one to two hours long and the group size was four to six coaches. Some coaches had participated in groups for several years and others for only six months.

Before launching our research project, we put aside ("bracketed") our own beliefs and assumptions relating to the research question. Based on our experience as coaches and coaching supervisors, we were aware that many participants in group supervision gain new insights, but we wondered how this learning happened and what this experience was like for practitioners. Interviews were held in three different languages (English, Spanish, and French) and recorded with permission on Zoom. Using Moustakas' (1994) method of analysis, the transcriptions were examined in the language recorded for meaning units, essential elements found across the described experiences.

## Key Findings

Three main magical ingredients of group supervision emerged from the interviews with study participants:

1   Learning occurred through hearing others' cases or from reactions to one's own case, an experience of "being witnessed" and "witnessing others."
2   Learning occurred through having an emotional experience facilitated by connection to group members.
3   Learning occurred through being both part of a group and observing the group's evolution as an entity.

Each of these findings will be discussed in more detail below.

### The Magic of Being Witnessed and Witnessing

Participants described the experience of bringing a case to the group and, through articulating that situation and hearing others' reactions, finding new meaning and potential next steps. Interestingly, there were several parts to this learning, which one participant described as "being witnessed." First, the coach gained perspective by stepping back to frame their topic for discussion with the group. Just this process alone – summarizing the key points and describing the situation as if from the outside – often allowed the practitioner to see things differently, with a fresh state of mind. Then the coach experienced new insights through hearing how others reacted or interpreted the case. This included not just group members' thoughts, but their emotional responses, somatic experiences, and even, as one participant commented, "their silence." Coaches described how complex situations called for multiple perspectives. As one person stated, "It was very powerful to have others look at my case. I realized that I had come with pre-conceptions, but I didn't see them. Hearing the perspectives of others, it struck me that I did not see the whole picture, or my part in things."

Revisiting a client situation through the eyes of others not only offered an opportunity to revise perceptions or assumptions, but often illuminated new actions that the coach could take. A participant expressed it this way: "Their questions helped me expand my vision of possibilities, to try things that would yield much richer work. The group's input granted me permission to do it differently." This experience could be liberating and energizing. As one coach stated, "I am normally very cerebral, but when I came out of the meeting, I felt it everywhere in my body." Comments like this revealed the magical nature of supervision.

In addition to "being witnessed," participants described learning through "witnessing others." Often, coaches could relate to the situation being outlined by another practitioner and, in some cases, this triggered a re-framing of their own experience. In addition to realizing that colleagues face similar challenges, the discussions frequently surfaced thoughts or emotions that, as one participant put it, "remain hidden." Being in the presence of another coach's struggle provided a vicarious re-experiencing of challenging situations, creating greater understanding, and even healing for practitioners.

In some instances, hearing about another coach's case introduced a totally new experience for participants. One person described this as, "almost pre-experiencing the situation." It was as if, using a magic wand, they had lived it themselves. This led to a greater awareness that was derived from envisioning themselves in the scene. As an example, a participant reported of the impact of hearing about a colleague's client whose family faced a deeply troubling event that irrevocably changed their lives. The incident stayed with him for months he said, reminding him in his work as a coach that "everyone has a story."

### *The Magic of Learning Through Emotional Connection to the Group*

In addition to gaining new insights about themselves, their clients, and the client system, participants described the emotional connection they experienced, something they did not anticipate when joining a supervision group. Several of the coaches mentioned not really knowing what they were getting into at first and having some trepidation about what supervision would involve. One person put it this way:

> When I first heard about coaching supervision, I thought, why would anybody want to do that? Maybe I thought it was like the Spanish Inquisition or something. But it is the exact opposite. It's being supported and really looking for you to grow.

Indeed, several participants described the bond they felt with their group and the way it allowed them to experience deep learning. The forces of competition and comparison, endemic in Western culture, as noted by Proctor (2008), were put aside in service of a shared desire to help each other develop. Particularly in the groups that continued for two years or more, an atmosphere of safety, openness, collaboration, and trust evolved. This connection between members, an emotional container, supported caring, and honest dialogue. As one person put it, the supervision group was "a wisdom circle of guardian angels."

Participants related how a spirit of camaraderie inspired them to be more vulnerable in the group, to share more fully, and to search inside themselves more deeply, both when witnessing and when being witnessed. The bond between members encouraged them not only to go to the "harder places," discussing the concerns that kept them awake at night, but also to places of celebration, of joy, acknowledging the fulfillment that drew them to coaching work in the first place. Several participants commented on the lack of judgment in supervision and the feeling of support they received from colleagues who understood the challenges of doing work of the heart and mind. This emotional connection seemed indispensable to learning about themselves as well as learning from others' situations in a manner that added to their experience as coaches. One participant stated, "There are topics that others bring to the session that also serve me, even if I have not lived those experiences. One becomes aware of subjects that often remain hidden."

### The Magic of Being Part of a Group and Seeing the Group Evolve as an Entity

The third main finding of our research was that participants experienced learning both through being a group member and seeing the group unfold as an entity itself. As mentioned previously, one of the benefits of group supervision is that it not only offers an opportunity to hear others' cases and interpretations, but also provides an in-the-moment view of group life. Participants described how they saw themselves in the group, their reactions to others, the roles that members took, the different styles of interaction, and how they experienced reactions from others. They also observed how the group evolved, becoming a self-sustaining system with patterns of its own, providing important learning that the coaches could transfer to complex systems in their work.

Although the supervisor carried out a valuable role in the group, several coaches discussed how each member had a part to play in creating the whole. This, they pointed out, did not necessarily mean that the group did not encounter conflict or tension. Inviting other perspectives can arouse angst when the reaction does not fit with one's own. As one participant commented, "Any dissatisfaction has nothing to do with whether or not the group is being run well. It has to do with everyone bringing different needs or interests." These differences potentially offered learning but needed to be navigated with care. One person put it this way: "It takes commitment and a willingness to be reflective about each other's nature and learning edges." Individuals also need be brave enough to be vulnerable and yet confident enough in themselves that they can choose from the feedback what will be most useful to them and their clients.

Participants remarked that despite these challenges, the experience of being part of a supervision group was worth the effort. One coach observed that even though he "was not a group person," he developed "some of the best relationships he has ever had." He offered the following reflection:

> Sometimes you get a talker in there, or you get someone who wants to be prescriptive. And then you know, you get someone who thinks he's got this role to bring some development to the group … . *But, when the magic is there, boy, the magic is there.*

## Implications/Discussion

What was striking in our study was the extent to which the group, both as an assembly of individuals and an entity, played a role in the learning experience of seasoned coaches. Not only did it support participants' desires to hear how colleagues might solve problems or make new meaning from reflection (the resolution and elevation functions described by Moral and Angel, 2019), but it met their emotional needs. The experience of connection in the group allowed coaches to step into more vulnerable places, where the learning could be highly personal. It gave them a sense of being cared for as a person who cares for others. Learning in a group also allowed them to see themselves as part of a system and enhanced their understanding of how systems work. As one participant commented, "We learned how to be in a group."

However, for "the magic" of group learning to be achieved, a healthy system is required. Interestingly, even though the groups we studied were not "authoritative," where the supervisor plays a central role, participants emphasized the importance of the supervisor's leadership and presence. Two main supervisory tasks were highlighted: (a) setting the scene by orienting the group to the work at hand; and (b) attending to group process, with a focus on individual as well as group needs.

### Setting the Scene

The coaches in our study in the Americas described how in the beginning they had little understanding of what supervision entailed. Some had fears about a forum in which they would be disclosing real-life challenges with other practitioners. It helped to alleviate concerns when the supervisor explained the purpose and format of the supervision, including the confidentiality of the process and the nonjudgmental approach. They felt relief in knowing that supervision involved some structure and guidelines for working together.

Participants also appreciated the supervisor setting the tone for working together during the session, what Passmore and McGoldrick (2009) referred to as "opening up the critical reflective space" (p. 151). This included ensuring clarity of the case to be discussed and the desires or needs of the coach who brought the topic. Participants described the impact of the supervisor's relaxed stance, a calming energy, which supported deeper exploration even when challenges arose. It was also helpful when the supervisor led them through a grounding exercise in the beginning of the session, inviting group members to be present to their thoughts, feelings, and somatic reactions. This supported bringing their here-and-now experience to the supervision.

### Attending to Group Process

Coaches particularly valued the role of the supervisor in "holding the container" and keeping things on track. Managing group dynamics was deemed vitally important, especially in the early stages when trust, safety, and emotional bonds had not yet formed. Despite a shared interest in learning, the different styles of participants could cause friction. Some people tend to dominate, while others may hold back. At times, group members might stray into unempathetic, projective, or judgmental responses. Emotions could run high, whether being witnessed or witnessing others. With the focus on developing self-as-instrument, not just problem-solving, coaching supervision can feel very personal. It draws on the immediate experience of the group, working with not just what can be seen from the proverbial balcony, but also with what is occurring on the dance floor as the group works together. As one person said, "It is all grist for the mill." The supervisor, as a guide, must attend to both the parts and the whole, intervening where necessary and modeling desired practices to curate a space that serves the learning needs of both individuals and of the group.

## Conclusion

Although this study involved a relatively small number of participants and focused solely on group coaching supervision, it revealed several valuable findings for coach practitioners and coaching supervisors. Perhaps most noteworthy was that supervision, with its experiential orientation, critical self-reflection, and reliance on generative dialogue, offers a way for coaches to learn in ways that go beyond the technical and practical knowledge available from books, webinars, and didactic training sessions. More than just adding new tools and techniques or solving the problem at hand, it probes and challenges practitioners' underlying assumptions and beliefs, exploring what Patterson described as "the place where our evolving roles meet our evolving souls" (p. 181). This kind of "emancipatory learning," where one breaks away from previous ways of thinking and being in the world, can be a powerful and profound experience (Mezirow, 2000, p. 10).

As this suggests, supervision has the potential to be transformative in all three primary functions: qualitative, developmental, and resourcing (Hawkins & Smith, 2006). Moreover, when conducted with a group, the learning can be exponential. There in resides the magic of group supervision. Not only do coaches expand their knowledge of self-as-instrument through their own cases, but they gain insight from others' situations and firsthand experience of the workings of a group. This develops what Hawkins (2019) has called "WeQ," the collaborative intelligence needed to address the challenges today in the work of coaches, that "mostly lie in the connections between individuals, between teams, and between organizations" (p. 66).

Apart from the professional development that supervision offers coaches, it is important to emphasize the emotional support that it provides. Coaching is a very human profession and to do good work and avoid depletion, practitioners must continuously nourish themselves. As Patterson (2019) so eloquently stated, "Supervision provides an oasis, mirror, and haven for leaders and people practitioners to come home to themselves, know themselves and others, emerging refreshed, renewed, reinvigorated and purposeful for skillful, wise, and elegant action" (p. 186).

Magic, indeed.

## Areas for Future Research

As discussed, the small size of this study means that our findings may be considered exploratory. Areas for future research include examining the learning experience of a larger pool of coaches or the experience of learning over time, a longitudinal study with groups that stay together for several years. It would also be interesting to compare the development of coaches who have attended group supervision with professional development gained in other forms of reflective practice, like action learning or intervision. Given the importance attributed to the supervisors in our study, it would be helpful to gain more insight as to how they can help (or hinder) the group in doing deeper work together. In addition, more robust research is needed regarding how learning in supervision is transferred to work with clients and client systems and its impact.

Supervision, in its application to the coaching field, is still in its early days in the Americas. In fact, it may be the best kept secret for continuous professional development. Group supervision, where multiple learning partners come together with a qualified supervisor, may just be the elixir for great coaching.

## References

Armstrong, H., & Geddes, M. (2009). Developing coaching supervision practice: An Australian case study. *International Journal of Evidence Based Coaching and Mentoring*, 7(2): 1–17.

Argyris, C., & Schon, D. (1974). *Theory in practice: Increasing professional effectiveness.* Jossey-Bass.

Association for Coaching (2019) Coaching supervision guide. Retrieved December 29, 2020 from https://cdn.ymaws.com/www.associationforcoaching.com/resource/resmgr/AC_Coaching_Supervision_Guid.pdf

Bachkirova, T. (2016). The self of the coach: Conceptualization, issues, and opportunities for practitioner development. *Consulting Psychology Journal: Practice and Research*, 68(2): 143–156.

Bachkirova, T., Jackson, P., & Clutterbuck, D. (2011). Introduction. In T. Bachkirova, P. Jackson, & D. Clutterbuck (Eds.), *Coaching and mentoring supervision: Theory and practice.* (pp. 1–11). Open University Press.

Bachkirova T., Jackson P., Hennig C., & Moral M. (2020). Supervision in coaching: Systematic literature review. *International Coaching Psychology Review*, 15(2): 231–253.

Berne, E. (1991/1993). *Transactional analysis in psychotherapy.* Souvenir Press.

Bion, W. (1961). *Experiences in groups.* Basic Books.

Bluckert, P. (2005). The similarities and differences between coaching and therapy. *Industrial and Commercial Training*, 37(2): 90–96.

Burke, M.A. (2020). Chasing the shadow: Coaching for equity in education. In T. Hildebrandt, F. Campone, K. Norwood, and E. J. Ostrowski (Eds.), *Innovations in leadership coaching: Research and practice.* (pp. 322–345). Fielding Graduate University.

Butwell, J. (2006). Group supervision for coaches: Is it worthwhile? *Journal of Evidence Based Coaching and Mentoring*, 4(2): 1–11.

Campone, F. (2020). Coaching in wonderland. In T. Hildebrandt, F. Campone, K. Norwood, and E.J. Ostrowski (Eds.), *Innovations in leadership coaching: Research and practice.* (pp. 418–436). Fielding Graduate University.

Carroll, M. (2007). One more time: What is supervision? *Psychotherapy in Australia*, 13(3): 39–40.

Carroll, M., & Shaw, E. (2013). *Ethical maturity in the helping professions.* Jessica Kingsley.

Cavanagh, M.J., Stern, L., & Lane, D.A. (2016). Supervision in coaching psychology: A systemic developmental psychological perspective. In D. A. Lane, M. Watts, & S. Corrie (Eds.), *Supervision in the psychological professions: Building your own personalized model.* Open University Press.

Cochrane, H., & Newton, T. (2018). *Supervision and coaching: Growth and learning in professional practice*. Routledge.

Cohen, Z. (2015, July/Aug). *Facing up to shame*. Coaching at Work. J. https://www.coaching-at-work.com/2015/06/18/facing-up-to-shame/

Corey, M. S., & Corey, G. (2006). *The process and practice of groups*. Thomson Brooks/Cole.

De Haan, E. (2011). Back to basics: How the discovery of transference is relevant for coaches and consultants today. *International Coaching Psychology Review, 6*(2): 180–193.

De Haan, E. (2017). Large scale survey of trust and safety in coaching supervision: Some evidence that we are doing it right. *International Coaching Psychology Review, 12*(1): 37–48.

De Haan, E., & Regouin, W. (1991). *Being supervised: A guide for supervisees*. Karnac Books.

De Haan, E., & Sills, C. (2010). The relational turn in executive coaching. *Journal of Management Development, 29*(10): 845–851. 10.1108/jmd.2010.02629jaa.001

European Mentoring and Coaching Council (2018). *Supervision*. Retrieved December 24, 2020 from https://www.emccglobal.org/quality/supervision/definition/

Grant, A. (2012). Australian coaches view on coaching supervision: A study with implications for Australian coach education, training, and practice. *International Journal of Evidence Based Coaching and Mentoring, 10*(22): 17–33.

Hawkins, P. (2019). Resourcing. In E. Turner & S. Palmer (Eds.), *The heart of coaching supervision: Working with reflection and self-care*. (pp. 61–82). Routledge.

Hawkins, P., & Schwenk, G. (2011). The seven-eyed model of coaching supervision. In T. Bachkirova, P. Jackson, & D. Clutterbuck (Eds.), *Coaching and mentoring supervision: Theory and practice*. (pp. 28–44). Open University Press.

Hawkins, P., & Shohet, R. (1989). *Supervision in the helping professions*. Open University Press.

Hawkins, P., & Smith, N. (2006). *Coaching, mentoring, and organizational consultancy: Supervision and development*. Open University Press.

Hawkins, P., & Turner, E. (2017). The rise of coaching supervision 2006-2014. *Coaching: An International Journal of Theory, Research, and Practice, 10*(2): 102–114.

Hawkins, P., Turner, E., & Passmore, J. (2019). *The manifesto for supervision*. Henley Business School.

Hay, J. (2007). *Reflective practice and supervision for coaches*. Open University Press.

Hodge, A. (2016). The value of coaching supervision as a development process. Contribution to continued professional and personal wellbeing for executive coaches. *International Journal of Evidence Based Coaching and Mentoring, 14*: 87–106.

International Coaching Federation. (2020). *Coaching supervision*. Retrieved December 23, 2020 from https://coachfederation.org/coaching-supervision

Jackson, P., & Bachkirova, T. (2019). The three Ps of supervision and coaching: Philosophy, purpose, and process. In E. Turner and S. Palmer (Eds.), *The heart of coaching supervision: Working with reflection and self-care*. (pp. 20–40). Routledge.

Kegan, R. (1982). *The evolving self*. Harvard University Press.

Lawrence, P. (2019). What happens in group supervision? Exploring current practice in Australia. *International Journal of Evidence Based Coaching and Mentoring, 17*(2): 138–157. 10.24384/v0d6-2380

Lawrence, P., & Whyte, A. (2014). What is coaching supervision and is it important? *Coaching: An International Journal of Theory, Research, and Practice, 7*(1): 39–55. 10.1 080/17521882.2013.878370

Lewis, L. (2013). Foreword. In E. Murdoch and J. Arnold (Eds.), *Full spectrum supervision.* (pp. xvii–xx). Panoma Press Ltd.

McAnally, K., Abrams, L., Asmus, M. J., & Hildebrandt, T. (2020). *Global coaching supervision: A study of the perceptions and practices around the world.* https:// coachingsupervisionresearch.org/wp-content/uploads/2020/02 Global_Coaching_ Supervision_Report_FINAL.pdf

McLean, P. (2019). *Self as coach: Self as leader.* John Wiley & Sons, Inc.

Mellor, K., & Schiff, E. (1975). Discounting. *Transactional Analysis Bulletin, 5*(3): 295–302. 10.1177%2F036215377500500321

Mezirow, J. (2000). Learning to think like an adult: Core concepts of transformation theory. In J. Mezirow & Associates (Eds.), *Learning as transformation: Critical perspectives on a theory in progress.* (pp. 3–34). Jossey-Bass.

Moral, M., & Angel, P. (2019). *Le coaching et sa supervision.* InterEditions.

Moustakas, C. (1994). *Phenomenological research methods.* Sage.

Moyes, B. (2009). Literature review of coaching supervision. *International Coaching Psychology Review, 4*: 162–173.

Norwood, K. (2020). Beautiful form watcher: Coaching for equity in education. In T. Hildebrandt, F. Campone, K. Norwood, & E. J. Ostrowski (Eds.), *Innovations in leadership coaching: Research and practice.* (pp. 346–370). Fielding Graduate University.

Passmore, J., & McGoldrick, S. (2009). Super-vision, extra-vision or blind faith? A grounded theory study of the efficacy of coaching supervision. *International Coaching Psychology Review, 4*(2): 143–159.

Patterson, E. (2019). Oasis for leaders and people practitioners. In J. Birch, & P. Welch (Eds.), *Coaching supervision: Advanced practice, changing landscapes.* (pp. 176–187). Routledge.

Potter, P. (2020). Becoming a coach. In T. Hildebrandt, F. Campone, K. Norwood, & E. J. Ostrowski (Eds.), *Innovations in leadership coaching: Research and practice.* (pp. 371–394). Fielding Graduate University.

Proctor, B. (2008). *Group supervision.* Sage Publications Ltd.

Salter, T. (2008). Exploring current thinking within the field of coaching on the role of supervision. *International Journal of Evidence Based Coaching & Mentoring, Special Issue, 2*: 27–39.

Schultz, W. (1958). *FIRO: The three-dimensional theory of interpersonal behavior.* Rinehart.

Taylor, E. (2008). Transformative learning theory. *New Directions for Adult and Continuing Education, 119* (Fall 2008): 5–15. doi 10.1002/ace.301

Tkach, J. T., & DiGirolamo, J. A. (2017). The state and future of coaching supervision. *International Coaching Psychology Review, 12*(1): 49–65.

Tuckman, B. (1965). Developmental sequences in small groups. *Psychological Bulletin, 63*: 384–399.

## Author Bios

**Lynn Harrison**, Ph.D., MCC, ESIA is an executive coach with 30 years of experience in management/consulting. Her background includes co-founding an international, franchised training organization, leading at the senior management level, and providing consulting services to executive leadership teams and boards. She is the Vancouver, Canada-based principal of Black Tusk Leadership, Inc., four-time recipient of the International

Coach Federation (ICF) Prism Award.Lynn has a Ph.D. in Organizational Systems and an MA in Applied Behavioral Science. She is a master certified coach (MCC) and a certified master corporate executive coach (MCEC) with the Association of Corporate Executive Coaches. She is accredited as coaching supervisor (ESIA) and has coaching certifications in Co-active Coaching, Ontological Coaching, Advanced Ontological Coaching, Boss Whispering, and Stakeholder-Centered Coaching.

**Martine Bizouard**, PEng, MBA, MCC, MP, ESIA is an executive coach and supervisor with 15+ years of experience in coaching plus 15+ years of experience in the corporate world and teaching in leading business school. She founded Terra Incognita, which provides executive advisory services to leaders and official elects, and all range of coaching services to corporations and administrations and mentoring and supervision to coaches.

Martine also holds an engineering degree and an MBA. She is trained in coaching and psychotherapy. She is a master certified coach (ICF) and master practitioner (MP-EMCC). She is accredited as coaching supervisor (ESIA-EMCC). She holds coaching certifications in various approaches.

Martine has volunteered as CEO in France of an international organization for leadership and policy-making.

**In addition, we would like to acknowledge Aida Frese (PCC, ESIA), our supervision colleague from Argentina, who conducted interviews with coaches in South America and helped to analyze findings.**

We also would like to thank Michel Moral, Peter Jackson, Pam McLean, Gary Metcalf, Terry Hildebrandt, Sarah Eustice, and Jonathan Passmore for their generous assistance with our study.

# 12 A Framework for Group Presence in Group Coaching Supervision

*Lynne DeLay and Ken Giglio*

> Be with those who help your being. Don't sit with indifferent people … your work is deeper.
>
> —Rumi, *The Essential Rumi*

## Introduction

The shared experience of presence—the awareness and deep connectedness of being in the flow of moments — is at the foundation of all effective coaching and coaching supervision (International Coaching Federation, 2019). Presence concepts, theories, and models define presence as either a solo or a one-to-one experience (co-presence; relational presence) that enhances work in relationships, whether therapeutic, coaching, or supervisory (Colosimo, 2013; Colosimo & Pos, 2015; Geller, 2001; Geller et al., 2010). Lacking in the coaching and coaching supervision literature, however, are references to group presence. This chapter presents a group presence framework and explores the experience of presence in group coaching supervision, focusing on such questions as: *What is presence within groups? How does it manifest? What enhances presence or inhibits it? What role/s do the co-facilitator supervisors play in generating presence? How do we apply group presence to the work of supervision through process and flow?*

Our framework evolved from a mutual interest and passion for educating coaches on reflective practice, particularly in the Americas. We are curious about how presence happens and flourishes as a beneficial experience for supervisors and coaches in a group setting. As such, we examine the current theories and concepts of presence, how this International Coaching Federation (ICF) core competency manifests between two experienced coaching supervisors, and how it is enhanced to foster deeper work in group supervision.

Co-facilitation is not new to the US or to psychology. In fact, it is common for a less experienced supervisor to work with a more experienced one until they have gained sufficient experience and confidence. Co-facilitation models are lacking in the supervision literature and writing on

DOI: 10.4324/b23130-15

co-facilitation and group presence in group coaching supervision is largely absent (Lucas & Whitaker, 2014).

As practitioners and educators in the field of coaching supervision, we believe that group supervision carries substantial benefits for coaches in the Americas. Effective group supervision delivers the core functions of supervision: Coach development, well-being and quality control that includes ethical judgment. In addition, group supervision remains more cost-effective than one-on-one work and continues to gain popularity in the Americas because it allows coaches to reflect together and learn from each other (Proctor, 2008).

This chapter explores various theories of presence and how it has evolved in coaching and coaching supervision in the Americas and across the world. Many of the foundational theories of presence are from the US (Silsbee, 2008; Strozzi-Heckler, 2014). These theories have influenced individual and group work in coaching and counseling. Presence is also central to the self as coach model (McLean, 2019).

Presence can be difficult to articulate, so later in the chapter we introduce music as a metaphor to help illustrate the concept and foster a more holistic understanding of presence in group supervision.

## The Facets of Presence

> Authentic Presence—Inviting and allowing another person to have his or her experience just as it is—this is perhaps the greatest gift anyone can offer.
>
> —John Welwood

The Merriam-Webster Dictionary defined *presence* as "the fact or condition of being present." Presence is also used to describe a "group of people," "a person or spirit that you cannot see but feel is near," and "the quality of making a strong impression" (Merriam-Webster Dictionary, 2021).

Table 12.1 shows how the different fields of coaching, coaching supervision, and psychotherapy have defined *presence* and its meaning within a professional context.

In reviewing the literature on *presence*, it has commonly been described as "a state of awareness in the moment" (Silsbee, 2008), "a state of profound contact and engagement" (Mearns & Cooper 2005, 2018), "the capacity to fully acknowledge, allow, and open to our immediate experience just as it is, without agenda, judgment, or manipulation of any kind" (Welwood, 2000), and "bringing our whole self into the encounter" (Geller & Greenberg, 2002).

Carl Rogers greatly influenced the psychotherapy, coaching, and coaching supervision fields with his theory and practice of unconditional positive regard, which is linked to therapeutic presence (Geller, 2013). Other related concepts of presence include moments of meeting and

*Table 12.1* Definitions of Presence

| Source | Definition |
| --- | --- |
| Blake et al. (2016) | Presence is an ineffable quality difficult to define; an inherently relational quality read primarily through non-verbal cues; others assess you as either having a strong presence, or not. It can be learned and embodied. |
| Bugental (1987) | Presence is a name for the quality of being in a situation or a relationship in which one intends at a deep level to participate as fully as she is able. Presence is expressed through mobilization of one's sensitivity - both inner and outer- and bringing into action one's capacity for response. |
| Curry (2003) | Presence is an affective quality with somatosensory components, felt by clients, which changes their state from suffering toward a sense of well-being. |
| Geller & Greenberg (2002) | Therapeutic presence involves bringing one's whole self into the encounter with the client, being completely in the moment on a multiplicity of levels, physically, emotionally, cognitively, and spiritually. |
| International Coaching Federation (2019) | Maintains Presence: Is fully conscious and present with the client, employing a style that is open, flexible, grounded and confident. 1 Remains focused, observant, empathetic and responsive to the client 2 Demonstrates curiosity during the coaching process 3 Manages one's emotions to stay present with the client 4 Demonstrates confidence in working with strong client emotions during the coaching process 5 Is comfortable working in a space of not knowing 6 Creates or allows space for silence, pause or reflection |
| Rogers (2007) | Presence is the quality of a therapist connecting with his/her patient. |
| Scharmer (2016) | Presencing – To sense, tune in, and act from one's highest future potential—the future that depends on us to bring into being. Presencing blends the words "presence" and "sensing" and works through "seeing from our deepest source." |
| Senge et al. (2008) | Presence is the core capacity needed to access the field of the future by being fully conscious of and aware in the present moment - an act of deeply connecting with any point in time; listening deeply; being open beyond one's preconceptions and historical ways of making sense; letting go of |

*(Continued)*

*Table 12.1* (Continued)

| Source | Definition |
| --- | --- |
| | old identities and the need to control; and making choices to serve the evolution of life … leading to a state of "letting come," of consciously participating in a larger field of change. |
| Shen et al. (2009) | Social Presence - Feelings of community and intimacy learners experience in an online environment; the subjective experience of being present with a "real" person in a technology-mediated environment and having access to his or her thoughts and emotions. |
| Siegel (2018) | Mental presence is a state of being wide awake and receptive to what is happening in the moment, within us, and between the world and us. |
| Silsbee (2008) | Presence is an internal state—the inclusive awareness of stillness, immediacy and possibility. As much a way of being as a way of doing. |
| Welwood (2000) | Unconditional Presence — The capacity to fully acknowledge, allow, and open to our immediate experience just as it is, without agenda, judgment, or manipulation of any kind. Here we are at one with our experience, without the subject/object barrier. This is an innate capacity of our being. |
| Yalom (1980) | Detached presence allows the therapist to be "in two places at once—at his or her own side and at the patient's side" (p.407). "Effective therapists … display a non-possessive warmth and a high degree of accurate empathy and are able to 'be with' or 'grasp the meaning' of a patient" (p. 401). "The therapist is interested in the 'you' of the patient, not only the 'you' that is present but the potential dormant 'you'" (p. 407). In this authentic encounter, the therapist strives for selflessness, indestructible caring, "being with," without prejudgment. |

moments of now (Stern, 2004), mutual intersubjectivity (Jordan, 1986), co-presence (Nuttall, 2019), linking (Rowan, 2005), and David Bohm's idea of dialogue (Science & Nonduality, n.d.). Additionally, the field of quantum physics also informs our understanding of presence through the concepts of nonduality and the interconnectedness of all things (Laszlo, 2007/2014; Science & Nonduality, n.d.).

In general, we can move from an internal state of presence to being present with others (co-presence) by practicing deep listening, authenticity, aligned communication, attention, allowing for deep connection and empathy, a sense of congruence, unconditional positive regard, limbic resonance, and dealing with uncertainty. References to group presence are largely lacking in presence literature. The concept can be inferred from individual and relational presence or co-presence writings; however, it is not covered in any focused way in the coaching supervision literature.

The accelerated shift to online supervision due to the COVID-19 pandemic has sparked interest in how presence is fostered in virtual environments (Geller, 2020). The concept of social presence, from the field of social psychology, can aid our understanding of how group presence can be fostered online (Oh et al., 2018). Social presence is the feeling of community and intimacy that learners can experience while working in an online environment (Shen et al., 2009). Studies have shown that it builds trust between people and groups as they interact and work using technology (Lu & Fan, 2016).

More directly informing and influencing our group presence framework is Scharmer's theory u (Scharmer, 2016), along with mindfulness and embodiment concepts and practices (Goldstein, 2016; Palmer, 2008; Welwood, 2000). Scharmer described presencing as "the blending of sensing and presence [which] means to connect from the Source of the highest future possibility and to bring it into the now" (Scharmer, 2016, p.161). Scharmer applied presencing to individuals and organizational structures, using terms such as "co-sensing," "co-presencing" and "co-creating" as the foundation for "the rise of the social space of emergence and creation." This "social space of emergence and creation" is integral to group presence. The bottom of the u in the model is the space of presencing, a space of not knowing, where a participant's intention is to listen deeply with an open mind, an open heart, and open will.

Not knowing is both a beginning and returning point for presence. Scharmer discussed "letting go" to "let come" as the way of presencing at the bottom of the u. While letting go of stories and biases, among other things, it is important to "let come," we view the group presence as a space of "letting be." By letting be, the group can hold a question without urgency, and explore a theme wherever it goes. Reflection in a space of "letting be" allows for the release of expectations, including the potential for "letting come."

Mindfulness is intrinsically linked to presence. Both are ways of being fully awake and aware in the moment. Mindfulness is an ongoing practice that can lead to a state of individual and group presence.

Among the myriad approaches and aspects of mindfulness, there are four "ways of being mindful," which are particularly valuable as co-facilitator tools to enhance group presence: **welcoming** with unconditional friendliness; **focused attention** on the process of reflection; **embodied awareness** of feelings and sensations; and **compassion** for self and others (Goldstein, 2016; Welwood, 2000).

Key to the practice of mindfulness is one's awareness and acceptance of bodily sensations and feelings in the moment. Group presence, therefore, relies on a collective somatic awareness, creating an openness to reflect and leverage group sensations and feelings.

## Group Presence as "Story-free" Ground

Coaching supervision heavily involves reflecting upon and processing stories. The coach comes with their own perspectives, thoughts, and emotions about what is transpiring within their client work (their self-story). The coach describes what is going on in the client's world from the client's perspective (the client's story), which includes their experience with organization's culture, strategy, and business (the system story).

As neuroscientist Lisa Feldman Barrett (2020) noted, our minds enable us to "live in a world of social reality" (p. 111) in which we construct our own stories. Reality may or may not be found in these stories as they are unpacked and reflected upon during coaching supervision. To capture the clearest view of what is happening with a coaching case or situation, we need a foundational space without stories. This could be our closest brush with reality. This story-less place or story-free ground is presence. Presence allows for the spontaneous unfolding of reflective dialogue without attachment or expectation. Individuals become aware of and release their stories first, and then the group becomes collectively aware through dialogue and presence practices. This intentional clearing of the ground where stories live and grow enables group presence to emerge. Presence then becomes the ground for the work of coaching supervision.

## Presence as a Competency in a System

*Maintains Presence* is one of the eight core competencies of the ICF, a professional coaching body with North American roots. ICF defined "Maintains Presence" as: "Is fully conscious and present with the client, employing a style that is open, flexible, grounded and confident" (ICF, 2019). Two of the six behavioral indicators that mapped directly to the group presence experience were: "Is comfortable working in a space of not knowing," and "creates or allows space for silence, pause or reflection" (ICF, 2019).

Coaches in the Americas closely align their coaching strategies and tactics with the ICF's competencies. As the coaching field is governed by professional associations, including the ICF, how these organizations define and measure presence matters to coaches in their work with clients and their credentialing. It is interesting to note that across three leading professional coaching associations—the European Mentoring & Coaching Council (EMCC), the Association for Coaching (AC), and the Association of Professional Executive Coaches and Supervisors (APECS)—none referred to presence directly in their standards. However, it is implied as a core skill embedded in their coaching competencies and supervision standards.

The challenge facing our field is moving from theory to practice: *As professional coaches and supervisors, how do we operationalize presence in individual and group work? How do we create a framework for group presence that facilitates impactful group supervision work?*

## Group Coaching Supervision Structure, Models, Approach

We would describe our approach to group coaching supervision as eclectic, creative, and agile. While fluent and experienced in applying several models, including The seven-eyed model (Hawkins & Shohet, 2007), for the purposes of this exercise we leveraged the Tri-lens Coaching Supervision Model™. The Tri-lens Coaching Supervision Model provides a framework for reflecting upon the three lenses of self, other, and system, while maintaining a mindful, centered space of attention and presence.

One primary structural consideration was whether to practice the framework with open or closed groups. While the group presence framework has been tested with closed groups, most of the examples in this chapter are from open groups. An open group allows flexibility and fluidity in membership as participants can commit to just one session at a time. This creates an opportunity to test the ability of group members, who typically do not know each other, to coalesce quickly and function as a collective whole using our framework. Also, the frequency of group presencing practices before and during the group supervision process accelerates a broadening of the field of awareness. In closed groups, deep listening and a sense of the collective emerge gradually as members learn to trust each other, and the co-supervisors model safety, respect and confidentiality. In open groups, we build on the facilitation technique of open space technology, which included four foundational principles: "Those who come are the right people," "whatever happens is the only thing that could have happened," "whenever it starts is the right time," and "when it is over, it is over" (Owen, 2008).

## Source of Case Examples

We have used our group presence framework in supervision groups with coaches from around the world. Many groups have been held with ICF chapters in the US as part of their ongoing mission to inform, educate, and provide real-time coaching supervision experiences. Over a period of two years, we've experimented and co-supervised 17 sessions using this model (12 in the US). Each time, we followed the same framework for setting the conditions.

## Music as a Metaphor

As a way of understanding our approach, we offer music as a metaphor, and refer to resonance using its musical meaning. To illustrate resonance, imagine two violins lying on separate tables separated by several feet. When we strike the string of one violin, the exact same string on the second violin vibrates. Their frequencies are aligned (Leeds, 2010). This can happen with people. Energetically speaking, like the violins, we vibrate in response to others. This is called sympathetic vibration. "Tuning" or the process of aligning frequencies is also discussed.

## The Group Presence Framework

We outline the framework for group presence, below. In each phase, we briefly explain our process and flow, describe how it relates to music metaphorically and experientially, to an extent. We also share a case example to illustrate the planning, structure, and flow of the group presence experience. Table 12.2 provides details of the framework's six phases and illustrates the flow from one phase to the next. This table also shows, by phase, the critical factors that enhance presence in group supervision, as well as those that inhibit or impede it.

## Phase One: Tuning of the Lead Violinists

### Process and Flow

Like the violin, which needs to be played frequently to maintain its resonant tone, supervisors must tune their resonant tone, listening to the sound of their own instrument, and adjusting the pitch as necessary. As two lead violinists, they provide the note to which the rest of the orchestra aligns. These are antecedents to presence. It starts before the group session begins. Presencing between individuals and within a group includes building psychological safety, mindfulness, and embodiment practices (Crane-Okada, 2012).

### Case Example

*It was 20 minutes before our group began. In preparation for co-facilitating the supervision group, we have just joined Zoom to co-presence with each other. Prior to our virtual connection, we each have centered in our own way. We took a few minutes and checked-in with each other and adjusted for any last-minute changes. When we felt fully connected, we mentally voiced our intention and began to align physically by rhythmically breathing together (breathing in on a count of four and out on a count of four) and created a sense of oneness with our in-breath and out-breath to mimic one body breathing. As we began to function as one body, we sensed ourselves moving beyond our individual egos to a larger co-presence. Now we were ready to engage with the group. We admitted the group as they arrived on Zoom.*

The strategy described above is one way to become attuned together. We encourage co-supervisors to experiment with different approaches and find what works for them. This is one way the partnership begins to emerge and a sense of oneness is created. We believe it is important to engage the physical body in order to embody presence as much as possible.

*Table 12.2* The Phases of Group Presence with Presence Enhancers and Presence Inhibitors

| Phase | Process and Flow | Presence Enhancers | Presence Inhibitors |
|---|---|---|---|
| 1 | **Tuning of the Lead Violinists** | • Co-facilitation role clarity and equal status affirmed<br>• Structure, process, and flow co-established for the group work<br>• Individual and shared mindfulness and embodiment practices<br>• Agreement between supervisors that each will attend to their own presence in preparation for and throughout the group work and call upon each other for support when needed in maintaining presence | • Not being fully in the moment with each other<br>• Lack of honesty, transparency, and acknowledgement of each supervisors' current state of mindfulness and presence, be it in sync or not<br>• Lack of awareness for each supervisor and within their co-facilitator dynamic of voices of judgment (VOJ), cynicism (VOC), and fear (VOF) (Scharmer, 2016) |
| 2 | **Group Tuning to Enhance Performance** | • Supervisors set intention for all to be fully present with each other in group presence by using attention and embodied awareness throughout the group's time together<br>• Supervisors lead group centering/mindfulness/embodiment practices<br>• Specific "seeing and sensing" each other practices, using eye contact, movement, gestures, all in service of being in the moment with each other (in-person or in a virtual application) | • Supervisors do not clearly communicate the shared responsibility of group presence, the "We in the Moment"<br>• Individual group members do not fully commit to and attend to their own mindful presence<br>• Distractions are not identified and managed and pull the group away from their attention with each other and the reflective work |

| 3 | The Musical Score | • Supervisors contract with the group as co-facilitators providing information on structure, models, and overall group process and flow<br>• Psychological contracting also covered to surface assumptions and expectations with the group to foster safety<br>• Agreement between all that re-contracting to foster safety and group presence is a shared responsibility and can be called upon at any time | • Supervisors are misaligned on how they will communicate and contract with the group<br>• Supervisors are not clear, or may not give sufficient time, in how they contract with the group, including psychological contracting<br>• Lack of attention to structure, process, and flow for the group work |
| 4 | The Solo Parts | • Acknowledgment by supervisors of the vulnerability present for coaches who share challenging coaching cases<br>• Group agreement on who will share their case and when<br>• Conscious approach of non-judgment by supervisors and group to what cases are presented | • Supervisors allow too much time for potential supervisee to share their case/s allowing too many details to enter the space<br>• Supervisor chooses the cases to reflect on versus the group<br>• Supervisors do not emphasize a welcoming and non-judgmental approach when sourcing cases |
| 5 | Group Improvisation | • Supervisors A and B hold their respective presence spaces with the supervisee and group as well as being aware of the overall group presence dynamic<br>• Supervisors practice self-observation to monitor their own presence, connection with each other and the group | • Supervisors and the group work from "effort" versus the "source" (Hawkins et al., 2019)<br>• Supervisors rush presence activities<br>• Group gets bogged down in the stories of the coaching cases versus examining the core elements to reflect on.<br>• Supervisors become distracted and lose their own presence |

*(Continued)*

*Table 12.2* (Continued)

| Phase | Process and Flow | Presence Enhancers | Presence Inhibitors |
|---|---|---|---|
| | | • Group offers empathy and support as well and are also willing to challenge to each other<br>• Supervisors collaborate with the group to reflect on the coaching work through guided awareness and "a discipline of attention" (Scharmer, 2016)<br>• Centering (presence) practices embedded into the structure of the group as the facilitators shift from working with the supervisee to the group | • Distractions are not identified and managed, which pulls the group away from their attention and presence with each other and the reflective work. Distractions could be technology related.<br>• Supervisor B pushes pace for group responses<br>• Supervisor A thinking ahead while listening to group comments |
| 6 | **The Musical Coda** | • Supervisors acknowledge the contributions of the supervisee, group, and each other in terms of the reflective work and the fostering and maintaining of group presence<br>• Final reflections captured by Supervisor A from the supervisee and from Supervisor B from the group | • Supervisors mismanage group time and rush the ending, bring their anxiety into the process and disrupting presence<br>• Supervisors allow individual group members to take too much time<br>• Supervisors allow the continuing of the case processing during the closing reflection rather than creating space for final remarks |

## Phase Two: Group Tuning to Enhance Performance

### Process and Flow

A group of six coaches and two coaching co-supervisors is like an ensemble or chorale group that needs to tune together before performing. We generally began with a large group (from 15–75 participants) from which we asked for volunteers. In soliciting volunteers from an open group, not only do we have an ensemble that has never played together, but the members typically do not know each other. As quickly as we could, vibrationally, we aimed to produce *group resonance* in the volunteer group. This required exquisite listening skills. As Daniel Siegel (2018) noted:

> "A system that is integrated is in a flow of harmony. Just as in a choir, with each singer's voice both differentiated from the other singers' voices but also linked, harmony emerges with integration" (p. 10).

In the same way that we ground and centered as facilitators, we invited the small volunteer group to individually center and then guided them in a group mindfulness exercise. With open groups, the tuning phase serves to intentionally align and connect the members, collectively. Our overarching goal was fostering group presence, which creates *coherence* among the group members (Yu, 2020). This coherence among the parts (group members) created alignment and alignment created resonance and presence. On a quantum level, some theorists have suggested that the connection (with each other and the field) was already there. Creating coherence was more a matter of getting beyond the individual so that our best and most natural self could emerge.

As the coaching co-supervisors centered and grounded with the group through the mindfulness exercise, psychological safety was created, opening everyone to deeper levels of connection with each other and the larger system or field (Edmondson, 2018). Like the violins that open to their full resonance, individuals in a group could fully allow themselves to open to self and others. When the group achieved this centering, they felt free to take interpersonal risks and any fears or resistance were released. Group members felt accepted and safe. Judgment was suspended. Neurologically, entering this phase has been associated with the release of oxytocin, which enhances trust (Glaser, 2016).

### Case Example

*As group members arrived, we engaged them in light-hearted banter and created a welcoming and friendly atmosphere. When the group was complete (at 60 people), we reminded them of the purpose of our session. We opened the floor to volunteers and six coaches stepped forward. We invited the members who were not in the small group to mute themselves and turn off their cameras. This left only the six volunteers and the two co-supervisors with their video and audio on.*

*As the six volunteers settled, one coaching supervisor acknowledged the courage it took to volunteer and thanked them for participating. We shared that we would first spend time connecting and then share contracting information about how the group would work. The group gave permission to proceed.*

*One coaching supervisor led the group in a mindfulness centering exercise. Breathing and guided imagery were used to steady the attention of the coaches and to deeply connect them in the present moment. Next, we transitioned to an activity in pairs in which coaches looked directly into each other's eyes (held for a few seconds so each person felt "seen") and while doing so, mentally sent positive regard or appreciation to everyone including the co-supervisors. We reminded them that by volunteering we were being helpful to each other and this assistance was always a gift.*

*Everyone came together during this activity. We noticed people smiling with softer eyes and faces, relaxed and lowered shoulders, slower breathing, and someone spontaneously made a heart with their two hands. With this increased collective awareness and alignment, we all became relaxed and more open.*

### Optional Tuning Activities

Another option for collective work is to breathe deeply together on the in-breath and out-breath, rhythmically as one body (as described above). For those preferring movement, the group can physically move in unison using simple movements in dance-like fashion. This can involve hands, arms, legs, body swaying, and other movements. There is also sound: The group can hum or sing a simple tune together. Regardless of the activity, each introduces a vibrational energy into the working space and serves to connect the group members. The group's collective intention and unified movements co-create the space. At the quantum level, anything we consciously focus on attracts that energy into the space.

## Phase Three: The Musical Score

### Process and Flow

In Phase Three, just as musical groups need a musical score or roadmap that informs them when and how to play together in harmony, so does a supervision group. When the group was relaxed and aligned, we moved to general contracting including clarifying our different roles and how the two co-supervisors would interact with the supervision group (Cochrane & Newton, 2018). This included agreement on the role of the volunteer coach, how the remaining group would work with the volunteer supervisee, time boundaries, and anything else group members wanted to address to be totally available, relaxed, and safe. We reminded the group that we would need a volunteer to discuss a case with Coaching Supervisor A; Coaching Supervisor B, we explained, would work solely with the group members not directly presenting a case. The group members were asked to listen deeply and pay particular attention to what arose internally in their minds and in their bodily sensations. This reflection in action, as Schon (1983) highlights, allowed for insights and learnings to surface for members as the dialogue unfolded. Deep listening and focused attention are also mindfulness approaches that generate group presence.

As the group's reflective process continued, the coaching supervisors paid particular attention to any anxiety that arose within the group or individual members. Our aim was to be aware of any factors that could hinder presence, including anxiety about the group process and expectations. We explained that there was nothing they could do or feel that was "wrong," even if they noticed nothing. All things are data in supervision, as Shohet (2020), noted. Stressing this point reduced potential performance anxiety and alleviated concerns of being judged or compared to other group members. We addressed any questions and then began the work by asking for a volunteer supervisee.

### Case Example

*The volunteer group was now relaxed and connected. One coaching supervisor explained that Coaching Supervisor A would work solely with the volunteer supervisee and Coaching Supervisor B would work with the remaining members. When Coaching Supervisor A worked with the supervisee, the other members were to simply listen and notice what arose in them. The coaching supervisor further outlined the back-and-forth movement between listening to the supervision conversation and the participation of group members led by Coaching Supervisor B. This back-and-forth between coaching supervisors would continue until the supervision was complete and another case was volunteered. The time allotted was two hours. Questions were addressed before moving on.*

## Phase Four: The Solo Parts

### Process and Flow

Now that the contracting was complete, we moved into what is known in music as the solo. We asked for a coach willing to share a case, situation, or pattern and work with Coaching Supervisor A. We have seen a wide range of topics presented for group reflection, from specific coaching engagements or situations arising within a case to patterns that repeat across a coach's caseload. Since our experience has been mostly with open groups and coaches unfamiliar with each other, we have observed that a warming up period is needed for coaches to bring forward some aspect of their work. Soloists are also familiar with the courage needed to perform a solo. They are in the spotlight with no place to hide. Everyone focuses on each note that the soloist sings.

Generally, we have found that only one or two coaches initially volunteer to share. To date, we have had no issues with a case being brought forward. If time remained after two coaches experienced supervision, we invited additional members to volunteer.

*Case example*

*General contracting was completed. We recognized initial safety was established by observing smiling faces, relaxed body language and verbal affirmations. Coaching Supervisor B asked the group, "Who would like to partner with Coaching Supervisor A and share a coaching case, situation, or theme for reflection?" After a bit of silence, one group member volunteered.*

## Phase Five: Group Improvisation

### Process and Flow

In Phase Five, supervision began. At some point, Coaching Supervisor A would pause and ask the supervisee if they would like input from the group. Once agreed, Coaching Supervisor A handed off facilitation to Coaching Supervisor B.

Coaching Supervisor B was now ready to engage with the observing group members who have witnessed the supervision. To start, Supervisor B invited the group members to pause and release what they just heard. This practice is like a rest in music. Rests are purposeful and integral to the music. Debussy wrote that music is not in the notes, but in the spaces between the notes (Mind Fuel Daily, n.d.). These spaces prevent the next note from getting acoustically entangled with the resonance trail of the last (Williamson, 2011). They create a meditative space where member attention can turn in on itself, onto the very process of listening itself. In this meditative space, the group members are asked to relax, take a few deep breaths, and re-center.

Let silence be the art you practice.

—Rumi, *The Essential Rumi*

From a psychological perspective, the silence served another purpose. Coaches have often spoken about how easy it was to fall out of presence. They have noted getting triggered by the client's story, distracting thoughts, fatigue, or physical discomfort. The recentering activity allowed them to be still, to achieve presence as individuals and as a group and to disengage for a moment from the conversation in order to clean their lens or mirror. From this space of group presence, they could also change the lens through which they responded. Thus, they could respond from a deeper, cleaner place and connect with what "want[ed] to emerge" in the moment.

When the group was ready to continue, Coaching Supervisor B, chose a question to ask the group members using the supervision discussion and the Tri-Lens Coaching Supervision Model to focus on coach (self), client (other), and organization (system).

This stage of Phase Five resembles improvisation and cannot be "scripted" except in the broadest of terms. The magic lies in how the different parts within the group respond to each other in the moment, as the group plays and transcends the confines of the score. In musical terms, the melody glides effortlessly among players. Each player takes their cue from the section heads (coaching supervisors) who listen for the music to be played and that neither know beforehand. There is a process of release, an experience of the unknown, a sense of "being in flow." All of this emerges in the present moment—the moment of now.

Below are sample questions to foster reflection by the group through the use of metaphors, vision activities, a focus on physical sensations, sentence completion, and other methods:

- What metaphor would you offer that connects with what you have heard from your colleague about their coaching situation?
- What one word comes to mind as you think about the *organization* that the client works in?
- When you reflect on the coach's *client*, what do you notice in your body and where?
- As I listen to the *coach* and their story, I notice … . (complete the sentence)

These questions prompted each group member to respond from a relaxed, more reflective place. Coaching Supervisor B completed this section by adding his or her response, and then handed back facilitation to Coaching Supervisor A.

Coaching Supervisor A asked the supervisee what responses resonated most with them and the two continued, using the group's offerings, until the next handoff to Coaching Supervisor B. Coaching Supervisor B repeated the re-centering activity, asked a different question, elicited responses, then added their own. The process was then repeated until Coaching Supervisor A and the supervisee agreed that the supervision was complete.

Another coach volunteered and Phase Five was repeated until all members had a chance for supervision in the allocated time.

### Case Example

*One coach stepped forward and briefly described a theme in his coaching that he wanted to reflect upon. His coaching work felt inconsistent, and he was questioning his value proposition due to a tendency to consult (telling) versus asking coaching questions. His clients liked the direct guidance, so the coach felt compelled at times to forgo asking questions. It "felt good" to be appreciated for giving direct guidance, and yet the coach was conflicted. Coaching Supervisor A asked him what question he would like answered and the coach replied: "How will I be able to monitor myself, be in command of myself, to put my best foot forward as a coach?"*

*Coaching Supervisor A continued with a few more questions and then asked the supervisee if he wanted input from the group. The supervisee agreed and Coaching Supervisor A turned the session over to Supervisor B. Supervisor B guided the group members in a three-breath breathing exercise and after some silence, asked the group: "After listening to this coaching situation, what image presents itself to you right now as you think about the coach and his situation?" After some silence, group members offered the image of scissors, a rabbit, and two people in a tug of war, among others. Coaching Supervisor B signaled the close of this part by sharing an image and handed facilitation back to Coaching Supervisor A.*

*Coaching Supervisor A guided the supervisee to center by consciously breathing together and then asked what images resonated with him. The supervisee resonated most with "two people in a tug of war," and the coaching supervision exploration picked up again, with insights emerging from the one-on-one dialogue between Coaching Supervisor A and the supervisee. Following a pause, Coaching Supervisor A again asked if the supervisee wanted input from the group. He agreed and the process was repeated.*

*After centering the group members, Coaching Supervisor B asked: "What one word arises for you when you think about the system the coach's client works in?" One group member responded "hierarchical," another responded "expert," until Coaching Supervisor B added the final response and then passed the supervision to Coaching Supervisor A. After centering, the supervisee was asked what terms resonated most with him. The new input was explored, and the handoff repeated until Coaching Supervisor A asked if the supervisee felt complete or if he needed anything else for closure before the session was ended.*

## Phase Six: The Musical Coda

### Process and Flow

After a brief centering exercise, Coaching Supervisor B picked up with the remaining group members on the last round and reminded them that when one member of the group worked, they all worked and learned. This section resembles a coda in music where a signal is given that the composition is ending. The group was asked to share one personal lesson from the group's work that would be useful for their own coaching. Each member shared their insights and learning. Coaching Supervisor B thanked the group for their contributions and closed the session. This was an important step and helped group members who have been listening and contributing to receive something, as well.

### Case Example

*In the process of closing the supervision session, Coaching Supervisor A asked if the supervisee had made a shift during the group reflection process. This shift could be within themselves (self as coach), about their client relationship, the system, or any combination of the three. After ending the one-on-one dialogue with the supervisee, Coaching Supervisor A handed the session to Coaching Supervisor B who reiterated that group supervision enabled all members to learn together. Coaching Supervisor B then asked the group: "From the cases we have discussed, what key learning are you taking away that is useful to your work as a coach?" One member shared: "I need to pay more attention to contracting." Another offered: "I can be braver in my interventions." Still another said: "This session helped me see how I get in my own way." Coaching Supervisor B closed the group by thanking everyone. The group supervision experience was concluded.*

## Conclusion

Presence is essential to creating a meaningful and impactful relationship with coaching clients. Presence is also crucial for coaches to meaningfully reflect on their coaching work. The group presence framework within a group supervision format creates a process and flow for presence to manifest, first between co-supervisors and then the entire group. In this deep collective awareness, coaches and coaching supervisors are steeped in presence, allowing for the functions and benefits of supervision to be fully realized.

Intentionally setting presence and group presence as an experiential entry point, particularly in open groups, facilitates supervisors and coaches to ground themselves and thoroughly explore whatever emerges. We suggest that the group presence experience, over time, will develop the ICF's maintaining coaching presence competency. This will provide coaches and facilitators with the ongoing practice and experience needed to deepen their ability to maintain presence (Siminovitch & Van Eron, 2008) and regain it more quickly. Like a muscle, it becomes stronger and more responsive with practice.

Focusing on group presence in open groups allows group members to function more quickly on a collective level and conduct deeper group work. We hypothesize that the structure of the group process and dialogue, with its intentional and consistent focus on presencing practices, facilitates the establishment of group presence. Given that open groups allow for a great deal of flexibility, this may warrant more exploration.

Finally, this approach simplifies and clarifies the role of each coaching supervisor for themselves and the group. This simplicity allows the coaching supervisors, particularly Coaching Supervisor A, to bring the full power of their attention and presence to themselves and the supervisee. Coaching Supervisor A is freed from switching roles and shifting focus between the supervisee and tother group members. Since there are two co-supervisors, the other group members can be continually supported and attended to by Coaching Supervisor B. Practicing group presence generates deeper group work, demonstrates the power of deeper reflection, facilitates ongoing personal development, and ultimately benefits the clients we serve. It is a skill that is transferable from group to one-on-one supervision settings. For coaching supervisors looking to experiment with working together, this framework offers a powerful approach for working collaboratively.

There is a need for qualitative research to better understand the impact of group presence on coach well-being, professional development, ethical practice, and their overall quality and maturity as coaches.

## References

Blake, A., Strozzi-Heckler, R., & Haines, S.K. (2016). Somatics, neuroscience and leadership. *Strozzi Institute*. https://strozziinstitute.com/somatics-neuroscience-and-leadership-2/

Bugental, J. F.T. (1987). *The art of the psychotherapist.* W.W. Norton & Co.

Cochrane, H., & Newton, T. (2018). *Supervision and coaching: Growth and learning in professional practice.* Routledge.

Colosimo, K. (2013). *What does therapist presence look like in the therapeutic encounter? A rational-empirical study of the verbal and non-verbal behavioral markers of presence.* [Master's thesis, York University]. York Space Repository. https://yorkspace.library.yorku.ca/xmlui/bitstream/handle/10315/27553/Colosimo_Ken_A_2013_Masters.pdf?sequence=2&isAllowed=y

Colosimo, K. A., & Pos, A. E. (2015). A rational model of expressed therapeutic presence. *Journal of Psychotherapy Integration, 25*(2): 100–114. 10.1037/a0038879

Crane-Okada, R. (2012). The concept of presence in group psychotherapy: An operational definition. *Perspectives in Psychiatric Care, 48*(3),:156–164. 10.1111/j.1744-6163.2011.00320.x

Curry, D. (2003). *Healing presence: Experiencing the medicine of the naturopathic relationship. An organic inquiry.* [Doctoral dissertation, Saybrook Graduate School and Research Center]. Dissertation Abstracts International. B64/06, 2585. UMI No. AAT3094683.

Edmonson, A. C. (2018). *The fearless organization: Creating psychological safety in the workplace for learning, innovation, and growth.* (1st ed.). Wiley.

Edmondson, A. C. (2018, November 14). How fearless organizations succeed. *Strategy + Business.* https://www.strategy-business.com/article/How-Fearless-Organizations-Succeed?gko=63131

Feldman Barrett, L. (2020). *Seven and a half lessons about the brain.* Houghton Mifflin Harcourt.

Geller, S. M. (2001). *Therapists' presence: The development of a model and a measure.* [Doctoral dissertation, York University]. National Library of Canada. http://citeseerx.ist.psu.edu/viewdoc/download?doi=10.1.1.427.3025&rep=rep1&type=pdf

Geller, S. M. (2013). Therapeutic presence as a foundation for relational depth. In R. Knox, D. Murphy, S. Wiggins, & M. Cooper (Eds.), *Relational depth: New perspectives and developments.* (pp. 175–184). Basingstoke: Palgrave.

Geller, S. M. (2020). Cultivating online therapeutic presence: Strengthening therapeutic relationships in teletherapy sessions. *Counseling Psychology Quarterly.* 10.1080/09515070.2020.1787348

Geller, S. M., & Greenberg, L. S. (2002). Therapeutic presence: Therapists' experience of presence in the psychotherapy encounter. *Person-Centered and Experiential Psychotherapies, 1*(1-2): 71–86. 10.1080/14779757.2002.9688279

Geller, S. M., Greenberg, L. S., & Watson, J. C. (2010). Therapist and client perceptions of therapeutic presence: The development of a measure. *Psychotherapy Research, 20*(5): 599–610. 10.1080/10503307.2010.495957

Glaser, J.E. (2016). *Conversational Intelligence: How Great Leaders Build Trust and Get Extraordinary Results.* (1st ed.). Routledge.

Goldstein, J. (2016). *Mindfulness: A practical guide to awakening.* Sounds True.

Hawkins, P., & Shohet, R. (2007). *Supervision in the helping professions.* (3rd ed.). Open University Press.

Hawkins, P., Turner, E., & Passmore, J. (2019). The Manifesto for Supervision. Henley Business School and Association for Coaching.

International Coaching Federation. (2019, October). *Updated ICF core competencies.* https://coachfederation.org/app/uploads/2020/07/RevisedCompetencyModel_July2020.pdf

Jordan, J. V. (1986). The meaning of mutuality. *Work in progress,* 23: 1–11. https://www.wcwonline.org/vmfiles/23sc.pdf

Laszlo, E. (2007). *Science and the akashic field: An integral theory of everything.* (2nd ed.). Inner Traditions.

Laszlo, E. (2014). *The self-actualizing cosmos: The akasha revolution in science and human consciousness.* Inner Traditions.

Leeds, J. (2010). *The power of sound: How to be healthy and productive using music and sound.* (2nd ed.). Healing Arts Press.

Lu, B., & Fan, W. (2016, March). Social presence, trust, and social commerce purchase intention: An empirical research. *Computers in Human Behavior,* 56: 225–237. 10.101 6/j.chb.2015.11.057

Lucas, M., & Whitaker, C. (2014). A model of co-facilitation for supporting group coaching-supervision. *International Journal of Evidence Based Coaching and Mentoring,* 12(2): 1–9.

McLean, P. (2019). *Self as coach, self as leader: Developing the best in you to develop the best in others.* (1st ed.). Wiley.

Mearns, D., & Cooper, M. (2005). *Working at relational depth in counselling & psychotherapy.* (1st ed.). SAGE Publications Ltd.

Mearns, D., & Cooper, M. (2018). *Working at relational depth in counselling & psychotherapy.* (2nd ed.). SAGE Publications Ltd.

Merriam-Webster Dictionary. (n.d.). Presence. In Merriam-Webster.com dictionary. Retrieved January 8, 2021, from https://www.merriam-webster.com/dictionary/presence

Mind Fuel Daily. (n.d.). *The space between the notes.* www.mindfueldaily.com/livewell/the-space-between-the-notes/

Nuttall, M.D. (2019). Co-presence and the transpersonal field according to R.D. Laing: Pointing towards holism. *Journal of Transpersonal Psychology,* 51(2): 225–241.

Oh, C. S., Bailenson, J. N., & Welch, G. F. (2018). A systematic review of social presence: Definition, antecedents, and implications. *Frontiers in Robotics and AI,* 5: 114. 10.3389/frobt.2018.00114

Owen, H. (2008). *Open space technology: A user's guide.* (3rd ed.). Barrett-Koehler Publishers.

Palmer, W. (2008). *The intuitive body: Discovering the wisdom of conscious embodiment and aikido.* (3rd ed.). Blue Snake Books.

Proctor, B. (2008). *Group supervision: A guide to creative practice.* (2nd ed.). SAGE Publications Ltd.

Rogers, C. R. (2007). The necessary and sufficient conditions of therapeutic personality change. *Psychotherapy: Theory, Research, Practice, Training,* 44(3): 240–248. 10.1037/0033-3204.44.3.240

Rowan, J. (2005). *The transpersonal: Spirituality in psychotherapy and counseling.* (2nd ed.). Routledge.

Rumi, J.A. (2004). *The essential Rumi.* HarperOne.

Scharmer, O. (with Senge, P.). (2016). *Theory u: Leading from the future as it emerges.* (2nd ed.). Berrett-Koehler Publishers.

Schon, D.A. (1983). *The reflective practitioner: How professionals think in action.* Temple Smith.

Science & Nonduality. (n.d.). *David Bohm, Implicate order and holomovement.* https://www.scienceandnonduality.com/article/david-bohm-implicate-order-and-holomovement

Science & Nonduality. (n.d). *Nonlocality gets a boost - David Bohm revisited.* https://www.scienceandnonduality.com/article/nonlocality-gets-a-boost-david-bohm-revisited

Senge, P. M., Scharmer, C. O., Jaworski, J., & Flowers, B. S. (2008). *Presence: Human purpose and the field of the future.* Doubleday.

Shen, K., Yu, Y., & Khalifa, M. (2009, January). Knowledge contribution in virtual communities: Accounting for multiple dimensions of social presence through social identity. *Behavior and Information Technology, 29*(4). 10.1080/01449290903156622

Shohet, J., & Shohet, R. (2020). *In love with supervision: Creating transformative conversations.* PCCS Books.

Siegel, D.J. (2018). *Aware: The science and practice of presence – The groundbreaking meditation practice.* TarcherPerigee.

Siegel, D. (2019, January 9). Interpersonal connection, compassion, and well-being. *Embodied Philosophy,* (10). https://www.embodiedphilosophy.com/interpersonal-connection-compassion-and-well-being/

Silsbee, D. (2008). *Presence-based coaching: Cultivating self-generative leaders through mind, body, and heat.* (1st ed.). Jossey-Bass.

Siminovitch, D. E., & Van Eron A. M. (2008). The power of presence and intentional use of self: Coaching for awareness, choice, and change. *International Journal of Coaching in Organizations, 6*(3): 90–111.

Stern, D. N. (2004). *The present moment in psychotherapy and everyday life.* W.W. Norton.

Strozzi-Heckler, R. (2014). *The art of somatic coaching: Embodying skillful action, wisdom and compassion.* North Atlantic Books.

Welwood, J. (2000). *Toward a psychology of awakening: Buddhism, psychotherapy and the path of personal and spiritual transformation.* Shambhala Publications Inc.

Williamson, V. (2011, April 2). *The music of silence.* Music Psychology. https://musicpsychology.co.uk/the-music-of-silence/

Yalom, I. D. (1980). *Existential psychotherapy.* (1st ed.). Basic Books.

Yu, A. E. (2020). Co-creating a new shared reality: Exploring intersubjectivity in executive coaching relationships. In T.H. Hildebrant, F. Campone, K. Norwood, & E. Ostrowski (Eds.), *Innovations in leadership coaching: Research and practice.* (pp. 202–221). Fielding University Press.

# 13  An Exploration of Group Supervision

*Damian Goldvarg and Lily Seto*

Newer coaching supervisors are often looking for examples of coaching supervision. It might be useful to note that in recent years, an increasing number of coaches in the Americas (North, South, and Central) have trained as coaching supervisors. This example is offered as one model for a coaching supervision group process, albeit not the sole model used by coaching supervisors in the Americas. The authors introduce a group supervision session as a learning experience. The group consists of three coaches who graduated from the University of Southern California Professional Coaching Program, which is offered in partnership with the Goldvarg Consulting Group. One coach has two years of coaching experience and the remaining two coaches each have one year of experience.

The three supervisees (e.g., coach participants) were brought together expressly to record a session for the purposes of writing a book chapter. The coaches who participated in the group consented to being recorded and sharing their names for the purposes of this chapter. All agreed to using the session as the basis for a book chapter. It was explained that if any of the coaches were uncomfortable sharing the session, they could email their concerns to the authors and their recording would be deleted; no questions asked. The first draft of the chapter was shared with the coaches to ensure that they were comfortable with what was being presented. All of the participant coaches agreed that the chapter could proceed.

In this chapter we examine a single session of group coaching supervision and identify key elements of the group supervision process.

## Session

Although the three coaches were acquainted by graduating from the same coaching program and working for the same organization, they had not directly worked with each other. This was the first time they participated in group coaching supervision together.

The session was conducted virtually and took place April 2019. Goldvarg was the coaching supervisor. The group session lasted approximately one hour.

DOI: 10.4324/b23130-16

As experienced coaching supervisors, Goldvarg and Seto bring over eight years of group supervision experience to the session process and review. The authors evaluated the transcript of a group supervision session by identifying elements highlighted in the *EMCC Supervision Competence Framework* (2019), seven-eyed model of coaching supervision (Hawkins & Schwenk, 2011), and best practices and literature on group supervision. It is worth noting that the ICF, which is the largest coach credentialing organization in the Americas, does not offer a similar set of standards for coaching supervision. Thus, at present, the EMCC standards and associated frameworks are the main option for professional coaching supervisors.

## Evaluation Approach

The elements of the *EMCC Supervision Competence Framework* (2019) that we explore are standards related to working with groups. Facilitating group supervision involves the ability to skillfully handle supervisees and group dynamics, enabling all present to benefit from supervision. This is fostered by facilitators who (EMCC, 2019, p. 11):

- Contract with the supervision group to create a safe space for all members
- Work in service of the group as a whole as well as the individuals within it
- Support the supervision group through the stages of its development
- Adapt the supervision process according to group dynamics
- Elicit individual contributions
- Notice and draw attention to the effect of "parallel process" within the group
- Effectively manage time throughout the session

The seven-eyed model is comprised of seven modes (or "eyes") that a coaching supervisor can use with a coach to foster reflection and insight into the coach's engagements with their client(s) and systems within which they work. These seven modes are (Hawkins & Schwenk, 2011):

1   The client and their context
2   The coach's interventions
3   The relationship between the coach and the client
4   The coach's experience
5   The relationship between the coach and the supervisor, and potential parallel processes
6   The supervisor's self-reflections
7   The wider context

## Group Supervision Session

### Contracting

The first group supervision competence requires that the coaching supervisor "contracts with the supervision group to create a safe space for all members" (EMCC, 2019, p. 11). As the coaching supervisor for the session, Goldvarg began the session by explaining coaching supervision and emphasized that it is a reflective practice between colleagues that takes a systemic perspective and takes into account three systems: coach-client, coach-supervisor, and the overall context. He further explained that supervisees did not have to necessarily present a problem; they might spend their time validating what was already working well in their coaching practice.

Goldvarg made sure to offer key ground rules. Ground rules or group agreements are key to creating a safe space in the session that invites vulnerability and builds trust within the group. Additionally, group agreements address confidentiality, being present, respect, participation, collaboration, and being supportive. The coaching supervisor modelled respect and collaboration by asking the group several times, if there was anything else they needed to help them work at their best during the session. Two participants responded with requests to finish on time. This request was honored; an example of supporting one of the group's agreed upon "rules." As they wrapped up discussion of ground rules and moved forward, everyone expressed a willingness to be open and vulnerable.

Goldvarg further detailed the supervision process and explained that groups usually have three to seven participants. Generally, not all coaches have time to present a case in a single session. However, in this particular session, it was established among the group that the hour would be divided among three participants to allow each coach 20 minutes to present. The order in which each coach presented was agreed upon by participants. Although it was established that each coach would bring one case at a time, everybody was invited to engage and participate by sharing their thoughts and insights during the process. This is an example of the *EMCC Coaching Supervision Competency Framework* (2019) approach: *Effectively manages time throughout the session.*

Proctor (2008) suggests that the group supervisor should have a leadership role during the session to provide structure to the encounter and create safety for all participants:

> Leadership is needed to clarify rights and responsibilities and develop trust so that they can reveal their work in a rounded manner ... In the busy life of group supervision, think of them (working agreements) as like the walls of a bouncy castle. They hold the boundaries in a springy way and generate energy. In order to do that, they need to be well constructed and reliable. They also need readjusting in the light of experience. (p. 53–54)

A group contract should exist to maximize the group experience (Carroll & Gilbert, 2011). Carroll and Gilbert recommend the group contract include issues regarding how to give feedback, not to hold bad feelings, and how to relate theoretical concepts to their practice. They reinforce the importance of raising these issues at the outset of the group session to provide clarity on how to work together.

Following the contracting part of the session, the supervisor asked the first participant, Brooke to present her case, how long she had been working with the individual, and any background information that she wanted the group to know. This demonstrated the seven-eyed model's, eye 1: *Who the client is and what she is bringing to supervision* (Hawkins & Schwenk, 2011).

### Brooke's Case

Brooke mentioned that her client was not getting the management jobs that she applied for. The client wanted to look into why she was being passed up on jobs, learn what she could do differently, and work on a plan to move forward. Brooke and her client have been working together for four months, meeting every two or three weeks.

The group supervisor asked Brooke: "What should we know about the client?"

Brooke shared that her client was having some "aha" moments and wanted to gain understanding of what she needed to do differently. Her question for supervision was about how to move the client forward:

> We recycle some of the same conversations over and over again where she [the client] gets some insights. But in the subsequent sessions, sometimes we're talking about a slightly different topic, but the same concept. I don't see her as truly transforming … and some of the concepts and things that she seems to have "aha" moments with seem fleeting because in a subsequent session, we are talking about the same topic again. I'm not sure how to move her to see the bigger picture or help her to see where she's recycling the same topics over and over.

### Coaching Supervision Process

After a coach presents their case, there is usually a round of clarifying questions that help everyone to better understand what is happening. In this case, the supervisor asked clarifying questions to collect further information to better understand the case, not to provide hypotheses or to explore the issue(s), yet.

At this point, another participant said, "I have a similar issue, so I'm also interested in what tools I can use to see the situation from a different perspective."

This comment illustrates how groups invite participants (e.g., supervisees) to learn from each other's cases. The supervisor explained to the group that often group supervision normalizes common experiences. In this way, people realize they are not alone and that their colleagues may have similar challenges. The richness of group supervision allows people to learn not only from presenting their own cases, but also from listening and participating in their colleagues' cases.

The supervisor noted that, "By clarifying, you start seeing things." This means that clarifying questions are also a way to start looking at the situation from different perspectives, even though the goal of this part of the process is to get a deeper understanding of the case presented before jumping to explore the issue further (Hawkins & Schwenk, 2011).

This clarifying process provided Brooke with some insight.

One of the participants shared, "My clarifying question is: Did she recognize this in the conversation with you, that she is talking about a similar conversation from the past?" Brooke responded, "I'm going to say no and actually this is a light bulb for me because I really feel like I have not pointed out this pattern to her."

## Role of Other Participants in Group Supervision

After clarifying the case, Goldvarg asked Brooke what she needed from the group: "What would you like from your colleagues here? Because in supervision, we may need different things at different times. So today, right now, from this group, what do you need?"

This question is an important part of contracting because it clarifies the unique needs of the coach in addressing this particular case or situation. Contracting is dynamic and contracting questions are asked throughout the supervision session, not just at the beginning.

Brooke indicated that she wanted to explore patterns. The supervisor followed up and asked: "Today, what do you need from your colleagues around patterns?"

To which Brooke responded:

*I think maybe I have not taken her [the client] to the next level, digging deeper into her feelings and emotions about things. And partly I think that's because I feel like that will get her off track, but at the same time I think that's an area that I haven't focused on with her enough. It's not that I don't do it, cause I have another client where we've done that. But this particular client, I'm having trouble thinking of going to that next deeper level about her emotions of how she feels about her current job or her lack of movement or being able to get a promotion. I've been more pragmatic with her in terms of skills and competencies and we've really been at that level rather than delving a little bit deeper. So, I guess from this group, maybe any insight into when you've worked with a client and then you recognize that maybe you haven't gone deep enough ... any ideas or insight on how to transition?*

Another participant responded by sharing an experience with a client where she visualized stepping out her body and observing from afar:

> *I'm having trouble with one of my clients because she's unemotional. She says she cares, but she doesn't show it. One of the techniques that I've used a couple of times with other clients that I tried on her was to have her visualize stepping out of her body and being an observer from afar and taking a look at this person that she sees to see if she can give another perspective or another reason for some of the things that are happening or maybe be her own mentor, but step out of herself and probe. And I think maybe I didn't use silence enough. I think if I just was still and didn't try to jump in and was quieter and just waited, she might have come up with more stuff. So I'm now thinking, oh, this is helpful for me cause I'm realizing something that maybe I hadn't done.*

After each member of the group participated, the supervisor intervened and shared his own observations and hypothesis. This is an example of the *EMCC Coaching Supervision Competency Framework* (2019) approach: *The group supervisor elicits individual contributions.* In this case, the group supervisor not only invited the participants' perspectives, but also reinforced a point from one of the participants about moving from the "what" to the "who." The supervisor highlighted what Kevin had said: "The other possibility is that she is so focused on the "what" versus the "who" … because my hypothesis is that maybe the client is not getting the jobs because they know what she is doing, and she needs to focus on how she is showing up."

The supervisor shared a hypothesis about why Brooke's client was focused on doing versus being. He said:

> *"My hypothesis is that maybe she is not getting the jobs because of not what she is doing but how she is showing up and how she is perceived as someone that does not show emotions. I wonder about you giving feedback about your own experience of her."*

The supervisor then invited Brooke to move the focus from the client to herself and asked how she relates to risk taking. This demonstrates the seven-eyed model, eye 4: *What is happening to the coach working with the client* (Hawkins & Schwenk, 2011).

Brooke responded positively to everybody's comments and said:

> *Talking about this has made me see that in fact, I might not be serving her well by not taking that risk. I'm willing to take the risk now that I hear that I might be contributing to her not realizing and seeing more possibilities and growing more from this experience. Even though she sees the coaching as a very positive thing and she feels like she's learned a lot, I think there's more that could be done. She's not maximizing where she wants to be. I'm aware that I need to*

*now figure out the best way to approach it with her, in a way that she wants to continue on and that we can get to the next level and see if she wants to go there.*

The supervisor asked, "How do you relate to risk taking?" This points to questions around eye 4: What is happening for the coach? Also, what similarities can be drawn between the coach's and client's experience? (Hawkins & Schwenk, 2011). This process is called identification or parallel process because the coach resonated in a similar way to how the client behaved by playing it safe and not taking risks (Hawkins & Schwenk, 2011). At this point, Brooke realized that she needed to take more risks and that the risks were worth taking.

## Follow up

The group supervisor noticed that time was coming to a close for the first participant and suggested that the group start to wrap up the first case. This is an example of the *EMCC Coaching Supervision Competency Framework* (2019) approach: *Effectively manages time throughout the session.*

The supervisor engaged the participants for a final round and finished Brooke's case by asking: "One last round from the participants. Anything else you want to say about this case before we wrap up?"

Janette shared that the exploration of the case helped her with her own case: "I think it's similar to the client that I was going to bring up ... this has already helped me with my client that I was going to talk about."

The supervisor closed that portion of the discussion and reinforced how group supervision worked and how a case discussion was a good opportunity for all participants to learn, not only the one bringing the case.

This is what Proctor (2008) calls the supervisors' dual responsibility: "The supervisor has a dual responsibility. She is responsible for enabling and ensuring that good enough supervision is being done in the group. That responsibility carries with it the care for each individual's learning and development needs" (p.10).

### *Janette's Case*

Janette presented her case next:

> *This person is having difficulty making career and business decisions. The way she shows up is not the way she feels inside ... her face doesn't show emotions. She is not an emotional person, so she does not go deep. She stays in the 'what' but her request is about the 'who' and yet she doesn't want to go there.*

This demonstrates the seven-eyed model, eye 1: *Who the client is and what she is bringing to supervision* (Hawkins & Schwenk, 2011).

## Contracting

After Janette presented her case, the supervisor asked "What do you need from us?" (Hawkins & Schwenk, 2011). Janette replied:

> *"What do we do with people who can't connect with themselves? What questions*
>
> *can I ask? Techniques, approaches that would be helpful."*

The group supervisor asked for any clarifying questions. One was posed: "To what extent is the client aware that the lack of emotion is impacting how she is being perceived or how it impacts relationships?"

Janette responded, "The client said: 'This is my face; this is the way I am, very stiff, frozen'."

One participant asked Janette, "Is there an expressed desire to change?" Janette answered, "Only in the first session, then not so much."

Another clarifying question was asked, "How does she perceive her own willingness to change?"

Janette responded, "She said she is willing; however, she seems more focused on issues in her job and how to make some big decisions right now … she wants to be perceived as she cares and not as a pushover."

The group supervisor asked Jannete about the contract she had with the client. This is important because many times the contract is not clear or not used as a guide for the exploration of the coaching process.

Janette responded, "She wanted to explore where to go in her life."

The group supervisor shared an observation about the case: "It sounds like you are stuck." Janette agreed.

At this point, the supervisor introduced the concept of a parallel process. This is an example of the *EMCC Coaching Supervision Competency Framework* (2019) approach: *Notices and draws attention to the effect of 'parallel process' within the group.*

The group supervisor defined parallel process and explained that the coach repeats in the here and now [i.e., in the group supervision session], what happened in the session with the client. He said: "We may be stuck here and now in the same way your client was feeling. Was the client also feeling stuck?"

This demonstrates the seven-eyed model, eye 5: *Relationship between the coach and supervisor* (Hawkins & Schwenk, 2011).

Mattison (1977) hypothesized that the way in which group participants react and interact often mirrors the issue with the client that the counselor (coach) is presenting (parallel process). Proctor (2008) noted that "paralleling may happen all the time, but if not focused on, it is unrecognized" (pg.109).

The supervisor also shared that he felt stuck, "As the supervisor, I am feeling the same way. I am stuck." This demonstrated the seven-eyed model, eyes 5 and 6: *Observation from the supervisor on what is happening to him* (Hawkins & Schwenk, 2011).

The group supervisor then engaged the other participants by asking: "When you are stuck, where you don't see where to go, what do you do? How do you get unstuck?"

Kevin replied:

> *When I feel stuck, I am trying too hard to bend the situation the way I want it to go. I have a perception, or I think things should go in a certain direction … my own bias sometimes gets me stuck and I wonder if this might be happening with you.*

Brooke followed with, "When I am stuck, I have a perception I have to go in a certain direction, an opinion, my own bias may keep me stuck as well."

Janette validated her colleagues' comments and confided that she felt insecure with this client, who she perceived is very introverted and closed up. Janette shared: "I feel inadequate. What can I do to touch her? I need another approach to open up in a way that she will feel more comfortable, less stressed."

The group supervisor shared his own reaction (Hawkins & Schwenk, 2011) and used a metaphor:

> *I wonder what we may not be seeing here that may help you get unstuck. You started to see something about your style and what works for you. The image that came up for me was of "armor" protecting herself. You used the word protection. How do you go through that protection, her fear; what are her fears? Connection between who she is and who she wants to be. And this challenge that you are having in connecting with her; does she have this issue with others? Is this a good place to start?*

Using metaphors is a way of unlocking an unconscious way that the client is viewing a situation. In *Metaphors in Mind*, Lawley and Tompkins (2000) make the point that "metaphors carry a great deal of information in a compact and memorable package" (p. 9).

Once Janette validated her colleagues' comments, she then suggested that she would assess where her client was to consider any questions she may not have asked.

The supervisor followed up by asking Janette, "Who do you want to be as a coach for her?"

Janette did not answer the question. Instead, she answered with what she would do: "I really want to be a facilitator for her to open channels, windows to see new possibilities. Be able to move from being stuck."

It might have been useful to explore this metaphor of opening channels more fully, so she could move forward.

The supervisor engaged the participants one last time for this case and asked, "Any reactions?"

Brooke said, "I sense that there is discomfort for Janette and wonder how that impacts what they both want to accomplish."

Janette agreed and realized that she needed to notice things more and not try too hard. She shared that at the end of the last session with her client, it felt important to share resources and her client found this valuable:

> *I agreed to play the role of a mentor or an advisor and send her some resources that she might find useful. She immediately texted me back and she was very surprised by how quickly I found something for her and that she found it very valuable. So, you know, I let my guard down and I had said I'm no longer coaching. And that's where we ended up having a little bit of a connection.*

As Janette shared her desire to provide value through her coaching, the group supervisor reinforced the role of the coach and how it differentiated from the role of a consultant. This is a recurrent topic in supervision, in particular with newer coaches.

Janette shared that she needed to be comfortable sharing resources, and at the same time follow the rules of coaching. It was discussed that perhaps by using a different hat, a coach could move into a different role that provided value to the client.

The supervisor reinforced that coaching is not about giving advice, but rather sharing resources and best practices after the client has done most of the work. The supervisor closed Janette's case by acknowledging her willingness to be vulnerable especially in a group setting.

Vulnerability is key in conversations that we have in supervision. It allows for learning and growth. In groups, we take vulnerability to a larger forum. Sharing honestly and authentically requires some risk taking. In her research, Brown (2018) discovered that "the foundational skill of courage-building is the willingness and ability to rumble with vulnerability" (p, 11). She further defined vulnerability as "the emotion that we experience during times of uncertainty, risk and emotional exposure" (Brown, 2018, p. 19). In a project called "Aristotle," a team at Google concluded that successful group or team learning came from group members feeling safe enough to take risks and be vulnerable with each other (Inc., 2021).

### Kevin's Case

Kevin had participated in group supervision in the past. When he presented his case, we noticed a difference in how comfortable he was sharing his case and how he asked for what he needed from the other participants.

During his case presentation, Kevin shared:

> *My client is getting value; she wanted to work on her professionalism working with donors. We've had two sessions so far, the first session focused on appearances, the second session is on who she is being. The question I bring to*

*the group is how to stay in the present; she goes to the past to look at her future. I am a coach not a therapist. The focus is on who she wants to be. I explored emotions, and if they were helpful or not helpful to the situation at hand. Am I allowed to do that? How do I keep bringing her to the present and future instead of going to the past?*

The supervisor asked Kevin what he wanted from the group, to which Kevin responded: "I need help figuring out how to stay in the present and ask about what she [the client] is experiencing."

The supervisor asked for clarifying questions. One of the participants asked, "What are the triggers and how does she flip back to the past?"

Kevin responded, "She came from humble beginnings and now contrasts that with working with her very rich clients."

Janette asked how his client's past is helping her meet her goals. Kevin responded that it would be a good question to explore in the next session with her.

The supervisor then shared what he noticed and his own reactions. He noted that it was a good question to ask the client how the last (his past) comment related to the topic of coaching agreement, to bring her back to the present.

At this point, the supervisor took on the role of teacher and shared:

*Sometimes clients are attached to the past to explain their current life. Sometimes therapy may be required if something is incomplete and there is a need that is more than coaching. Sometimes people talk a lot about the past, to give meaning and to understand the present but if they are attached to the past and cannot let go, then therapy may be needed. Another issue is that when a client spends too much time talking about the past; is he or she avoiding the present by going to the past?*

The supervisor then invited reactions.

Kevin agreed and explained that for him, going to the past is a way to understand the present.

The supervisor asked another question: "Why are you bringing this up?"

Kevin responded:

*I love the rules. I'm a coach. I'm not a therapist. My focus is to support you to what you want to be in your future self. I think the way that I have managed it is often that it brings up emotions and I present those emotions as helpful or not helpful to the situation. I think that's the way to go; it's always a balance because I don't want to dwell in her past, but yet we always go there and I think for her, that's helpful. As a coach, I want someone to say whether I'm allowed to do that or not. That's what I would like from us. I think ways to take what she's expressing and make it valuable for a coaching session, so she wants to talk a little bit about, oh, I'm that way because when I was a child or my mother treated me a certain way, and I want to be able to say I understand but at the same time I want to make sure that we don't stay there. So, I'm always looking for ways to bring what she's experiencing to the present and future.*

*And I love the fact that while our first session was about appearances and then the second session had nothing to do with appearances, but it was about who she was being. So, my sense is she's doing work in between sessions. So, the question I bring to the group is not so much a concern of how to do this correctly but how a lot of our discussions inevitably go to her past. And she uses a lot of her past to make sense of her future and why she is the way she is and how she needs and wants to be different.*

The supervisor then explained the concept of transactional analysis and wondered how that might be related to the case presented. With newer coaches, supervisors may need to take a more didactic role, clarifying the role of coaching. This points to the role of the supervisor in knowing when to shift into the more didactic role of the formative element of supervision (Proctor, 2008). Because the participants are newer coaches, the supervisor thought that transactional analysis would be a useful tool to introduce into the session. He shared:

*I want to introduce you to the concept of Transactional Analysis. How many of you have heard of this idea that when we relate to someone, we may relate as a parent or child? So many times, in relationships, when we relate to each other, we may be relating in these patterns instead of treating each other as two adults, she (your client) may be seeing them (the donors) as parental figures, or they are donors that are inviting her into a child state. How do you relate to this Kevin?*

Kevin responded:

*I think that that is definitely there, an over respect, over deference to some people in her life that she's working with and that she brings these issues or concerns to the table to discover how she wants to improve upon the relationships. That's a good point … I don't know how to delicately bring that to light, what we're describing here but that's definitely some of the things we've talked about.*

The supervisor replied:

*If you go to YouTube or Google, there are many resources on transactional analysis and sometimes you can share a video with a client and ask, 'Do you see any familiar patterns here?' And then if you do, 'What will it require for you to relate as two adults instead of as parental or child figures?'*

The supervisor once again asked for reactions from other participants.

Janette noticed that transactional analysis was relevant to other relationships in her life, which was a broader application of the group supervision conversation:

*It triggered something in me. I'm now thinking of relationships that I have with some of my peers or friends. And there are times when I feel like a parent, and sometimes I actually feel like a child and that I'm being parented. It's fascinating how that comes into play within friendships and relationships, even in the workplace. So that might be something to explore.*

Kevin replied: "I am learning that I don't need to be afraid of the past. There just needs to be some separation."

The supervisor acknowledged Kevin's reflection as they worked together to wrap up his case. Then, to close the group supervision session as a whole, the supervisor asked participants what they learned from the session.

| | |
|---|---|
| *Janette shared:* | "I learned a lot and I'm interested in learning more about transactional analysis in relationships. I want to take away to not be parental, and to treat everyone on an equal level; to be mindful of that." |
| *Kevin noted:* | "I learned that being brave, sometimes challenging, and redirecting with a question, going deeper; bravery helps to be of better service to our clients." |
| *Brooke replied:* | "I learned a lot. I need to do more reflection and journaling about each client, and how I am performing." |

All the group supervision participants agreed with Brooke, and the supervisor closed by thanking everyone for their participation and willingness to be fully engaged and vulnerable during the session.

## Conclusion

In this supervision session, we observed a group conversation where typical coaching issues were brought to the session, such as feelings of feeling stuck, not making progress, not going deep enough due to client defensiveness, coaches' insecurities, and differentiating coaching from consulting and therapy. The coach participants were able to be vulnerable and share openly in part because of the psychological safety that was created at the beginning of the supervision session, agreed upon and supported by the group.

Other benefits of establishing a group agreement are described by Proctor (2008):

> If the supervisor can encourage an atmosphere of empathy, respect and authenticity, the process of negotiation prepares for and being the supervisor's task. At the same time the process builds a group working alliance which is founded on the shared vision and experience of the group (p. 60).

Several key elements of supervision were exhibited throughout the group session, such as setting up ground rules, checking in with supervisee(s) during the process, every coach sharing their case and actively participating, and the supervisor engaging other participants to co-supervise by sharing questions, observations and learnings. These are examples of the *EMCC Coaching Supervision Competency Framework* (2019) approach: *Notices and draws attention to the effect of 'parallel process' within the group* and *the group supervisor elicits individual contributions*. This is how we identified, throughout the evaluation, the competencies being demonstrated.

Similarly, we witnessed how some of the eyes of the seven-eyed model were used in the session to help foster reflection and insight within the coaches (Hawkins & Schwenk, 2011). These moments of gaining a new perspective resulted not only from the supervisor engaging with the participants, but also from the participants engaging with one another. This is a participative style of supervision. While the supervisor is tasked with striking a balance between the individual bringing a case and the other coaches who are learning from the case, group supervision can be good entry point for coaches who are new to supervision. Hearing cases from other coaches and learning of common struggles or joys can offer a sense of community and a great resource for coaches, especially those newer to the profession.

Finally, we would like to acknowledge that this example and analysis represents our own work as pioneers of supervision in the Americas. The process may be similar to work done in other parts of the world, but the content is unique to local systemic issues. We adopted the EMCC supervision competency model in our work because it aligned with our systemic work and because it's the current global standard. We know of one other coaching supervision competency model developed by the Association for Coaching (the only other association that provides coaching supervision accreditations worldwide) and it is very similar to the EMCC model.

We are aware of the limitations of our research. This is a single example from among many possibilities, conducted with a very small, select group all of whom were trained by the supervisor. Thus, the example may have limited application to groups following different models or facilitated by supervisors with different orientations.

*Special thanks to Kevin Corbett, Janette C. Brown, and Brooke Baldwin our coach participants and to Sarah Eustice for her superb research and editing skills.

## References

Bordin, E. S. (1983). A working alliance based model of supervision. *Counseling Psychologist, 11*(1): 35–43.

Brown, B. (2018). *Dare to lead.* Random House.

Carroll, M., & Gilbert, M. (2011). *On being a supervisee creating learning partnerships.* Vukani Publishing.

European Mentoring Coaching Council [EMCC]. (2019, June). *Supervision competence framework.* European Mentoring Coaching Council. https://www.emccbooks.org/product/supervision-competences

Hawkins, P., & Schwenk, N. (2011). The seven-eyed model of coaching supervision. In T. Bachkirova, P. Jackson, & D. Clutterbuck (Eds.), *Coaching and mentoring supervision theory and practice* (pp. 28–40). McGraw-Hill Education.

Hawkins, P., & Smith, N. (2013). *Coaching, mentoring and organizational consultancy: Supervision, skills & development* (2nd ed.). McGraw-Hill House.

Hawkins, P., & Turner, E. (2020). *Systemic coaching: Developing value beyond the individual.* Routledge.

Inc. (2021, Jan 5). *Google spent 2 years studying 180 teams. The most successful ones shared these 5 traits.* Inc. Magazine. https://www.inc.com/michael-schneider/google-thought-they-knew-how-to-create-the-perfect.html

Lawley, J., & Tompkins, P. (2000). *Metaphors in mind: Transformation through symbolic modeling.* Developing Country Press.

Mattison, J. (1977). *The Reflection process in casework supervision.* Institute of Human Relations. Tavistock.

Proctor, B. (2008). *Group supervision. A guide to creative practice.* Sage.

Stewart, I., & Joines, V. (2012). *Transactional analysis: A new introduction to transactional analysis.* Lifespace Publishing.

## Author Bios

**Damian Goldvarg** has 30 years of experience in executive assessment and coaching, leadership development, talent management, facilitation, strategic planning, and team building services. Originally from Argentina, he has extensive experience working with people from different cultures and social backgrounds. He has worked with individuals and organizations in over 60 countries, including the Americas, Europe, Africa, and Asia, offering services in English, Spanish, and Portuguese.

Damian is a master certified coach and received his Ph.D. in Organizational Psychology from Alliant University in California. He is also a professional certified speaker (CSP) and an accredited coach supervisor (ESIA) and facilitates certifications on professional coaching, mentor coaching, and coaching supervision. He was the 2013–2014 International Coaching Federation Global President and received the 2018 ICF Circle of Distinction Award for his contribution to professional coaching worldwide and the 2019 Supervision Award from the European Coaching and Mentoring Council.

**Lily Seto** is a global leadership coach and coaching supervisor with many years of experience. She holds a Masters in leadership and training and holds memberships and credentials with the International Coaching Federation (ICF-PCC) as well as with the European Mentoring and Coaching Council (EMCC), Supervision ESIA and senior individual coaching and team coaching. Lily has been facilitating both internal and external supervision groups since 2013. She is also the co-lead for the Americas Coaching Supervision Network, which has over 300 members from 25 countries.

# 14 Supervision in the Americas: Working with Virtual Technology

*Damian Goldvarg and Eve Turner*

## Introduction

This study addresses a gap in the literature of virtual coaching supervision with particular emphasis on the Americas. It draws on the experience of 20 of the most experienced coach supervisors working in the Americas who were interviewed one-to-one in early 2021. The growth in supervision globally has been well documented (e.g., McAnally et al., 2020; Hawkins & Turner, 2020) and the COVID-19 pandemic has made the use of virtual technology in working widespread globally (Turner & Goldvarg, 2021). But our research shows that virtual working for those in this study was very much part of their standard practice. This may be because supervision started later in the Americas: The first coaching supervisors were trained in 2013. The use of virtual technology was already prevalent by this time and used more routinely by those developing a supervision practice.

The research for this chapter was conducted during the COVID-19 pandemic, an event that brought about a huge increase in the use of virtual technology. The dramatic shift toward virtual working was reflected by changes in the stock and revenue of Zoom (an online video system), which rose 591% (Novet, 2020); in the third quarter of 2020, their total revenue reached $777.2 million, a 367% increase year-over-year (Zoom, 2020). The participants were part of a transformation in the first 20 years of the 21st century where, "4.66 billion people were active internet users as of October 2020, encompassing 59% of the global population" (Clement, 2021), compared to less than 7% in 2000 (Roser et al., 2020).

The purpose of this chapter is to contribute to the understanding and practice of virtual working in coaching supervision. In particular we aim to:

- Establish how widespread virtual working is among supervisors
- Share what participants saw as the advantages and disadvantages of virtual supervision compared to other forms
- Synthesize the top suggestions for improving the effectiveness of virtual working

DOI: 10.4324/b23130-17

# Methodology

The 20 participants were selected for the breadth and depth of their coaching supervision experience. The most experienced supervisors had 15 years and up to 1500 hours of supervisory experience. The remaining participants had between three and 11 years of experience. The average was just below 7 years of experience and 431 hours of supervision delivery. Supervisors were located in the US (14), Canada (3), Argentina (1), Brazil (1), Mexico (1).

All of the participants were interviewed using a semi-structured interview protocol. All the comments were entered into Word and manually coded according to their content.

# Results

In terms of technology, most participants reported using Zoom, Microsoft Teams, Skype, Facetime, and Webex video software approximately 95% of the time. Zoom was the most favored when a preference was given. The phone was also used, albeit much less frequently.

Supervisors generally enjoyed their virtual work and expressed a preference for working virtually. The main reasons given were: Comfort, working from home, not needing to travel or drive, not being in traffic or needing to park, having more flexibility of scheduling, working across different time zones, and the opportunity to work with anybody in the world. Additionally, participants talked of being more present, meaning that the person they were working with was closer to them, visually, when they were in front of the screen. During face-to-face work including work in groups, some supervisees may be more distant. One said, "I like being in the first role versus being in the back of a Broadway play." Interestingly, some supervisors reported that they became so used to virtual work they didn't even remember what it was like working face to face.

Some, however, did express reservations about working virtually and not being in-person. They commented on the importance of meeting a supervisee in-person for an exchange of energy. There was also mention that meeting face to face allowed the supervisor (or coach) to observe the whole body instead of only what was visible on screen. This limitation was coupled with perceptions that somatic work was more easily done in-person. As one participant described:

> In group supervision when people can touch and move their chairs, you get to see the whole-body seating in a chair, easier to look at the people. I can look at image but when face to face, I can take the whole person and several people at the same time.

Two supervisors shared stories and described that their perceptions had changed when they met with supervisees face-to-face. That said, several participants believed that it was still possible to create a conscious connection virtually.

## Advantages of Virtual Work

"It is fabulous working virtually."

Participant responses can be grouped under five main themes: Efficiency, global reach, connection, creativity, and self-awareness.

### Efficiency

Efficiency was one element highlighted above that participants related to less travel. Others related it to time boundaries as people showed up ready to work and do so with less "chit chat," while maintaining connection. From some participants there was a sense that ordinary daily life didn't show up in the virtual environment and therefore, work together could begin more quickly. Others described how easy it was to record a session or chat and then share as a resource for others to take away. For example, one participant noted that "in three seconds, I got a poem to the group. I can't do that in-person."

### Global Reach

The simplicity of setting up a virtual group makes it possible to deliver effective, group supervision across regions and time zones. Participants are able to connect with people from all over the world and have a group that brings diversity to their practice. One participant described how they were able to "move during the pandemic and nothing changed." Another added, "I love working virtually. It is global." Virtual working also allowed more people access to supervision: "We can reach more people." The ability to work in different time zones enabled for greater diversity and allowed this to be an intentional factor behind supervision work.

### Connection

Supervisors talked of seeing people in the context of their work and home environment, and felt there was an added richness in seeing their background. Many participants felt it was possible to craft a sacred space where people could be with each other and connect. Some also referenced how affordable it was to connect. For example, there were no transportation costs to meeting, so it made access easier. Respondents were keen to emphasize that meaningful work could be done virtually: "The most important thing is that … in a virtual environment, you can do good, important work!" Another stated: "We can still show emotions, be vulnerable."

*Creativity*

Creativity was illustrated in many references in the research. Participants were finding new ways of being creative and experimenting, for example showing pictures, using images or music, using chairs to represent others. One supervisor mentioned going for a walk with their supervisee during a one-two-one session, which allowed both to use what was being seen independently to stimulate the conversation. Other elements mentioned were the ability to take advantage of the platform, such as using the chat function and the ease with which it was possible to "share documents or work on documents in real time or open a model or tool that I want to share with someone, quickly showing in screen. This is not as convenient, face-to-face."

*Self-awareness*

Working virtually allowed some supervisors to "stay closer to myself. In person there is a tendency to focus on them, different emotional field, I feel I can look around the room, be better grounded, see other things." Some found they were more able to "tune into" mode six of the seven-eyed model (Hawkins & Shohet, 2012) and concentrate on what was going on in themselves, as the supervisor (pp. 101–103). As described by this participant: "Being attuned to my body, pick up what my supervisee may be feeling and experiencing, being aware, having antennas that pick-up information, share it if it is in the service of the supervisee, relationship." Other participants described feeling that something in the consciousness was extended beyond physicality when working virtually.

## Disadvantages of Virtual Work

Here the participant responses can be grouped under these main themes: Physical implications, body language, ethics, creativity, and distractions.

*Physical Implications*

Participants described that there were challenges with sitting in front of a screen, "A lot of hours sitting in the same place without moving, my eyes get tired." Some detailed a need to deliberately take action to counter this: "I need to look for ways to walk and exercise between sessions for my body and my eye." There could be greater challenges in reading body language, "I miss some of the nonverbal clues." Another believed that "We live in our bodies, working face to face you can use that more effectively. Sensing people, energy feels more complete." It could also take more effort to retain presence: "As supervisor, I need to work hard on being present." Others noted challenges around organization, specifically the challenges of starting on time and honoring time and agreements when some people had arranged sessions back-to-back.

### Body Language

In the virtual environment, participants needed to find different ways to be with and hold intense emotions. Some shared that it required even more sensitivity, and there was a need to be careful with what was present and not miss subtleties. In virtual working there may be a delay in picking up on emotional issues. As several participants highlighted, supervisors need to create safety and one felt it "takes a longer time to create safety and extra time to build rapport." There was also reference to the importance of paying attention to differences in culture. One supervisor mentioned that in some countries it might be inappropriate to show your face or home.

Some supervisors found it more challenging to do somatic work. Supervisors could not fully observe body language and the signals that might be provided, as they mostly only saw from the head up, not the whole body. "You may not get the body language, they can't see if I am tapping my foot." This also worked the other way round: "You might not see them crossing their legs and might not even see crossing arms," so there was a sense of limited access to the whole human experience. And as one said, there's "definitely no sense of smell involved!"

Another challenge supervisors described was picking up on the supervisee energetically or "how they feel, what you feel, what you picked up, the 'vibe', what you pick up from them." However, some felt that while they recognized "It is not the same energetically … I feel it does not stand in the way" of the work. This was linked to an inability to use ones full senses, with no option to be physical, touch, embrace: "I am limited to audio and visual."

### Ethics

While it was seen as an advantage to see people in context, there was consideration and sometimes concern about what might be going on in the supervisee's physical context. Questions arose like, "what is in the room?" and "who can hear?" And participants described a need to prepare the physical environment. Confidentiality was key to this and supervisors felt it was important to work on this and be intentional about it. Some participants had a sense that some people became too casual, and were concerned that the virtual environment could lead to privacy issues and might not feel like a professional environment. This was partly tied to the need to create a safe environment and to contract, e.g., regarding permission to record.

### Distractions

Participants described a range of distractions both physical and technological. Examples ranged from children coming into the room to a front doorbell ringing. Technology could also prove problematic. This could be because Internet connections were poor and intermittent or resulted from people being unfamiliar with the new technology (or both). And from a diversity perspective, one participant voiced concern that some clients and coaches, such as Indigenous communities, might not have adequate access to wi-fi technology and be disadvantaged as a result.

### Creativity

Participants also linked working virtually to challenges in creativity. Some referenced exercises that were done in person that couldn't be done virtually: "I tried and some exercises are difficult relating to somatic work, and there is a difference." Another stated, "I need to be creative and there are limitations such as working with Legos. But in my place, I have different tools." One respondent recognized that while working virtually might not be quite as easy, some of the creative challenge "may be my own resistance." However, certain tools were difficult to share: "The magic box, figures to represent, it is easier in person."

## Recommendations for Working Virtually

In the final section of our research, we asked participants to share their suggestions for how to make virtual work as effective as possible. The recommendations build on themes mentioned earlier. We have collated these under three main headings, starting with the need for preparation and then embracing building the relationship and finally, attending to and expanding the field. Technology appears under the first main heading, but is essential to all three. After these recommendations, we draw from other work to make further suggestions.

### Preparation

#### Body Language

In considering our body language, the experienced supervisors in the Americas urged us to be intentional about paying attention to the whole body and applied that to both the supervisor and the supervisee. As supervisors, they suggested we spend more time getting centered, focused, quiet, and present to allow us to be most reflective. They encouraged supervisors to be aware of their face and body language and how they come across. Then in working with our supervisees, we can encourage them to do the same by asking what is going on their body, what their body is saying, and what they are noticing. We can ask the supervisee to take into account both their face and body language. As one supervisor mentioned, we need to read body language more thoroughly and look for small changes that will allow us to get more information.

*Technology*

Technological preparation is key, and this starts with ensuring there is good Internet access and checking we have everything set and ready, such as knowing that our microphone and camera are working. This creates "the right conditions to work." Participants also stressed the need to have a backup phone line ready in case there are Internet problems and to know who is calling whom and on what number! Being familiar with how the technology works is part of this preparation. For example, know how the supervisor or the supervisee can turn off self-view in Zoom, if that is distracting. As one participant shared, "I like the idea of hiding yourself, so you only see the other person."

Participants highlighted the importance of contracting in advance, particularly when working in groups and establishing clear expectations such as having cameras and audio on or off. Different groups may have different expectations. By contracting, we can co-create what happens and set mutual expectations. The contracting extends to recording and as an additional safeguard, it was recommended that supervisors ask for permission before recording each time. Participants also recommended that the agreement also include leaving electronic distractions off during the session such as turning off email notifications and avoiding multitasking. These guidelines will help supervisors avoid any awkwardness and ensure "you are not distracted by other stuff." Participants also emphasized a need to pay attention to our own background and any noise or distracting actions going on, so that people can concentrate and hear us clearly.

*Self-care*

Supervisors stressed the importance of having regular breaks to avoid virtual fatigue with a "need to be alert to this, as it can be exhausting being in video conferencing all day." This includes allowing a break of at least 15 minutes between clients as part of taking care of ourselves between calls and avoiding "the rush of going from meeting to meeting in Zoom." Similarly, they recommended ensuring that supervisors don't work for more than two hours without taking a longer break. They also urged supervisors to "allow sufficient time to connect, join, and breathe together at the start" of a session.

A further way of providing self-care is to regularly look away from the screen and help the eyes focus on different focal points. As one participant described: "Do not be afraid to go away from the screen, keep soft eyes, open, receptive versus pinpoint focused." Linked to self-care was the recommendation that supervisors pay attention to time differences when scheduling sessions. This includes choosing a time of day that works for us. One respondent said, "I do sessions early in the morning, so I am not tired. Not at the end of the day."

*Efficiency*

To enhance effectiveness and efficiency, they recommended always leaving the camera on, ensuring microphones are open, being sure we are in a quiet space, and setting up a work environment that will most support us and our supervision efforts. There was also a theme of not letting working virtually "be in the way." This mode of work is enabling us to serve others in need and it is what the world needs us to do today. There was a shared belief that virtual working would continue post-pandemic and possibly increase, given people are increasingly comfortable with this format and understand its benefits. Given the global nature of our work, participants recommended sending invites as calendar invitations to ensure they are scheduled in the right local time and sending emails with online meeting details (such as Zoom login information) as a back-up.

### Establishing a Safe Relationship

*Building the Relationship*

When meeting virtually, we need to make time to connect as human beings and get to know one another rather than just getting straight down to work. This includes devoting time before a session to our mental and physical preparation, as mentioned above. We are each different and knowing ourselves, we need to consider how much preparation we need and how to ready ourselves most effectively (e.g., by meditating).

In contracting, we also need to use our agreements to create safety for individuals and groups, as this allows work to go deeper. One supervisor mentioned how contracting is necessary to explore implicit expectations. There is a desire to be open to what works for clients, and clearly share how technology will be used and technical issues will be handled. For example, if a client is disconnected from a session, will they have the option of re-admittance (through a waiting room in Zoom) or are they blocked from re-entry ("locking the room" in Zoom). Questions supervisors can pose include: "How do you feel about the virtual environment"; "Do you have any reservations"; "What might we take for granted that needs to be explicit"; "What is the impact of virtual working on you?" These questions can be used when contracting to capture what might be "in the room." Everyone has a different preference; therefore, experience and expectations need to be clear. Through our contracting we can invite members to share the whole experience of what is happening and honor any differences.

*Ethics*

Supervisors stressed the importance of making sure we are working with someone who is trained as a supervisor. They also mentioned the need to take time, both as a supervisor and with your supervisees, to identify and reflect on bias and any beliefs about working virtually. Part of our self-work is to ensure that we show up authentically, trust the process, share what happens, and aim to be aware of own blind spots. There are also practical elements: Being explicit about what data may be recorded, how data will be stored and secured, being clear about who will have access to it, and what information will be transmitted in emails. As one participant said, "Discuss breach of confidentiality, how to manage recordings in group supervision, and how secure the recording and its transit is."

### Attending to and Expanding the Field

#### Creativity

There is a sense that creativity in virtual working is both key to successful supervision and feasible with some forethought. Participants encouraged supervisors to be more intentional about using technology, open to creativity, and alert to different approaches. The importance of modelling creativity was clear to participants: "Don't be afraid to try things, including new things and encourage supervisees to try new things too." Another advised: "Try new things, don't be afraid the supervisee will not see these the same. Have faith that the supervisee will co-discover together with you and have faith the work needed will be done." A number of techniques were suggested including Mural (an online whiteboard) and two chairs (to "bring" someone else into the room). Another participant shared: "Invite supervisees to move – to walk around, to get into their bodies, and not only use their mind." Contract around and set up the use of drawing. Participants noted the importance of forethought and preparation, "When using tools, ensure that the supervisee has these in advance such as 'Points of You', or Magic Box."

#### Cultural Differences

There was reference above to different cultural considerations encountered by participants, such as the appropriateness of showing our face and home during sessions. This led participants to emphasize the need to be present and sensitive to different cultures when working virtually and ensure this always informed our ways of working. This requires us to be more present to build trust and ask the client what they need to be present. As authors, we would also recommend that supervisors be present and sensitive to cultural differences in the acceptability of eye contact.

#### Energy Work

Participants were very alert to energy in working virtually and stressed the need to "watch the energy in the room and never underestimate the field, the energy, use your intuition." Supervisors mentioned paying attention "to how safe the individual or group feels. And pay attention to what you are seeing, conscious of the environment you want to create, or evoke." Another wrote, "Working virtually, I found myself thinking 'embody presence more, be more conscious around energy.' There is something before the start, taking time to center. What I am picking up in terms of their energy? Checking energetically, what is going on?" Some respondents were self-conscious they might miss things, so they recommended supervisors adopt a reflective practice themselves, reviewing sessions, doing written reflections on the quality of the presence. "What do you see as patterns, cadence of interactions? Building a muscle. What distracts you in the moment?" And finally, respondents reminded us to slow down as we can have a tendency to go in a rush. In virtual work, it is essential to create silence to pause, just as in face-to-face work.

*What else?*

In a short piece written around the time of the first COVID-19 pandemic lockdown in the UK, Hawkins and Turner (2020) drew on their experiences of running virtual sessions globally for some years. Their additional considerations included considering the appropriateness of what people see behind you, including what is written on book covers! Our visibility is another theme that captures the importance of arranging our screens and cameras so at least our faces and hands are in the frame (we have probably all experienced many cut-off chins and missing necks!). They also suggested noticing how light falls at different times of day, so we are neither too bright nor in shadow. One aid to address this can be positioning directional lighting on either side of the screen. Given how often we have all experienced technical issues, it is sensible to predict and prepare for these so we are not adversely affected at the time and can retain a calm exterior!

When working with groups it can be extremely helpful to create opportunities for the sort of social bonding that is commonplace when we meet face-to-face—those conversations over the coffee machine! One method is to put people into small breakout rooms as they arrive for "coffee" so people can catch up and just have a chat, without the conversation being content driven by the day's topic. Hawkins and Turner (2020) also encouraged sufficient comfort breaks. This also allows for the very necessary rest we need for our eyes. Studies during the COVID-19 pandemic lockdown have shown that increased screen time has had negative consequences for children's eye health, including large increases in new cases of myopia (Freund, 2021). All those using screens for long hours are advised to "look up from the screen more often, let your eyes wander and spend more time outdoors."

To this we would add one practical consideration that has emerged as a potential issue over time: Ensuring we have the most up-to-date software downloaded, including for the video system we are using. Doing this, and encouraging our supervisees to do the same, can save time and make communication easier and more secure.

Finally, while we may not be able to meet our supervisees, we can still bring in nature and let ecology be a partner to our supervision. At its simplest, this may be simply looking out the window and sharing what we see, hear, and feel. One of us also regularly does walking sessions, with trusty mobile and headphones. We walk for the duration of the session and share what we see, hear, and feel and are enriched by how it adds to our understanding and appreciation of the situation and brings in new perspectives.

## Conclusion

The results from our study show that coaching supervisors considered virtual work beneficial as it can save time and money and allow professionals to work with colleagues all over the world. However, supervisors also identified a range of challenges that included technology, ethical considerations, and distractions. One element that wasn't raised in the Americas study as compared to prior research (see Turner & Goldvarg, 2021), was that of the world environment. None of our participants mentioned the link between how virtual work limited the necessity of travel and decreased our environmental footprint.

Our research was only conducted with supervisors, and a future study might ask coaches the same questions and gain insights into their experience of virtual working, particularly as it relates to their supervision sessions. Might their experiences differ? It would also be interesting to understand what supervisors and supervisees experience as the "best" virtual backgrounds. One of the authors sat in on a virtual workshop about health and well-being in which a main presenter had their wine collection in the background and wondered what impression the presenter created by doing so. This raises more questions about what makes for a most effective work setting. We also note that the preference for virtual working among supervisors in the Americas suggests we will need to pay attention to our vision and eye health as part of our well-being.

Our study shows that virtual working in supervision is already well established in the Americas. For several supervisors, virtual supervision is the only supervision they know. Our hope is that future training for coaches and supervisors will take that into account and explore what best practice means and how to achieve it with those in training, including what might be the advantages, any pitfalls and how to make the most of the medium. There is also a need for more research on creativity in virtual supervision. We are sure many more tools will become available to support our clients in the future, from virtual reality communication tools to sophisticated whiteboard systems to systemic constellations. While there are obviously physical limits when it comes to visually reading body language, other limits may only be in our imagination!

## References

Clement, J. (2021). *Worldwide digital population as of October 2020*. Statista. https://www.statista.com/statistics/617136/digital-population-worldwide/

Freund, A. (2021, January 21). *COVID-19 and eyesight: Myopia on the rise during lockdown*. DW: Made for Minds. https://www.dw.com/en/covid-19-and-eyesight-myopia-on-the-rise-during-lockdown/a-56301421

Hawkins, P., & Shohet, R. (2012). *Supervision in the helping professions* (4th ed.). Open University Press.

Hawkins, P., & Turner, E. (2020). Working from home. In K. McAlpin, & D. Norrington (Eds.), *Surviving the coronavirus lockdown and social isolation*. Wordcatcher Publishing. www.wordcatcher.com/LetsResetNormal

McAnally, K., Abrams, L., Asmus, M., & Hildebrandt, T. (2020). *Global coaching supervision: A study of the perceptions and practices around the world*. https://coachingsupervisionresearch.org/wp-content/uploads/2020/02/Global_Coaching_Supervision_Report_FINAL.pdf

Novet, J. (2020). Zoom's astronomical growth rate appears to be moderating; shares fall. *CNBC*. https://www.cnbc.com/2020/11/30/zoom-zm-earnings-q3-2021.html

Roser, M., Ritchie, H., & Ortiz-Ospina, E. (2020). Internet. *Our World in Data*. https://ourworldindata.org/internet

Turner, E., & Goldvarg, D. (2021). Supervising virtually. In T. Bachkirova, P. Jackson, & D. Clutterbuck (Eds.), *Coaching & mentoring supervision: Theory and practice* (2nd ed.). Open University Press.

Zoom. (2020). *Zoom reports results for third quarter fiscal year 2021*. https://investors.zoom.us/node/8261/pdf

## Author Bios

**Damian Goldvarg** has 30 years of experience in executive assessment and coaching, leadership development, talent management, facilitation, strategic planning, and team building services. Originally from Argentina, he has extensive experience working with people from different cultures and social backgrounds. He has worked with individuals and organizations in over 60 countries, including the Americas, Europe, Africa, and Asia, offering services in English, Spanish, and Portuguese.

Damian is a master certified coach and received his Ph.D. in Organizational Psychology from Alliant University in California. He is also a professional certified speaker (CSP) and an accredited coach supervisor (ESIA) and facilitates certifications on professional coaching, mentor coaching, and coaching supervision. He was the 2013–2014 International Coaching Federation Global President and received the 2018 ICF Circle of Distinction Award for his contribution to professional coaching worldwide and the 2019 Supervision Award from the European Coaching and Mentoring Council.

**Eve Turner** researches and writes on various subjects including supervision, systemic coaching, eco-conscious coaching and supervision, ethics and contracting including books, articles, and chapters. Her most recent, best-selling book is co-authored with Peter Hawkins, *Systemic coaching: Delivering value beyond the individual*; her first was co-edited with Stephen Palmer, *The heart of coaching supervision: Working with reflection and self-care*. A fellow at Henley Business School and the University of Southampton, Eve is an active volunteer within the profession. Chair of the professional body APECS (Association of Professional Executive Coaching and Supervision) she has also co-founded the Climate Coaching Alliance www.climatecoachingalliance.org. Eve also set-up in early 2016, and leads, the Global Supervisors' Network, a unique, free-of-charge, participative personal and professional development network for supervisors worldwide working in coaching, coaching psychology, mentoring, and consultancy: www.eve-turner.com/global-supervisors-network.

An accredited master executive coach and master supervisor, Eve has won several awards including the EMCC 2018 Supervision Award and its 2015 Coaching Award, four from Coaching at Work magazine, the 2018 Contributions to Coaching Supervision Award, the 2015 and 2019 Best Article Award, and the 2020 Contributions to Climate Coaching Award, and received the BPS Special Group in Coaching Psychology's 2008 award for a distinguished research project.

# 15 The Creative Journey in Coaching Supervision

*Susie Warman*

## Introduction

When my daughter turned eight, she invited friends over for a pajama party. As her birthday was the day prior to Halloween, I decided to entertain them by dressing up as a witch and making up scary stories to tell. The girls could not blink while I was talking; the costume seemed so real that even my daughter didn't recognize me. The story ended up being scary, relative to the audience. Consequently, I had another challenge: None of them were able to fall asleep. Worried that I could be facing a long night ahead, I made my way to the kitchen and came back with a "special drink" (liquid yogurt with green food coloring), and told them that if they drank it, all of their fears would fade away. Once again, they fell for my story and "voilà," in a blink of an eye, they were all experiencing REM state of sleep. Today, 25 years later, we still laugh about that night.

Time has taught me that children's minds can shift from reality into fantasy in a blink, sometimes without them realizing it. Lahad (2000) recommended that we, adults, think more like children and allow ourselves to come and go from reality into fantasy without fear.

Not so long ago, as I was leading a group supervision, I had the intuition that the supervisee was being too rational and needed an image to build up his train of thought. It was once again close to Halloween and that creative Halloween night 25 years ago came to mind. I told the group, "while listening to our supervisee, if you could disguise as someone or something that would better represent our supervisee's case, what would you dress up as, and why?" The results were fantastic! The supervisee began surfacing and acknowledging personal beliefs, integrating rich learnings and insights, which had been previously invisible to her.

Creating a visual representation for our supervisee fostered collaboration that was expressed in a non-rational way. By being creative in coaching and supervision, we can unlock blind spots, and penetrate locked doors in our clients' minds.

Throughout this chapter, reflections will be shared on how clients can bring deep thoughts into their coaching and supervision journey. I'll also

DOI: 10.4324/b23130-18

explore the impact that play, metaphors, and other methods can have in disclosing powerful parallel processes on supervisees. Informing this chapter and my insights are data collected from an online survey and personal interviews, and assessments of 20 supervision recordings that had been obtained from Goldvarg Consulting archives and public supervision demonstrations. Throughout the chapter, I also share findings, conclusions, techniques, and insights from colleagues who participated in the research study as well as insights taken from the recordings. Excerpts from a supervision session that portrayed the use of diverse creative techniques have also been included.

Hypothesis: Being creative in a supervision session helps the supervisee go deeper and gain awareness and understanding, which otherwise might not be available. By utilizing unconventional methods, supervisees can surpass unconscious barriers and overcome an unwillingness to face vulnerability.

> *"Creativity is contagious, pass it on"*
> --Albert Einstein

### How does Creativity Interact with our Brain?

There has been a lot of interest in learning about creativity over the past 60 years. A lot of debate and research studies have been generated to understand what is really triggered in our brain when being creative. Neuroscience studies suggested that to be "creative" entails our brain's left and right hemispheres becoming equal partners. Each hemisphere functions differently. People are either left- or right-brained, meaning that one hemisphere is usually more active than the other. If you are mostly analytical and methodical, you are considered to be left-brained. Otherwise, if you tend to be more creative, artistic or intuitive, you are considered to be right-brained. Lahad (2000) suggested that to use both realms creates a dialogue between them. Notwithstanding, recent research has suggested that creative thought is a result of several large-scale networks interacting in the brain's cortex. Kaufman's (2013) neuroscience research on creativity suggested that the right brain/left brain distinction is not able to offer us the full picture of how creativity works in the brain. He maintained that we cannot separate both realms as creativity does not involve a single brain region or single side of the brain.

Gash (2017) brings an interesting view to the working of the brain. He posited that the left-brain right-brain concept should only be seen as a metaphor as the whole brain is involved in creative thought and action.

### Defining Creativity

According to Wikipedia (n.d.), the term *creativity* comes from the Latin term *creare*, "to create, make." Creativity is a phenomenon whereby something new and somehow valuable is formed. In order to create "something new," we need to be curious and open our minds, hearts, eyes, and ears to everything around us. To be "creative" we also need be "courageous," approaching our fears as an invitation to stretch ourselves above and beyond. Our fears may appear in the form of either a lack of success and inability to translate ideas into a transformational process, or as not being "good enough." I always encourage people to try new things as long as they are safe and purposeful. Fun, new resources brought into session will create a common bond between supervisor and supervisee, which may normalize the process. Take a dive in your inner self by introspecting: What is my fear asking from me? How can I attain the courage needed? Is there anything I need to let go? Am I protecting something? What may be my blind spot?

*"A person who never made a mistake never tried anything new"*
--Albert Einstein

We must keep in mind that comfort is the killer of creativity. Be open to experimenting and exercising the mastery skill of simply not knowing. Supervisees may find discomfort in availing themselves to different methods such as metaphors or "play spaces" that we bring to the session. Once the shared sense of psychological safety is established, supervisees are able to bring their true selves into the room. Self-compassion plays an important role within ourselves, too. Permitting ourselves to make mistakes or be mistaken, makes us stronger.

Creativity in coaching and supervision is related to engaging through imagery, play, and other tools that bring magic to the session, creating a state of deep reflection and learnings for our clients.

The concept of creativity has drawn attention in our profession over the past few years. Supervision, being so open and free, permits innovating that may produce deep insights in the supervisee.

Being creative also helps us as supervisors, to bring our whole selves to the session as an instrument for learning. The possibility to look into different systems may appear to be permitting parallel processes to show up and stimulate reflection. Research has proven that practicing "creativity" in supervision increases energy, enhances intuition, self-confidence, and vulnerability; hence, it fosters deep learnings. I have discovered that the more creative these methods are, the more fun the learning becomes.

## Research Study

I began conducting research using interviews and a survey from our supervisor network in the Americas. Almost 50% of participants were based in US and Canada, the rest were in Latin America. Listening to a vast amount of supervision recordings was helpful for drawing conclusions. Aside from the hypothesis testing, I had two additional goals. My first objective was to understand what is required from supervisors to feel confident in bringing creative techniques into our sessions. My second objective was to have our colleagues share their creative techniques and use of metaphors, which could complement the wider group. The results yielded as expected, a general consensus that we each are creative in different ways.

### Information Gathered in our Research

I posed the following questions to study participants:

- How much more do supervisors prefer being creative rather than utilizing traditional techniques?
- How creative are supervisors?
- How much risk are supervisors willing to take in experimenting with new techniques?
- What "creative techniques" have been utilized in supervision sessions?
- To what extent have metaphors been used within supervision sessions?

Based on these data, 57% of the supervisors had between three and four years of experience as supervisors, while 21% had under a year of experience (see Figure 15.1). Most of the supervisors (71%) felt confident trying creative techniques during sessions. In our sample, more North Americans used creativity in sessions than did Latin American coaches. I was gratefully surprised that the years of experience as a supervisor had no effect on taking risks during sessions and trying something different! However, it was found

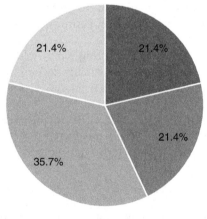

■ <1 year   ■ 1-2 years   ■ 3-4 years   ▪ >5 years

*Figure 15.1* Time that I've been a Supervisor? (24 answers).

that 29% of the supervisors utilized creativity occasionally, yet not on a regular basis. Some reasons stated were "I feel uncomfortable," "I can't find the right metaphor, prefer not to use," "worried that it might not work," "I don't know when to use them," and "just haven't try it yet." We asked the 71% who did use creative techniques, to share the impact of these technique on their supervisees, and provide examples. Most agreed that it usually shifted the conversation in new directions and allowed insights and generative learning to become apparent, which otherwise may have never surfaced. It is a way to discover more opportunities.

Through this methodology, supervisees can discover how to use personal resources to understand personal challenges and engage further. This is especially true if the method mixes up the format of how we "normally" interact. It enables supervisees to break through barriers or patterns that are holding them back. Most importantly, it enables prospects to see and embody new possibilities, following which energy shifts and optimism increases.

As an outcome of the research, I broke down different "creative techniques" into the following categories:

1   **Use of Metaphors**

   a   **By Clients:** Inviting client to create a metaphor
   b   **By Supervisor:** Supervisor sharing a metaphor

2   **Images:** Pictures, postcards, images, drawings, white board, art, visualizations, or meditation
3   **Narrative:** Storytelling, role playing, acting, or constellations
4   **Play; crafts and objects:** Play-Doh, Lego, cubes, Playmobil, magic box, mural, hats, or costumes
5   **Music and corporal movements:** Expressing emotions with music, asking client to use physical movement, inviting a client to engage in an imaginative journey.

I share more examples below on how coaches and supervisors have used some of these tools.

## The Power of Metaphors

Sullivan and Reese (2008) in their research, explain how metaphors are the language of the unconscious mind where words stand for symbols of something else. In this sense, images have potential information embedded in them. A figure of speech by which a word or phrase stands for something else. My research showed that 95% of supervisors and coaches felt comfortable using metaphors as a tool (see Figure 15.2) and used them frequently during coaching and supervision. Metaphors are present in many ways in our everyday language. We often use expressions such as: A weight

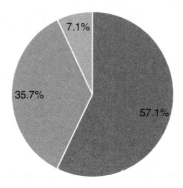

■ Always ■ Often ■ Sometimes ■ Seldom ■ Never

*Figure 15.2* Do I Feel Confident Utilizing Metaphors in My Supervision Sessions? (24 Answers).

is lifted; we are living on a rollercoaster; he or she broke my heart; you light up my life; you are my sunshine; I'm breaking apart; let's do an ice breaker, I'm drowning in a sea of grief; hope is on the horizon; a needle in a hay stack; knot in my stomach; hit a brick wall; fishing for compliments; wading through mud; spreading my wings; and heading in different directions.

Do these sound familiar? As noted, combinations of simple words are being used to portray colorful pictures. A metaphor is a figure of speech containing an implied comparison. According to Your dictionary (2020), the definition of a metaphor is "a word or phrase used to compare two unlike objects, ideas, thoughts or feelings to provide a clearer description." The word metaphor itself comes from a Greek term meaning to "transfer" or "carry across." In this sense, according to Wikipedia (2020), metaphors "carry" meaning from one word, image, idea, or situation to another, and linking them.

According to that definition, the purpose of the metaphor is to carry precious information, inviting us to shift our state from the left brain thinking (logical) to the conscious mind, and access to other sources of information. Metaphors can unlock our unconscious mind by comparing the known to the unknown, the abstract to the concrete. As a result, good metaphors help the supervisee understand something they otherwise might not, creating vivid messages in our minds. Kaufman and Gregiore (2015) refer to a "seed moment," when the first seeds of an idea are shown. New ideas appear suddenly and a supervisee can build over them. According to one participant in our study, being creative helps coaches take a step and jump over internal barriers, expressing the unspoken, sharing deeptriggers or hidden emotions, externalizing complex perceptions, and making sense of them. This further integrates body, heart, and mind, and helps the supervisee embark on a transformative journey in the session.

The use of metaphors makes sense in our profession. Being that our clients are creative and resourceful, metaphors help us bring them from a rational way of thinking into exploring new ideas. The supervisor must not only explore what is happening to the supervisee, but also ask systemic questions about all of the systems impacting our client's process. How are other stakeholders impacted in the relational system of the client? Hopkins and Turner (2020) have conducted extensive studies into systemic coaching that can inform these efforts.

## Using Metaphors in Coaching & Supervision

1  **Supervisee using metaphor:** Inviting the client to create a metaphor. If you were to come up with an image, picture, symbol that could represent what XY might look like, what would that be? In this way, we are bringing the subconscious into the room. For example, if you were a book, what book would you be? What resonates with you? We could also look into other systems and ask: "If you would be dancing with X, how would the dance be?" To get a systemic view, we could ask: "If you were watching the dance of your client with their stakeholders or with you, from a theatre balcony, what would you see?" Alternatively, we could ask: "If you were to be watching your relationship with your client from a drone, what would you be seeing?"

2  **Supervisor offers metaphor:** In this case, the supervisor asks permission to share a metaphor with the client. After hearing it, the client might reply, "well it is not quite that, but it is this … " Thus, providing input. When sharing a metaphor, we must always follow it with a question such as "how does this land on you?" Or "of what has just been said, what resonates with you?"

## Why Use Metaphors

Benefits of using metaphors include the following:

1  Creates rapid understanding
2  Challenges self-disclosure. Using images or language can be easier for our client when talking through sensitive topics, bypassing intense emotions
3  Changes relationship to an issue when currently stuck
4  Accesses unconscious resources of new information held at the bottom of the iceberg
5  Utilizes symbols and images that have potential for information on them
6  Explores other interconnected systems
7  Helps illustrate a point

I have added a number of examples of metaphors and creativity used by supervisors during our research in Appendix 1.

## Serious Play in Supervision

Learning and discovering through play can be meaningful and powerful. Sanbar (2020) shared how he utilizes "play" in supervision sessions. Here are some of his thoughts:

> *We might believe that to reflect and gain awareness around difficult cases or recurring themes, it takes up a similar degree of pressure and weight that may have created the situation, but as Einstein postulates, "we can't solve problems by using the same kind of thinking we used when we created them." Instead of leaning into the gravity of the moment, it may be levity that is needed. This kind of levity in supervision may take the form of playful experiments or crafty tinkering. To add more of Einstein's views, it is play that is the highest form of research. Thus, if you continue certain that play is something that only children do, you are still thinking in the adult mindset that created the aforementioned. Research suggests that as adults, we are 96% less creative than we were as a children, partially because as children we had not learned to burden ourselves by barriers, self-doubt, or even worse, self-judgment. Play unburdens us. This form of play isn't frivolous play for the sake of play, this is serious play. Serious play may use tools such as LEGO® or doodling to bring the whole self into the room by way of hands-on thinking. When we use these tactile tools, we meaning-make through metaphors, which we know are so valuable to the supervision journey. Other playful experiments might be facilitated through improvisation or role-playing which allows for just enough discomfort that we let go of the "shoulds and musts" that sometimes dominate our adult minds. The key to creating a playful reflective space that elicits a generative experience or heightened awareness is to effectively frame the activity and then, with clear psychological contracting, allow for as much freedom as possible. Like the small but sturdy walls of the park's sandbox, the child is free to frolic within the play space knowing where the limits are and thusly unburdened by the fear of the unknown.*
>
> *This freedom within the frame is what allows for developmental theorist Erik Erikson to assert that the playing child advances forward to new stages of mastery and the playing adult steps sideward into another reality. When the right amount of play is effectively facilitated in supervision, the adult experience and childlike wonder converge which brings about that creative genius within. When it comes to creative problem-solving in supervision, play is the way* (Sanbar, personal communication, 2020).

## Practicing Creativity in Supervision

I am often asked about how supervisors can practice creativity during coaching supervision. Here are some strategies and approaches, gathered through conversations with other supervisors.

- Inquire and experiment. Be an explorer, experimenter, and have the will to master the unknown. Even if the activity fails, there is much to be learned and incorporated into the client-supervisor relationship.
- Bring awareness
- Use intuition to inquire
- Co-create and check for learnings
- Hold the space and listen deeply
- Have a mindset of play and curiosity
- Don't be fearful about making mistakes
- Take risks, be courageous
- Dare to go into the unknown
- Be attentive of language and body language
- Experiment alternate paths
- Brainstorm, there are many ways to look at the same thing.
- Practice, the brain adapts to the new information.
- Be willing to get out of your own comfort zone.
- Have a growth mindset and be playful. Holding fast to the belief that we don't have to have the answers, allows possibilities to emerge during dialogue.
- Be open to lean into child-like wonder and have the humility to know that failing is a great path to creative success.
- Trust the process, the supervisee's creativity and relationship
- Create a space of vulnerability and intimacy
- Create serenity
- Let go of your fears

## Group Coaching Supervision Demonstration

The following session took place at the Third Annual Supervision Conference in 2020, organized by America's Coaching Supervision Network. What is unique about this session is the use of six creative techniques. I have edited and selected certain sections to best represent the goals of this chapter. Moreover, for confidentiality, I have changed the names of the supervisors and the supervisee.

List of participants:

Supervisor 1: S1
Supervisor 2: S2
Supervisee: Daniella
Group participants: Marc, Jessica, Ariella, and Lila

*After contracting, laying ground rules, performing centralization exercise, and going through the structure of the session, the session begins with a check in.*

S1: I am going to ask each of the participants to share, only with a movement (no words), how are you present now. *All share.*

S2:  We will start by asking Daniella to share a case that she is working on in order to, together, explore the challenges. Daniella, are you ready to share case's highlights in around four minutes?

*Daniella explains her case.*

S2:  Daniella, what would you like to attain from this group/session? How would you like us to support you?

DANIELLA:  I want you all to be authentic and challenge my train of thought; also, I want to have fun and laugh while doing so.

S2:  And in terms of what you would like to achieve from this conversation? You already shared some context, but what do you really want to get from this group?

DANIELLA:  My goal is to absorb in my body the sense of possibilities for this client.

S2:  Thank you, Daniella. We are going to move on into an exercise which uses pictures that S1 is going to explain.

S1:  Thank you for sharing the background and context of the case. Daniella, I'm going to show you a set of 20 pictures. I want to know which ones, if any, resonate to you. Let's flip through the whole deck, I will pass through all of them at once. Then, for a second time, we will flip through them, one-by-one, and ask you to stop me wherever reflections come to mind, and how they stimulate your thinking. To other participants, you will have an opportunity to share which picture, only one, provides some answers to the thinking of Daniella's case and share the reasoning behind it. Ready, Daniella! Here we go. *(The supervisor shares images, twice, as explained above.)*

DANIELLA:  That one!

*She chooses an image of a rabbit with big ears*

S1:  Can you explain what resonates in you?

DANIELLA:  The power of attention and connection. That is what I see here, and it is about valuing the practice that keeps making us better all the time; yet, we don't notice how we progress until after the fact. That is what I see in this picture.

S1:  I am hearing that you don't notice how we progress real-time. How do you introspect on this?

DANIELLA:  It's not knowing about your progress, rather learning to live the experience, and appreciate the learning. That is what I am getting.

S1:  Is it ok if I keep on showing more pictures?

DANIELLA:  Yes! Go on … this one.

*Image of rafters in turbulent waters*

DANIELLA: Yes! This is one relates to the environment as a whole –the noise comes together in while getting equipment, answering to government, having financial ability to do what's needed, as well as the competition at large, sailing instructors and coach. That is where I am, and the reality of studying her, her family, and the surrounding noise serves it all. *(There is a long silence.)*

S1: I will now open it up to the participants to share insights. Marc, would you like to start?

MARC: When I heard Daniella speak out and explain the picture, I saw the wealth of the experience knowledge she brings to the table time after time, and also this notion of how much I bring. Her hands are full. How much should I give or take? And the idea of abundance and balance she is trying to strike by bringing an empty hand, and an empty heart, of possibilities of the unknown.

LILA: This one resonates in my body because what I hear is Daniella looking to take in her body the sense of possibility, and here I saw a vast of possibility with the guys flying together in this adventure. I think Daniella is in an adventurer with her client. Together, in the same level, learning from each other and discovering the whole picture.

ARJELLA: The empty chairs image. Possibility came to mind by sitting on the different chairs/ different rows. They seem to be mixed up but they each offer a possibility. If you want to get a sense and embody possibility, how would it look like? And if you move to a chair, what would these different roles represent from this new perspective? Then, move to another chair, and another, and envision which chairs are there for you to expand your perspective.

JESSICA: I noticed all of baskets look empty, but still carry a great feeling of possibility of filling them up. How is she going to carry all the baskets? Then, I thought … maybe you are carrying a huge number of options. When you mentioned you wanted to solve all of them, my train of thought was: Is that actually possible? Should she focus on what you and your client together see as the most intentional focal point, and then, move on to the next?

S1: Daniella, of what you just heard, what resonates to you?

DANIELLA: This was a beautiful exercise! All the pictures talked to me. Marc you made me cry; hence, that is where the heart is. This mixture of creating the space with the clarity of each role, the chairs, and the one by one that Jessica brings, in order for me to get to the skydivers that Lila contextualized … Beautiful! This brings me to ahhh (aha moment)

*She breathes deeply.*

*After some more reflections, we moved onto the next exercise.*

S2:   We will give you five minutes to prepare how each of you could use, in your own creative way, expressions to exploration.

JESSICA:   Daniella, hold your hand onto your heart and notice the sensation. I use it as a preparation for myself. Shake up a bit, stand up, move your leg. Let go of what just happened, and stay with what will happen right now - connect to your soul.

DANIELLA:   Love it, reminds me of what I'm letting go, and it is the connection. I am the medium for my client; thus, plays perfectly.

JESSICA:   It is very touchy to be in that space of possibility.

DANIELLA:   Letting go of my mind, I'm usually too much planning.

S2:   What are you present to now?

DANIELLA:   It never ceases to amaze me how simplicity is so powerful.

ARIELLA:   I grabbed some objects: a razor, ruler, glue, tiny box, etc. (*she picks one of the objects*). Inside, there is a crystal and beneath it your heart, where there are many meanings and there is one that is "clarity" but it is in here, deep inside. Hold on to the space of possibilities.

S2:   Daniella, do you want to share your reaction?

DANIELLA:   The feeling talks to me more than the words. It is a sense of tranquility. My shoulders dropped and clarity is in my heart. And that is already what I do, it brings tears in my eyes that "I always want more … " Thank you. (*She breaks into tears.*)

DANIELLA:   I am a cryer.

S2:   A lot of us connect with that experience.

ARIELLA:   Create the possibility to honor yourself in this story.

DANIELLA:   And that is exactly one of my learnings, ahhhhh.

MARC:   Take a moment to look at my Lego® construction. Building of the initial picture that I choose of the fragments that were there, the image of the wind that change the unknown. To our past, our future. Some pieces are in front of us, some behind. There is a shark of profit that chases us under the water, but we are faster than such shark, we know the wind, we trust the wind. We can look behind and ahead of us, and we are aware of ourselves and how we put ourselves in the middle. How we want to show up.

DANIELLA:   Incredible, the shark for me was the connector with the ecological part and honoring how this sport is truly resonating with what COVID-19 has brought to me. Thank you very much for helping me honor the past and the future, and bringing one to the other.

LILA:   I would like to invite Daniella to let go of her whole body. Take the sense of possibility. I invite her to create a shape that enables this sense. Create in your body possibilities.

DANIELLA:   (*Makes body movements to represent possibilities.*) I feel the radiation of the wisdom in my heart.

DANIELLA:   I think it is a stunning closure.

S1: One more round, what have our learnings been?

*Everyone shares their learnings.*

DANIELLA: I am struck by the combination of abundance and simplicity, and I am taking away this learning around shining my light with humility in service of my client and others. Many times, I am beyond careful of these lights, and it is in placing at service to bring the light to others.

*Closure of the session*

What was most amazing about this session was the collaborative experience and partnership the whole group of supervisors built. The group developed a field of togetherness and connection in the service of the supervisee, allowing the supervisee to feel safe and supported. We all learned from each other. The deep insights the supervisee had were the result of the many creative techniques that coaches brought to the session, from a non-verbal check in, to the use of images, lego play, visualizations, and use of objects through meanings and movements. Supervisors used themselves as instruments so the supervisee was able to visualize, in her very own way, much more than words could ever reflect in a session. Toward the end of the session she said: "The feeling talks to me more than the words." Through metaphors and play, the supervisee was able to look at her inner self exploring the different players in the system. The parallel processes were very powerful to her.

In the Appendix, I have collected a number of examples of how coaching supervisors have used metaphors and creativity during supervision. Consider them a grain of inspiration for the development of your own creative approach. Uniqueness will not only surface in creating new ideas or building upon others, but also during deep listening and intuitive questioning. The seven-eyed model, developed by Bachkirova, Jackson, and Clutterbuck (2011), is considered a very effective methodology to follow in a supervision session. Nonetheless, the magic of your session will appear when you add up the secret sauce in your own special and unique way!

Wrapping up and going back to the original hypothesis, I can conclude that there is no doubt that being creative in supervision opens the unconscious barriers and strengthens our willingness to face vulnerability, bringing new insights and awareness to the session.

To finalize the chapter, I invite everyone to have the courage to follow your heart and intuition to bring new ways for supervisees to connect with their inner self, and hold their space for new discoveries, while having fun and being creative!

*"Logic will get you from A to B. Imagination will take you everywhere."*
--Albert Einstein

My deepest gratitude to all the supervisors who participated in this survey, interviews and demonstrations, giving me permission to share their names: Dr. Damian Goldvarg, Lily Seto, Marcela Fernandez, Tere Entremayor, Geoff Duncan, Paul Sanbar, Nathalie Dubah, Adriana Rodriguez, Alicia M. Aguero, Martine Bizouard, Traci Manalani, Fernanda Bustos González, Eliane Fierro, as well as to those who decided to remain anonymous. Also, my special appreciation to Enrique Alvarez, who supported me in executing the aforementioned research.

## References

Bachkirova, T. Jackson, P., & Clutterbuck, D. *Coaching and mentoring supervision: theory and practice*. McGraw-Hill.

Creativity. (2020). In *Wikipedia*. https://en.wikipedia.org/wiki/Creativity

Gash, J. (2017). *Coaching creativity. transforming your practice*. Routledge.

Hawkins, P., & Shohet, R. (1989). *Supervision in the helping professions*. Open University Press.

Hawkins, P., & Turner, E. (2020). *Systemic coaching: Delivering value beyond the individual*. Routledge.

Kaufman, B. S. (2013). *The real neuroscience of creativity*. Boston Review.

Kaufman, S., & Gregiore, C. (2015). *Wired to create*. TarcherPerigee.

Lahad, M. (2000). *Creative supervision: the use of expressive arts methods in supervision and self-supervision*. Jessica Kingsley Publishers.

Metaphor. (2020). In *YourDictionary*. https://www.yourdictionary.com/metaphor

Metaphor. (2020). In *Wikipedia*. https://en.wikipedia.org/wiki/Metaphor

Seto. L., & Geitner. T. (2018). Metaphor magic in coaching and coaching supervision. *International Journal of Evidence Based Coaching and Mentoring, 16*(2): 99–111. https://radar.brookes.ac.uk/radar/items/50d60ec2-19e7-40eb-8ec1-5ab226abc32e/1/

Sullivan, W., & Reese, J. (2008). *Clean language: Revealing metaphors and opening minds*. Crown House Publishing.

## Appendix 1. Examples of Metaphor Usage and Creativity

The following are methods by which supervisors have utilized prior described techniques as coaching tools.

- Imagine yourself as an animal/fictional character, and place yourself in the relevant setting, considering all the system interactions – behaviors, beliefs, and feelings.
- Gauge on a dashboard to represent status of self-compassion, self-care, self-awareness, among others. In response to the emotional state, ask questions such as: What does equanimity mean for you? What allows you to recognize balance in a certain moment? If these elements were represented on a dashboard, what would you see there now?

- Have the client imagine they are running a marathon and frame questions according to the challenge. For example, what motivated you to prepare for this moment? How will you feel as you cross the finish line? Was this journey eye-opening? What where you required to leave behind? Who was rooting for you?
- Share with the supervisee a metaphor that could bring insight to them and after, ask questions such as: How does it land in you? In what form does this resonate for you? What are your insights of what I just shared?
- Ask the supervisee: If you were to be a book, TV show, fruit basket, a dance, movie or song, which one would you be and why? The conversation becomes richer as thoughts and reflections in the group are exchanged.
- The Mask: Perform an exercise by which supervisees write down words to describe their "public persona" on the outside and their "inner persona" on the inside. In group supervision, there has been a lot of thought leadership in both creating the mask and having others respond to what they perceive.
- The White Board: Have the client draw themselves in relation to their system as it produces faster, deeper, more actionable results. Studies show clients are eager to take actions by the time the session is over.
- Utilize images to describe how a client sees a current situation. This has helped the individual express incapacity to feel in certain moments.
- Through usage of Playdoh®, the coach builds the goal and is able to mold around, in order to test psychodynamic relationship and reflect upon roadblocks, actions and inactions.
- Describe relationships in the system through Playmobil® has helped uncover the unseen. It is also a great tool for constellations in a group supervision.
- Ask the client to complete a sentence. For example "I feel as … ." "I wish I … … "
- Build a story. Use objects to represent the story or situation the Supervisee brings. Offer to include missing people or create an alternative story line, as parallel processes often unfold data.
- Draw pictures randomly and have the supervisee connect them to the situation, enabling parallel processes to interlink the systems involved.
- Guide a visualization that allows everything that needs to be in the room to get expressed. The visualization should include thoughts, feelings, somatic experience smell, and memories, among others. All of this to bring up to life the situation, and facilitate connecting the dots.
- Multiple voices technique: This methodology is based on the work of Tom Andersen, in which each member embodies the individuals that appear in the system of the supervisee. The conversation that is produced while the supervisee remains as an observer, provides great insights to supervisees.

- Use of Quan Yin (the goddess of mercy in Tibetan Buddhism) cards where by each of them holds a message or saying. The supervisee interprets the message and explores what resonates to them, creating a spiritual connection.
- LEGO® Serious-Play methods and MURAL collaborative white boards, mostly for group supervision. Whether they are building mental models with LEGO® or elaborating on metaphors, once a mental image of their case has been created and expanded upon, it becomes easier to recognize relationships among the systems being discussed.
- Magic Box: Seto and Geitrner (2018) share how metaphors can be used in the Magic Box. This process allows the supervisee to embody the situation in symbols and access conscious and unconscious associations. In addition, the supervisor may use the seven- eyed model to unpack various relationships represented in the supervisee's symbolic landscape, and notice their own reactions with regards to what supervisee is saying and depicting. The aforementioned tool can be placed in action with both individual supervisees, as well as group supervisions. If a supervisee doesn't own a Metaphor Magic Box, they can collect 12 small items to use. The supervisor may invite the supervisee to build the scenario which they are intended to reflect upon. Analysis can be done during "construction," or after completion. Areas of inquiry may include:

  i   What items does the supervisee choses to represent themselves and others;
  ii  Randomness or significance to how items are placed and the proximity between them;
  iii Are there any patterns that emerge from the picture;
  iv  Does the supervisee discover feelings aor sensations that emerge as discussion of the metaphoric landscape takes place;
  v   Items that arise as the supervisor assesses significance to the scenario;
  vi  Situations happening in the picture that may also be playing out in the here and now;
  vii If the client were able to physically stand and move around the picture, what other information might become available from another angle or perspective.

- Story telling: Supervisor suggests in group supervision to craft a story together, in which each individual tells a part of a story that can bring to insights to the supervisor. The outcome of the story is then created by the person being supervised. Each member begins by connecting the previous chapter, with their own, in order to build the full story. After the supervisee marks the end to the story, the supervisor enacts a line of questioning that facilitates lessons learned and insights.

- Points of You®: A tool that can be utilized to bring out new emotions and insights to our mind and heart. Points of You® is a company engaged in helping people assess things from a different standpoint, one previously undiscovered. The magic comes out when you look at the photos, read the stories full of metaphors and interact with the words. The games are based on associative links between photographs, themes and issues that have been chosen.
- Share the case, during a group supervision, and have the coach listen to a conversation between supervisors without any intervention with regards to their view of the cause or hypothesis. At the end, ask the supervisee: What did you take from listening to the conversation?
- Supervision SPA: One participant in our research has created a three-day retreat at her house by the lake in Valle de Bravo, Mexico, in which a group of six supervisees undergo a series of activities such as meditation, visualizations, mindfulness, forest walks, forest bathing, sailing, and supervision experiences. The goal is integrating the mind and body, creating an overall experience of accomplishment, self-caring, self-compassion, self-awareness and learnings.

## Author Bio

**Susie Warman** is a master certified coach certified by the International Coaching Federation, mentor coach and supervisor certified by Mentor and a coach supervisor (ESSIA) accredited by the European Mentoring and Coaching Council (EMCC) and Center for Creative Leadership. Susie is a sociologist by formation and holds Masters degrees in both history and coaching. Furthermore, Susie is a Ph.D. candidate in history at the University of Minnesota, specializing in education.

Susie is the Founder and Director of Blue Wing Coaching (www. bluewingcoaching.com), a Mexico and Florida-based consulting firm focused on coaching, leadership development, and developing high performing teams. For two decades, Susie has worked with multinational and local companies in a vast array of industries. She is known for her capacity to understand the client's needs, as well as for her human touch, solid principles, and values.

Her specialties lie within executive coaching, leadership development, high-performing teams, and coaching facilitation. In addition to individual coaching, Susie offers workshops on topics such as effective communication, conflict management, change management, leadership skills for the c-suite, organizational culture change, effective team building, career transition, and Emotional Intelligence.

Susie is also coach trainer for the visually impaired, having trained over 25 blind coaches and incorporated them into the labor force.

# Section III

# How We Learn

# 16 Understanding the Developmental Journey of the Coach Supervisee

*Pamela McLean*

## Introduction

The organization I've led for three decades, Hudson Institute of Coaching, has been a contributor in the field of coaching since the inception of the field and like so many others, we've been committed to high quality coaching focused on the development and growth of client(s) and systems. In-depth learning for a coach begins by cultivating an understanding of one's inner landscape, identities, and narratives that lead to the development of the coach's awareness of self and subsequent conscious use of self in the work of coaching. This deliberate approach requires a carefully crafted evidence-based curriculum with a developmental focus, accompanied by experiential learning and ongoing experiences that support a coach's incremental growth and maturation. Upon completion of an accredited coach training program, the journey of development is in the early stages of formation. The distance from novice to mature coach is long and it requires opportunities to continue to develop one's regular reflective practices that optimally include input from experienced practitioners. Supervision has long been an important part of learning and developing in one's craft in many fields and it is emerging in the Americas as an important element in a coach's development toward maturity. Coach supervision, whether in an individual or group format, provides deliberate learning and reflection opportunities allowing the coach to evolve and deepen capacities over the course of their coaching journey.

Over the past ten years coach supervision has played an increasingly important role in providing deliberate processes to support a coach's development post-program. While the Americas have been slower than our European counterpart to adopt supervision as a standard practice, the tides are shifting and the growing emergence of supervision in this region of the globe is evidenced in recent studies and throughout this book (McAnally, Abrams, Asmus, Hildebrandt, 2020). This is good news for this relatively recent field of study and practice that seeks to secure its place as an important contribution to humankind; and it is an important advancement for practitioners who want to mature and do their best work.

DOI: 10.4324/b23130-20

In our organization, we made a commitment to coach supervision before it was a standard practice in the Americas; in large part because of our background and grounding in psychology and related fields and because it was clear the journey to maturity is a long one that requires more than accumulating coaching hours! We were convinced this practice would be foundational in the development of coaching maturity in the profession. We embarked on our journey convening a subgroup of our faculty including eight credentialed, experienced coaches. This group engaged in a year-long coach supervision certification through Ashridge University under the direction of Erik DeHaan, Ph.D. Over the course of the year we experienced the impact this had on our own work and we were optimistic it could serve our community of coaches equally as well.

Today we have a group of credentialed coach supervisors who provide year-long coach supervision groups to growing numbers of our coach graduates and we regularly hear anecdotal comments and feedback about the value they receive from their coach supervision. Last year we determined we had been providing coach supervision for a long enough period of time that we could take a step back and learn from our supervisees. We wanted to better understand how the experience of coach supervision was impacting their developmental journey. This was the genesis for this study.

I set out to investigate three aspects of the supervision experience including:

1   What can we learn about the specifics of the developmental path of the coach through the lens of the coach supervision experience?
2   What can we learn about how a coach's capacity to use one's self, as instrument, in coaching evolves and grows through supervision?
3   What can we learn about the optimal duration of time a coach spends in coach supervision to mature in their work?

Equipped with a group of credentialed coach supervisors and 75 coach supervisees with a minimum of one full year of monthly supervision, as well as many with over five years in monthly group coach supervision; this research study was conducted.

## Brief Review of Relevant Research on Skill Development

A brief review of relevant research on the developmental journey of a learner provides a useful foundation for this study. The development of mastery or maturation has been examined across related fields and research suggests a predictable progression of skill development that has a nested quality wherein early levels of development are continually embedded as the learner progresses toward mastery and maturation.

Howell's (1982) early model outlines the four stages each learner must pass through to reach mastery and provides a view into the broad developmental journey common for any learner acquiring a deep competence in a particular field of study. He traces the learner's development from the earliest stage wherein the skill deficit is not recognized to the final stage where so much practice and learning has occurred that the work becomes second nature. Howell's study identifies four stages progressing from novice to master including:

- Unconscious incompetence: The unconscious incompetent lacks the skill and knowledge-based competencies needed in a particular area of study and is completely unaware of this insufficiency.
- Conscious incompetence: The conscious incompetent is aware she lacks the skills required to perform at a high level in a particular area and experiences the anxiety that accompanies this awareness.
- Conscious competence: This stage evolves over time and practice and the more sophisticated and demanding the skill set, the longer the time investment before reaching a meaningful skill level.
- Unconscious competence: This fourth stage is the level of mastery that no longer requires focused attention, becoming so natural that the elements are now elusive and intuitive. Leonard (1992), Gladwell (2008) and others cite 10,000 hours of time and practice as required to reach a meaningful level of mastery in any complex task Table 16.1.

## Howell's Model

*Table 16.1* Coach's Development through Howell's Model

| Unconscious Incompetence | Conscious Incompetence | Conscious Competence | Unconscious Competence |
|---|---|---|---|
| An experienced leader who believes she generally coaches every day, and the skills are second nature. | The novice coach understands all that is required to become a coach and is hyper-alert to all there is yet to learn. | The coach who has engaged in enough practice and skill building to begin to feel confident about their level of competence, but remains highly alert to all of the skills and uses of self that can be utilized at each step of the way in coaching | The coach well on the journey to mastery, no longer monitors each intervention, each use of self and all which informs any particular approach. Instead, at this stage the coach is fully present and so skilled that work feels almost intuitive. |

While Howell provided an early view into the general developmental path from novice to master, others have continued to study this incremental phenomenon in the fields of counseling and coaching.

Building on the work of Hogan (1964); Stoltenberg, McNeill & Delworth (1998, 2008) carefully investigated a supervisee's stages of development in the field of counseling, as observed in the supervision milieu. This led to the development of their well-known Integrated Development Model (IDM). The IDM model emphasizes the need for the supervisor to use approaches and interventions that correspond with the level of the supervisee's development. The model describes three levels of development as follows:

> Level One: supervisees are early in their development exhibiting high motivation as well as high anxiety and a fear of evaluation.
> Level Two: supervisees are growing in experience and oscillating between confidence and motivation depending upon the particular successes they are experiencing with their clients.
> Level Three: supervisee have sufficient experience to exhibit a sense of security and confidence along with increased objectivity.

Megginson and Clutterbuck (2009, 2016) developed a model specifically focused on coach maturity and articulated four mindsets which the supervisor can identify through the observation of the sorts of questions the coach asks about their work. Their model tracks a sequential developmental progression leading to maturity.

Megginson and Clutterbuck (2009) Four Stages of Coach Maturity Table 16.2.

*Table 16.2* Megginson and Clutterbuck (2009) Four Stages of Coach Maturity

| Coaching Approach | Style | Critical questions |
|---|---|---|
| Models-based | Control | How do I take them where I think they need to go? How do I adapt my technique or model to this circumstance? |
| Process-based | Constrain | How do I give enough control to the client and still retain a purposeful conversation? What is the best way to apply my process in this instance? |
| Philosophy-based | Facilitate | What can I do to help the client do this for themselves? How do I contextualize the client's issue within the perspective of my philosophy or discipline? |
| Systems eclectic | Enable | Are we both relaxed enough to allow the issue and the solution to emerge in whatever way they will? Do I need to apply any processes at all? If I do, what does the client context tell me about how to select from the wide choices available to me? |

Bachkirova's (2011) work in developmental coaching places an emphasis on use of self as instrument, stressing the importance of the practitioner's development and writes *"It is the coach as a person, rather than the application of particular techniques or methods, that makes a difference in coaching practice."* She underscores that with each new layer of development, the coach expands her ability to see and understand more aspects of themselves and their clients.

Hawkins' (1985, 2012) 7 eyed supervision model is widely recognized and used by coach supervisors around the globe. Hawkins and Shohet (2012) pull the developmental progression thread through the 7 eyed model noting that early in the supervisee's development the focus is on mode 1, the client, wherein the supervisor is helping the supervisee *"to attend to what is, rather than to premature theorizing and over-concern with their performance"*. Once this terrain has been thoroughly developed, it possible to move to Mode 2, where the focus is on examining the coach's interventions. They further note *"as the supervisees become more sophisticated, then Modes 3 through 7 become more central to the supervision"*.

Hawkins and Shohet (2012) integrate the findings of Hogan (1964), Worthington (1987) and Stoltenber and Delworth (1987) and create a combined developmental model with four major stages of supervisee development. Their model progresses from self-centered to client centered; laying the groundwork for the integrative stages of process or relationship centered and context centered.

While it is beyond the scope of this study, Hawkins and Shohet (2012) note that these developmental stages parallel a supervisor's development as well, and Stoltenberg and Delworth also suggest it is difficult to provide supervision to others until the supervisor has reached higher levels in their own development.

With Howell's early backdrop tracing the broadly sequential developmental journey to maturation, combined with the current models focused on the development of the coach; I sought to ascertain the impact the coach supervision experience can have on the coach's development with these inquiries on my mind:

1   What can we learn about the specifics of the developmental path of the coach through the lens of the coach supervision experience?
2   What can we learn about how a coach's capacity to use one's self, as instrument, in coaching evolves and grows through supervision?
3   What can we learn about the optimal duration of time a coach spends in coach supervision to mature in their work?

## Study Design

76 coach supervisees, all graduates of our year-long coach certification program, were asked if they would be willing to participate in this research

project by completing an online questionnaire that predominantly consisted of open-ended questions. These supervisees were located throughout the globe and 60 of the 76 coach supervisees completed the survey. Given the 60 coach supervisees participating in the study had all completed Hudson's year-long leadership coaching program; they share common models and language, and, in many cases, they knew one another prior to enrolling in a supervision group. The 60 respondents in this study have all been in year-long monthly group coach supervision spanning a range from a minimum of 1 full year to over five years.

The coach supervisors share many factors in common including: PCC or MCC credential, at least one (in many cases, two) coach supervision credential(s), active engagement in their own coach practices and monthly group supervision, all sharing a common coach methodology and developmental perspective, and all conversant in Hawkins' 7 eyed supervision model.

I collected only two demographic facts including number of years coaching and number of years in group coaching supervision. I used the Self as Coach model (Mclean, 2011; 2019) as a starting point for exploration of the coach's development because all participants share this model and it broadly describes key domains of the coach's inner landscape that supports deliberate use of self Figure 16.1.

I asked the coach supervisees to choose from this model, the two areas relative to use of self, wherein they believe they have developed the most in through their supervision experience. The areas included: presence, empathy, range of feeling, boundaries, and courage. I then asked the following open-ended questions:

*Figure 16.1* Self as Coach.

1   In what ways has your supervision experience strengthened your capacities in the two areas of development you chose?
2   In what ways have you experienced your own development in the two areas you chose and, if possible, offer an example of the impact in your coaching?
3   Have you become more aware of how your own narrative can impact your coaching through your coach supervision experience? If yes, might you share what you have noticed and learned in this regard?

### Three Groups of Supervisees

The 60 respondents were distributed into three groups spanning a range of 1 to 5 or more years of monthly group supervision as follows:

*Early-Stage Supervisees*: 23 participants had experienced 1–2 years of coach supervision
*Mid-Stage Supervisees*: 12 participants had experienced 3–4 years of coach supervision
*Later-Stage Supervisees*: 25 participants had experienced 5 or more years of coach supervision

This distribution of number of years in coach supervision provides the opportunity to examine trends over the course of several years in the developmental journey of a coach supervisee.

Across all groups of coach supervisees, presence was the competency chosen the most often. Two other areas, boundaries and courage trailed behind and other dimensions trailed even more. This emphasis on presence was so dominant, that I chose to focus on examining this singular competency area of development along with their reflections on the impact of their narrative in the qualitative study of their responses.

### The Qualitative Analysis Process

I utilized the work of Boyatzis (1998) on transforming qualitive information in research through the use of thematic analysis and code development as well as particularly helpful discussions with an experienced research methodology consultant, Francine Campone. I arrived at using a conceptual formation of clusters using a developmental hierarchy.

I thoroughly studied, sorted, and categorized the open-ended responses of all 60 participants to determine whether or not observable broad themes and patterns were discernable. Once I identified a clear pattern that could be coded, I sought a second opinion from a research expert to monitor any bias I might inadvertently possess.

The thematic patterns I identified linked to the coach's development of presence as well as the impact of the coach's narrative led me to create three levels that had a developmental and progressively nested quality. These three levels include:

*Level 1: Self Awareness*: What's happening in me? How am I doing? Am I adding enough value for my client?
This level is characterized by the coach's reference to self in their development and includes anxiety about how the work is going, how they are doing in the work, and concerns about adding value. This level also finds the coach listening to the client's situation through the coach's own narratives, their biases, judgments, and experiences.

*Level 2: Client Awareness*: What's happening with my client? What is she experiencing and needing?
This level is characterized by the coach's reference to the client and a growing attention to the other and all that can be observed. At this level the coach appears more equipped to notice and manage biases and judgments of her own that might interfere with understanding her client's experience.

*Level 3: Relationship Awareness*: How are we working together in dialogue and in exploration?
This level is characterized by a synthesis of self-awareness and client awareness; allowing the coach to begin to explore the nuances of the interaction together. Increased attention is placed on 'the dance' more than the "dancers." At this level, the coach is able to explore and consciously use dynamics that arise in the dance between supervisor and supervisee.

The thematic coding allowed me to identify patterns across the three groups of coach supervisees including Early-Stage supervisees with 1–2 years of supervision; Mid Stage supervisees with 3–4 years of supervision; and Later Stage supervisees with five years or more of supervision.

## The Findings

Closely aligned with existing research on the coach's development, I found a discernable progression focused on the development of levels of awareness, most particularly in Levels 1, 2, and 3, over the course of several years in supervision wherein the focus of awareness evolved as follows:

Level 1:   Awareness of self, was dominant in the Early-Stage Supervisees
Level 2:   Awareness of client, emerged in the Mid-Stage Supervisees
Level 3:   Awareness of relationship, grew in dominance in Later-Stage Supervisees

**Finding #1: Early-stage supervisees predominantly focus on Level 1: Awareness of Self—What's happening in me? How am I doing?**

Early-Stage Supervisee's were primarily focused on development at Level 1: Awareness of Self. These coach supervisees had been in supervision for a minimum of one year and up to two full years. The dominant theme for these coaches was self-referential in nature, with an ever-growing awareness of self. The vast majority of coded comments focused on what the supervisee was noticing or becoming increasingly aware of relative to themselves—their reactions, concerns, judgments and feelings—all coming into full view for these supervisees. The main themes in this early-stage group included performance anxiety, awareness of their own narrative as their frame of reference and as an impediment, and a deepening awareness of their urges—to rescue, to wish for everyone to be happy, etc. The coding details (see appendix 1) included 22 examples of Level 1 awareness, 3 examples of Level 2 awareness and no incidents of Level 3. Coded representations of Level 1 Awareness of Self in this group of early-stage supervisees are reflected in these examples of self-observations.

Dealing with my performance anxiety:

- How am I doing?
- What's happening for me?
- My inner critic gets in the way.
- Am I adding any value for my client?
- I'm noticing how my expectations of progress are always present.

Recognizing how my narrative gets in my way:

- I'm noticing my stories impact how I proceed in coaching.
- I keep using my own life experiences as a frame of reference.
- I am noticing what I bring into the coaching that comes from my narrative, not from my client.
- I am learning to notice how my judgments get in the way.

Noticing my urges:

- I am learning that I often want to rescue my clients.
- I like to be upbeat and I am learning how that gets in the way of meeting the client where they are.

These early-stage supervisees frequently referenced the role supervision and their supervisor played in their development as a coach. Some examples of their comments are included below:

- The trained ears of my supervision group enable me to see and hear and challenge my stories.
- My group coach supervision empowers me to feel comfortable with my discomfort in my coaching sessions.
- My supervision experience has helped me notice when I am over-identify with my client, this impacts my work.
- My supervisor has helped me explore the limits of my range of feelings.
- My supervision experience has helped me see much more quickly, how often I am trying to 'get somewhere' with my client instead of trusting the process of unfolding.
- Through supervision I have become much more aware of when my stories get in the way of the coaching.
- Through supervision, I have developed reflective practices that have aided in my awareness.

### Finding #2: Mid-stage supervisees place a growing awareness on Level 2: Awareness of Client—What's happening with my client? What is she experiencing and needing?

Mid-Stage Supervisee's demonstrated an appreciably growing focus on an awareness of what is happening for the client represented in the coding as Level Two: Awareness of Client. While the Level 1 Awareness of Self remains very present, the awareness of what is happening for the client rises significantly. In this mid-stage group of supervisees, the supervisee is able to place a growing focus of attention on the client, noticing what's happening for the client and what the client is needing. The coach's more conscious management of performance anxieties, judgments and biases found in Level 1, enables this stronger awareness of the client. The central theme is an expanding shift in the coach's focus, managing one's narrative and one's urges to be present to the client at this new level of awareness. The coding data (appendix 1) provides a view into the overlapping nature of development. The coding details include 12 examples of level 1 (awareness of self), 9 examples of level 2 (awareness of client), 3 examples of level 3 (awareness of relationship) and no examples of level 4 (broader xxx. While level 1 focused on the supervisee's awareness of self remains strong, the supervisee's awareness of the client (level 2) has grown substantially and there are a few examples of awareness of the integration (level 3). The nested quality of development begins to emerge for the mid-stage supervisee.

Examples of this growing shift of awareness focusing on the client:

- I have grown to be more focused on my client's story and less worried about how my client may be judging me and/or my competency as a coach.
- I find myself more connected to my clients, but no longer pulled in. I see the person; I see their challenges.

- I initially felt a need to rescue or advise. Recognizing that I was triggered, I was able to be with the client and provide the space for her to process her next steps.
- I can recognize what is mine and what is the clients.
- Supervision has increased my presence with clients and my ability to really notice what is coming up for the client.
- I have been able to coach from the outside, helping a client see their behaviors and not get wrapped up in a client's story and emotions.

These mid-stage supervisees frequently referenced the role supervision and their supervisor played in their development as a coach. Some examples of their comments are included below:

- Observing how each member of our supervision group shows up, the role they play and the impact each has, has been a great self as instrument learning for us all.
- As I listen to the cases we explore, mine or others, I see how we, as coaches show up in the relationship and that has made me more aware and more curious about what is showing up for me.
- I have realized that I can think I am very clear about a situation or a topic, only to then expand my arena of awareness. The next time I have a similar situation, I get to apply the learning from supervision and start from the more expanded arena.

### Finding #3: Later-stage supervisees demonstrate awareness at three levels of development in a sequential and overlapping dynamic. Awareness of self, client and the relationship are dynamically interacting.

The later-stage supervisees provide a view into the overlapping and sequential nature of their development. These supervisees now seem able to focus equally in three levels of development with an ability to fully focus their awareness on the interaction between coach and client, the co-creation of the work, the nuances, and the art of 'the dance' in the work. They are equally able to notice what's happening inside themselves as coaches while observing what is occurring for the client; all the while they appear able to ask themselves how the coach-client relationship is unfolding and how they are co-creating the work. In this later-stage supervisee group, the earlier levels of development appear to be fully nested into this later stage. This is clearly seen in the coding. In this Later-Stage Supervisees group, there was nearly equal attention to awareness at three levels of development with coding detail revealing 10 examples of level 1 (awareness of self), 11 examples of level 2 (awareness of client) and 10 examples of level 3 (relationship awareness) (see appendix 1).

Comments illustrating the nested quality of all levels of development:

- I have a much broader range of awareness of what is going on in me, my client, the field between us, and capacity to use those insights in support of the client's vision.
- I have much greater trust in my intuition and the emergent and can flow with a session. The impact has been we find our way to what matters most for the client in terms of insight and the change that is trying to emerge.
- I have learned to suspend any judgments while not abandoning my discernment. An example is not being afraid to mention noticing the elephant in the room, even if that means I ask a question that causes an awkward silence. I am more comfortable with that silence now, to allow the client to come forth.

Examples of comments demonstrating Level 3 awareness:

- I am more aware in the moment of my response to what is happening with the client and with myself during the conversation.
- I am noticing a sense of freedom and fluidity in my sessions.
- I see myself more as the instrument, not the solution. I continually reaffirm the partnership aspect of the coaching relationship.
- I need to take care I remain curious- even though I have a lens with which I can spot patterns, systems and themes that clients may not see, I have learned to be a curious explorer with clients, to make sure I don't judge that there are patterns where none exist, or worse yet, hop over the fence to start weeding in my client's garden instead of my own.

## Conclusions

I began with three exploratory inquiries in this study: a) What can we learn about the specifics of the developmental path of the coach through the lens of coach supervision? b) What can we learn about how a coach's capacity to use one's self, as instrument, in coaching evolves and grows through supervision? and c) What can we learn about the optimal duration of time a coach spends in coach supervision to mature in their work?

My study design included three groups and four levels of development: My first exploratory inquiry in this study focused on what can we learn about the specifics of the developmental path of the coach through the lens of coach supervision? My observation from the qualitative data provided by 60 coach supervisees is that there is a wealth of learning that is valuable in understanding both the development of a coach's maturity and the role supervision can play in that journey.

First, a predictable nested and overlapping developmental progression emerged in this study. The early-stage supervisee's reflections and comments about their development are almost exclusively focused on Level 1's awareness of self, wherein emphasis on performance anxiety is most prominent and frame of reference is self-focused. The mid-stage supervisee's reflections and comments about their development balances a focus on Levels 1 and 2, holding their attention on themselves as well as their clients. The later-stage supervisees reflections and comments about their development traverses all three levels from awareness of self to awareness of the interactive quality of the coach-client relationship.

This developmental progression is useful for both the supervisee and the supervisor. For the supervisee, there is a sense of normalcy in the unfolding path of development and there is reassurance that there is a predictable nature to development that is hastened and deepened through the reflective nature of supervision. For the supervisor, it emphasizes the importance of understanding the supervisee's level of development. This needs careful exploration in the contracting conversation, and an observational eye early in the supervision to choose the right approaches and interventions as supervisor to maximize the learning experience and support the developmental progression of the supervisee.

Second, the developmental journey of these coach supervisees appears to substantiate a nested overlapping and agile quality. The progression of the supervisee's development from Level 1 through Level 3 from self to the relationship, is intersecting and sequential without being linear. The progression found in the qualitative responses of these supervisees tracks quite closely to the model adapted by Hawkins and Shohet emphasizing the passage from self-centered to client-centered to relationship focused Figure 16.2.

The second exploratory inquiry focused on the ways a coach's capacity to use one's self, as instrument, in coaching is enhanced through supervision. Bachkirova (2011) underscores that with each new layer of development, the coach expands her ability to see and understand more aspects of themselves and their clients. This developmental layering is evidenced in this study. The anecdotal comments made by supervisees relative to the impact of supervision on their developing awareness captures the value supervisees place on the supervision experience. Evidence that supervision has enhanced this group of supervisees conscious and deliberate 'use of self as instrument' is found in each level in these reflections:

Level 1:     Awareness of Self

- Through supervision, I'm much more aware of my tendencies, and have learned to manage them – sometimes in the moment, sometimes after further reflection.

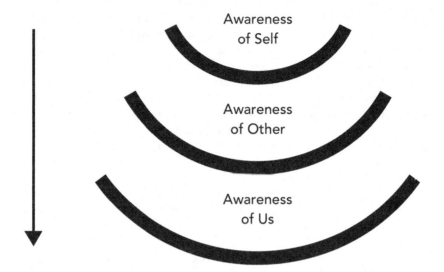

*Figure 16.2* Nested Layers of Development for the Supervisee.

- My group coach supervision empowers me to feel comfortable not knowing.
- My supervision experience has helped me notice when I am pushing my agenda.
- My supervisor has helped me explore the limits of my range of feelings.
- My supervision experience has helped me more quickly see, how often I am trying to solve or rush to find a solution.
- Through supervision I have become much more aware of when my stories get in the way of the coaching.

Level 2:    Awareness of Client

- As I listen to the cases we explore, I see how we, as coaches, show up in the relationship and that has made me more aware and more curious about what is showing up for me.
- In supervision, my arena of awareness expands beyond myself and on to my client's full experience.

Level 3:    Awareness of the Relationship

- Supervision has enabled me to be self-aware of any dynamics at play, to focus on being curious while putting my own self-identification in its place in the coaching relationship.

- Supervision has strengthened my courage to turn up the heat when that's what the client seems to need, while cultivating my capacity for presence.
- Through supervision, I'm much more aware of my tendencies, and have learned to manage them – sometimes in the moment, sometimes after further reflection.

This finding is helpful for the supervisee and supervisor, as it allows both parties to observe the developmental trajectory and adjust the learning contract as well as the supervisor's interventions to align with the emerging growth edges evolving during the supervision.

The final exploratory inquiry focused on exploring the impact of the duration of a supervisee's engagement in supervision.

Any conclusions are necessarily circumspect given this is a single study with 60 respondents; yet the progression of the coach's development in this study spans several years before supervisees reach a layered awareness at all three levels. It is also notable that the first level, awareness of self, comprises much of the developmental work identified by those in the early-stage supervisee group and the progression to awareness of the client followed by the integrative awareness of the interaction is only evidenced in this study after 2–4 years of supervision. This finding may suggest coach supervision that allows a supervisee to travel the developmental journey from novice to maturity takes several years to achieve. The early self-referential focus appears to be a predictable early stage that is present for at least two years as the dominant area of development and only as that begins to recede does the coach move to a growing awareness of other and finally the relationship.

## Implications

### Coach Supervisor Implications

First, the findings in this study emphasize the importance for the supervisor to fully understand the stage of development of the supervisee. The initial exploration of this can occur during the contracting conversation; and once the supervision begins, the supervisor may observe additional nuances that allow supervisor and supervisee to create a developmental plan that aligns and supports the supervisee's stage of development.

Second, the findings emphasize the need for the supervisor to tailor supervision interventions that will best correspond with the supervisee's level of development. This study, and previous research, provides ample evidence the early coach and supervisee is anxious about 'getting it right', adding value and being evaluated. This suggests the supervisor needs to provide plenty of support while also helping the supervisee explore what is unfolding internally. In general, when the supervisor is alert to the unique stage of development of each supervisee, it allows the supervisor to choose interventions and approaches that will fully foster the appropriate layer of development and enable the supervisee to deepen their awareness of self, sufficiently to move progress on their journey to maturity.

### Coach Training Implications

First, in coach training, there may be value in examining the overall architecture of program curriculum to ensure emphasis is placed first on awareness of self, before moving to next level awareness's of the other, the relationship and the larger contexts. This could include curriculum emphasizing the nested developmental layers that occur as the coach matures. Any observed coach practice sessions might focus on emphasizing awareness of self, exploring what is happening inside the coach rather than focusing solely on the actions they took or competencies they exhibited.

Second, given the importance of the coach's awareness of social identity in one's self and those we coach; these findings may prove valuable in explicitly drawing attention to the depths of work we need to do as coaches to develop a thorough awareness of our self, our social identity and our narratives before turning our attention to the coachee. When the coach takes the time to fully explore this terrain and uncover their inevitable blind spots, it lays the foundation for a differentiated view of the other with an ability to separating one's own social identity, biases and values from those of the client.

Third, the field of coaching may be served by further examining the critical role coach supervision plays in the development of the coach. We might finally begin to consider coach supervision to be an ethical practice, an essential requirement of our work and a developmental journey without a destination—no certificate, no requirement of hours —just a commitment and a practice to be at our best in our work as coaches and able to be aware of our self, our client and the unique qualities of the relationship.

## References

Bachkirova, T. (2011). *Developmental coaching: Working with the self.* NY: Open University Press.

Boyatzis, R. E. (1998). Transforming qualitative information. *Thematic analysis and code development.* California: Sage Publications.

Clutterbuck, D., Whitaker, C., et al. (2016). *Coaching supervision: A practical guide for coach supervisees.* NY: Routledge

Gladwell (2008). *Outliers: The story of success.* NY: Little.

Hawkins, P., & Shohet, R. (2012). *Supervision in the helping professions.* (4th ed.). Maidenhead: Open University Press.

Hogan, R.A. (1964).Issues and approaches in supervision. *Psychotherapy: Theory Research and Practice I,* 139–141.

Leonard, G. (1992). *Mastery.* SF: Plume.

Mclean, P. (2011). *The completely revised handbook of coaching*. San Francisco: Jossey Bass.

Mclean, P. (2019). *Self as coach, self as leader: developing the best in you to develop the best in others*. New Jersey: Wiley.

McAnally, K., Abrams, L., Asmus, M., & Hildebrandt, T. (2020). Global Coaching Supervision: A Study of Perceptions and Practices Around the World. https://coachingsupervisionresearch.org

Megginson, D., & Clutterbuck, D. (2009). *Coaching and mentoring: Further techniques*. London: Butterworth-Heinemann

Megginson, D., & Clutterbuck, D. (2016). *Coaching and mentoring: Further techniques*. NY: Routledge

Stoltenber, C., & Delworth, U. (1987). *Supervising counselors and therapists*. San Francisco: Jossey-Bass

Stoltenberg, C.D., McNeill, B., & Delworth, U. (1998). *IDM supervision: An integrated developmental model for supervising counselors and therapists*. San Francisco:Jossey-Bass.

Worthington, E. L. (1987). Changes in supervision as counselors and supervisors gain experience: A review. *Professional Psychology: Research and Practice, 18*(3): 189–208. 10.1037/0735-7028.18.3.189

## Appendix 1: Content Coding Table

| | Level 1: Awareness of Self Coding: comments and reflections representing a self-referential orientation | Level 2: Awareness of Client Coding: comments and reflections representing a client or 'other' orientation | Level 3: Awareness of Relationship Coding: comments and reflections representing integrated interaction created between coach and client |
|---|---|---|---|
| Early Coach Supervision Group (n = 24). 1–2 yrs. in yr.-long group supervision, meeting monthly | 22 | 3 | |
| Mid Coach Supervision Group (n-12). 3–4 yrs. in yr. -long group supervision, meeting monthly | 12 | 9 | 1 |
| Later Coach Supervision Group (n=24). 5 or more yrs. in yr. -long group supervision, meeting monthly | 10 | 11 | 10 |

## Author Bio

**Pamela McLean**, Ph.D., Master Coach and Coach Supervisor, is CEO of The Hudson Institute of Coaching, an organization with 35 years of experience providing a full suite of coaching services inside organizations. McLean brings years of experience as a clinical and organizational psychologist, a master coach, coach supervisor and leader in the field of coaching.

McLean authored The Completely Revised Handbook of Coaching (2012) examining key theories and evidenced based research informing the field; and Self as Coach, Self as Leaders (McLean, 2019) examining the coach's need to build awareness of one's internal landscape to consciously and deliberately use one's self as an instrument in coaching.

Pam is a Board Member of The Association of Learning Providers. She has served on Harvard's JFK Women's Leadership Board, the faculty of Saybrook University in San Francisco, California, the Editorial Board of IJCO, and the Board of LikeMinded in San Francisco. She lives in California and enjoys all things related to weekend cooking, gardening, birdwatching and traveling to new places around the globe.

Consultative conversation with Francine Campone. December 30, 2020.

# 17 Remaining Relevant and Fit for Purpose: A Core Challenge for Coaching

*Angela Wright*

## Introduction

How do coaches and coaching remain relevant and fit for purpose? And what part might coaching supervision play? According to the Oxford English Dictionary (n.d.), if something is fit for purpose it is "well equipped for its designated role or purpose." In law, a fit for purpose obligation typically imposes a higher duty than that of exercising "reasonable care and skill." This raises the question: What does this mean in the context of coaching? Are we, as coaches, well equipped for our designated role or purpose? And how do we become or remain so?

The need to navigate, respond, and adapt to our increasingly complex, interconnected, and uncertain world have been identified as core challenges for leadership and coaching (Cavanagh, 2013; Wright et al., 2019). If coaches are to support leaders, organizations, and broader stakeholders in this ever-changing context, we too must develop our "own personal and collective capacity to understand, critically consider and integrate multiple perspectives on coaching issues and the coaching process" (Wright et al., 2019, p. 108).

Consistent with the qualitative, developmental (or formative), and re-storative functions of supervision, (Hawkins & Shohet, 2006; Inskipp & Proctor, 1993), it is my belief that the primary purpose of supervision is to help coaches "to see" more than they can currently see in themselves, others and the systems in which they operate, and that "through dialogue in supervision, the coach and supervisor are able to make visible those things that the coach cannot yet see; those things that they are blind to; those assumptions they subconsciously hold; those things that are not in the coach's current frame of reference" (Wright et al., 2019, p. 109).

This chapter draws on my own experience of living, working, and training as a coach on three continents, along with my practice as a coach, coach supervisor, and educator, globally. It also draws on current coaching literature and research, including my own recent research on coaching supervision in the US between 2017 and 2018 (US study) (Wright et al., 2020; Wright, 2021).

First, this chapter will provide an overview of the US study. Extrapolating from that research and my lived experience, I have identified

DOI: 10.4324/b23130-21

four key areas for further exploration in this chapter: 1) the capacity for systemic and network thinking; 2) the critical importance of personal as well as professional development; 3) the role of the internal coach and the coaching ripple effect; and 4) understandings of supervision and who needs it. I will provide a brief outline of each area and make links to the relevant literature, identify some of the key issues and challenges in practice and share examples of the value of supervision in each context. Each area will also be discussed from an ethical and legal perspective, before a more detailed exploration of the importance of developing ethical maturity, legal awareness, knowledge, sensitivity, and judgment. Finally, hypotheses around the impact of contextual factors, including current coaching discourses and global differences will be explored.

The purpose of this chapter is not to critique existing narratives and perspectives. Rather, the aim is to highlight a number of key areas that may be critical to our individual and collective evolution in order to stimulate dialogue as to how coaches and coaching remain relevant and fit for purpose and the part that coaching supervision may play in achieving this.

## US Coaching Supervision Research

In 2016, I invited coaches to join the first coaching supervision groups offered to members by a professional body in New York City. While the general response to the invitation was one of curiosity, one comment in particular, "We don't need supervision. Take your ideas back to Europe," was the catalyst for the US study. Reflecting on this response, I realized that it was perhaps not only indicative of a level of misunderstanding, confusion, and resistance in the marketplace, but also a reflection of the clumsiness of my approach. Inspired by Hodge's (2016) research, I decided to undertake a research project whereby coaches were provided with the opportunity to engage in supervision so that they could make up their own minds about its true value (Wright et al., 2020; Wright, 2021).

Coaches were invited to participate through an advertisement on the websites of the Association for Talent Development, the International Coaching Federation (ICF) and through posts on LinkedIn. More than 100 coaches inquired or applied to be part of the project. Of those, 45 coaches participated. The participants represented a mix of internal and external coaches with various levels of experience and diverse backgrounds in coach training. Advertising through ICF increased the representation of ICF accredited coaches. Each participant committed to undertaking two, one-hour virtual coaching supervision sessions with the same supervisor.

The aim of the research was to contribute to the evidence base for coaching supervision in the U.S. by exploring: 1) the potential value and benefits derived from supervision; 2) the impact of a systemic developmental approach; and 3) whether understandings of supervision changed as a result of the experience (Wright et al., 2020). Pre and post data were collected and analyzed using a thematic analysis methodology (Braun & Clarke, 2006; Harper & Thompson, 2012). Further details on the research, our findings, and the systemic developmental approach used are discussed elsewhere (Tennyson, 2021; Wright et al., 2019). While initially conceived as a study of coaches in North America, four coaches from other geographic locations also participated. In the following sections of this chapter, I explore four selected areas that emerged during the research that also have been evident in my practice as a coach supervisor in the US.

## The Capacity for Systemic and Network Thinking

Linear, models-based approaches (Clutterbuck & Megginson, 2011) such as GROW (Whitmore, 1992) were the hallmark of early approaches to coaching. More recently, interest has grown in the broader context of coaching, including more systemic perspectives (Cavanagh, 2006, 2013; Lawrence, 2019; Lawrence & Moore, 2019; O'Connor, 2020) and discourses around network coaching (Western, 2017). Despite these shifts in thinking, coach education, training, assessment, and accreditation reflect an outdated and arguably unhelpful paradigm—one that reduces coaching to a mechanistic process that is at odds with the complexity of the coaching dynamic itself, the context in which coaches work, and the challenges faced by their clients (Bachkirova & Lawton Smith, 2015; Cavanagh, 2013; Garvey, 2017; Lane, 2017).

My experience working with, supervising, and educating coaches suggests that a prevalence of coach training organizations are still teaching proprietary models, usually some derivative of GROW. Clutterbuck and Megginson (2011) have described this as models based coaching, where following the model is more important than exploring the client's world. They have also suggested that this narrow perception of coaching leads to the 'dangerous myth' that a good coach can coach anyone. I would go further and argue that such narrow, linear approaches may potentially to do harm, in certain circumstances. Spence et.al. (2006) in their article, *Duty of care in an unregulated industry* explored the legal ramifications of failing to recognize mental health issues in coaching and considered the extent to which coach training assists coaches in discharging their duty of care. "Sticking with" the model in such situations (either due to lack of awareness or to alleviate the coach's anxiety) and failing to take into account other relational or systemic factors raises a number of ethical and legal issues.

Working with a supervisor who takes a more holistic view of the client, the coaching relationship, and the broader environment (i.e., one who has an in-depth understanding of system and network dynamics) may help facilitate a broader and more nuanced understanding of the issues and challenges coaches face in their practice. As part of a systemic developmental approach (Wright et al., 2019), these theories were both explicitly and implicitly used as part of the US study.

One of our key findings in the study was the emergence of a new "bigger," systemic perspective. Supervision appeared to help coaches "to see" more (Bachkirova, 2008) in their inner, outer, and relational worlds. Respondents reported being able to see patterns in their coaching, gaining a better understanding of the coach and client relationship and the broader aspects of the coaching environment: "Coaching supervision allows us to 'look, think outside the rut,' to view patterns that were unrealized," "it afforded me a panoramic view on the issue I was presented with - how I saw and approached the problem." Another respondent commented:

> *The coaching supervision helped me deal with the issues I faced by helping me to see other points of views; see the bigger picture. I would not have been able to 'see' beyond my issue had I not spoken about my concerns during the coaching supervision session.*

In addition to increased awareness and perspective, the participants also reported that this led to new opportunities and possibilities for action: "[Supervisor] has shown me new doors that I did not know were there ..." and "every conversation opened new possibilities for me."

While supervision and reflective practice may enhance a coach's capacity to "see more," the use of system and networked approaches to coaching are not without their challenges. These approaches require a coach to understand and work with multiple complexities in a system and to take and integrate multiple perspectives. This may raise complex ethical and legal issues around a coach's level of competence, challenges around confidentiality, managing multiple stakeholder perspectives and questions as to who is the client: the coachee, the organization or the broader system? (Wright & O'Connor, 2021). It may also raise systemic ethical challenges that go beyond the individual (Western, 2017) in recognizing that coaching is part of a wider social context.

## Personal and Professional Development

Over the last few years there has also been a noticeable shift from skills and performance coaching to more developmentally focused coaching (Bachkirova & Baker, 2018; Berger, 2006) that draws on theories of developmental psychology (e.g., Bachkirova, 2011; Cook-Greuter 2004; Kegan, 1994; Torbert 1991; Wilber, 2000). Developmental coaching has been described as coaching that addresses the current needs of the client with a view to increasing their overall capacity to engage with the challenges of life and to create a better platform for further growth (Bachkirova, 2021). This is sometimes referred to as vertical development (Cavanagh, 2013).

Consistent with criticisms in the leadership literature (Avolio et al., 2009; Lichtenstein et al., 2007; Uhl-Bien et al., 2007), Kegan (1994) contends that there is a "mismatch" between the expectations we have of our leaders and their level of cognitive development. I have argued elsewhere that if coaches are to support leaders in meeting current and future demands they must engage in self-reflection and engage in coaching supervision as part of their ongoing development (Wright et al., 2019).

Supervision may help coaches actively engage in their own developmental process through the integration of learning, experimentation, and reflective practice that takes them beyond their "growing edge" (Berger, 2006). Supervision may also help coaches reflect on their own developmental level and consider its impact on their coaching—what does it enable and what does it constrain? Such considerations highlight the importance of development of "self as instrument" (Bachkirova, 2016). The systemic developmental approach used in the US study also drew on Kegan's (1994) adult development theory.

Participants in the US study reported that increased self-awareness, including recognizing their own blind spots, and a greater understanding of the coaching relationship dynamic (de Haan, 2017) helped them reframe their perspective on coaching challenges and issues: "Supervision … help [ed] identify where my personal perceptions and/or challenges might be contributing to the issue(s)."

Participants also reflected on their "inner critic," reporting an increased appreciation of their own background and values leading to greater confidence as coach: "I left each of the sessions with more confidence in my ability to handle these challenges," and "I have more confidence and feel more comfortable with flexing my approach and also committing to really defining very clearly, my coaching approach."

Often this new found confidence led to a sense of being less constrained by the original model or approach in which they were accredited or trained, perhaps representing movement on the continuum of coach maturity (Clutterbuck & Megginson, 2011): "I now have more confidence in myself as a coach and I feel liberated in that I don't have to fit myself into some box others have said is "real coaching." Another respondent shared:

> *I see myself with greater clarity and compassion, with a better understanding of where I fit in the world. I was draining my emotional capacity from making myself fit into a very narrow space as a coach, even to the point of questioning the coaching profession as a career choice. I now have a renewed sense of who I am, expanding the space for me to be that person and continue growing.*

Others described an increased level of congruence between their coaching, values, and sense of "self" (Jackson & Bachkirova, 2019): "[Coaching Supervision helped me] define my approach in a more detailed manner, so that I am in alignment with my values and sense of self."

Moreover, the participants reported greater reflexivity and breadth of perspective, which may also be reflective of an evolution of complexity in thinking and meaning making (Bachkirova & Baker, 2018; Berger, 2006;

Kegan, 1994): "New insights did emerge as I was able to connect a few patterns of thought/behavior from multiple settings to current situations," and "it's not so much that I'll "do" something differently, but rather I'll "be" someone different. From there, everything else flows."

There are a number of issues that may be more complex in the practice of developmental coaching. For example, the blurring of boundaries between coaching and therapy, the identification of mental health issues, the effects of parallel processing (Bachkirova & Baker, 2018), challenges around ethical issues and the development of ethical maturity (Lane, 2011), and the stage of development of the coach vis-a-vis the client (Laske, 2006). Each of these issues may raise similarly complex legal issues (Wright & O'Connor, 2021).

## The Role of the Internal Coach and the Coaching Ripple Effect

Over the last few years there has been an increase in the use of internal coaching (Maxwell, 2011; St John-Brooks, 2018). An internal coach has been described as a coach employed by an organization who provides coaching to employees in that same organization. (Maxwell, 2011). Drivers for this increase in use have included reduced costs (as compared to the use of external coaches) and opportunities to scale and expand coaching programs. Internal coaches also cited their knowledge of internal resources, ease of observation, opportunities for learning reinforcement, and institutional knowledge (including of power dynamics and culture) as benefits.

Some US organizations have been slow to incorporate supervision into the coaching offerings and practices despite evidence of its value (Champion, 2011; Lucas, 2012; Robson, 2016; Tennyson, 2021; Wright et al., 2020). Yet, internal coach participants in the US study stated they felt supervision had a positive impact, including immediate ripple effect on others in the organization. For example, through sharing new knowledge and perspectives:

> *As there is a ripple effect in coaching per se, there is also this effect in having coaching supervision in order to enhance the effectiveness of other coaches in the corporate environment where I work by disseminating knowledge and/or by letting people know what I have discussed during the supervision session and how it could be put into practice.*

Despite the perceived benefits of internal coaching, it is not without its challenges. Internal coaches often work in complex organizational settings where they need to manage multiple internal relationships and stakeholder perspectives, and where there are both seen and unseen power dynamics at play. For many, a multiplicity of roles may cause conflicts of interest, confidentiality issues, as well as issues around boundary management. Boundary management also arises in the context of mental health issues and in managing the boundaries of a coach's competence. In some instances, there may also be less opportunity to build coaching capability depending on the nature of the role and other competing demands. Further, institutional knowledge can be a double-edged sword. It raises questions as to what biases, perceptions, perspectives, and assumptions are being brought to the coaching and to a coach's decision making; and what part the coach plays in the systemic pattern of interactions that play out in the organization (Wright, 2020; Wright & Tennyson, 2021).

There are a number of ways to manage these challenges, including developing a robust organizational coaching philosophy and purpose, guidelines, policies and practices, use of contracting, setting expectations, and agreeing on important aspects of the coaching engagement up front (e.g., around reporting and confidentiality). A coach who is a member of a coaching body can refer to its code of ethics for support and guidance. However, internal policies, initial contracting, and codes of ethics will never be able to cover every situation that an internal coach might face. Engaging in reflective practice and supervision can be beneficial in helping internal coaches navigate ethical and legal challenges related to their often multiple roles, competing commitments, expectations, and demands.

The internal coach participants in the US study reported the value of discussing issues and reflecting on challenges with an external coach supervisor: "It gives me the space to open up in a way that I may not open up to someone inside the company where I work to gain that unbiased opinion ... guidance as to my coaching practice." Another noted: "I was able to discuss these with an 'external' coach supervisor who had no bias in our conversations which was good in terms of what we discussed and potential ways to deal with this."

More specifically, they suggested that the supervision allowed them to take a bigger perspective on the organization and to gain a better understanding of the influence of cultural issues and power dynamics, including the impact on coaching outcomes and the expectations the organization had of coaching: "It helped me look at the bigger system in which I work and bring these issues to the team for discussion as to what we might change in order to make the impact of coaching even better than it is today." Another stated:

> One of the key insights was to look into the broader aspects of the coaching environment in which I work, i.e., the systems/corporate culture and this helped me understand why certain coachees perhaps behaved like they did during my coaching sessions.

Investing in coaching supervision that supports the normative (ensuring work is professional and ethical), developmental (developing both personal and professional skills, understanding, and capacities), and restorative functions (providing emotional support) of internal coaches, may also assist an organization discharging its duty of care to the coach, coachees, or employees and the broader stakeholders they serve (Wright & O'Connor, 2021). This is discussed further, below.

## Understandings of Supervision and Who Needs It

While coaching supervision has existed as a distinct practice since 2006 (Armstrong & Geddes, 2009), there still appears to be some confusion between supervision and other modalities such as coaching, mentor coaching, training supervision, and coach the coach. (Bachkirova, 2011). The US study highlighted some of these misunderstandings.

A number of coaches chose not to join the study because they felt that they were too experienced to need supervision: "I am a master coach, I don't need supervision" and "I have been coaching successfully for 20 years, why would I want to be supervised by you?"

This has been described by McGivern (2009) as the "vanity trap." Participants who chose to join the study however, expressed a different perspective, including the need to develop "self as instrument": "No matter how much experience you have, there will be always blind spots you won't be able to see by yourself in your practice." Another respondent shared: "As a coach, the most important instrument is self. If we're unable to have space to work out our own challenges, confusion, doubt, etc., it is hard to be as effective as possible."

Moreover, a number of participants also commented on the necessity of continuous learning beyond their initial coach education. Supervision was seen by many as crucial development for both new and experienced coaches alike: "It's important to understand that [it] is not enough getting a coaching certificate. The importance of keep polishing our coaching skills is essential in order to become a better coach" (sic).

Many participants shared that they felt the insights they gained from the supervision sessions provided them with a perceived "missing link" between theory, their training and practice (Hawkins, Turner, & Passmore, 2019). As one shared:

> To me this was the missing link. I'd had recordings evaluated and received peer feedback through reciprocal peer coaching, but I felt I needed guidance in some of the practical areas that go beyond the simple mechanics of coaching or coaching theory and research … a way to bring those together. I have a lot of theory from my PhD in organizational psychology, and a lot of the brass tacks from my coaching program. But [Supervisor] really helped me with some nuances that aren't obvious from my training and previous experiences and I can only imagine that I'm just at the tip of the iceberg right now. I think there is much more to learn.

While training, learning activities, practice hours, and self-reflection are essential components of our development, a number of participants in the US study described them as insufficient:

*I have done significant training, but no learning has made more impact on me as a coach than supervision. I am committed to continuing coaching supervision as there is no more effective way of ensuring I provide the most effective coaching to my clients.*

Misunderstandings were also evident in the reasons a number of the participants did not continue with the study. Responses included: "I don't have anything to bring" and "everything is going well following our last call," highlight the challenges of supervising the "everything-is-fine" coach (Bachkirova, 2019). It is also possible that coaches who contend that they do not need supervision or do not face any issues or challenges in their practice are engaging in self-deception. While this concept may elicit a strong reaction in some coaches, to shy away from it is to miss an opportunity to improve quality of practice (Bachkirova, 2015).

Changes in understandings of supervision as a result of participating in the US study were clearly evident. Participants were not only able to compare and contrast supervision to other modalities, but clearly articulate its differing uses, values and benefits. As one participant described:

*My understanding has changed due to participation in this project because I saw it as a more evaluatory experience, similar to the ICF Coaching Competencies and whether or not I was meeting them. Instead, my experience was that I got to look at certain nagging doubts I have about my coaching, unrelated to the competencies, and the ability to get support and clarity on those doubts.*

To assume that we are too experienced, knowledgeable, or successful to reflect on our practice raises a number of potential ethical and legal issues, not least in relation to managing the boundaries of our competence. This also includes the promises we make around the outcomes of our coaching services (e.g., return on investment), the way we "hold ourselves out" (e.g., master coach), and the way we market our services, including the assertions we make about our qualifications and experience. Each could lead to potential claims of breach of contract, breach of duty of care, or misrepresentation (Wright & O'Connor, 2021).

When considering the boundaries of our competence, it is important to balance our ethical responsibility and accountability with the need to engage in experiential and transformative learning so as to enhance our professional development. Supervision has an important role to play in managing this tension (Carroll, 2006).

## Development of Ethical Maturity, Legal Awareness, and Judgment

Each of the four preceding sections have identified a number of ethical and legal issues. This emphasizes the importance of developing ethical maturity and legal awareness, knowledge, sensitivity, and judgment, referred to collectively as legal thinking.

Good coaching is underpinned by the highest standards of competence, responsibility, and sound ethical judgment. However, unlike professions such as medicine, law, and psychology, coaching is an unregulated industry with no universal standard of practice or code of ethics (Wright & O'Connor, 2021). As such, we have no clear or definitive guidance as to the standard and scope of our professional responsibility. While existing codes of ethics may provide a recourse and direction in times of uncertainty, they cannot provide guidance on the myriad of ethical dilemmas coaches inevitably face. For internal coaches, codes may also conflict with internal policies, practices, or expectations. Supervision may help coaches navigate the boundaries of their own competence, explore ethical issues, and develop their ethical maturity (Lane, 2011; Lane & Cavanagh, 2021).

Despite the inextricable link between ethics and law, the development of legal thinking appears to be an overlooked aspect of our development as coaches. It appears that very few training programs address the legal implications of coaching in any meaningful way. It is in this context that supervision has an essential role to play in the development of legal thinking (Wright & O'Connor, 2021). While legal issues could (and I believe should) form a core aspect of the education and training of coaches, the law is complex. Coach education can never cover the plethora of situations that a coach is likely to encounter. In this way, it is similar to the necessary limitations of ethical codes.

From establishing businesses, marketing services, contracting with clients, safeguarding confidential information, intellectual property and personal data, to the retention and disposal of documents post engagement, legal considerations arise in almost all aspects of coaching and supervision practice. It is incumbent on coaches and supervisors to consider the laws in the jurisdictions in which they work. In fact, there is an established legal principle in most jurisdictions that ignorance is no defense. This is of critical importance (Wright & O'Connor, 2021) and highlights the need to develop every supervisor's legal thinking.

Consistent with the accepted functions of supervision (Hawkins & Shohet, 2006; Inskipp & Proctor, 1993), ethical and legal issues may be identified that the coach may not be aware of as part of the normative function. Supervision may enhance a coach's ethical maturity and legal thinking as part of the developmental function. It may also support a coach when navigating potential ethical and legal issues as part of the restorative function. Moreover, this co-created dialogue may help both the coach and supervisor increase their awareness, reflexivity, and critical thinking around potential ethical and legal issues.

Given the growth and evolution of coaching, supervisors have an increasingly important role to play in the development of ethical maturity and legal thinking. This is even more important for internal coaches given their potentially overlapping roles, responsibilities and boundaries, and multiple expectations and demands. Ethical issues did arise in the US study although they were often not described in those terms and in some instances not recognized at all. There was also at least one instance in which a participant was unaware that their intended practices had the potential to do serious harm in breach of their duty of care.

Supervision, with an appropriately qualified supervisor, may help a coach: Recognize red flags that indicate the relevance of legal issues; determine their capability of working with the level of complexity the issues present and; know where to refer should specialist advice be required. Importantly, it may also be prudent for all coaches (and organizations using or purchasing coaching services) to seek the support of a supervisor as evidence that the coach and organization has taken all reasonable steps to uphold their duty of care (Wright & O'Connor, 2021).

In the following section, the potential impacts of contextual factors and coaching discourses on the understanding and uptake of supervision in the US are explored.

## Impact of Coaching Discourses, Coaching Body Politic, and Global Differences

Dominant discourses in any industry, discipline, or profession are important because they shape perceptions and practices. The term discourse "aims to expose how institutionalized patterns of knowledge and power are embedded in our social world, and shape and limit both how we think and our social relations" (Western, 2017, p. 42). Importantly, as these discourses shape and influence social and professional norms, they become invisible to us. This chapter attempts to identify coaching discourses that may have an impact on attitudes and approaches to coaching supervision in the US.

One of the dominant discourses in coaching is the managerial discourse, which emphasizes scientific rationalism—"if it can't be measured it doesn't count"—and is premised on the belief that we can control or manage our environment. This sits well with goal focused, time measured, and mechanistic approaches to coaching. It may also help explain why there has been some resistance to more systemic and networked approaches, since they challenge long held paradigms that assume organizational systems can be objectively evaluated or controlled. I am not sure if the management discourse is more prevalent in the US. It is certainly consistent with an often-heard comment: "We need proof - that's corporate America."

It has also been suggested that the word 'supervision' has negative connotations, particularly in a US context. As one participant commented:

*The word "supervision" gave me the idea that I was going to be supervised or watch by someone 'senior' than me. The connotations from that word were rather 'cold' and negative. However, once I experienced it, I understood it to be more like an equal relationship between two coaches where knowledge and wisdom are shared with a little coaching. It is definitely a positive experience.*

It is difficult to draw conclusions based on the limited sample size (41 US-based coaches). Furthermore, participants in the US study were self-selecting. Coaches with the greatest levels of resistance to supervision may have been less inclined to apply to participate and therefore, less represented in the sample.

One factor that would appear to have an influence on discourses around coaching supervision, particularly in the US, is the Coach Body Politic (CBP). The CBP explores the relationship between coaching organizations including coach providers, accrediting and training institutions, and coaching practice (Western, 2017). Little has been theorized about this important concept (de Haan, 2008) despite its influence over how coaching is practiced. This is all the more troubling given coaching bodies are self-appointed and accountable only to themselves. This is a fact that still seems to elude many in the coaching industry, particularly those new to the field.

ICF's position on supervision continues to evolve. It now recommends supervision as an important element of a coach's professional development, learning, and growth. It is not however, a requirement for individual accreditation unlike a number of other coaching bodies (e.g., EMCC and the Association for Coaching). While I would not advocate that coaching supervision be mandated for fear it could become a "box checking" exercise, the fact that it is not a requirement likely has a far greater impact on understandings and uptake in the US given the ICF's dominance in the region. Consistent with observations by Hawkins and Turner (2017), those who participated in the US study from other regions were more familiar with coaching supervision and were more likely to have experienced it.

The collective conversations we have as coaches, particularly on social media may also have a profound impact on our thinking and practice as coaches. One conversation that is of particular relevance in the present context is what I might term the "anti-supervision/pro coach mentoring" conversation. One social media post in particular attempted to instill fear into practitioners by suggesting that the use of the title "supervisor" confers legal liability in a way that coach mentoring does not. This assertion is debatable, especially since a mental health professional's liability is inversely proportional to the supervisee's level of skill and experience (Werth et al., 2009). This issue is discussed further in the chapter, Supervising Legally (Wright & O'Connor, 2021). Interestingly, the post's author did not refer to other titles (e.g., master coach, coach mentor) and the implications they may have on the scope and standard of a coach's duty of care.

Are such claims born of fear and protectionism? Rather than debate titles and legal culpability, we should accept that as coaches, consultants, mentors, and supervisors, we all have moral, ethical, and legal obligations. We cannot avoid liability. Cries that "coaching is not therapy," that "we deal with the future not the past," "ask don't tell" and "supervision is psychological (and dangerous), and coach mentoring is not" are unhelpful. We are not above the law. As such, we need to reflect on the nature of our responsibilities and educate ourselves accordingly.

Other influences may emerge as a result of coaching related surveys. While often well intentioned, these can sometimes be unhelpful in the context of supervision given the level of misunderstanding in the marketplace. Confusion with other modalities (e.g., training supervision, coach mentoring, etc.) in the mind of the respondents renders data potentially meaningless and often counter-productive. For example, if a respondent is confusing coaching supervision with mentor coaching, data collected on the uses and benefits of "supervision" may not accurately reflect their perspectives.

It has also been suggested that the gap is widening between academia and coaching bodies with negative consequences for the field of coaching, including a lessening of cross fertilization of ideas. My observation in the US is that the converse might be the case. While there are exceptions, it appears that many university coaching programs in the US are either accredited by or aligned with the ICF. If this is indeed the case, this situation is equally worrying since too close a relationship between coach training providers and coaching bodies may lead to collusion, partisanship, a lack of criticality or independent thought (Bachkirova & Smith, 2015).

Supervision has an important role to play in raising our individual and collective awareness and helping us "to see" those things that influence the way we think and practice. In addition to reflecting on the impact of coaching discourses, this also includes thinking critically about our philosophical underpinnings and the theoretical perspectives, models, and approaches we draw on. The participants in the US study reported and appeared to demonstrate increased critical thinking. In fact, a number of coaches described how supervision kept them abreast of the latest research, but also allowed them to be more selective and not to "jump on the bandwagon."

## Conclusion

In this chapter, I attempted to answer the question: How do coaches and coaching remain relevant and fit for purpose and what part might coaching supervision play? Extrapolating from research and observations in practice, I've explored the capacity for systemic and network thinking, the importance of personal and professional development, the role of the internal coach and understandings of supervision and who needs it. This has highlighted the role supervision may play in developing a coach's capacity including the critical importance of developing our reflexivity, critical thinking, personal, and ethical maturity. Of equal importance, yet often overlooked, is the need to develop our legal awareness and judgment. Hypotheses around the impact of contextual factors and coaching discourses on understandings and uptake of supervision in the US have also been discussed. These discussions are critical to consider as they not only shape our thinking and practice today, but exert a powerful influence on how our industry will evolve in the future. Engaging in reflective practice and supervision may also help us make visible the discourses and contextual factors that influence our thinking and why, so that we may transcend subsystem allegiances and ideologies and recognize our interconnectedness and common purpose.

This chapter is a starting point. Each of the areas discussed deserve greater attention and require further investigation by researchers and practitioners. Indeed, it is hoped that the coaching industry will think more deeply about 1) how coaches can best remain relevant and fit for purpose; 2) the role of coaching supervision in supporting these goals; and 3) the impact of supervision on the evolution and longevity of the coaching industry.

# References

Armstrong, H., & Geddes, M. (2009). Developing coaching supervision practice: An Australian case study. *International Journal of Evidence Based Coaching and Mentoring*, 7(2): 1–17.

Avolio, B. J., Walumbwa, F. O., & Weber, T. J. (2009). Leadership: Current theories, research, and future directions. *The Annual Review of Psychology, 60*: 421–449.

Bachkirova, T. (2008). Coaching supervision: Reflection of changes and challenges. *People and Organizations at Work*, 16–17.

Bachkirova, T. (2021). *Developmental coaching: Working with the self.* Open University Press.

Bachkirova, T. (2015). Self-deception in coaches: An issue in principle and a challenge for supervision. *Coaching: An International Journal of Theory, Research and Practice, 8*(1): 4–19. doi: 10.1080/17521882.2014.998692

Bachkirova, T. (2016). The self of the coach: Conceptualization, issues and opportunities for practitioner development. *Consulting Psychology Journal: Practice and Research, 68*(2): 143–156.

Bachkirova, T. (2019). *Supervising the 'everything is fine' coach.* [Conference presentation]. Oxford Brookes University Coaching Supervision Conference, Oxford, U.K.

Bachkirova, T., & Baker, S. (2018). Revisiting the issue of boundaries between coaching and counselling. In S. Palmer, & A. Whybrow (Eds.), *Handbook of coaching psychology: a guide for practitioners.* Routledge.

Bachkirova, T., & Lawton Smith, C. (2015). From competencies to capabilities in the assessment and accreditation of coaches. *International Journal of Evidence Based Coaching and Mentoring, 13*(2): 123–140.

Berger, J. G. (2006). Adult development theory and executive coaching. In D. R. Stober, & A. M. Grant (Eds.), *Evidence based coaching handbook* (pp. 58–97). Wiley.

Braun, V. and Clarke, V. (2006). Using thematic analysis in psychology. *Qualitative Research in Psychology, 3*(2): 77–101.

Cavanagh, M. (2006). Coaching from a systemic perspective: A complex adaptive conversation. In D. Stober, & A. M. Grant (Eds.), *Evidence based coaching handbook* (pp. 313–354). Wiley.

Cavanagh, M. (2013). The coaching engagement in the 21st Century: New paradigms for complex times. In S. David, D. Clutterbuck & D. Megginson (Eds.), *Beyond goals: Effective strategies for coaching and mentoring*. Gower Publishing.

Carroll, M. (2006). Supervising executive coaches, *Therapy Today, 17*(5): 47–49.

Champion, C. K. (2011). Beyond quality assurance: the Deloitte internal coaching supervision story. In T. Bachkirova, P. Jackson, & D. Clutterbuck (Eds.), *Coaching & mentoring supervision: Theory and practice* (pp. 281–289). Open University Press.

Clutterbuck, D., & Megginson, D. (2011). Coach maturity: An emerging concept. In D. Brennan, & L. Wildflower (Eds.), *The handbook of knowledge-based coaching: From theory to practice* (pp. 299–313). Jossey-Bass.

Cook-Greuter, S. R. (2004). Making the case for a developmental perspective. *Industrial and commercial training, 36*(7): 275–281.

de Haan, E, (2008). *Relational coaching*. Wiley and Sons.

de Haan, E. (2017). How supervisors attend to coaches, so that they attend to leaders. *Coaching Perspectives, 15*: 6–8.

Fit for purpose. (n.d.). *Oxford English dictionary lexico*. https://www.lexico.com/definition/fit_for_purpose

Garvey, B. (2017). Issues in assessment and accreditation of coaches. In Bachkirova, T., Spence, G., & Drake, D. B. (Eds.), *The SAGE handbook of coaching*. SAGE.

Harper, D., & Thompson, A. (2012). *Qualitative research methods in mental health and psychotherapy: A guide for students and practitioners*. Wiley-Blackwell.

Hawkins, P., & Shohet, R. (2006). *Supervision in the helping profession*. Open University Press.

Hawkins, P., & Turner, E. (2017). The rise of coaching supervision 2006–2014. *Coaching: An International Journal of Theory Research and Practice, 10*(2): 1–13.

Hawkins, P., Turner, E., & Passmore, J. (2019). *The manifesto for supervision*. Association for Coaching and Henley Business School.

Hodge, A. (2016). The value of coaching supervision as a development process: Contribution to continued professional and personal wellbeing for executive coaches. *International Journal of Evidence Based Coaching and Mentoring, 14*(2): 87–106.

Inskipp, F., & Proctor, B. (1993). The art, craft and tasks of counselling supervision. Part 1: Making the most of supervision. Cascade.

Jackson, P., & Bachkirova, T. (2019). The 3 ps of supervision and coaching: Philosophy, purpose and process. In E. Turner, & S. Palmer (Eds.), *The heart of coaching supervision: Working with reflection and self-care*. Routledge.

Kegan, R. (1994). *In over our heads: The mental demands of modern life*. Harvard University Press.

Lane, D. (2011). Ethics and professional standards in supervision. In T. Bachkirova, P. Jackson, & D. Clutterbuck (Eds.), *Coaching and mentoring supervision*. Open University Press.

Lane, D. (2017). Trends in eevelopment of coaches (education and training) Is it valid, is it rigorous, is it relevant? In T. Bachkirova, G. Spence, & D. B. Drake (Eds.), *The SAGE handbook of Coaching*. SAGE.

Lane, D., & Cavanagh, M. (2021). Supervising ethically. In T. Bachkirova, P. Jackson, & D. Clutterbuck (Eds.), *Coaching and mentoring supervision* (2nd ed.). Open University Press.

Laske, O. E. (2006). *Measuring hidden dimensions: The art and science of fully engaging adults. Volume 1*. Interdevelopmental Institute Press.

Lawrence, P. (2019). What is systemic coaching? *Philosophy of Coaching: An International Journal, 4*(2): 35–52. 10.22316/poc/04.2.03

Lawrence, P., & Moore, A. (2019). *Coaching in three dimensions: Meeting the challenges of a complex world.* Routledge.

Lichtenstein, B., Uhl-Bien, M., Marion, R., Seers, A., Orton, J., & Schreiber, C. (2007). Complexity leadership theory: an interactive perspective on leading in complex adaptive systems. In J. K. Hazy, J. A. Goldstein, & B. B. Lichtenstein (Eds.), *Complex systemsleadership theory: New perspectives from complexity science on social and organisational effectiveness.* ISCE Pub.

Lucas, M. (2012). Exploring the double-value of supervision: A developmental perspective for internal coaches. *The International Journal of Mentoring and Coaching, 10*(2): 21–90.

Maxwell, A. (2011). Supervising the internal coach. In T. Bachkirova, P. Jackson & D. Clutterbuck (Eds.), *Coaching & mentoring supervision: Theory & practice.* Open University Press.

McGivern, L. (2009). Continuous professional development and avoiding the vanity trap: an exploration of coaches' lived experiences of supervision. *International Journal of Evidence Based Coaching and Mentoring* (Special Issue 3): 22–37.

O'Connor, S. (2020). Systemically integrated approaches to coaching: An introduction. *Philosophy of Coaching: An International Journal, 5*(2): 40–62. 10.22316/poc/05.2.04

O'Connor, S., & Cavanagh, M. (2013). The coaching ripple effect: The effects of developmental coaching on wellbeing across organisational networks. *Psychology of Wellbeing: Theory, Research and Practice, 3*(2): 1–23.10.1186/2211-1522-3-2

Robson, M. (2016). An ethnographic study of the introduction of internal supervisors to an internal coaching scheme. *International Journal of Evidence Based Coaching and Mentoring, 14*(2): 106–122.

Spence, G. B., Cavanagh, M.J., & Grant, A.M. (2006). Duty of care in an unregulated industry: Initial findings on the diversity and practices of Australian coaches. *International Coaching Psychology Review, 1*(1): 71–85.

St John-Brooks, K. (2018). *Internal coaching: The inside story* (2nd ed.). Routledge.

Tennyson, S. (2021, in press). Applying a systemic developmental approach to coaching supervision: Experiences from the U.S.A.

Torbert, W. R. (1991). *The power of balance: Transforming self, society, and scientific inquiry.* Sage.

Uhl-Bien, M., Marion, R., & McKelvey, B. (2007). Complexity leadership theory: Shifting leadership from the industrial age to the knowledge era. *The Leadership Quarterly, 18*: 298–318.

Werth, J. L. Jr., Welfel, E. R., & Benjamin, G.A.H. (Eds.), (2009 ). *The duty to protect: ethical, legal, and professional considerations for mental health professionals.* Washington, DC: American Psychological Society.

Western, S. (2017). The key discourses of coaching. In T. Bachkirova, G. Spence, & D. B. Drake (Eds.), *The SAGE handbook of coaching.* SAGE.

Whitmore, J. (1992). *Coaching for performance: A practical guide to growing your own skills.* Nicholas Brealey.

Wilber, K. (2000). *Integral psychology: Consciousness, spirit, psychology, therapy.* Shambhala Publications.

Wright, A. (2021). Research matters: What's in it for us? *Coaching at Work, 16*(1): 56–57.

Wright, A., McLean Walsh, M., & Tennyson, S. (2019). Systemic coaching supervision: Responding to the complex challenges of our time. *Philosophy of Coaching: An International Journal, 4*(12): 107–122. 10.22316/poc/04.1.08

Wright, A., & O'Connor, S. (2021). Supervising legally. In T. Bachkirova, P. Jackson, & D. Clutterbuck (Eds.), *Coaching and mentoring supervision* (2nd ed.). Open University Press.

Wright, A., & Tennyson, S. (2021 in press). Team coaching in a professional services firm: A case study of internal and external team coaching in a complex adaptive system. In D. Clutterbuck, E. Turner, & C. Murphy (Eds.), *The team coaching casebook.* McGraw Hill.

Wright, A., van Vliet, K., & Tennyson, S. (2020, February 15). *Experiencing coaching supervision: A study in understandings of supervision, value & benefits* [Conference presentation]. University of Sydney Evidence Based Coaching Psychology Conference, Sydney, Australia.

## Author Bio

**Angela Wright**, based in New York, is a partner at CEC Global with extensive experience coaching and supervising individuals, groups, and teams, including providing supervision to internal and external coaches and leading reflective practice groups for leaders. She co-facilitates the Oxford Brookes University Advanced Professional Program in Coaching Supervision in the US and is part of the faculty on the Masters in Executive Coaching and Organizational Consulting at New York University. In 2018 she received the EMCC Coaching Supervision Award. Angela is actively engaged in research, including research in coaching supervision. She was part of the writing team on the world's first ISO (International Organization for Standards) aligned guideline for the training of coaches and the provision of coaching services. She has also published articles and book chapters, presented at international conferences on coaching and coaching supervision. Prior to her coaching career, Angela practiced as an attorney where she specialized in disputes around professional responsibility, corporate governance, breach of duty of care, conflicts of interest, and ethical issues. She holds an LL.B, LL.M, J.D., and an M.Sc. in Organizational Coaching Psychology. Her Ph.D. focuses on how coaches and coaching will remain relevant and "fit for purpose."

# 18 Introducing Supervision into Training Programs for Professional Coaches

*Elena Espinal and Adriana Rodríguez*

## Introduction

This chapter navigates the relevance of including supervisory processes in the training of professional coaches and analyzes the impact this has had on the development of a coach's being, doing, and relationship with the client.

To enter into this chapter, we invite you to acknowledge a coach's journey as a path of no return. Regardless of the professional experience, those who are truly committed to coaching must recognize the need to participate in ongoing learning and development activities, and engage in reflective practices that allow them to "go deeper and discover themselves and their impact on others, and how they are impacted by others, so that they are serving their client from the stance that they hold" (Hullinger, 2020).

We consider reflective practices, particularly supervision, as a fundamental component that needs to be included from the very beginning of a coach's training.

European coaching associations, such as the Association for Coaching (AC) and the European Mentoring and Coaching Council (EMCC) have established guidelines and competencies for supervisors, and include supervision as a mandatory process for their professional coaches (Association for Coaching 2021, International Coaching Federation 2021; EMCC, 2021). On the other hand, associations based in the Americas, such as the International Coaching Federation (ICF) or Federación Internacional de Coaching Ontológico (FICOP), have not yet established requirements for coaches to undergo a supervision process once they are practicing professionally.

In light of this situation, we pose these questions: How can we accelerate the process of supervision adoption in the Americas? How can we better promote the benefits of supervision and encourage coaches to adopt it as an inalienable practice for their professional lives?

Team Power is a company that has been devoted to training coaches over the last 23 years. It has done so in Argentina, with recognition from both the ICF and Argentina's Department of Education, and in partnership

DOI: 10.4324/b23130-22

with FICOP. Team Power has also delivered baseline coach training and coaching specialization programs in México with the endorsement of ICF.

We believe that coaching enables people to relativize their perspectives and explore other, more powerful points of view that can enable them to create the future they want, and relate better to others and the world around them.

Like most Latin American training centers, we are deeply influenced by Existentialist and Ontological interpretations of humans and language that seamlessly align with the general guidelines of coaching. Also, these philosophies serve as a foundation for generating deep reflection on the world and the way we observe, so that we can deepen and foster conversations much more oriented to the observer ("who"). We believe that action is a byproduct of our way of observing and not an end in itself, as depicted in behavioral coaching proposals that focus more on the way of dong things ("how").

The Ontological source facilitates the learning and understanding of the work of a coach, whose mission is not to solve situations but to accompany the client into the discovery of new ways of interpreting (being), and consequently, of doing.

Our personal experience with supervision empowered us to recognize our own models, in our use of power and how our story influences the client and the client's influence on us. We wondered, how much could supervision improve the quality of the profession? This question stemmed from our observations that when a coach undergoes regular supervision, their presence and awareness deepens and sharpens.

Drawing on this experience, we decided to conduct a pilot project to analyze the impact of supervision in our students' coaching practices. To do so, we included supervision in Mastering Coaching Skills, our program aimed at training and improving the quality and depth of coaching processes for professional coaches.

Throughout this chapter, we depict how this pilot project was carried out, the benefits students reported from the supervisory processes, differences the mentors observed, and the impact this process had on the coaches. We also share some recommendations for those trainers who want to include supervision in their training programs.

Our purpose is to open up dialogue in the Americas about the significance of supervision as a reflective process and as a foundation component in the training of professional coaches.

## Supervision: A New Step in Building our Profession

Thirty years ago in the Americas, coaching was perceived as a mystical art, exercised only by some privileged people who had a special ability to "listen beyond," using intuition as guidance for the conversation. No agreement was established and there was no way to measure whether the client gained something really empowering from the session or not.

Even today, many coaches still mistake their service, believing their involvement aims at "solving" the issue the client faces, forgetting their commitment is to partner with the client to shift the position from which the client experiences to a place of power, enabling them to change their actions accordingly, and achieve results.

The emergence of competency models from organizations like the ICF greatly advanced the practice. The ICF model (2020) provided a technical profile and a frame that made coaching easier to learn. Coaching became a practice that could be learned and applied all over the world. It accounted for the transformation of an art into a technique, expanding and popularizing the profession worldwide so that clients know what they can expect from a coach, whether their coach is an Associate Certified Coach (ACC), Professional Certified Coach (PCC), or Master Certified Coach (MCC) practitioner.

As with any new way of observing, competencies opened a new world of action and simultaneously closed other possibilities. Talking only about competencies casts a shadow over the singularity and the art of a conversation, which varies depending on who the coach is, the quality of relationship that they are able to establish with their client, their own history and their own relationship with the future and the uncertain. That is to say, the competencies are focused more on doing, than on being. Ultimately, if a coach's practice is essentially based on the doing, the coach's training will necessarily be, too. When competencies were introduced, mentoring gained relevance, as it helped coaches to develop and consolidate the competencies. Mentoring emerged as an arena for strengthening the coach-competence axis.

The risk we face when using a competency-based training that offers students only coaching and mentoring practices, is to train highly skilled coaches who will not necessarily become wise observers. We remain unaware of our impact in the client's world and how our personal and unique listening is the source of the questions we are offering to our client. This awareness can only be achieved by a reflective practice focused on the being of the coach.

This quest to incorporate *being* into the coaching profession is evidenced in the update of the competencies by the ICF, including the competency "Embodies a coaching mindset" (ICF, 2021), inviting the coach to participate in ongoing reflective practices to enhance their practice.

It is also increasingly common to hear how coaches have introduced reflective practices, including meditation, yoga, journaling, or bodywork into their profession. In coach training programs, we have observed how widely these practices are promoted. Yet, working alone does not nurture critical reflection. "Introspection and intersubjective reflection without critical self-analysis is … of limited value and open to the charge of self-indulgence ... we need others to clarify and challenge tacit assumptions, the existence of which we may be unaware" (Finlay, 2008).

It is at this point that supervision becomes essential.

The supervision process allows a more powerful learning than the one accrued in many years of individual experience as a coach. Supervision focuses on the coach as a being and the being of the coach in the relationship.

It also fosters reflexivity: "Reflexivity is the process of 'stepping back' from a situation we are involved in ... here we examine ourselves to gauge our values, assumptions, behavior and relationships, and thereby monitor our learning and develop our intra-personal and inter-personal skills" (Lawrence-Wilkes, 2015).

Today we know that supervision was proposed to challenge the way of being a coach.

## A Pilot Project to Increase Consciousness about the Importance of Supervision

Supervision became a recurrent topic in conferences and the experiences of coaches who underwent supervision revealed its value. Today, no one dares doubt that coaching conversations (and their outcomes) are shaped by the individuals who participate in them. This is the context created and the culture and backgrounds in which coach and client live.

As we trained certified coaches to increase their competency level, we decided to analyze the impact of supervision on their learning and their coaching practices. Our program, Mastering Coaching Skills, has been successfully delivered to professional Spanish-speaking coaches for more than nine years and has reached nearly 600 graduate coaches.

Over eight months, coaches participate in live webinars with certified coaches, who offer practical experiences. They also participate in online meetings to deepen in their being as coaches, carry out more than 70 coach practice sessions, and strengthen their competencies through individual and group mentoring processes.

We began with the hypothesis that by including coaching supervision in regular coach training programs, coaches would be more effective in coaching sessions, and they would strengthen competencies linked to the being of the coach and their relationship in the coaching process, such as embodying a coaching mindset, presence, and trust. Furthermore, if supervision had the potential to improve our quality as coaches, it would be desirable to be exposed early in our professional training.

To measure the impact of supervision and test this hypothesis, we set up two groups: One receiving supervision and one not receiving supervision. Our plan was to compare and contrast these groups.

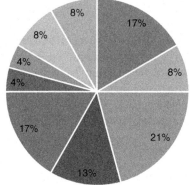

*Figure 18.1* Country of Residence.

Note: *Country of residence of participants, the percentage includes both group A and group B participants.*

## Beginning of the Pilot Process

We invited coach–supervisors to participate in the project through three individual supervision sessions and one group supervision session. We also invited 29 active students from the Mastering Coaching Skills program to participate.

Twenty-four students agreed to participate, assembling a diverse group. The entire research group was made up of students from Argentina, Chile, Spain, the US, Mexico, Panama, Peru, the Dominican Republic, and Venezuela (see Figure 18.1). Students were training as ontological, life, transformational, and organizational coaches, among others (see Figure 18.2). They worked full or part time as coaches (see Figure 18.3), and had a professional experience varying from 20 to 1,000 hours of coaching processes (see Figure 18.4).

Once they consented to participate, we divided students into two groups: Group A, the unsupervised group and Group B, the supervised group. Group A would participate in all the regular activities of the program. These included 12 live sessions, four in-depth sessions with a master coach, eight group mentoring sessions, three individual mentoring sessions, 12 online activities, 12 recordings for self-assessment and feedback from peers, seven follow-up sessions, and 72 practice sessions as coaches. Group B would participate in these activities and would participate in three individual supervision sessions and one group supervision session.

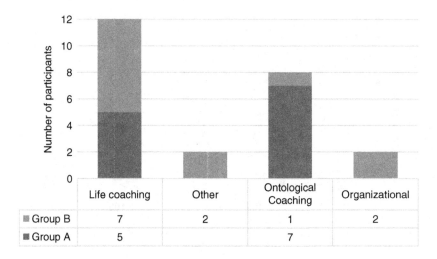

| | Life coaching | Other | Ontological Coaching | Organizational |
|---|---|---|---|---|
| ■ Group B | 7 | 2 | 1 | 2 |
| ■ Group A | 5 | | 7 | |

*Figure 18.2* Professional Coach Training.

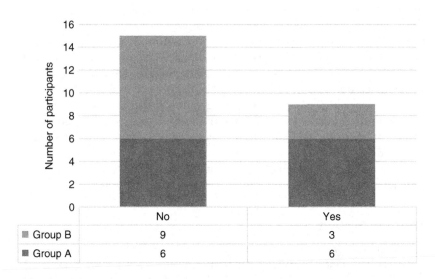

| | No | Yes |
|---|---|---|
| ■ Group B | 9 | 3 |
| ■ Group A | 6 | 6 |

*Figure 18.3* Participants Who Make a Living from Coaching.

To ensure the highest objectivity in the results produced by the students and the mentors who participated in the project, we kept the membership of both groups confidential.

To assess the impact of supervision and identify the baseline development of participants, two questionnaires and an initial interview were administered to both groups. The first was a demographic questionnaire that

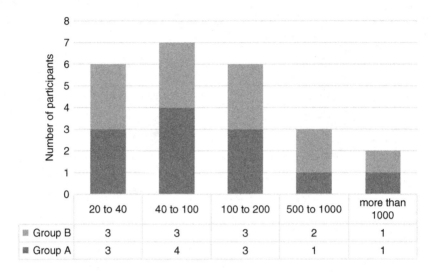

*Figure 18.4* Coaching Experience Hours.

gathered information on country of origin, current residence, educational level, current profession, professional training as a coach, coaching experience, and previous participation in supervisory processes. The second was a self-evaluation questionnaire about their practice as a coach. Through the self-evaluation questionnaire, participants rated the effectiveness of their competencies as coaches to identify their main concerns and evaluate their practice. Once the groups were arranged and questionnaires were completed, all the students in Group A and Group B were interviewed by the coordination team, to gain greater clarity and explore the information collected.

To maintain confidentiality, students learned their group assignment only after completing the questionnaires and the initial interview.

## Framing Session

A framing session was held with students of Group B where they were told about the differences between mentoring and supervision. Also, participants got clarification about the goals of supervision, the issues that might be addressed, and the commitment needed by the group in attending such sessions.

From that first meeting, we identified how unaware coaches were about supervisory practices. Only two participants reported previously participating in a supervision session, and had clarity about what to expect.

At the end of the framing session, we randomly assigned students and supervisors and requested they commit to the following: During individual supervision sessions, participants were free to select the topic they wanted to address. These could include ethical dilemmas about a coaching session, difficulties, fears, doubts, personal barriers, limitations to their effectiveness, emotions, or general aspects of their practice as coaches. In group supervision, coaches would jointly decide the main topic to be addressed. At the end of each session, they were expected to submit a questionnaire documenting the main insights and discoveries of the session.

During the four months of this pilot project, three follow-up sessions were held with supervisors to collect information on the scope of the sessions, the main topics addressed, and the learning reported by students.

Once the supervision process was completed, a final interview and questionnaire were administered to all participants (Groups A and B) to identify the progress obtained and to compare and contrast the results with baseline questionnaires and interviews.

Additionally, mentor coaches were asked to assess the increase in coaching competencies for students in both groups based on ICF PCC markers.

## Results

Information and insights were classified into three main topics: The impact of supervision on the most frequent fears and concerns that coaches face (based on Steinfeldt, 2015); the impact on the coaching relationship (exploring the most frequent situations that a coach endures during the process); and the impact of supervision on coach effectiveness, as defined by ICF competencies.

## Impact of Supervision on Common Fears and Concerns

In the initial questionnaire, participants across both groups expressed that their main concern in a session was "to achieve a change in the way the client observes himself/herself or the situation he/she is facing" and that "the client attains his/her goal through the coaching session/s" (see Figure 18.5). Additionally, 58% of the participants reported their main fear was "failing clients/not providing value" (see Figure 18.6).

To scrutinize these fears, we asked coaches what they expected of themselves during a session and their main concern regarding the session. Participants shared their interest in ensuring their client "gets something valuable," "gets something different from when he/she arrived," also "to accompany in an appropriate way," "to do it well," and "to be useful."

Valuable, adequate, useful? Have we taken the time to ask our clients what this means to them? Or is it that we measure the success of a coaching session using our own standards and expectations? How much do these qualifiers guide our performance as coaches? How much do they limit us?

Thirty-three per cent of the coach participants expressed that they do not

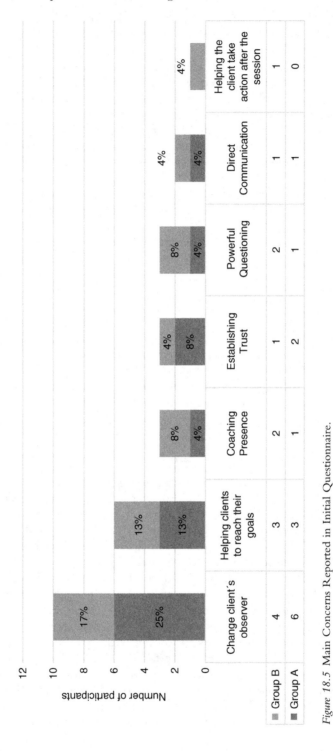

*Figure 18.5* Main Concerns Reported in Initial Questionnaire.

Note: *Main concerns reported in initial questionnaire, the percentage shown represents all participants.*

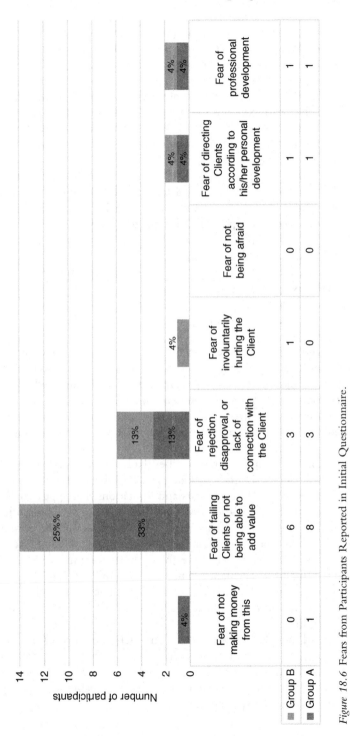

*Figure 18.6* Fears from Participants Reported in Initial Questionnaire.

Note: *Fears from participants reported in initial questionnaire, the percentage shown represents all participants.*

share these concerns with other people; 38% indicated they do share their concerns with a coach in their personal processes, 38% share with a mentor and 50% share with other colleagues. None of the participants reported sharing their concerns with a supervisor who is, indeed, the ideal person to address these issues.

At the end of the project, 50% of coaches from Group B indicated how in supervision they had explored the fears of "failing clients/not providing value," "fear of rejection/disapproval/loss of connection with the client" and "fear to the lack of professional worth, not being able to make a living from coaching" (see Figure 18.7).

However, in the final interview with each supervisee and supervisor, we identified that these were not the only fears addressed in the sessions. There was yet another fear that was explored: "Fear of being vulnerable."

Coaches who received supervision recognized the value they received when the supervisor shared their own experience, mirroring what happened to the coach in their conversation.

As supervisors, we have said many times "this has happened to me too," "I understand how you feel," "in my experience ..." This is because supervision is a space to share openly, to allow ourselves to be vulnerable and pave the way for coaches to open up to new levels of intimacy with their own clients.

Coaches who received supervision realized they felt empowered to "share with the client what happens to me," "create a more human, vulnerable space," "relate to others with compassion," and "show what I feel, observe and perceive from intuition." In the words of a supervisee: "I realized that what I am is what I can then offer my clients; it is not enough to ask about emotions, we need to express what we are perceiving and feeling in the session itself."

Mentors confirmed this, expressing they had observed a new level of presence in the coaches, signified by being aware of the kind of relationship they were establishing and of the fears and limitations that appeared.

Trainees who underwent the supervision process showed a significant change that had to do with "transference," involving dominant personalities of men and women. Understanding this phenomenon freed them in their coaching so they felt more powerful when questioning and emancipated from the quest for acceptance. They left "the child" aside. They were then able to orchestrate an adult relationship with the client: A relationship between equals, without subordinating themselves or trying to impose a way of being with the client.

Other learned models, materialized in fears such as the fear of not being able to add value to my client (poor self-esteem) or the fear of not being enough for the client, were recurring thoughts. Therefore, we consider presence and self-confidence two of the greatest capabilities developed through the supervision experience.

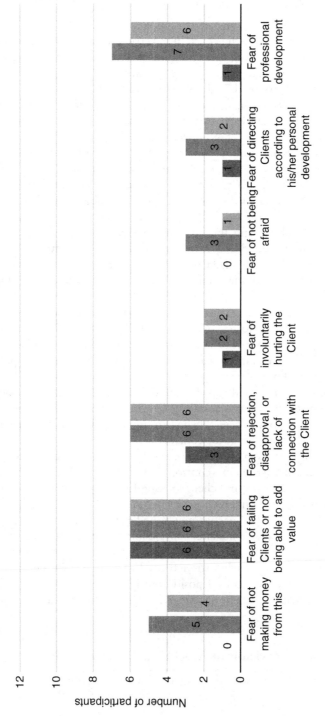

*Figure 18.7* Group B Comparison of Fears.

Note: *Comparison of fears reported by participants in group B in the initial and final questionnaire.*

## Impact of Supervision on the Coaching Relationship

Unlike other practices, one of the primary targets of supervision is exploring what happens to the coach in the coaching relationship. We wanted to identify how exploring these judgments about the relationship with the client impacts the effectiveness of the coach.

To do so, we proposed 33 different scenarios that a coach may face as the focus of the work during a coaching session. At the beginning and end of the process, we asked each participant (Groups A & B) to identify how often they experienced these situations.

When comparing and contrasting the results from the unsupervised group (Group A) and those who received supervision (Group B), we identified that Group B reported a displacement greater than 10% in 3 scenarios: Scenario 2, "I think I don't know the subject and that makes me feel insecure"; scenario 20, "If any client issue affects me, I avoid showing myself vulnerable during the coaching session"; and scenario 25, "I am concerned about not adding value for my client" (see Figure 18.8).

Participants also recognized one of the main benefits gained in supervision as coaches was their ability to open themselves up to being vulnerable and allowing others to be vulnerable.

In the words of one student: "Supervision allowed me to look deep inside what happens to me as a coach. I found the benefits of sharing, recognizing that I am part of a community, and feeling trust and empathy. I learned to be vulnerable and caring to others with respect, and opened up to share my feelings."

Coaches who received supervision also expressed how this process allowed them to "feel more comfortable with their own limitations," "experience greater confidence," "believe more in themselves and have greater self-assurance," and "let go of control."

In the words of a supervisee: "Thanks to the supervision process, today I trust myself and I let go my control over the results. It is not my aim to resolve. I try to be with my client looking for a new way of observing the situation, where he could feel more powerful."

In total, 50% of the coaches mentioned having greater self-confidence and self-assurance as coaches after supervision. Mentors also noted that trust is one of the competencies in which they observed the biggest impact from supervision. That is, coaches strengthened their power by being less self-demanding—empowered by a position of not knowing—which enabled a conversation with the client that was characterized by broader openness and curiosity.

## Impact of Supervision on Coaching Competencies

Hawkins et al. (2019) state that supervision is essential for quality coaching and "is a key element in the action learning cycle that connects the

| No. | Scenario | Grupo A | Grupo B | Both groups | Difference between group B and A |
|-----|----------|---------|---------|-------------|----------------------------------|
| 20 | If any client issue affects me, I avoid showing myself vulnerable during the coaching session | 13% | 25% | 19% | 12% |
| 25 | I am concerned about not adding value for my client | 12% | 24% | 18% | 11% |
| 2 | I think I don't know the subject and that makes me feel insecure | 5% | 16% | 11% | 11% |
| 8 | I don't think I have the necessary tools to be effective with a client | 4% | 11% | 7% | 7% |
| 5 | If the client seems lukewarm, I do not trust that he/she can resolve the situation on his/her own | 6% | 11% | 8% | 5% |
| 16 | I have generated such a close relationship with my client that our sessions seem like a friends talk | 2% | 6% | 4% | 5% |

*Figure 18.8* Displacement Reported by Participants in Coaching Sscenarios.

Source: *Displacement reported by participants comparing initial and final questionnaire. The percentage shown was determined by group.*

competencies we learn on coaching training, with the practice of working with a great variety of clients and client organizations" (Hawkins et al., 2019).

This pilot project began at the end of 2019, before the transition of the ICF eleven competences model into the new model of eight competencies (ICF, 2020). Therefore, when referring to competencies, we will alternate between both models.

As we seek to strengthen the connection between a coach's competencies and supervision, during the initial survey, we asked participants to rate how effective they felt in each of the coaching competencies. The competencies with highest effectiveness declared by participants at the beginning of the project were: Establishing trust and intimacy or cultivate trust and safety, meeting ethical guidelines and professional standards or demonstrates ethical practice. All were rated higher than eight (based on a 1–10 scale in which 10 was "highly effective").

At the end of the project, we asked students to once again evaluate their effectiveness in each competency. In both groups, participants rated all competencies higher than eight (see Figure 18.9).

The competencies in which the unsupervised group (Group A) reported greater effectiveness were coaching presence or maintains presence, active listening, establishing trust and intimacy with the client or cultivates trust and safety, and meeting ethical guidelines and professional standards or demonstrates ethical practice. All of these competencies were rated higher than nine. These same competencies also rated higher in the group that received supervision (Group B), along with another competency, creating awareness or evoking awareness (see Figure 18.10).

We asked supervisees if they could identify which competencies in their practice were directly impacted by supervision. Their answers included: Creating awareness or evokes awareness, coaching presence or maintains presence, establishing trust and intimacy, and cultivate trust and safety. At the end of the study, we asked the supervisees if they could identify which competencies' effectiveness did supervision directly impact? Their answer was creating awareness, coaching presence and establishing trust and intimacy with the client, according to 58% of the respondents (see Figure 18.11).

Mentors validated this information in their final evaluations. By using a final coaching recording, they observed a displacement increase in Group B in the effectiveness of the competencies coaching presence or maintains presence, establishing trust and intimacy, or cultivate trust and safety and establishing the coaching agreement or establishes and maintains agreements.

The greatest impact reported by students in Group B related to being and the co-creation of the relationship. This connects closely to new ICF Competency "Embodies a Coaching Mindset" (ICF, 2021):

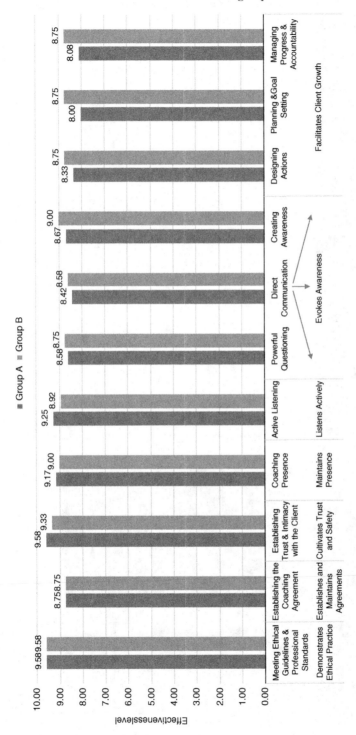

*Figure 18.9* Effectiveness in ICF Coaching Competencies.

Note: *Effectiveness reported by students in their ICF competencies during the final questionnaire. Effectiveness was evaluated in a scale from 1 to 10 (10 being the highest).*

| Comparison with 8 ICF Core Competencies Model | 11 ICF Core Competencies Model | Group A | | Group B | | All participants | |
|---|---|---|---|---|---|---|---|
| | | Final questionnaire | Displacement reported by participants compared to initial questionnaire | Final questionnaire | Displacement reported by participants compared to initial questionnaire | Final questionnaire | Displacement reported by participants compared to initial questionnaire |
| Demonstrates Ethical Practice | Meeting Ethical Guidelines & Professional Standards | 9.58 | 0.92 | 9.58 | 0.83 | 9.58 | 0.88 |
| Establishes and Maintains Agreements | Establishing the Coaching Agreement | 8.75 | 1.92 | 8.75 | 1.42 | 8.75 | 1.67 |
| Cultivates Trust and Safety | Establishing Trust & Intimacy with the Client | 9.58 | 1.50 | 9.33 | 0.83 | 9.46 | 1.17 |
| Maintains Presence | Coaching Presence | 9.17 | 1.33 | 9.00 | 1.17 | 9.08 | 1.25 |
| Listens Actively | Active Listening | 9.25 | 2.00 | 8.92 | 1.08 | 9.08 | 1.54 |
| Evokes Awareness | Powerful Questioning | 8.58 | 2.17 | 8.75 | 2.67 | 8.67 | 2.42 |
| | Direct Communication | 8.42 | 2.17 | 8.58 | 1.08 | 8.50 | 1.63 |
| | Creating Awareness | 8.67 | 1.75 | 9.00 | 2.00 | 8.83 | 1.88 |
| | Designing Actions | 8.33 | 2.17 | 8.75 | 1.50 | 8.54 | 1.83 |
| Facilitates Client Growth | Planning & Goal Setting | 8.00 | 1.75 | 8.75 | 1.75 | 8.38 | 1.75 |
| | Managing Progress & Accountability | 8.08 | 1.92 | 8.75 | 2.08 | 8.42 | 2.00 |
| Total average | | 8.68 | 1.87 | 8.86 | 1.56 | 8.77 | 1.71 |

*Figure 18.10* Effectiveness Displacement in ICF Coaching Competencies.

Note: *Comparison of effectiveness identified by coaches in the initial and final questionnaire on their ICF competencies. Effectiveness was evaluated in a scale from 1 to 10 (10 being the highest).*

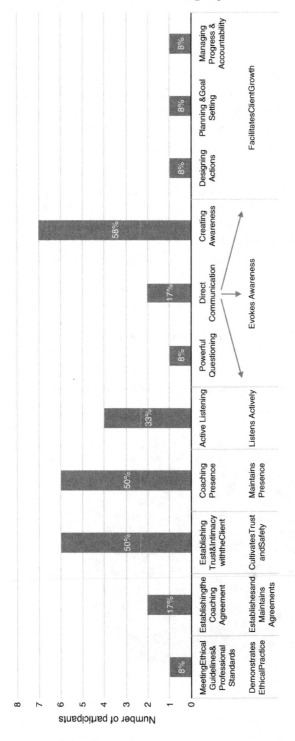

*Figure 18.11* Impact of Supervision in ICF Competencies by Group B.

1   Acknowledges that clients are responsible for their own choices
2   Engages in ongoing learning and development as a coach
3   Develops an ongoing reflective practice to enhance one's coaching
4   Remains aware of and open to the influence of context and culture on self and others
5   Uses awareness of self and one's intuition to benefit clients
6   Develops and maintains the ability to regulate one's emotions
7   Mentally and emotionally prepares for sessions
8   Seeks help from outside sources when necessary

Finally, we asked coaches who received supervision if this process had an impact on the results obtained in their training. A full 82% of participants in Group B reported that supervision had a direct influence on the results obtained in Mastering Coaching Skills, and 18% reported that supervision greatly influenced them (see Figure 18.12).

All (100%) of the participants who received supervision recommended including it in training programs.

When referring to their improvement after supervision (based on the final interview), 100% of participants recognized an impact on their way of being coaches: Reflection on their practice, strengthening their identity as coaches, and having compassion for themselves. Fifty percent mentioned having more confidence and self-assurance as coaches and trusting their

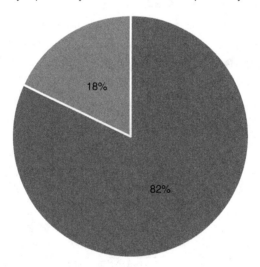

*Figure 18.12* Impact of Supervision in ICF Competencies by Group B.

Note: *Impact of supervision in Mastering Coaching Skills program identified by participants in Group B.*

processes, and 25% reported that supervision impacted their direct work with the client.

## What We Learned and Subsequent Actions

There was a time when mentoring filled up spaces that clearly belonged to supervision. Our own training as supervisors allowed us to clearly differentiate between the two functions, with two distinct ways of being: Mentoring is focused on the use and development of competencies; supervision focuses on facilitating reflection and the creation of awareness by the coach. Additionally, supervision enables the provision of feedback on certain psychological aspects that govern the coach's behavior which, in some cases, call for a referral to a specialist.

This last point is especially relevant in the present time. In recent years, as we experience adverse situations such as the COVID-19 pandemic, our way of looking has changed. It has led us to observe and consider much more seriously the effects of trauma in relationships, which are triggered in certain situations, but may go unnoticed. Yet, such traumas are ultimately present in coaching relationships.

Students in the Mastering Coaching Skills program already had open spaces to share as a group. What changed in supervision was the focus on themselves, on their being as coaches, instead of on their effectiveness in the competencies.

Supervisees were able to acknowledge their emotions and revisit those that were blocked and often thwarted their effectiveness in client sessions. The quality of their sessions was definitely boosted thanks to a more systemic look. Above all, as we experienced a few years ago, supervision meant a human and confidential space where coaches could open up to vulnerability, to emerge strengthened not only as professionals, but also as individuals.

Among the most significant result of this project was the development of high levels of self-awareness in the coaches and the personal work they took on, themselves. In doing so, they acknowledged that the only "tool" they actually had for coaching was their own being, the relationship they were able to create and their own emotions and feelings during the session, which were openly offered to the client.

If we intend to create a profession with a solid foundation, then we should consider including supervision in the professional development of coaches.

Practicing the possibility that our way of looking, and even our moods and emotions, are part of our relationship with the world and with others, enables us to foster the wisdom of making our judgments more flexible. It also enhances our understanding of others and to encourage them into a change, transitioning into more powerful beings who are more aware of the future each one creates.

As of 2020, we offer supervision in all our coaching training programs. In the beginning, we added supervision as an optional process in our

Mastering Coaching Skills program. This offered students the option to participate in four group supervision sessions, of two hours each, in groups of five individuals. Coaches could decide when—or even if—to begin this process.

By implementing supervision, we created a revealing space where students from different groups gathered to talk about what happened to them in their sessions and allowed themselves to be vulnerable, achieving a multiplier effect in their learning and gaining maturity as coaches. The phenomenon of mingling more experienced coaches (500+ hours of practice) with novice coaches (<100 hours of practice) sets up a mosaic of incredible color and diversity.

We realized the first step for supervision was to gain recognition by including it in coaching baseline training. This allows coaches to feel comfortable requesting supervision as a methodical and habitual practice, just as they do coaching and mentoring.

After conducting supervisory processes for two generations, we can confirm the impact supervision has on the development of the being and on strengthening the competencies of the "coach's mindset" of presence, trust, and listening. Above all, we can confirm that supervision helps students establish deeper relationships, in which they are more open to sharing vulnerability with their clients.

This is why, from 2021 onward, we have decided to include supervision as a comprehensive part of the Mastering Coaching Skills program.

## Conclusion

When interviewing supervisees, they were explicit about how free they felt in their "being as a coach." The creation of this bond is based on being less afraid and transcending limiting conversations. It would be interesting to be able to measure any shifts in clients' perceptions and levels of satisfaction as the relational space created by the coach, changed before and after supervision.

It is also important to note that while noticeable improvement was attained, even among coaches with over 500 hours of practice, the effectiveness of the supervision process on novice coaches did not go unnoticed. For the veteran coaches, the phenomenon of "who-I-am-being-with-the-other" was much more evident and paved the way for advanced questioning, directed to the "who" instead of to the "what."

Novice coaches tend to ask questions related to the "what," as their fear of not being efficient fuels an attempt to "solve the client's issue." Knowing all this, the participants are motivated and convinced to take up the role as a professional coach.

After the pilot project and the implementation of supervision in our programs, we realized that supervision involves being authentic, acknowledging our emotions, and becoming vulnerable and compassionate with ourselves. It is not possible to work as a coach without being involved with our emotions and, at the same time, being of service to the client. Supervision empowers coaches as "the tool" for powerful coaching sessions with their clients.

## References

Association for Coaching. (2021). *AC coaching supervision principles framework*. https://cdn.ymaws.com/www.associationforcoaching.com/resource/resmgr/Accreditation/Coaching_Supervisor_Accreditation/Supporting_Documentation/Principles_Framework_CSA.pdf

EMCC Global. (January 2021). *Supervision*. https://www.emccglobal.org/quality/supervision/

EMCC Global. (January 2021). *Competences*. https://www.emccglobal.org/quality/supervision/competences/

Farmer, S. (2012). How does a coach know that they have found the right supervisor? *Coaching: An International Journal of Theory, Research and Practice, 5*(1): 37–42.

FICOP. (January 2021). Federación Internacional de Coaching Ontológico Profesional. https://www.ficop.org/

Finlay, L. (2008). *Reflecting on 'reflective practice'*. The Open University.

Goldvarg, D., & Perel, N. (2012). *Competencias de coaching aplicadas*. Editorial Granica.

Goldvarg, D. (2017). *Supervisión de coaching*. Editorial Granica.

Hawkins, P., & Smit, N. (2006). *Coaching, mentoring and organizational consulting, supervision and development*. McGraw-Hill.

Hawkins, P., Turner, E., & Passmore, J. (2019). The manifesto for supervision. Association for Coaching, and Henley Business School.

Hullinger, A. M., DiGirolamo, J. A., & Tkach, J. T. (2020). A professional development study: The lifelong journeys of coaches. *International Coaching Psychology Review, 15*(1): 7–18.

International Coaching Federation. (2020). *ICF core competencies rating levels*. https://coachingfederation.org/app/uploads/2017/12/ICFCompetenciesLevelsTable.pdf

International Coaching Federation. (2021). *ICF Updated ICF Core Competencies*. https://coachingfederation.org/app/uploads/2021/03/ICF-Core-Competencies-updated.pdf

Lawrence-Wilkes, L. (2015). *The reflective practitioner in professional education*. Palgrave Macmillan.

Steinfeldt, J. (2015). *What are coaches afraid of? An exploration of courage and the path to coaching mastery*. University of Pennsylvania.

Turner, E. & Palmer, S. (2018). *The heart of coaching supervision: Working with reflection and self-care*. Routledge.

Wolk, L. (2008). *Coaching el Arte de Soplar las Brasas*. Gran Aldea Editores.

Wolk, L. (2013). *Coaching para coaches*. Gran Aldea Editores SRL.

## Author Bios

**Elena Espinal**, (MCC), MC, Ph.D., has been one of the first coaches in the world to earn the title of Master Certified Coach, she is the founder and former Director of the Instituto de Capacitación Professional, the first institute to deliver the Career of Coaching in all the Americas; and has studied and worked with Jim Selman and Fernando Flores.

For the past 25 years, Elena has worked, with Fortune 500 companies, governments, and non-governmental organizations, with outstanding results for her clients.

Elena is the author of the book: *Crafting the future*, and specializes in future design for governments and organizations.

She is passionate about serving the communities she belongs to and is a committed advocate for the establishment of diversity and inclusion. Elena created "Coaching con vision" (coaching with vision) and empowers blind coaches to work in organizations in Latin America.

**Adriana Rodriguez** is a Professional Certified Coach (PCC), with wide experience in executive and team coaching within Fortune 500 companies. She has worked for more than 25 years in the organizational world, and has held management positions in training, and human and organizational development. Adriana is also mentor coach, supervisor and trainer for professional coaches in Latin America.

Adriana is Co-Director of Team Power where she leads transformation processes, accompanying leaders, and empowering teams to create futures not previously contemplated.

Companies find in Adriana a committed partner, an articulator who sets everything in motion, attentive at every moment to what may be needed, as well as someone who challenges others because she truly believes in their greatness and possibilities.

# Conclusion

*Francine Campone, Joel DiGirolamo,*
*Damian Goldvarg, and Lily Seto*

The Introduction to this book began with a landscape. As the contributions of our diverse authors were assembled, we found instead an ocean of voices. The authors brought not only their own voices, but shared the voices of coaches and coaching supervisors. As we reflect on the chapters in this book, we can feel the vibration, the voices speaking, the energy in the work of the coaches, supervisors, and clients. This energy is palpable—rivers filling this ocean of energy that is the development of the human potential. It is clear that the momentum for coaching supervision in the region is building. We see it as a maturation of the profession in the Americas.

Many of these voices are new, first time authors who are bringing fresh perspectives and experiences to the coaching supervision field. We did not request specific chapters from any of our colleagues, but we did encourage their participation. Several of the authors collaborated with colleagues based in Europe. We accepted all fully formed chapter proposals and focused on what made them unique to the Americas to the extent that was possible.

Some authors shared their experiences conducting individual and group supervision; some shared their innovative practices, such as offering supervision to participants in their training programs. Others offered new models of coaching supervision. Authors predominantly shared their work experiences and some conducted research to collect data and bring a glimmer of light to coaching supervision in the Americas. It is not always clear what is unique to the Americas in some chapters; however, the voices and perspectives of the authors authentically reflect their experiences in this region. Some chapters speak to the heart of systemic issues faced by supervisors in the Americas, such as important diversity and equity issues.

In all oceans, some currents are stronger than others. In this chapter, we look at three broad currents and themes that emerged in this work—diversity, organizational work, and coach development—and we consider the implications for new work in the field of coaching supervision. As the editorial team, we represent a partial cross-section of voices in the Americas and recognize that the voices of BIPOC and other groups are not yet fully reflected in the literature of coaching and coaching supervision. While we drew on our individual histories, perspectives, cultural orientations and experiences to explore themes, we also recognize the limitations of our own perspectives. This chapter concludes with an invitation to readers to explore the unchartered waters of coaching supervision in the Americas: Topics and themes that were not addressed as well as suggestions for future research.

## Culture, Diversity, and Coaching Supervision

In the Americas, we find great diversity in terms of culture, geographic spread, languages, and industries. Coaching supervision is a relatively new source of coach development and many opportunities exist to develop it further with an Americas flavor or flavors. For example, in many parts of Europe, supervision draws heavily on models and methods in psychology and has a strong personal development orientation. Here in the Americas, coaching and coaching supervision have more hybrid roots that include psychology, organizational development, entrepreneurship, philosophy, and other disciplines. Thus, we need to be sensitive to the potential for transdisciplinary models of coaching supervision, which incorporate culturally oriented principles and practices along with a strong business orientation.

We considered the question: Are current models and methods of coaching supervision truly transcultural? Some chapters in the book have added nuance and perhaps new dimensions to existing models; others demonstrate the adaptability and universality of existing models. Escalante brings forward the complexity of diversity, noting that "the Americas hold a kaleidoscope of cultural heritage and values." Her multi-systemic field includes consideration of spirituality as well as both the conscious and unconscious impact of cultural influences. Lowish, Seto, and Prefontaine note a dynamic range from spirituality to the impact of intergenerational trauma and cultural disruption. Chapters also indicate a strong Ontological orientation in Latin American coaches, with acute attention to language and meaning-making.

Language also matters with respect to the term "supervision." Several chapters document the extent to which the term "supervision" poses a challenge for acceptance and adoption in the Americas. Goldvarg and Seto, in particular, share the experiences of coaching supervisors and note that while they individually educate and promote the practice, it will take time for all coaches to recognize the benefits of supervision and become ambassadors for the practice. The ICF endorses coaching supervision as an avenue for on-going professional development and promotes its value and benefits.

While these chapters highlight the complexity of culturally attuned coaching supervision, other chapters point to the extent to which the EMCC standards of professional practice and the widely known seven-eyed model of coaching supervision (Hawkins & Shohet, 2000) seem to translate well with little or no adaptation. With the increased use of virtual technology during the pandemic year, Goldvarg and Turner's offering may translate well globally with the proviso that attention to cultural norms and technological access are given consideration. The chapter on creativity reinforces the universal value of play. As the prevalence of coaching supervision in the Americas grows, we anticipate that the flavors of the Americas contexts will influence and shape new iterations.

## Coaching Supervision in Organizations

The second theme invited the authors to reflect on internal coaching and the value proposition of coaching supervision for organizations. While three of the chapters describe barriers to the use of coaching supervision in the Americas, one chapter describes two successful cases of its use in organizations in the US. This reflects the ambivalence about coaching supervision that is widespread in organizations across the Americas.

We see a dynamic tension between the value proposition for organizations—quality control, ethical compliance, and market value—and the value for coaches in their own words- supportive, restorative, clarifying. Three chapters suggest that organizations consider the value proposition for coaching supervision as one of quality assurance, resolution of ethical dilemmas and distinction for the organization's market position. One chapter, where a coaching vendor platform is positioning supervision as a value-add proposition to organizational clients, demonstrates how the organizational value proposition for coaching can further serve the wider client base. In many cases, persuading corporate and governmental organizations to embrace coaching supervision required demonstrating value and managing scale. This may be less of a challenge when organizations have an established and well structured program for coach development. We strongly suggest that as internal coaching and coach development programs are created, supervision be included from the outset so that both coaches and organizations can experience immediate benefit.

In addition to the value proposition for organizations, coaching supervisors found a need to address the value proposition for participating coaches. Tennyson notes that coaches in the US came to supervision with a desire to learn "best practices" and practical actions. This focus evolved over time through experience. Coaches who have participated in supervision see the benefits of being resourced, having space to think through ethical dilemmas, and learning from others. This aligns with a greater emphasis on the resourcing and restorative function of coaching supervision. Harrison and Bizouard's study of coaches' lived experience of supervision noted the power of the group process in fostering a sense of being witnessed, developing self as instrument, and the value of emotional support. The implication for coaching supervisors is a need to be aware, when proposing supervision to organizations, that there are two needs to be addressed: Meeting the organization's brand and quality interests and articulating the potential benefits to the individual coaches. For both, intentional and systematic education is needed and, with respect to encouraging coach participation, experience is most persuasive. As the trend toward internal coaches grows, there is an opportunity for coaching supervisors to leverage these brief examples to encourage the incorporation of supervision as a foundational element of internal coaching programs.

## Supervision and Coach Development

The final theme invites consideration of ongoing learning and professional development. We are in a period of transition to a time when coaching supervision is expected of all coaches. During this period of transition, education will be paramount—educating clients and sponsors, as well as educating coaches as to the value of supervision. Supervision is useful for coaches at all levels of experience. Using the model of Kadushin (1976) and Proctor (1987) of professional development, support, and quality control, it doesn't take a stretch of the imagination to envision how coaches at all levels might find benefit.

As long-time coach educators, mentors, and coaching supervisors, this is of particular interest and concern. The updated ICF Core Competencies specify as part of the Coaching Mindset that coaches "engage in ongoing learning and development as a coach; develop an ongoing reflective practice to enhance one's coaching; and remain aware of and open to the influence of context and culture on self and others." Nonetheless, opportunities for continuing coach development tend to focus heavily on training in specific coaching models or certifications in various assessments rather than on cultivating critical reflective practice or self-development.

The landscape of coach education in the Americas is extremely diverse, ranging from brief, proprietary model skills training to graduate programs of a year or more. One of us (Francine) constructed a high-level overview of 107 ICF Accredited Coach Training Programs (ACTP) that highlighted the tension between a technical-pragmatic orientation and a developmental-transformative paradigm for coach development.

Coach training programs included proprietary coach training schools, university based or university affiliated programs, and consulting organizations that have coaching and coach training in their service organizations. Nine programs trained coaches for specific coaching niches: Family recovery, clergy, end of life care, services for the deaf, healthcare, education leadership, wellness, and spirituality. Of the more general coaching sector programs, 64% indicated they prepare coaches to work in diverse sectors. The remaining programs specified training coaches for leadership, executive, business, and organizational work. Slightly over half of the ACTP programs (52%) describe the training content as consisting of the ICF competencies plus the program's unique model, drawn from diverse sources. Of the remaining program descriptions identifying a specific orientation (in addition to the ICF competencies), the predominant model is Ontological (24%), especially in Latin America. Neurolinguistic Programming (NLP) was the second most frequently identified model (10%). Four programs specified integral theory, with the remaining orientations including Gestalt, Adlerian, and Eriksonian models; positive psychology; relational, process, and solution focus models; evidence-based coaching; Asian philosophy; Emotional Intelligence; spirituality and Christian theology. We suggest that strongly encouraging coach training graduates to engage in regular, ongoing supervision would strengthen the adoption of a coaching mindset beyond the constraints of a specific coach training model or toolkit. This would also enable coaches, regardless of their initial training, to adapt situationally and respond authentically to each unique client and encounter.

The developmental journey of coaches is little addressed in the literature and McLean's chapter suggests a continuum of coach development that appropriately matches the coach's developmental needs. As coaches complete programs that incorporate coaching supervision, they will have experience and practice in reflective learning from their own experiences, offering an avenue for ongoing development as they progress along their own developmental path. Coaching supervision provides a different approach to coach development, one that expands the coach's frame of reference and capacity for systemic thinking and ethical management of complex coaching situations and engagements. Espinal and Rodriguez's example of integrating coaching supervision into their training program situates coach self-development and critical reflective practice at the center of coach education. We suggest that coaching supervision provides a supportive process that deepens the practitioner's coaching mindset and expands the coach's ability to work effectively in a complex and diverse environment. Coaching supervision is an excellent tool or program for us to use for support, as a healing space, and as a community to work together to support all manner of diversity of individuals. Group supervision, especially, can enhance creativity and gather diverse thoughts and views. And finally, all coaches should be lifelong learners, continually seeking new experiences, paradigms, models, tools, and more.

Given the nuances and complexity of diversity in the Americas, coaches and supervisors need to respond to micro and macro aspects of systems with attention to organizational and individual cultures, worldviews, and norms. This is especially important with regard to relational dynamics, including psychological contracting, and ethical choices. More nuanced systems thinking includes spirituality, philosophical orientation and history. As coaches' and coaching supervisors' work becomes increasingly unrestricted by geography, this degree of attunement is essential.

It is our hope that as more coaches experience supervision and realize its benefits, the idea of supervision as reflective learning will become more accepted and the negative connotation of the word will decrease. Integrating coaching supervision into coach education can prepare the ground for this by providing early exposure to supervision and differentiating it from mentoring. As noted in several chapters, coaches found that supervision builds confidence. As learners strive to meet the performance expectations for certification, supervision can provide confidence-building support and foster resilience.

## Unchartered Waters

Collectively, these chapters offer a panoramic view of the racial and cultural diversity, organizational cultures, and educational perspectives that influence coaching supervision in the Americas. Yet there is much more awaiting exploration. We leave with many big questions. How will coaching supervision in the Americas evolve? Will it become more mainstream as in Europe? Will it take on a flavor of its own? Is supervision in the Americas different from supervision in other parts of the world? What are the similarities and differences? What are the unique challenges of supervisors in the Americas? What is the unique contribution of supervision in the Americas to the coaching supervision practice worldwide?

We look forward to the continued journey. We note four areas for further research and exploration.

## Expanding the Cultural Horizons of Coaching Supervision

Diversity and inclusion are central themes. We see a need for supervision models that are more inclusive of other cultures and perspectives and less about European perspectives. This suggests noting and reflecting on different frameworks for diversity such comparing the melting pot model of the US with that of multiculturalism in Canada. Reflecting Indigenous culture, for example, would entail bringing more of our ancestors and nature into supervision in a much more holistic way. Special interest groups for Black and Indigenous coaches and coaching supervisors could be created to provide an opportunity for these individuals to focus on topics and issues they have in common.

Internal coaches especially need greater attunement to cultural diversity, particularly in global organizations. In a global and virtual world where coaches and coaching supervisors work across geographic and continental borders, there is a greater need for understanding how to be culturally fluid and responsive. Supervision, as reflection on action, offers a pathway for coaches to learn from their cross-cultural encounters and adjust standard models and practices accordingly.

Developing alternative models would also require re-thinking models and methods of research. Scholar-practitioners in the field are encouraged to explore the literature of decolonizing methodologies and contribute theories and models that diversify the literature of the field.

## Value for Coaches and Organizations

We see a need for research on how coaches and coaching companies in the Americas might position supervision as a value add and part of their business proposition. The term "supervision" remains an obstacle to acceptance, as well as a source of confusion about the distinctions between supervision and mentoring. Further research that documents the value of coaching supervision for organizations would be beneficial as would broader education regarding the distinctions of mentoring and supervision. In considering the restorative function of coaching supervision, we would welcome more research on the benefits of coaching supervision in times of turmoil, such as the recent COVID-19 pandemic.

As internal coaching grows, more research is needed to provide evidence of best practices. Research on the role of coaching supervision with internal coaches can build evidence of the challenges those coaches face and document benefits to the organization. As governmental oversight of corporate practices waxes and wanes in the US, internal coaches will have a particular need for a safe, caring, and trusted space in which to think through ethical challenges and align with accepted practices in the coaching field. We would welcome research that considers the efficacy of internal supervisors compared with external supervisors for internal coaches.

Given the increasing interest in organizations developing internal cadres of coaches, sometimes as an add-on to their current responsibilities, how might coaching supervision help ensure internal coaches are fit for purpose in their coaching roles As coaching supervision is adopted for internal coaches, there might be research that demonstrates the value supervision adds to the organization's investment in coaching. As chapters on coaching supervision within organizations indicate, group supervision seems to be the preferred mode, being the most cost-effective and perhaps providing the greatest flexibility. As both group and team coaching supervision require greater sophistication and specific skills in supervision practice, it will be important to document the skills and competencies required of supervisors providing these services. There are some initial training offerings in these specializations and we look forward to forthcoming data from these programs.

Team coaching has increased in popularity in recent years. The ICF team coaching competencies have identified the use of a co-coach when working with teams. The two coaches may trade roles frequently and allow each other to observe the process and both may provide some of the functions of a supervisor in this team coaching role. The advent of team coaching supervisors should bolster the adoption of supervision overall. We look forward to the expansion of team coaching supervision eagerly await research in this domain.

## Quality

Training schools are beginning to integrate coaching supervision as part of their programs. Research could be conducted around the difference that coaching supervision makes to coach development and the development of a coach mindset that supports continuous learning and reflection. Such research might broaden the understanding of continuous learning for coaches beyond additional workshops, training for use of proprietary instruments, or certifications.

As McAnally et al. note, there are no training or education requirements in order to call oneself a coaching supervisor in the Americas. As happened in the field of coaching, a broad, strategic and sustained effort by the coaching community, including professional organizations such as the ICF, is needed to educate coaches, coach educators, and coaching providers as to the value and benefits of working with credentialed supervisors. There is also opportunity for the development of supervision of supervision to ensure consistent rigor to our profession. Now that there are approximately 300 coaching supervisors in the Americas, how do we continually develop as a community and as a discipline? One strategy may include growing the practice of supervision of supervision as well as specialized courses beyond initial certification training. The opportunity exists to develop criteria, value and other standards around coaching supervision that are unique to the Americas. The Americas Coaching Supervision Network, as it continues to grow, intends to serve as a nexus for developing and supporting the coaching supervision community in the Americas.

## Ways of Working

In our initial call for proposals, we suggested a few topics that were not addressed in the responses, leaving these open for further exploration. These included supervision and sustainability (including the role of supervisors in addressing climate change issues) and supervision and technology. Apart from one chapter in this book, we see many possible avenues for exploring the uses of technology and virtual work in coaching supervision. Even before the onset of COVID-19, it appeared that many supervisors in the Americas had experienced virtual work compared with European colleagues. Given the varied cultural norms about interpersonal relationships and communication in the Americas, it would be useful to better understand how working virtually might impact the relational dynamics between coach and supervisor. What adaptations of virtual working might be culturally responsive? How might technology be used to enhance the coaching supervision experience?

A related area of curiosity is the future role supervisors may take in supporting coaches to adopt new technologies, some which may support administrative functions, supplement coaching services (such as software to generate reports or help clients track their progress), or provide automated coaching (Artificial Intelligence [AI] coaching) between human-to-human coaching sessions. It will be useful to consider how to ensure that coaching supervisors are up to speed on useful technologies. We don't yet know how practitioners and clients in the Americas have adapted to the use of technology when compared with our counterparts in Europe and the UK. Exploring this might point to further opportunities to maximize the benefits of technology and virtual working.

Research is still needed around the efficacy of individual versus group coaching supervision. There are questions about the value of group supervision compared with individual supervision. We note that current group supervision books are adapted from clinical supervision practice so there are opportunities to expand and diversify theories, models, and methods of working with groups.

In his poem about the ocean Pablo Neruda refers to "the sea's university." In undertaking this book project, we set out on our own uncharted journey to hear the voices from this vast sea called the Americas. While we have not yet mapped the ocean in this book, we have moved beyond the known horizon of coaching supervision and we invite readers to join us in continuing the journey.

## References

Hawkins, P., & Shohet, R. (2000). *Supervision in the helping professions.*Open University Press.

Kadushin, A. (1976). *Supervision in social work.* Columbia University Press.

Proctor, B. (1987). Supervision: A co-operative exercise in accountability. In A. Marken & M. Payne (Eds.), *Enabling and ensuring: Supervision in practice* (2nd ed.). National Youth Bureau.

# Index

Page numbers in italics indicate a figure and page numbers in bold indicate a table on the corresponding page.

Printed in the United States
by Baker & Taylor Publisher Services